W9-BBB-642

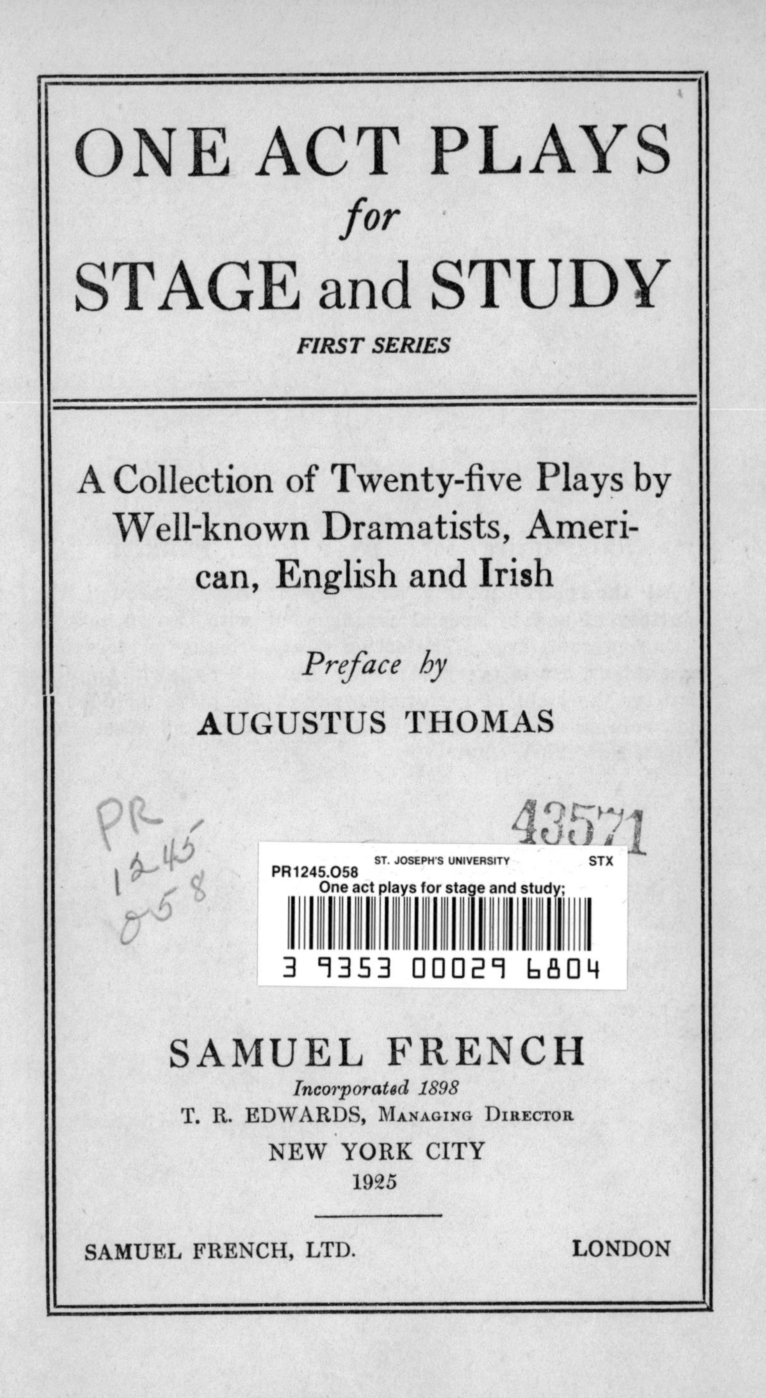

# ONE ACT PLAYS
*for*
# STAGE and STUDY

***FIRST SERIES***

A Collection of Twenty-five Plays by Well-known Dramatists, American, English and Irish

*Preface by*

**AUGUSTUS THOMAS**



SAMUEL FRENCH
*Incorporated 1898*
T. R. EDWARDS, MANAGING DIRECTOR
NEW YORK CITY
1925

SAMUEL FRENCH, LTD. LONDON

*Sixth Printing*

# CONTENTS

# PREFACE

In the Savoy Hotel, London, one afternoon nearly fifteen years ago—perhaps quite fifteen years—Charles Frohman gave an American author the 'script of a one-act play to read. It was "The Twelve Pound Look," by J. M. Barrie, soon to be done in London, and Mr. Frohman thought it might be useful in America for Miss Barrymore.

Later Mr. Barrie came into the room and the American writer embarked upon the presumptuous task of persuading Mr. Barrie to make a four-act play of the 'script instead of having it done in its one-act form. It seemed to the American that the story outlined, the events referred to, and the consequences given, were enough for a full evening's play. What he said made no change in Mr. Barrie's decision, but it did invite some ideas about playwriting. The American had quoted Mark Twain's remark to the effect that for him a "good short story was a novel in the cradle," and that a little care and nursing would develop it. For Mr. Barrie a one-act idea was essentially a one-act idea and there were plays that were inevitably one-act plays and not more. In his opinion, "The Twelve Pound Look" was such a play.

Had an Englishman and an American been discussing short stories instead of short plays, the chances are that their positions would have been reversed.

The one-act play, however, has never had much of an American professional market. The curtain-raiser is relatively an English institution. It comes of climate and of differing dinner hours. In the London season it is still daylight at a quarter of nine o'clock. The "stalls" fill at that hour, but the pit and the gallery have had supper at six-thirty and the curtain-raiser is for them.

In an American volume like the present one addressed to the reading public and to amateur players and student play-makers, the one-act play has its proper and important place.

To the reader it offers the same quick introduction of characters, the rapid complication of relationships and ensuing situations, and the prompt extrication that make the short story popular. It is read at a single sitting and thereby fills the requirement that Poe somewhat arbitrarily imposed on poem and story.

For the player, one-act plays have the value of letting him assume in a season four or five times as many characters as the same time and study given to full-length dramas would permit. The usually shorter casts make their planning and preparation simpler, and a combination of them for an evening's program eliminates those risks that are supposed to attend a venture where the eggs are all in one basket.

The ostensible purpose of amateur players is to find for themselves and to give to others entertainment. It is probably true, however, that their real urge is that same inborn desire that drives and sustains the professional player; not vanity, not love of applause, not remuneration, but a deep-seated wish for self-expression. Many of us think and say that a prime luxury of life is "to be one's self." In a measure that is so, but to be one's self gives only a fraction of the relief and development that are found in occasionally or frequently being somebody else. In our day-dreams and through our reading, both of news and romance, we are constantly in our imaginations putting ourselves in the other fellow's place, but this substitution is necessarily imperfect, momentary, and often tantalizingly vague. The definite study of another personality, and, better yet, the definite assumption of it and expression in and through it, is a relief measurable in psychical and physical improvement, a vicarious outlet that we never know in any other way after we cease to be children and no longer play at pirate, policeman, or "lady come to see."

To the player, the great value of the play, long or short, is there—the lesser values of study, speaking, carriage, self-expression, and the like, are obvious and not negligible, but while these accomplishments seem to abide and to be the greater acquisitions it is a question if they are not all outweighed by the circulating expression referred to.

A similar reflection applies to the friends and patrons before whom performances are given. They, too, find in the mimic life they look upon an almost equal vicarious relief. Something is done, something is said—thoroughly done and outrightly spoken—that they have thought upon and waited for and wished to have realized. The mirror has been held as 'twere up to Nature, "virtue has been shown her own feature, scorn her own image, and the very age and body of the time his form and pressure."

This is all, of course, upon the presumption that the play is not utter trash, but has in it some truth.

As we read the list of writers whose playlets have been here assembled, we gather a fair confidence that real value is offered—or if not, and if all these Olympians have been caught nodding, we can solace ourselves with the general respectability of the company and thank the publishers for their good intentions.

AUGUSTUS THOMAS.

# THE MAN UPSTAIRS

COMEDY IN ONE ACT

## AUGUSTUS THOMAS

Augustus Thomas was born at St. Louis in 1857. As far back as his seventh year he was interested in theatrical matters, so that it is not surprising that "dialogue seemed" to him "the most natural literary vehicle." . . . "I began writing plays," he says, "when I was about fourteen years of age. . . . In 1882 I made a dramatization of Mrs. Burnett's 'Editha's Burglar.' With this as a curtain-raiser and a rather slap-stick farce called 'Combustion,' I made a tour of the country with a company that I organized, and with which I ran in debt several thousand dollars." For over thirty years Mr. Thomas has furnished the American stage with effective plays depicting various phases of contemporary American life. He is in the best sense of the word a man of the theater, a skilful and painstaking playwright, and a commentator as well, on the life and manners of his fellow-men.

Owing to the peculiar conditions of the American theater, Mr. Thomas has written very few one-act plays. The only one of these that has ever appeared in print is "The Man Upstairs," published for the first time in a private edition for use in the training camps of this country during the late war, and here first published for the general public.

Following is a list of Mr. Thomas' published plays: "The Earl of Pawtucket," "Mrs. Leffingwell's Boots," "The Other Girl," "The Witching Hour," "The Copperhead," "As a Man Thinks," "Alabama," "Arizona," "Oliver Goldsmith," "In Mizzoura," "The Harvest Moon," "The Man Upstairs."

References: Montrose J. Moses, "The American Dramatist;" Richard Burton, "The New American Drama;" Barrett H. Clark, "A Study of the Modern Drama."

# THE MAN UPSTAIRS*

CHARACTERS

Mr. Ruggles
Mrs. Ruggles
Mary
Mr. Frisbie
Mrs. Frisbie

Scene: *The Ruggles' Apartment.*

Time: *The present.*

Scene: *Apartment of Mr. and Mrs. Ruggles. Window right; portieres left. Door in the back.*

Discovered: *Mr. and Mrs. Ruggles at table. Chafing dish and dishes on table.*

Ruggles. (*To wife, who is blowing at alcohol lamp.*) Don't, don't do that, my dear.

Mrs. Ruggles. (*Pausing.*) Why not? (*Blows.*)

Ruggles. (*Anxiously.*) Because I tell you not to. You may kill yourself. (*Wife looks at him.*) I don't mean by blowing, but you're liable to inhale that flame.

Mrs. Ruggles. Nonsense—I'm not a child.

Ruggles. But burning alcohol isn't a good thing for an adult. It's mighty easy to inhale that blue flame—you can't tell where it's going. Besides, nobody "blows out" a chafing dish. These little hoods turn over the lights and extinguish them. (*Works extinguishers.*)

Mrs. Ruggles. Well, I didn't want it lighted anyway!

Ruggles. Very well, only never try to "blow it out" again.

Mrs. Ruggles. Dear, dear, Frederick, how many more times are you going to say that? You must see that

I'm nervous and tired and you must know that I didn't want the chafing dish lighted, and you might see that I'm doing the best I can under dreadfully trying conditions.

RUGGLES. My darling, compose yourself; I'm only suggesting that you refrain from suicide—and with the friendliest intentions.

MRS. RUGGLES. Where is the book?

RUGGLES. Here. (*Hands large cook book.*)

MRS. RUGGLES. (*Reading.*) Eggs—ah grattin——

RUGGLES. *Au gratin*, my love.

MRS. RUGGLES. (*Looking at him.*) Frederick— (*Pause.*) Haven't I all I can do without your interruptions? (*Pause.*) *Au gratin.* (*Looks at him.* RUGGLES *lights cigarette.*) Frederick, I won't have you smoking that cigarette before we've finished our dinner. (RUGGLES *throws cigarette in fire. Mrs. Ruggles reads.*) "Knead well together one tablespoonful of bread-crumbs." (*Looks about.*) Frederick, I've left the bread-crumbs in the kitchen. Will you get them for me? (RUGGLES *exits* L. *looking at watch.* MRS. RUGGLES *continues.*) "Two ounces of butter, three chopped anchovies"—Now I wonder if he got the chopped anchovies? (*Looks after him and continues reading.*) "One chopped shallot." (*Speaks.*) What is a shallot? (*Reads.*) "Three raw egg yolks, a good pinch of salt, half a pinch of white pepper and a pinch of grated nutmeg." (*Speaks.*) I'm *sure* he didn't *get* all these things. (*Reads.*) "When ready, put these ingredients into a silver baking-dish with one ounce of butter at the bottom." (*Re-enter* RUGGLES *with dish of bread-crumbs.*)

MRS. RUGGLES. Frederick, did you get the chopped anchovies?

RUGGLES. No—you asked me to get the bread-crumbs from the kitchen table. (*Sets dish down.*)

MRS. RUGGLES. I mean from the grocer's?

RUGGLES. (*Sits.*) No.

MRS. RUGGLES. Well, the book says— (*Reads.*) "Three chopped anchovies and one chopped shallot"—what is a shallot?

RUGGLES. I'm sure *I* don't know. It sounds like a sailing vessel. (*Rises and gets book.*)

MRS. RUGGLES. Doesn't the grocer know what it is?

RUGGLES. Judging solely from appearances, I should say he didn't.

MRS. RUGGLES. Didn't you ask him?

RUGGLES. No.

MRS. RUGGLES. Well, well, what *are* we to do?

RUGGLES. Personally I feel inclined to take the definition in the dictionary. It says here— (*Reads.*) "Shallot" —pronounced shal*lot;* a small kind of onion"——

MRS. RUGGLES. *But*, Frederick, I sent you to the grocer's to get *everything* for eggs *au gratin.*

RUGGLES. Well, I got a dozen eggs and a pound of the best American *gratin.* You didn't say anything about asking the grocer what kind of an onion a chopped shallot was—or anything else.

MRS. RUGGLES. Didn't you look in the book?

RUGGLES. No.

MRS. RUGGLES. (*In despair.*) Then we can't have the eggs gratin.

RUGGLES. (*Taking cigarette.*) Very well, dear, I'll try to bear up under it. We've had our canned soup and our canned salmon, and that ought to be enough for anybody.

MRS. RUGGLES. (*Ready to cry.*) I don't care, Frederick —they were *hot.*

RUGGLES. (*Reassuringly.*) My darling, they were *red* hot. I never had a *hotter* dinner in my life—and now a little coffee and a cigarette and I'll——

MRS. RUGGLES. But you said *canned.*

RUGGLES. Did I? Well, I meant *un*canned.

MRS. RUGGLES. It isn't my fault if the cook leaves us.

RUGGLES. Not at all. It's *mine*—entirely mine, my dear.

I should have made the home happier for the cook, I suppose. Do you know that during her entire three weeks I never even held her hand?

MRS. RUGGLES. Don't be absurd, Frederick. But I can't help it if the old cook leaves us and the new cook doesn't come; we should have gone out to dinner.

RUGGLES. Quite true. I dressed to go, but you thought it was a good chance to try a chafing dish.

MRS. RUGGLES. You said you knew something about a chafing dish.

RUGGLES. I said I knew how to make a welsh rabbit in a chafing dish.

MRS. RUGGLES. But we can't dine on a welsh rabbit. (*Pause.*) Can we?

RUGGLES. (*Quickly.*) No—no—no—of course we can't.

MRS. RUGGLES. You've been just as hateful as you could be all day.

RUGGLES. Why have I, dear? I thought I was angelic at breakfast. I said I'd never tasted better boiled eggs anywhere—except in a railroad depot.

MRS. RUGGLES. And when I was asking the janitor to get us some milk you said I was waiting to see that horrid creature above us.

RUGGLES. No. I *asked* you if you were waiting—simply *asked*, my love.

MRS. RUGGLES. Goodness, Frederick, how you exasperate me. Isn't *that* an insinuation that I was waiting to see him?

RUGGLES. Not necessarily.

MRS. RUGGLES. I can't step onto the landing, but you think I'm waiting to see that man upstairs going out or coming in—and I haven't seen him for a week.

RUGGLES. Well, that's too bad.

MRS. RUGGLES. (*In tears.*) Frederick, I won't have you talk to me in that heartless manner. It's bad enough to have the work of the entire flat on my hands without your brutality. (*Weeps.*)

RUGGLES. Why, Olive— don't, now don't do that. (*Tries to embrace her.*)

MRS. RUGGLES. No— you can't abuse me into desperation and then smooth it all over with a little palavar.

RUGGLES. But, dearie.

MRS. RUGGLES. *No, don't talk to me.* (*Exits* L.)

RUGGLES. (*Looking after her then at table.*) Damnation! (*Pause.*) One can of salmon, fifty cents—one can of soup, forty cents—eggs, thirty cents—alcohol, sixty cents—*cheese,* twenty-five cents—chafing dish, fifteen dollars. Seventeen dollars and something. We could have gone to the Ritz, had a private room and come home with our feet out of the taxi windows—metaphorically speaking—for that money. (*Pause—to portieres.*) I say, Ollie—let's put on our bonnets and go downtown for a little whirl. Come on, dear, and we'll forget all about the disagreeable day. (*Pause.*) Eh? (*Please.*) Ollie—don't you hear me?

MRS. RUGGLES. (*Off-stage, angrily.*) Yes, I hear you.

RUGGLES. Oh, do you? (*Turning away sulking.*) Well, I just wanted to be sure of it. (*Puts on hat.*) Didn't want to take any snap judgment on you. (*Puts on overcoat.*) I think *I'll* go. (*Pause. To portieres.*) Ollie—third and last call—*I'm* going downtown. Will you go with me? (*Pause.*) Oh, very well—don't sit up, dear—I may stop at the club. (*Exits slamming door. Enter* MRS. RUGGLES *at portieres.*)

MRS. RUGGLES. (*Looking at door.*) Frederick— (*Louder.*) Frederick— (*Still louder.*) Frederick— (*Pause.*) If he's really gone I shall never speak to him again. (*Goes to door—listens—opens it.*) Frederick— (*Pause.*) I can't call through the hallways for him. (*Shuts door.*) That's what a woman gets trying to save two or three dollars for a man —(*Indicates table.*) That's his gratitude. (*Knock at door.*) Oh, come back, has he? Isn't that a man all over— too much a moral coward to carry out his threat.

(*Knock.*) Well, I'll not answer him. (*Sits.*) He'll find I'm not in a playful mood. (*Pause. Ring.*) Why, I wonder if that is someone else? (*To mirror, fixing hair.*) I look a fright. (*Opens door.*)

MARY. (*Outside.*) Good evening—does Mrs. Ruggles live here?

MRS. RUGGLES. I am Mrs. Ruggles.

MARY. I'm the cook. Mrs Ericson, the Swedish intelligence office, sent me here.

MRS. RUGGLES. Yes? Come in. (*Enter* MARY.)

MRS. RUGGLES (*Sitting.*) Are you a good, plain cook?

MARY. I am, ma'am. There's me character.

MRS. RUGGLES. (*Taking letters.*) Can you make desserts—pies—and cakes—and puddings?

MARY. Oh, yis, ma'am.

MRS. RUGGLES. Sit down. (MARY *sits.*) What are your wages?

MARY. Eighty dollars.

MRS. RUGGLES. Eighty dollars, eh?

MARY. Yes, ma'am—I usually get eighty-five, but Mrs. Ericson said you'd only pay eighty.

MRS. RUGGLES. You're not a Swede?

MARY. No, ma'am.

MRS. RUGGLES. Well— (*Pause.*) What is your name?

MARY. Mary Nolan, mum.

MRS. RUGGLES. Well, Mary, we want a girl that can cook and who will do light house-work, too. You see, it's a small flat—with every convenience, and——

MARY. How many in the family?

MRS. RUGGLES. Two only—myself and husband.

MARY. Are they no children?

MRS. RUGGLES. No children.

MARY. Does you have much company?

MRS. RUGGLES. Scarcely any.

MARY. Is the laundry done out?

MRS. RUGGLES. Yes.

MARY. What time does the gintleman go to work?

MRS. RUGGLES. At nine—we breakfast at eight-thirty.

MARY. Does he come home to lunch?

MRS. RUGGLES. No, we have only two meals a day.

MARY. At what time have yez dinner?

MRS. RUGGLES. At six-thirty.

MARY. Well, I'm used to me Thursdays out.

MRS. RUGGLES. Very well.

MARY. And every other Sunday.

MRS. RUGGLES. (*Pause.*) Very well.

MARY. The janitor isn't a nigger, is he?

MRS. RUGGLES. No, the janitor is named Murphy.

MARY. That's good. (*Pause.*) Has the cook's room an outside window, ma'am?

MRS. RUGGLES. Yes. To the rear—it looks onto a court.

MARY. Is there a fire-escape?

MRS. RUGGLES. Two of them.

MARY. Very well, mum—I like your looks.

MRS. RUGGLES. Thank you, Mary. I'm sure we can get on together.

MARY. Have you a picture of the gentleman?

MRS. RUGGLES. No, I have not.

MARY. Oh, well, I daresay he's a noice man. Do yez eat in this room? (*Looking at table.*)

MRS. RUGGLES. No. We had a little luncheon here to-day by the grate fire.

MARY. Yis—well, mum, I couldn't come and do all that work for eighty dollars—sure I thought there was another girl.

MRS. RUGGLES. Well, what would you expect, Mary?

MARY. I gits eighty-five as a regular thing.

MRS. RUGGLES. Very well—we will pay eighty-five.

MARY. All right, then—we kin try fur a week. (*Rises.*) Is there a gas stove in the kitchen?

MRS. RUGGLES. There is.

MARY. Very well, mum.

MRS. RUGGLES. When can you come, Mary?

MARY. Would Wednesday do?

MRS. RUGGLES. I should like you at once, if possible. I'd like you to get the breakfast to-morrow.

MARY. I couldn't get here in time, mum. I'm stoppin' with me cousin in Jersey City.

MRS. RUGGLES. Can't you go over there to-morrow some time after breakfast and so stay here to-night?

MARY. (*Slowly.*) Oh, yis, mum. (*Quickly.*) Thin me wages begin to-day?

MRS. RUGGLES. (*Rising.*) Yes. Your room's the other side of the hall—next to the bathroom.

MARY. Thank you, mum. I'll take off me things. (*Exit.*)

MRS. RUGGLES. Well, there's a cook at last. Frederick might have shown a little more patience with the situation. (*Calls.*) Mary.

MARY. (*Off-stage.*) Yes, mum?

MRS. RUGGLES. I'm going out for a little while.

MARY. All right, mum. (*Enters.*) What shall I say if anyone calls?

MRS. RUGGLES. (*Going off.*) No one *will* call. (*Exit.*) My husband may come home. If he does, just say that I didn't know when I'd be back.

MARY. All right, mum, and I'll clear up these things.

MRS. RUGGLES. Yes.

MARY. Is there any tea in the house, mum? I feel that faint. (*Re-entering.*)

MRS. RUGGLES. Plenty, Mary. Good night.

MARY. Good night, mum. I'm to tell your husband you didn't know whin you'd be home?

MRS. RUGGLES. Yes. (*Exit.* MARY *fastens door.*)

MARY. (*Clearing table.*) Monday was always my lookey day! Eighty-five dollars and two in the family. (*Smiles.*) It's four months since I had work at sixty. (*Exit with tray. Rattle of key in door, then rattle of knob. Enter* MARY.)

MARY. Sure, someone's at that door. It's lucky I fastened it. (*Door rattles again.*) I wonder if the missus forgot something. (*Starts to door. Bell rings,* MARY *jumps back, gathers courage and opens door. Enter* FRISBIE *with valise.*)

FRISBIE. (MARY *nods.*) Hello—new maid! How long have *you* been here?

MARY. I jist come, sir.

FRISBIE. Where's my wife?

MARY. She's gone out, sir.

FRISBIE. Where?

MARY. I don't know sor.

FRISBIE. (*Removing coat.*) Hang that up—in the wardrobe. (*Exit* MARY. FRISBIE *opens valise and gets smoking jacket, throws shirts, etc., about. Re-enter* MARY *who busily picks things up.*)

FRISBIE. (*Standing in shirt sleeves.*) Didn't she get my telegram this afternoon saying I'd be home tonight?

MARY. I only came after dinner, sor.

FRISBIE. What made Sophie leave?

MARY. Is her name Sophie?

FRISBIE. (*Taking off shoes.*) Whose name?

MARY. Your wife's.

FRISBIE. No, that was the old cook's name.

MARY. Oh—I don't know, sor.

FRISBIE. (*Putting on slippers.*) Didn't my wife leave any word for me?

MARY. She said you might come, sor, and to say she didn't know when she'd be back.

FRISBIE. Didn't know when she'd be back?

MARY. No, sor. She looked like she'd been crying, sor.

FRISBIE. Crying, eh? That's strange. What happened during—oh, I forgot you've just come. (*Goes to mantel, picks up cigarette—looks at it—smells it.*) Was there anybody with her when you came?

MARY. No, sir.

FRISBIE. Well, what is there to eat in the house?

MARY. There's a little soup, sor—and some salmon—and eggs and cheese.

FRISBIE. Well, get me some.

MARY. Here, sor?

FRISBIE. No, in the dining room.

MARY. The missus said yez had only two meals a day.

FRISBIE. Oh, did she? Well, I want something now, no matter what she said about the meals.

MARY. (*Going.*) Yes, sir——

FRISBIE. And, say— (MARY *turns.*) What's your name?

MARY. Mary Nolan, sir.

FRISBIE. All right, Nolan, see if there's any beer in the ice-box—bring me a bottle while the lunch is getting ready.

MARY. Yes, sir. (*Exit.*)

FRISBIE. (*Back to cigarette. Pause.* ) Now, who the mischief has been smoking these things? And a fire in the grate. Nell's putting on a few lugs while I've been gone. (*Re-enter* MARY.)

MARY. There's no beer there, sir.

FRISBIE. Oh, hang it—and I asked Nell never to be without it.

MARY. There's four of these, sir. Will one of thim do?

FRISBIE. (*Taking bottle.*) Four? Champagne! (*Scratches chin—looks at bottle—looks at cigarette—back at bottle.*) Bring me a glass.

MARY. (*Going.*) Yes, sir. (*Exit.*)

FRISBIE. (*Cutting Seal.*) Four of them—quarts—I wonder if there's been a case. (*Reads label.*) Brut! (*Thinks.*) On the few occasions that Nell's been lucky enough to guess champagne—and get it—she's wanted a sweet wine. Who's been here that had to have Brut? (*Enter* MARY *with two glasses.*)

MARY. Which of these is right, sir?

FRISBIE. Put 'em both down. (MARY *sets glasses on table.*) Maggie——

MARY. Mary, sor.

FRISBIE. (*Pouring wine.* ) Yes, Mary. I suppose my wife told you that seven o'clock in this house means seven o'clock. (*Pause.*) We have breakfast at seven sharp.

MARY. We'll have breakfast, sor, at half-past eight.

FRISBIE. *My* breakfast is at *seven.*

MARY. The missus said breakfast at eight-thirty, sor.

FRISBIE. I don't care a damn what she said— (*Loudly.*) I'll have my breakfast at seven. (*Enter* RUGGLES.)

RUGGLES. I beg your pardon.

FRISBIE. Well sir? (*To* MARY.) That will do. (*Exit* MARY.)

RUGGLES. (*Looking after* MARY.) I thought I was in my own apartment—my name is Ruggles.

FRISBIE. (*Agreeably.*) Yes, I know you by sight, Mr. Ruggles. Your flat is just below.

RUGGLES. How stupid of me. You are Mr. Frisbie, I believe?

FRISBIE. Yes sir.

RUGGLES. Then my flat *is* below. You must excuse my rude intrusion.

FRISBIE. (*Smiling.*) Don't mention it, sir. Quite a natural mistake. Will you have a glass of wine?

RUGGLES. No, thank you; good night.

FRISBIE. Good night. (*Exit* RUGGLES.)

FRISBIE. Damn fool—doesn't know his own house; bursting into other people's like a mad bull. (*Drinks, takes paper, draws chair to fire, arranges bottle, lights cigar —sits.*) Now, where the deuce can Nell have gone? Crying, eh? Cigarettes and champagne. (*Pours it.*) Brut champagne. (*Enter* MRS. RUGGLES. *Starts at sight of* FRISBIE.)

FRISBIE. (*Rising.*) Good evening.

MRS. RUGGLES I beg pardon—I must have made a mistake. (*Looks about.*) I thought I was in my own flat.

FRISBIE. You are Mrs. Ruggles?

MRS. RUGGLES. Yes.

FRISBIE. Your flat is just below. Won't you sit down? (*Indicating wine.*)

MRS. RUGGLES. Oh, no—I— But there certainly is a mistake. These *are* my rooms. That is my sofa—that is my folding bed. (*To portieres.*) Mary.

MARY. (*Off-stage.*) Yes, mum.

MRS. RUGGLES. Never mind. (*Turning to* FRISBIE.) That is my cook. It is you who have made the mistake, sir.

FRISBIE. What! (*Rushes* L. *to portiers.*) Well, hang me, if I haven't—I thought this was the fifth floor.

MRS. RUGGLES. (*Agitated.*) This is the *fourth* floor, sir.

FRISBIE. Well, you really must excuse me—my name is Frisbie—I live——

MRS. RUGGLES. I know—you live in the flat above. Please go.

FRISBIE. I've unpacked my satchel—your husband was just here.

MRS. RUGGLES. (*Startled.*) My husband!

FRISBIE. (*Taking off smoking-jacket.*) Yes, I told him you lived downstairs. He's probably asleep there by this time—where's my coat? (*Exit* L.)

MRS. RUGGLES. (*Following to curtain.*) Please—please hurry, Mr. Frisbie—I shouldn't tell you of it, but my husband is foolishly jealous of *you.*

FRISBIE. (*Off-stage.*) Jealous of me! Here, Bridget—Maggie—Murphy—gimme my shirts.

MRS. RUGGLES. Oh, please—please go, Mr Frisbie.

FRISBIE. (*Appearing left in shirt-sleeves, with arms full of papers.*) My dear madam, compose yourself. I want my shirts. I haven't got a thousand. (*Exit. Enter* RUGGLES *on the bounce.*)

RUGGLES. *Well, sir!* (*Sees wife.*) Ha—where is he? (*Re-enter* FRISBIE *in shirt-sleeves, with coat, dressing-coat and satchel.*)

MRS. RUGGLES. Frederick——

FRISBIE. (*Dropping things.*) See here, Ruggles——

RUGGLES. You damned scoundrel. (*Men clinch and tussle.* MRS. RUGGLES *screams.*)

RUGGLES. I've caught you—caught you both together. (*Scuffle during which* MRS. RUGGLES *calls "Oh, Frederick" and* FRISBIE *cries "See here, Ruggles." Re-enter* MARY.)

MARY. Here, here, what d'ye mean? (*Parts them. To* RUGGLES.) Get out of this! Get out, ye loafer, or we'll trow ye downstairs. Does ye take this for a free-and-aisy?

MRS. RUGGLES. No, no, Mary. *This* is my husband.

MARY. Sure, *he* told me *he* was. (*Men glare and clinch again, but do not struggle.* MARY *acts as peace-maker.*)

FRISBIE. I never mentioned—the lady's *name.* You told me that you were the new cook and that *my* wife had gone out——

RUGGLES. Whom did you take *my* wife to be? A new chamber-maid?

MRS. RUGGLES. I wasn't here, Frederick.

MARY. Sure, *she'd* gone out.

FRISBIE. And left word she didn't know when she'd be back.

RUGGLES. Left word! For whom?

MRS. RUGGLES. For you Frederick.

FRISBIE. I thought I lived here—this wretched woman *said* I did.

MARY. Holy murder! *I* told you ye lived here? Divil a word of it, mum.

RUGGLES. You told me that *I* lived downstairs.

FRISBIE. Well, damn it, I thought you did. I supposed I was in my own flat, didn't I?

RUGGLES. Did you suppose this was your own wife?

FRISBIE. Not for a second, sir. I saw the mistake as soon as the lady came in and I began hustling to get out.

MRS. RUGGLES. I've just come in, Frederick, dear. You must believe me. Haven't I, Mary?

MARY. (*To* RUGGLES.) This livin' minute.

RUGGLES. You should have known my servant, sir.

FRISBIE. Damnation! *You* didn't know her—you saw her bring me wine.

RUGGLES. Well, I thought it was *your* wine.

FRISBIE. So did I. And asked you to join me. Would I have tried to detain you if everything had not been on the level? (*Pause.*)

MRS. RUGGLES. It's a perfectly natural mistake, Frederick. We musn't misjudge Mr. Frisbie.

RUGGLES. Of course not. (*Smiling.*) You must see, Mr. Frisbie, that the first glance at the situation justified my—animation.

FRISBIE. Why, you're not to blame, sir—I've been away for a week and was in such a hurry to see my wife that I walked up instead of waiting for the elevator. New girl—wife not home—and there you are—Murphy here put all my shirts away.

MRS. RUGGLES. Where are Mr. Frisbie's things?

MARY. In the bureau; sure, the dirty wans I throwed in the wash.

MRS. RUGGLES. Get them.

MARY. Yes, mum. (*Enter* MRS. FRISBIE.)

MRS. FRISBIE. Mr. Frisbie! What does this mean?

FRISBIE. Why, my dear.

MRS. FRISBIE. Where is your coat, sir? Why! Have you been drinking, Mr. Frisbie? (*Sees wine.*) There, there.

RUGGLES. Let me explain, madam. I came in just as Mr. Frisbie was trying to put his coat on, and——

MRS. FRISBIE. He was drinking with her——

MRS. RUGGLES. Mrs. Frisbie—your husband!

MRS. FRISBIE. Don't talk to me, you impudent woman—how dare you! (MRS. RUGGLES, MARY *and* MRS. FRISBIE *all talk at once.*)

MRS. RUGGLES. (*In trio.*) You are utterly mistaken, Mrs. Frisbie. There's been a misunderstanding everywhere.

Mr. Frisbie came into our apartments thinking they were his——

RUGGLES *and* FRISBIE. Ladies—ladies— (*Women stop talking.*)

RUGGLES. Perhaps if you would let us explain— (*Women resume talking.*)

RUGGLES. (*Loudly to* FRISBIE.) Come, have a drink.

MRS. RUGGLES (*In trio.*) Don't raise your voice at me—you don't know anything about it and you won't listen. Be still or I shall have my servant put you out. Every woman in the building has warned me against you as a mischief-maker. Be still, you shan't call me names in my own house!

MRS. FRISBIE. (*In trio.*) I had a telegram from my husband that he would be home to dinner. I nearly starved waiting for him. To think of his being down here drinking wine with a depraved person whose husband will permit such conduct. I've had my ideas about my husband. You're always in the elevator or the hall when he's about, and he's always talking—talking—talking about you. I shall move out of this flat and get a divorce.

MARY. (*In trio.*) Sure, mum, I'm the new cook! Whin your husband came in I thought he was Mrs. Ruggles' husband. Sure, I brought him the wine—he asked for beer, but there was none in the box. He took off his coat and shoes, and I put his shirt in the wash. For didn't I think he was the master—and I put the clean things in the bureau. Thin when Mr Ruggles came in and they flew at each other like two Donnybrook chickens—sure, I had to take both of them by the collars. (RUGGLES *and* FRISBIE *at beginning of trio give up in despair and pleasantly take a drink.*)

(*As women still keep on talking*)

CURTAIN

# THE MAYOR AND THE MANICURE

COMEDY IN ONE ACT

## GEORGE ADE

George Ade was born at Kentland, Indiana, in 1866. He began his literary career when he was still working for the Chicago Record (1890-1900). It was during the years that followed that he achieved national fame as the author of the "Fables in Slang" which are characterized by a distinctly American type of humor. At the same time, however, he wrote plays and the librettos of comic operas, of which latter "The Sultan of Sulu," "The Sho-Gun," and "Peggy from Paris" exercised widespread influence throughout the country. "The County Chairman" and "The College Widow," in particular, were real contributions to the American theater, which in the early years of the present century was not especially rich in genuine native drama. Mr. Ade has been equally successful as a writer of one-act plays, of which "Nettie," "The Mayor and the Manicure" and "Marse Covington" are the best-known. It is only within the last year that Mr. Ade has allowed his plays to be published, but in spite of the fact that these were written some time ago, it is evident to any reader of them, that George Ade the dramatist is a figure of importance.

Following is a list of George Ade's published plays:

"The County Chairman;" "Father and the Boys;" "The Sultan of Sulu;" "Just Out of College;" "The College Widow;" "Nettie;" "Marse Covington;" "Speaking to Father;" "The Mayor and the Manicure."

# THE MAYOR AND THE MANICURE*

## CHARACTERS

THE HONORABLE OTIS MILFORD, *Mayor of Springfield.*
WALLIE MILFORD, *his son.*
GENEVIEVE LE CLAIR, *a manicure.*
RUTH FOSTER, *engaged to* WALLIE.

PLACE: *Springfield—any State.*
TIME: *Now.*

SCENE: MAYOR'S *private office in office building. The essentials are entrance from street or outside, either at* C. *or* L., *and a practicable door leading off* R. *into an inner office. At* C. *flat-top desk with books and papers, desk telephone with insulated wire leading from it down over side of desk in plain view of front. This need not be an insulated wire; it may be a soft cord, one that can readily be cut with a pair of scissors. There are chairs at each side of the desk, although it is not essential to the action that there be more than three on the stage, one at* R. *of desk, one at* L. *At* L. *on the wall is a dummy telephone connected by insulated wire laid across the floor and over the desk, and there connecting with push-button so that telephone can be rung from the desk.*

*On the walls may be lithographs of the* HON. OTIS MILFORD. *Above the picture "People's Choice for Governor" and below "The Hon. Otis Milford." Have several of these displayed, wherever there is room on the wall. The* MAYOR *may have bouquet of flowers on his desk, the month being June, and if there are windows, the outside light effects may be high, as the time is supposed to be about eleven o'clock in the morning.*

*At rise of curtain* RUTH, *in street costume with parasol, standing between desk and door at* R., *talking off through door at* R., *which is standing open.*

*Suggest for curtain music: "What's the Matter with Father?" and "Boola-Boola."*

RUTH. (*Talking off* R.) Mr. Milford!

MILFORD. (*From within*) Well?

RUTH. If you're so awfully busy, *I'll* go down to the station and meet him.

MILFORD. (*Gruffly*) All right—all right.

RUTH. Shall I bring him up *here?*

MILFORD. Sure—haven't seen him for a year.

RUTH. All right.

(GENEVIEVE *enters* L. GENEVIEVE *must indicate by manner and costume that she is of the extremely artificial and "flit" description. Gown, parasol, style of dressing hair, hat, etc., all of the most ultra and showy kind. Nothing grotesque or impossible, but loud and showy. Her manner somewhat affected,* GENEVIEVE *starts across* R. *as* RUTH *starts* L. *and they discover each other—the desk between them. Slight bus. of surprise.*)

GENEVIEVE. Is this the Mayor's office?

RUTH. (*Looking at her wonderingly*) Yes.

GENEVIEVE. Is the Mayor in?

RUTH. He's in there—(*Pointing with parasol toward door* R.)

GENEVIEVE. Thanks. (*Starts to cross.*)

RUTH. (*Continuing*) —but I don't think you'd better go in. He's very busy just now—may bite your head off.

GENEVIEVE. (*Smiling in a superior sort of way*) Indeed?

I've never met the Mayor. Do you know him quite well?

RUTH. (*Speaking out with great frankness*) Oh, yes, indeed. I'm—— (*Hesitating.*)

GENEVIEVE. (*With sudden interest in her*) Oho! Is it possible that *you* are the young lady who is going to —— (*Pause.*)

RUTH. I thought everyone knew *that*—that is, every one in Springfield. I guess you don't live in Springfield.

GENEVIEVE. (*Amused, and rather patronizing the girl*) No, indeed! So you are going to marry——

RUTH. Wallie—he's the only son.

GENEVIEVE. Really! (*Then glancing at lithographs on wall, up and behind desk to* R.) The Mayor is a candidate for Governor.

RUTH. (*With enthusiasm*) Oh, yes, and everybody says he'll get it.

GENEVIEVE. (*Hesitating, and then looking at* RUTH *keenly*) Is—ah—the Mayor well-to-do?

RUTH. Well-to-do? He's terribly rich. He owns the street railway, and the telephone company, and the evening paper, and the box factory, and about half the buildings on Main Street.

GENEVIEVE. (*Bus. of being much interested and pleased at the news*) I'm glad to hear it.

RUTH. I'm going to the train. (*Starts for door left.*)

GENEVIEVE. Just one more question. (RUTH *stops.*) Mr. Milford's son. Just home from college, I believe?

RUTH. No—he stopped over at Binghampton. I'm going to the train *now* to meet him. (*Running quickly out of door* L.)

(GENEVIEVE *laughs to herself in a highly gratified manner and walks across* R. *rapping on door with parasol, or rather poking it, standing off a good safe distance as if somewhat apprehensive.*)

MILFORD. (*From within—loudly*) Well? Well? Well?

GENEVIEVE. (*Alarmed, but bracing up*) Mr. Milford.

MILFORD. (*Impatiently*) Haven't you gone away yet? What do you want now?

GENEVIEVE. (*Standing several feet away from the door and calling back at him*) I want to see *you.*

MILFORD. When I'm busy, you know better than to hang around here—— (*Opens door and steps out—sees* GENEVIEVE*—stops, startled.*) Oh!

(MILFORD *has a couple of sheets of paper in left hand and pencil in the right. He is of the florid, well-fed type—well dressed, but not in fastidious taste. A little carelessness in attire—rumpling of hair, pulling up of cuffs, etc., might emphasize rough and ready character of man. Avoid making him too sleek, pale and well-groomed.*)

GENEVIEVE. (*In sweet and insinuating tones and bus. with eyes*) Is this Mayor Milford?

MILFORD. (*Looking at her a moment before answering, and then, rather gruffly*) Yes ma'am that's my name, but I don't want to subscribe for any books.

(GENEVIEVE *has package of letters in her hand.*)

GENEVIEVE. I am *not* a book agent.

MILFORD. Sellin' tickets for a benefit?

GENEVIEVE. No, indeed.

MILFORD. Mebbe you're one of these lady reporters?

GENEVIEVE. (*Blandly*) Not at all.

MILFORD. All right—I'm glad to see you. (*Abruptly*) Sit down! (*Starts for chair back of desk.*)

GENEVIEVE. Mr. Milford, I—— (*Puts handkerchief to her eyes, bus. of trying to control emotions.*) I have come to see you on a matter of great importance.

MILFORD. All right! All right! (*Going behind desk. After another suspicious look at her, evidently having sized her up from her dress and manner*) Here—here ——Don't weep! Save your tears till you've told your story! I s'pose it's got something to do with a man.

GENEVIEVE. (*Simpering*) Yes, sir.

MILFORD Sure thing! Hold your horses while I telephone. (*Picks up telephone receiver and talks into 'phone*) Hello, hello! Give me the Evening Courier. —Hurry up—this is the Mayor.—Evening Courier? City Editor.—Hump yourself—this is the Mayor!— City Editor? This is the Mayor. Take this down. Ready? (MILFORD *holds up sheets and reads what he has written into the 'phone deliberately, as follows*—) "Walter Gillespie Milford, only son of the Mayor, arrived in Springfield this morning, having recently completed his course at Atwater College." (GENEVIEVE *is listening with interest.*) "He made a brilliant record both in scohlarship and athletics." (GENEVIEVE *cannot control herself, but bursts out an "Ha! Ha!"* MILFORD *looks at her.*) What's the matter?

GENEVIEVE. (*Restraining herself*) Never mind. Go ahead.

MILFORD. (*After giving her another hard look, resumes reading into the 'phone, holding the copy in front of him*) "Young Mr. Milford will immediately take charge of some of his father's most important business interests, and when the Mayor is elected Governor this Fall he will take *entire* charge. As we have already announced, he will shortly lead to the altar one of Springfield's fairest daughters." (*Very promptly on this cue, and just as* MILFORD *is hanging up receiver,* GENEVIEVE *screams and makes a bluff of falling back, half fainting, in her chair.*) Madam, you seem to enjoy doing that. What's the trouble this time?

GENEVIEVE. (*Bus. of extreme agitation—trying hard to appear surprised*) Oh! Oh! Why did you speak those cruel words?

MILFORD. *What* cruel words?

GENEVIEVE. Your son—you say he is going to be married?

MILFORD. Yes, ma'am—what of it?

GENEVIEVE. He never told me!

MILFORD. (*Looking at her hard and critically*) Mebbe not—couldn't tell everybody.

GENEVIEVE. He deceived me!

MILFORD. Who deceived you! That kid of mine? Ha! (*Laughs.*)

GENEVIEVE. I am here to appeal to you—his father.

MILFORD. Say—who are you—what's your name?

GENEVIEVE. Genevieve LeClair.

MILFORD. Circus name!

GENEVIEVE. I am a poor manicure girl.

MILFORD. Girl, eh?

GENEVIEVE. I went to Atwater to work——

MILFORD. (*Drily*) Atwater to work—the college boys! Sure thing! I beg your pardon. Go right ahead—don't let me interrupt your story.

GENEVIEVE. I met your son—he pursued me.

MILFORD. Pursued you? Great Scott!

GENEVIEVE. He bought me presents.

MILFORD. Hold on! *I* bought the presents—*he* merely delivered them.

GENEVIEVE. He made love to me—I thought he intended to marry me.

MILFORD. Marry you—— You're old enough to be——

GENEVIEVE. (*Bristling up*) I beg your pardon—I didn't come here to be insulted.

MILFORD. Why did you come here?

GENEVIEVE. To demand justice—or—

MILFORD. Damages.

GENEVIEVE. (*Haughtily*) Yes, sir—damages.

MILFORD. Now we're gettin' down to business. (*Looks at watch.*)

GENEVIEVE. I followed your son.

MILFORD. Yes—you followed him so fast you got here ahead of him.

GENEVIEVE. (*Taking letters from purse*) I have the letters he wrote me——

MILFORD. (*In dismay*) Letters—did that young pinhead——

GENEVIEVE. You'll enjoy hearing them—when they're read at the trial.

MILFORD. Trial?

GENEVIEVE. For breach of promise.

MILFORD. Now, hold on just a second! Let me see if I understand this case. College boy with too much money to spend—meets blonde manicure—out in the buzz-wagon—down where the near-beer flows—I'm afraid to go home in the dark. Wise manicure learns that papa has money—decides to get some of it. Am I right?

GENEVIEVE. (*On her dignity*) The facts will come out at the trial.

MILFORD. (*Smiling grimly*) There isn't going to be any trial.

GENEVIEVE. Isn't there?

MILFORD. No, ma'am.

GENEVIEVE. There will be, unless——

MILFORD. Now, Cleopatra—— (*With gesture of apology.*) Give me that name again. (*Hand to ear.*)

GENEVIEVE. (*Haughtily*) Genevieve LeClair.

MILFORD. All right, Genevieve. Before I go any further with you I'll get Atwater on long distance—talk to the Chief of Police and get a line on you.

(GENEVIEVE *is frightened and startled.*)

GENEVIEVE. That will take too long. I can't wait.

MILFORD. Take only a minute. I own the telephone company. (*Taking receiver off 'phone. Cheers heard outside.*) Aha! (*Replacing receiver.*) Papa's baby boy has arrived. (*He jumps up and runs up stage to look out of window.*)

(GENEVIEVE *rises at* R. *of table, first looking over at him.*)

GENEVIEVE. (*As if speaking to him, but not so that he hears*) You'll not telephone if I can help it. (*Looks *down at table, picks up scissors, cuts wire, bearing down on desk to do so. Replaces scissors.*)

(RUTH *enters from* L. *door joyously. Noise subsides.*)

RUTH. (*Jumping up and down*) He's here! He's here!

MILFORD. *Yes*—I see he's here.

RUTH. All the boys from the academy at the train—they all got out and yelled—— (*Imitating*) "What's the matter with Milford?"

MILFORD. (*Enthusiastically*) That's the stuff! (*Turning, sees* GENEVIEVE—*dryly to* RUTH) I know what's the matter with him.

RUTH. (*Seeing* GENEVIEVE) Oh, I forgot someone was here.

MILFORD. (*Explaining to* RUTH) Yes, lady dropped in to turn over some very important papers to me—real estate deal.

RUTH. Oh! (*Goes up to window.*)

MILFORD. (*Going toward* GENEVIEVE) Madame, I'll ask you to step into my private office just a minute while I discuss a few family affairs.

GENEVIEVE. (*Rising*) I didn't come here to be put away in any private office.

MILFORD. (*Crossing to door* R.) I know you didn't, but you'll step in there just the same. (*Opens door.*) This way. (*Pause.*) Please. (*She hestitates and they glare at each other, and then she moves to door at* R., *turns.*)

GENEVIEVE. I'll not be kept waiting long—understand that. (*Quick exit.*)

MILFORD. Yes—er—you'll find a Youth's Companion on the table there. (*He closes door* R. *and goes to desk.*)

RUTH. What a peculiar woman.

MILFORD. All these business women are peculiar—very eccentric. I'll telephone the glad news to Wallie's mother. (*Reaching for 'phone.*)

RUTH. (*Looking out of window or off* L.) This will be a happy day for Mrs. Milford.

MILFORD. I hope so. (*Into 'phone*) Hello!

RUTH. (*Still looking off*) There's a crowd around him—all shaking hands. (*Runs down, puts arms around* MILFORD, *gives him a squeeze.*) Oh! (*Then quickly back to window.*) Aren't you proud of him?

MILFORD. I'm proud, all right, but I'm trying not to show it. (*Into 'phone again*) Hello! (*Pause.*) Hello! (*Loud.*)

RUTH. (*Coming down* L.) What's the matter?

MILFORD. If I didn't own the telephone company, I'd say the service was rotten. Hello! Say, Central, wake up! (*Gives the 'phone an angry jerk and pulls up the severed cord.*)

RUTH. Why—it's broken!

MILFORD. (*Looks at severed cord*) Well, I'll be—— (*Then picking up scissors, looks at them for marks made by cutting; then shakes fist at door* R.) Look at that—I've worn it out talkin' to office-seekers! Here! You've got a cab waiting—drive up and tell my wife——

RUTH. Why don't you use the other 'phone?

MILFORD. What other 'phone?

RUTH. That one. (*Indicating one at* L.)

MILFORD. Never mind that. You jump in the cab——

RUTH. But, Mr. Milford—(*Persistently*)—why don't you 'phone?

MILFORD. (*Losing his patience—rising*) If you must know—that isn't a 'phone at all—it's a dummy!

RUTH. Dummy?

MILFORD. Man in politics has dozens of people coming to pester him every day. When I want to get rid of any one, I call myself up on the telephone like this. (*Pushing button on side of desk. 'Phone rings. Note: This push-button must be placed so that* MILFORD, *in reaching for it, must make the movement evident to everyone in front.)*

RUTH. (*Puzzled*) Call yourself up—how?

MILFORD. (*Annoyed at her persistence*) Why, don't you see? I touch this button, so—— (*Bus.*) 'Phone rings. I rush over, pretend to get an important call. Get rid of pest. Great idea, eh?

RUTH. (*Crossing to button*) All you have to do is to push the button, and—— (*Bus. of trying it. 'Phone rings. Laughs.*) Well, if that isn't the funniest——

MILFORD. I know—but you jump into that cab—(*Pushing her off door* L., *speaking after her*) Tell my wife that our innocent offspring has arrived. (*Closes door. Crosses and locks door* R. *Orchestra begins softly music of "Boola."*) Now, Genevieve, you are sequestered for a few minutes. (*Starting for desk.*)

WALLIE. (*Enters* L. *door*) Dad! (*Throwing aside hat.*)

MILFORD. (*Meeting him in front of desk*) Wallie, my boy, I'm glad to see you. How are you? (*Bus. of embracing him.*)

WALLIE. Finer'n silk—glad to get home.

MILFORD. I'll bet you are. Got your degree, did you?

WALLIE. I'm a Master of Arts.

MILFORD. Master of Arts, eh? I suppose you have mastered all the arts. The art, for instance, of inhaling cigarettes—the art of puttin' down fifteen balls in one run—the art of——

WALLIE. (*Interrupting laughingly*) Oh, you're like everyone else—you think us college fellows don't work —I've had a very—busy—year.

MILFORD. Yes; so I understand! Hope you didn't study too hard.

WALLIE. No—I took good care of myself. (*Sits on desk, removing gloves.*)

MILFORD. That's very gratifying. No shenanigan?

WALLIE. What do you mean?

MILFORD. I mean—you haven't been buying lemonade and lobsters for any chorus ladies——

WALLIE. Certainly not.

MILFORD. (*Sitting right of him on desk, aside*) Certainly not—how foolish of me to ask. (*Turning to* WALLIE) Milliners?

WALLIE. Why, no!

MILFORD. Dressmakers?

WALLIE. Dressmakers?

MILFORD. (*Offhandedly—explosively*) Manicures?

(WALLIE *chokes, rises and looks at his father frightened.*)

WALLIE. W—what do you mean?

MILFORD. Nothin' at all—just want to make sure you'd been behaving yourself, that's all.

WALLIE. Why, Father, you know——

MILFORD. (*Impressively, placing hand on* WALLIE'S *shoulder*) Yes, I know that you've got the best mother a boy ever had. I know you're engaged to marry the sweetest girl in this town, and I hope that you haven't overlooked those two important facts while storing—(*Putting hand on head*)—this with rich and precious knowledge.

WALLIE. Of course, I spent a good deal of money.

MILFORD. Of course you did—that's all right, I'm not kickin'—(*Turning* R.)—as long as we don't have to spend a lot more.

WALLIE. I don't follow you.

MILFORD. It's all right—you're home now, and ready to settle down—get married and be a great business man.

WALLIE. Yes, Dad.

(GENEVIEVE *rattles door at* R. MILFORD *pretends not to notice.* WALLIE *looks* R.)

WALLIE. Some one at that door.

MILFORD. Did you hear it, too?

(GENEVIEVE *pounds on door. Brief pause.* GENEVIEVE *pounds again.*)

WALLIE. (*Puzzled*) There is somebody there. (*Crosses behind to* R.)

MILFORD. I believe there is.

GENEVIEVE. (*Calling*) Mr. Milford! Mr. Milford! (*Rattles door.*)

WALLIE. Why, it's a woman! (*Looking at* MILFORD *knowingly.*) How about it, Dad—have I caught you?

MILFORD. It looks that way.

(GENEVIEVE *continues calling and rattling door violently.*)

WALLIE. She wants to get out.

MILFORD. I wouldn't be s'prised.

WALLIE. (*Coming down* R.—*mischievously*) Say, Dad, I won't give you away——

MILFORD. My noble boy! (*Embraces him.*) I will admit to you—there is a woman in there. (WALLIE *laughs.*) But as a man of the world you can readily understand that a politician has to be mighty careful.

WALLIE. Sure! That's one of the things I learned at college.

MILFORD. You won't give me away, will you?

WALLIE. (*Earnestly—taking himself seriously*) Certainly not—I'm a good sport.

MILFORD. (*Shakes hands*) My dear sport, welcome to our family circle. Say—you let her out—she'll surprise you.

WALLIE. (*Crosses and unlocks door, throws it open, then politely*) Come out, Madam. (GENEVIEVE *stalks out.*) Genevieve! (*Falls back into* MILFORD'S *arms.* GENEVIEVE, *drawn up proudly, glares at him.*)

MILFORD. (*Pulling* WALLIE *to his feet, throws him around to* L.—WALLIE *falls on desk.*) If you're a good sport—now's the time to show it.

WALLIE. (*Hair mussed—weak, terrified*) Genevieve! What are you doing here?

GENEVIEVE. (*Very theatrical*) I'm here to see you—you have wrecked my life!

MILFORD. (*Mock-serious*) See what you've done—you've wrecked her life.

WALLIE. (*Disgusted.*) Huh!

MILFORD. Come over and sit down—both of you. (*Crossing to table—they do the same—*WALLIE *slowly and hesitatingly.*) Let's get at the facts. (WALLIE *crosses and sits* L. *of table,* GENEVIEVE *at* R. WALLIE *nervous and rattled—*GENEVIEVE *haughty and on her dignity.*) Now, then, did you make love to little Genevieve here?

WALLIE. Well, I—I chased around with her more or less. (*Hesitating and very nervous.*)

MILFORD. (*Pointedly*) Why—tell me that? Why?

GENEVIEVE. (*Half to herself*) The brute!

WALLIE. You see—mighty few girls in a college town—Genevieve was popular. To get ahead of the others I had to—to——

MILFORD. Lay it on thick—mush—taffy.

WALLIE. Yes, sir.

GENEVIEVE. I should say he did. He said that I was his affinity.

WALLIE. (*Doggedly*) I thought you could take a joke.

MILFORD. Joke! A woman never gets old enough to regard love-making as a joke. Did you spring that affinity chestnut on her?

WALLIE. (*Shame-faced—hesitating*) Yes, sir.

MILFORD. Don't you know that only married men go chasing after affinities?

GENEVIEVE. He just the same as proposed.

WALLIE. Not guilty! (*Emphatically.*)

GENEVIEVE. (*Indignantly*) You led me to believe——

MILFORD. (*Interrupting her—to* WALLIE) Anyhow, you wrote her. You—the son of a politician! In future tell 'em anything you want to—but—you get a rubber stamp!

WALLIE. I guess I made a fool of myself, but I didn't mean anything.

MILFORD. Of course you didn't. The chump who rocked the boat didn't mean anything.

WALLIE. I didn't suppose——

MILFORD. (*Interrupting*) Now see here—you've been studying for four years—you think you've learned—but there's one subject about which you'll never know much, if you study for forty years, and that is—woman! (*This very impressively, but don't take too much time.*) Woman was created merely to keep man guessing! I know—I've guessed! You wait outside five minutes and mebbe I can settle this thing for you. (WALLIE *goes to door.*)

GENEVIEVE. (*As they cross, aside—confidently*) Only one way to settle it!

WALLIE. (*In doorway*) I'm sorry to get you into trouble.

MILFORD. Yes—I—I appreciate your sorrow! (*Exit* WALLIE L. MILFORD, *after turning and staring at* GENEVIEVE, *who looks back at him defiantly, goes to desk, standing behind desk.*) Madam, you may be the best little manicure in the world, but you're not going to trim me.

GENEVIEVE. (*Confidently*) Indeed?

MILFORD. Indeed! You know that one word of scandal would break his mother's heart. (*Indicating* L.) You know that he's engaged to marry a sweet, innocent girl—you know that I'm making a fight for Governor and this thing has got to be kept quiet. Furthermore, you know that I've got a bundle and you figure that you can shake me down.

GENEVIEVE. (*Insolently*) What if I do figure that way?

MILFORD. I'll stand by that boy—right or wrong. But listen! If you were young and innocent, and I thought he'd wronged you, I'd make him toe the mark and do the right thing by you. But you are no spring chicken.

You've been up and down the road a good many times and know all the bumps.

GENEVIEVE. (*Trying to be indignant*) Mister Milford!

MILFORD. No fool college boy can take you by the hand and lead you anywhere that you don't want to go. You've got no more claim against that boy—

GENEVIEVE. (*Decisively*) 'We'll let the jury decide that.

MILFORD. Madam, you are four-flushing. You know this thing has got to be kept quiet. How much do you want for those letters?

GENEVIEVE. (*Much relieved, adopting business manner, rapping table with each word*) Ten thousand dollars.

MILFORD. If I pay you ten thousand dollars, will you destroy the copies?

GENEVIEVE. (*Startled, rising*) Copies?

MILFORD. (*Triumphantly—striking desk*) Aha — so you haven't any copies! It's very evident you've never played the game of politics—as we play it in my district. Rule number one is—lock the originals up in a safety deposit box and do business with the copies.

GENEVIEVE. (*Apprehensively*) Surely, you wouldn't——

MILFORD. I have only to ring for the police.—There'll be a little item in the evening paper—"Crazy woman calls on Mayor." You'll go out of town on the next train—police will turn letters over to me! You forget that I'm Mayor here—I own this town. (*All this is in a bluffing, bulldog fashion.*)

GENEVIEVE. (*Frightened*) Is that the way you treat women in this town?

MILFORD. That's the way we treat blackmailers. This may be a jay town, but we know all about the third degree.

GENEVIEVE. (*Losing her nerve, half aside*) Arrest me —run me out of town? (*Turning to* MILFORD) *You* wouldn't do that?

MILFORD. No—but I've got a right to. When a woman

kicks off her petticoats and starts to fight a man at his own game, she needn't expect any mercy.

GENEVIEVE. (*Struggling to keep up her courage*) Ha! You're trying to frighten me. (*Resumes chair.*)

MILFORD. I've called up Atwater.

GENEVIEVE. (*Sneeringly*) Oh—have you?

MILFORD. You cut this wire—(*Showing severed cord*)—but you forgot that other 'phone. (*Indicating one at* L. *Pushes button—'phone rings.*) Aha—there we are now! (*Hurries over to 'phone and takes down receiver.*)

GENEVIEVE. (*Apprehensive, but trying to keep up a front.*) No one can say a word against my character.

MILFORD. (*Into the 'phone*). Hello—Atwater? Chief of Police? This is Mayor Milford of Springfield. A woman calling herself Genevieve LeClair, claiming to be a manicure, is down here trying to hold me up. Who is she? (*Pause.*)

GENEVIEVE. (*Very nervous*) You have no right to insinuate——

MILFORD. (*Into 'phone*) Yes, she's a blonde—(*Pause as though listening.*) Oh, bleached, is she?

GENEVIEVE. (*Indignantly*) A lie—it's natural!

MILFORD. (*Into 'phone*) What is her real name? (*Pause.*) You don't say so! (*Bus. of alarm by* GENEVIEVE.) Has she ever been mixed up with any college boys? (*Pause.*) Get out! Dozens of 'em, eh?

GENEVIEVE. (*Emotional bus.*) I merely met them.

MILFORD. (*Listening intently at 'phone, and then loudly and distinctly*) Where is her husband? (GENEVIEVE *shrieks and sinks back, half fainting*—MILFORD *hangs up receiver and hurries over to her, alarmed.*) Madam, don't faint in here. (*Letters have fallen to floor. He picks them up, looks at them hesitatingly for a moment and puts them back in her lap and begins patting her hand.*) Here! Genevieve! Come to! (*Slapping her hand. She half-recovers and looks up at him, terrified.*)

Why should the mere mention of a husband cause you to keel over like that?

GENEVIEVE. (*Struggling*) I have no husband —he deserted me.

MILFORD. Well, when we get into court we'll let him tell the jury why he deserted you.

GENEVIEVE. It is cruel of you to dig up my unfortunate past.

MILFORD. It is foolish of you to have an unfortunate past—especially if you're goin' into court. (*Pause.*) Genevieve, you have made a nervy play for high stakes, but you can't put it across. I've got your number. (*Coming behind her, back of desk softly*) Don't you think you'd better turn those letters over to me—then quietly—(*Pause*)—waft out of town?

GENEVIEVE. (*Recovering herself, clutching letters with both hands—defiant manner*) No! Never!

(MILFORD *touches button on desk. 'Phone rings.* GENEVIEVE *startled.* MILFORD *hurries over and picks up receiver.*)

MILFORD. Will you excuse me while I seem to answer the 'phone once more? (*Into 'phone.*) Hello! Oh! Detective headquarters? (GENEVIEVE *starts.*) Yes, the woman is still here. (*Pause.*) No—no—I don't want to arrest her unless I have to. Yes—plain clothes man in the corridor—good idea! (*Hangs up receiver—turns.* GENEVIEVE *arises and starts across* L. *up stage to escape as* MILFORD *turns from 'phone and intercepts her.*) Hold on, we're not through yet, Genevieve. (*In front of desk.*)

GENEVIEVE. (*Coming toward him, imploringly*) Are you a gentleman?

MILFORD. No, ma'am, I'm a practical politician—also, I am the father of an irresponsible idiot who needs protection. Do I get the letters? (*She looks at him, frightened, and slowly extends letters. He takes them.*)

GENEVIEVE. You are not going to disgrace me—humiliate me?

MILFORD. Certainly not. (*Enter* WALLIE—*sees him*) Walter, come here. (WALLIE *approaches him and* GENEVIEVE *goes a step or two* R.) I'm ashamed of you—you have compelled me—me—a tender-hearted man who wouldn't harm a fly, to bluff and bullyrag a defenceless woman. I want you to apologize to this lady for trifling with her affections. (GENEVIEVE *is surprised.* WALLIE *hesitates.* MILFORD *is more emphatic.*) Go ahead. (*As* MILFORD *seats himself at desk and begins counting out money from drawer or tin box,* WALLIE *crosses, embarrassed, and faces* GENEVIEVE.)

WALLIE. (*With an effort*) Genevieve—I've—I've acted like a mutt. I was engaged to another girl—never thought you'd take it seriously. I—I—apologize.

GENEVIEVE. (*Brokenly*) It was my fault. I had no right—but I did care a lot for you—and when I heard——

RUTH. (*Running on, speaking as she enters*) Wallie! Your mother wants me to bring you right up in the cab. (*Sees* GENEVIEVE—*pause.* WALLIE *runs across to* RUTH.) Oh!

MILFORD. (*Rising*) Oh—Ruth! (*Indicating*) This is Miss LeClair. (*To* GENEVIEVE) Miss Foster—going to marry my son.

RUTH. I'm glad to meet you.

GENEVIEVE. Thank you. I—I wish you much happiness.

(RUTH *and* WALLIE *go up stage* L.)

MILFORD. Miss LeClair. (*Taking bundle of bills he has counted out—putting them in large envelope.*) Here is the amount we agreed on—one thousand dollars. I believe you'll find it correct. (*Offers it to her. She takes it, hesitatingly and surprised.*) I could have given you a check, but I am so well known in banking circles here in town I prefer currency.

RUTH. Come on, Wallie! (*Starts* L. *to go off.*)

WALLIE. (*Starting after her and then seeing 'phone on wall at* L.) Wait 'till I 'phone Billy Johnson. He doesn't know I'm home. (*He crosses her to 'phone.*)

RUTH. (*Laughing*) That isn't a telephone—it's just a dummy.

(WALLIE *pauses, surprised.* GENEVIEVE *suddenly interested.* MILFORD *making signs to* RUTH *to keep her quiet.*)

GENEVIEVE. Dummy? What do you mean?

RUTH. It isn't connected outside. (*Crossing back to desk.*) There's a wire over to the desk, and when Mr. Milford wants to pretend to get a message, he just pushes the button like this. (*Pushes button. The 'phone rings. Laughing.*) Isn't that a cute idea?

GENEVIEVE. Wonderful!

(MILFORD *is sitting in front of desk.*)

RUTH. (*Hurrying* L.) Come on, Wallie! Your mother is waiting. (RUTH *exits* L. WALLIE *starts to follow and turns.*)

WALLIE. Good-bye, Genevieve.

GENEVIEVE. Good-bye, Wallie! (*After they exit,* GENEVIEVE *crosses behind desk, finds button and presses it. Both grin. She extends hand.*) I'm glad to meet the real member of the family. (*They shake hands.*) Say, how did you know I was a grass widow?

MILFORD. Experience, Genevieve, experience.

GENEVIEVE. (*Insinuating*) Won't you come out and have lunch with me?

MILFORD. You trot along, Genevieve. You've got yours. I had mine thirty years ago.

GENEVIEVE. (*Goes to door, laughing heartily, turns and waves her hand at him*) Good-bye!

CURTAIN

# THE RED OWL

TABLOID MELODRAMA IN ONE ACT

## WILLIAM GILLETTE

William Gillette was born at Hartford, Connecticut, in 1855. Although he took an interest in the theater at a comparatively early age, he managed to receive an education at Yale, Harvard, and the Massachusetts Fine Arts Institute. Since 1875, when he made his début as an actor, he has followed the professions of actor, manager and playwright. His more successful work has been in his own plays, chiefly "Sherlock Holmes," "Secret Service," and "Held by the Enemy," and with his own extraordinarily successful adaptation of "The Private Secretary." The only published one-acter of Mr. Gillette's is "The Red Owl," here printed for the first time. It was very popular on the vaudeville stage for a number of years.

As a playwright Mr. Gillette has achieved distinction through an extraordinary ability to construct tense and moving dramas. "Secret Service" and "Held by the Enemy" are among the very few successful Civil War plays this country has produced.

Following is a list of Mr. Gillette's published plays: "Held by the Enemy," "Esmeralda," "All the Comforts of Home," "Secret Service," "Sherlock Holmes," "Too Much Johnson," "Electricity," "The Red Owl."

References: Montrose J. Moses, "The American Dramatist;" Richard Burton, "The New American Drama;" Barrett H. Clark, "The British and American Drama of Today."

# THE RED OWL*

## CHARACTERS

HERBERT BRANDT
DOROTHY BRANDT
EDWARD VOSBERG
CHARLES
POLICEMAN

SCENE: *The hall of the Brandts' house in a Suburban District of New York.*

TIME: *The present.*

*A large hall of a suburban house, handsomely decorated. Rich furniture of elegant appearance, with dark rich tones. No light or glaring colors. Dark reds prevailing. Woodwork heavy and dark like mahogany or dark oak.*

*Fireplace on right side well down with large mantel richly carved. A coal fire burning—throwing a strong red light. A door up Right above the fireplace, opening to a back hall-way.*

*Stairway up Right leading to a landing. A balustrade above, where the stairway lands.*

*Large window at Left well up—and obliqued. This is a French window, and extends down to floor.*

*The large front door of the house is at left below the window, and well down stage.*

*Cases with drawers, etc., up Center. A large red owl on a pedestal on one of them, so that it is well elevated and near enough to be in plain sight. Electric effect*

---

*to give a subdued glow to the owl's eyes—not too pronounced or unnatural, but as if it might be the reflection of the fire with an added greenish tinge. A high clock on the landing with a slow and very loud tick, the hands started at a quarter to one at rise of curtain.*

*A table to the Right of Center with a few books and magazines on it, and a revolver of good calibre.*

*A small table or stand down Left of Center, near front, on which is a handsome tea service including a burning alcohol flame under hot water kettle. Also a plate of dainty sandwiches.*

*A built-in lounge or settee above the fireplace and up under stairway or in front of it, making a comfortable fireplace seat or lounge with cushions, etc.*

*The room is only about half lighted, so that the red glow from fire will strike across. The lights increase gradually for about two minutes after the curtain rises.*

HERBERT BRANDT *is seated by the side of the table at Right of Center—red glow from fire upon him. His face is toward the front—the table upon his right, between him and the fire. There is a revolver upon the table, with a silver name-plate on it. A leather satchel with straps to go over shoulders—the kind used to carry valuables—lies conspicuously on table by his side. He has a large packet securely tied up and sealed, grasped firmly in his hands. He sits motionless, his eyes staring straight before him. The clock ticks slowly. There is a strange luminous glow in the owl's eyes. In* BRANDT'S *a fixed look of tense anxiety. He then fingers the packet nervously. Slight noise off stage—*BRANDT *starts slightly and instantly becomes alert, and, keeping his eyes on the French windows he nervously and hastily places the packet in the leather satchel on table. Fumbles for revolver, all the while keeping eyes to the left. He gets hold of the revolver and rises with it in his hand ready for instant use. Slight pause as he looks keenly. Then he cautiously crosses toward left,* *and goes to upper side of French windows. He cautiously draws the portieres back a little and looks into the garden, all the while holding the revolver ready. Slight pause. He starts to recross to table. Pauses. Turns head toward door down Left. Cautiously goes down Left and satisfies himself that the door is securely locked.*

*Sound of a door closing heavily outside.* BRANDT *starts and turns instantly. He stands with revolver grasped in right hand, not aimed but ready. Sound of approaching footsteps outside. Crosses close to door up Right.*

BRANDT. Who's there!

CHARLES. (*Outside*) May I come in, sir?

BRANDT. Who is it?

CHARLES. (*At door up Right*) It's Charles, sir—the butler.

BRANDT. Is that you Charles?

CHARLES. (*Coming into room and standing near the door.*) Yes, sir!

BRANDT. What are you doing here?

CHARLES. I—I came back, sir—(*Hesitates*).

BRANDT. What for?—What did you come back for?

CHARLES. I came back to see if—if you was in any trouble, sir!

BRANDT. (*Not quite sure of himself*) Trouble! What do you mean! I thought I sent you to town with the rest of the servants. I told you to stay there and look out for 'em!

CHARLES. (*Embarrassed*) Yes, sir. There's a train back to New York at one-fifteen in the morning—I can take it if you wish.

BRANDT. Well, I do wish! You get that train!

CHARLES. Yes, sir. (*After slight hesitation, he turns and is about to go.*)

BRANDT. See here! (CHARLES *stops*) What did you come back for? Didn't you get them all out of the house? Aren't the servants all out as I told you?

CHARLES. Yes, sir. They're all out. I took them in on the nine-forty.

BRANDT. Well, why didn't you stay there with them? What are you doing here?

CHARLES. I was afraid there was something wrong, sir—that is—I—I didn't know but you might need me, sir.

BRANDT. Oh—you thought I might need you? (*Looking at* CHARLES *sharply.*)

CHARLES. Well, I didn't know, sir.

BRANDT. (*After a slight pause*) That's all right. But I don't need you. (*Turning toward tea-table*) There's nothing wrong.

CHARLES. I'm very glad to hear it, sir.—I'll hurry for the train. (*Turning to go.*)

BRANDT. Oh—Charles!

CHARLES. (*Turning back*) Yes, sir.

BRANDT. Just see if my wife is upstairs.

CHARLES. Yes, sir. (*He goes quickly up the stairs to the balcony and looks off—then returns half-way down.*)

Mrs. Brandt is in her room, sir—shall I speak to her?

BRANDT. No. I only wanted to know where she is. (CHARLES *comes down stairs and moves toward door up Right.*) Wait a minute! My wife says her brother sent that bird to her. (*Indicating owl.*)

CHARLES. You mean the owl, sir?

BRANDT. Yes—that thing there. She says it came to-day—from her brother.

CHARLES. Yes, sir. Mr. Vosberg sent it. It came this afternoon.

BRANDT. Did he bring it himself?

CHARLES. No, sir. A man brought it on an express wagon.

BRANDT. Oh—he did, eh!

CHARLES. Yes sir.

BRANDT. What did you mean at dinner when you said there was something else in the house?

CHARLES. (*Surprised*) Said what, sir?

BRANDT. I asked you—at dinner—if the LaRose Claret was all gone.

CHARLES. Yes, sir.

BRANDT. You said it was—but there was something else in the house. Did you mean anything by that?

CHARLES. Yes, sir—I was referring to that California lot you were going to try.

BRANDT. (*Doubtfully*) You were, eh!

CHARLES. Yes, sir.

BRANDT. You didn't mean anything else?

CHARLES. Certainly not, sir.

BRANDT. Oh—(*Looks at watch.*) See here—you'll have to hurry for that train.

CHARLES. Yes, sir. (*Turns and goes out.*)

(BRANDT *moves over to door up Right to see that* CHARLES *is off. Sound of door closing outside.* BRANDT *turns away, and sees the owl again. A motion of disgust as he goes down to table and sits as before.*

*Enter* DOROTHY BRANDT *at the top of the stairs. She looks anxiously over the balustrade at* HERBERT *and after a moment starts down the stairway. When she is about half way down* HERBERT, *hearing her, springs to his feet, grasping the revolver as before, and facing up at the same instant.*)

HERBERT. Who's there! (DOROTHY *stops on the stairway frightened.*) Oh!—it's you! (*Lowers revolver, and speaks nervously*) I —I didn't know—(*Breaks off, breathless.* DOROTHY *recovers herself, and stands on the stairway looking at* HERBERT *with anxiety.*)

DOROTHY. Why, who else could it be?

HERBERT. Who?

DOROTHY. Yes! I'm the only one in the house!

HERBERT. You're not the only one outside of the house! (DOROTHY *glances round with a slight look of alarm. Then she comes down the stairway and pauses near the foot of it, glancing nervously to the left again. Turns to* HERBERT.)

DOROTHY. But nobody knows you've got the bonds!

HERBERT. Don't speak so loud! (*Glances down at satchel strapped to his side.*)

DOROTHY. But they don't—do they? (*Pause*) Does anyone know, Herbert?

HERBERT. (*In an undertone*) Of course someone knows!

DOROTHY. Who?

HERBERT. The men I took them from.

DOROTHY. They were officers of the law!

HERBERT. All the worse—that kind of an officer! They're out for money—that's what they're out for—and they might give me away! My mistake was in bringing the things out here at all! I ought to have stayed in town!

DOROTHY. (*Going to him*) Why, it's a great deal safer to be here—in your own house! I know it is!

HERBERT. That's what I thought—before I came. Now it looks different. I wish I'd gone to a hotel.

DOROTHY. Hotel! Why, they're full of thieves—we read of robberies in them every day!

HERBERT. Yes, but you can raise an alarm mighty quick! Suppose we 'phoned the police station here—it would take fifteen minutes to get a man!

DOROTHY. I wish you hadn't sent Charles away.

HERBERT. You never can tell about a butler! He made a remark I didn't like!

DOROTHY. But he couldn't have meant anything by that!

HERBERT. Well, I'm not going to take any chances! If there's anybody after it the first thing they'd do would be to get at the servants. That's why I got 'em all out of the house—every one of 'em! (*Moves nervously across to Right and turns. As he turns his eyes fall on the owl again.*) And that damned bird up there—I wish he was out of the house with 'em!

DOROTHY. You mean the owl?

HERBERT. That's just what I mean!

DOROTHY. Why, Eddie sent it to me!

HERBERT. Well, it's got on my nerves!

DOROTHY. But they're very rare—red ones! They're almost extinct!

HERBERT. They'd be entirely extinct if I had my way! I couldn't get away from his confounded eyes! Here—just look at him now—do you see what I mean?

DOROTHY. (*Looking at the owl with a shiver*) Oh dear, yes! (*With a sudden impulse*) Here! (*She hurries to the little stand down left and snatches up a large napkin or table cloth*) I'll cover him up! (*She throws the napkin over the owl so that it is draped in white like a ghost*) There! (*Returns*) Now it won't trouble you any more.

HERBERT. I believe that bird's a hoodoo! Your brother's trying something with us—you wait and see if he isn't!

DOROTHY. What—Eddie?

HERBERT. Yes, Eddie! You know well enough what he is!

DOROTHY. Herbert—you're too severe!

HERBERT. Anyone that treats his wife as he does—you can't be too severe!

(HERBERT *sees that he has hurt her, and goes to her quickly. Taking her in his arms.*) Here, here! For heaven's sake don't mind what I say tonight! Eddie's all right—and so is the owl—and nothing's going to happen!

DOROTHY. (*Looking up at him, and clinging to him affectionately*) No!

HERBERT. Of course not! (*Pats her affectionately*) But it's just as well for me to sit up and keep a lookout—you mustn't mind that!

DOROTHY. But you're wearing yourself out—

HERBERT. Oh, nonsense!

DOROTHY. (*Clinging to him*) Yes, you are—and it's because you're so frightfully overworked—just see what you're going through—sitting up all night to guard that. No sleep—and no appetite—and your nerves on the rack—and revolvers about—and—and—(*Beginning to break down.*)

HERBERT. There, there! (*Affectionately*) Now don't get going, will you! It's only one night!

DOROTHY. But how do we know it won't occur again?

HERBERT. It couldn't! You see—this package of stuff I've got in here came in late—(*Indicating satchel*) from Clemons & Co. Everything was closed—I couldn't even get into the inner office where the safe is. Then I tried to find someone else with a safe who'd keep it overnight for me—but they'd all gone—there was nothing else to do!

DOROTHY. Why didn't you make Clemons & Co. take it back and send it in the morning?

HERBERT. In the morning they'll be bankrupt!

DOROTHY (*Astonished. Looks at him an instant before speaking*) Clemons & Co.!

(HERBERT *nods.*)

HERBERT. All in! If we hadn't got it tonight we'd be out over a million!

DOROTHY. A million! Do you—do you mean it's as valuable as that!

HERBERT. Sh! (*Glances round*) If a man got away with it he'd make a haul—I can tell you that! Half of it's in money! (*An idea occurs to him.*) Here! (*Taking satchel from table*) I'll strap it onto me! (*He quickly buckles satchel to his side*) They'll have to get me first—and I'll be hanged if they do that!

DOROTHY. (*Going quickly to him*) No—no!

HERBERT. (*Taking her in his arms tenderly*) Good lord —what a fool I am to be worrying you about this! The thing for you to do is to run right upstairs and go to bed—it's long after midnight.

DOROTHY. No!

HERBERT. What's the good of your sitting up?

DOROTHY. That's my place, Herbert—by your side! All the books say that—and I think it's in the marriage service too! Yes, I really think I promised to sit up with you!

HERBERT. (*Laughing*) Oh, no, you didn't—you promised to obey me—and now is your chance to do it! My orders are—(*She stops his mouth with her hand.*)

DOROTHY. No, no! Don't say it Now listen! Do you want me to keep my word about obeying? Do you?

HERBERT. Yes!

DOROTHY. Then you mustn't tell me to do anything that I won't! So now (*taking her hand away*)—if there's any disobeying you'll make me do it by giving the wrong order, and it'll be entirely your fault!

HERBERT. But what's the use of our both sitting up?

DOROTHY. There isn't any use in it—and you're the one to go to bed, because I couldn't sleep! I couldn't sleep a solitary wink, so I'll sit here and keep watch—and you can leave the revolver, because I know how to use it as you very well know— seeing I beat you three the last time! Now please go up and get a little nap!

HERBERT. There's no nap in me—don't you see that? You couldn't keep my eyes shut with a steel spring!

DOROTHY. (*An idea suddenly occurring to her*) Oh!

HERBERT. What is it? (DOROTHY *leaves him and hurries up left and opens drawer of a table. She takes out a small box and holds it up triumphantly.*)

DOROTHY. Look! Just the thing! Those sleeping tablets!

HERBERT. No—I wouldn't take any of those things to-night!

DOROTHY. (*Approaches him*) But Dr. Ackerman said they were perfectly harmless! And the one you tried last Monday gave you a beautiful night!

HERBERT. It wouldn't do it now!

DOROTHY. Then you can take more—he said there was no harm up to six!

HERBERT. (*Interrupting*) I'm not going to take any sleeping tablets tonight, Dorrie! Now don't say any more!

DOROTHY. (*Disappointed*) Oh! (*She moves slowly away with the box as if to place it where she found it. Glancing toward down left she sees the tea service and sandwiches on the little stand and walks over to it, looking at it as she does so.*) Herbert! (*Turning to him.*) You haven't eaten a thing! And I don't believe you took any tea! Did you? (*She lifts the tea pot.*)

HERBERT. What good is tea?

DOROTHY. It's lots of good!

HERBERT. Oh, well—I'll drink it if you say.

DOROTHY. And awfully strong—it's been steeping half an hour! Will you have cream?

HERBERT. No, give it to me clear.

DOROTHY. Yes, that's better for you. (*Puts the spoon on the saucer and starts toward him with the cup of tea*) You know you—(*She stops with a sudden idea*) Oh, I—(*Glances back to the tea table and then at* HERBERT *again with a moment's indecision.*) Wait a minute—I—I forgot the—(*Starts back toward table*) I forgot the sugar!

HERBERT. You put it in—I saw you.

DOROTHY. (*Slightly nervous.*) It was only one lump—you like two. (*Sets the cup on the table.*)

HERBERT. Oh, I don't care!

DOROTHY. Well, you must have it right! (*She picks up the box of tablets, opens it quickly and, standing with her back to* HERBERT, *counts out three tablets and drops them into the cup. She hesitates an instant and then takes one more out of the box and puts it into the cup. This is done very quickly.*) What's—(*Speaks a little absently.*) What's the good of having tea at all—if you don't have it—if you don't have it the right way! (*She stirs the tea quickly and takes up the cup and saucer again, turning toward* HERBERT *and crossing toward him with it.*) There! (*Handing the cup to* HERBERT) I think it's—I think it's the way you want it! (*A little breathless on last few words but covering it quickly, and smiling at him pleasantly.*)

HERBERT. (*Taking the tea.*) That was a good idea of yours! Cheer a fellow up—and all that! (*He drinks tea.*)

DOROTHY. (*Slight nervousness*) Oh, yes! Is it—is it good at all?

HERBERT. (*Doubtfully. He drinks some more and sets the cup down*) I suppose it's stood too long, that's all. It has a sort of a taste like moth-balls.

DOROTHY. Now you're going to let me sit up with you a little while—aren't you?

HERBERT. All right—if you really want to!

DOROTHY. Well, I really do! Let's come round here by the fire! (*Arranges chair.*)

HERBERT. Don't turn the chair that way—I want to keep my eye on that window!

DOROTHY. (*Shivering.*) Now, Herbert! Don't let's get nervous again!

HERBERT. Well—I don't want anyone coming at me from behind, do I? (*About to sit*) See here—I'm going to take that owl off from there! (*Goes toward the owl.*) He's worse covered up than he was before!

DOROTHY. What difference can an owl make? (HERBERT *stops.*)

HERBERT. That's so! What difference can it make! I must be—(*Sits*) Dorrie, you know I was never this way before, you know that, don't you!

DOROTHY. Of course I do! (*Puts arm around his neck affectionately.*)

HERBERT. You see, when you get to thinking of the different ways they might get at you—

DOROTHY. Oh, yes! But don't let's think of it!

HERBERT. Why, coming out on the train there was a

man at the further end of the car—and—(*Pauses—a little drowsiness showing in his last few words.*)

DOROTHY. (*With some alarm, but keeping quiet*) Yes—at the end of the car—?

HERBERT. He was there, you know. And he got off when I did—and I thought he—I thought—(*Pause*) Do you know—I'm actually a little sleepy—I am, upon my word!

DOROTHY. Oh, are you?

HERBERT. (*Suddenly rising*) See here—this won't do!

DOROTHY. (*Looking up at him*) What won't do, Herbert?

HERBERT. I must shake it off! (*Tries to rouse himself.*)

DOROTHY. Oh, don't do that!

HERBERT. I tell you I must! This isn't any time for me to sleep!

DOROTHY. But a little nap would do so much good for you!

HERBERT. No, no! (*Moves about trying to rouse himself. Sits again near* DOROTHY.)

DOROTHY. If you could close your eyes for just a few moments it would make you feel so much better!

HERBERT. Do you think so?

DOROTHY. I know it! And I'll wake you up in five minutes if you say. And keep watch every second of the time! Oh, Herbert, do!

HERBERT. I suppose I might just close my eyes a minute or two! (*Rises slowly.*)

DOROTHY. (*Rising*) Oh yes! Come! (*Bringing him toward stairway.*) I'll fix you all comfortable, and put a rug over you—and then I'll come down and keep watch!

(*They are starting up the stairway together.* DOROTHY *stops and goes to electric button near foot of stairway and turns off light. Room is darker, now lighted with red glow of firelight.*)

HERBERT. What are you turning off the lights for?

DOROTHY. I'm going to sit in the library. I don't like to be in the hall. (*Starts up stairway.*)

HERBERT. Well, you'd better keep an eye on that window—the lock's no good!

DOROTHY. I can see it from the library just as well.

HERBERT. (*Turning and going up.*) Oh, all right! Isn't it odd how sleepy I got—all of a sudden!

DOROTHY. (*Following* HERBERT *up the stairs*) That's often the way! You know you're always sleepy at night the minute you open a book!

(HERBERT *and* DOROTHY *exit at the top of the stairs. Short pause. Loud ticking of clock, very slow swing of pendulum. A faint knock at the door to the left—pause. The knock is repeated a little louder but still subdued. After another brief pause* EDWARD VOSBERG *appears outside the window up left and is seen cautiously looking in. He soon begins to work at the lock or catch of the window, slipping a table knife in and about. After a moment or two the lock or catch springs back with a rather loud click. He pauses briefly, then carefully and noiselessly opens the window and comes into the room. After a glance about he turns back to the window, throws the knife out through it, and closes the sash, carefully adjusting the lock or catch as it was. Then he turns and looks cautiously about, advancing a little, glancing up the stairway, listening for sounds from above, etc. He is in evening dress, wearing an overcoat of fashionable cut, silk hat, etc. He has gloves on, wears patent-leather shoes and carries a cane. His face is rather repulsive, showing marks of dissipation. After satisfying himself that no one has heard him come in, he goes quickly down to the little table and looks about on it for something. Lights a match and looks again. Picks up the box of tablets with the evident satisfaction of finding what he is looking for, and examines it closely by the light of the match. Puts the box down again, shields match-flame with hands and crosses to the table. Holds burning match close to cup and looks sharply down into it, examining the dregs carefully. Blows out match and throws it away. Stands thinking an instant. Then turns and goes up above table, takes off opera hat and places it on mantel. Takes out cigarette-case and lights a cigarette; stands puffing it. While doing so his eyes light upon the draped owl. He takes the cigarette out of his mouth and stands staring at it in surprise. Then he goes over and looks at it closely.)*

VOSBERG. Ha, ha ha! They didn't like it! (*Looks about the room again as if for an explanation of the phenomenon. His eyes are arrested by something on the table. He goes over and sees that it is a revolver, and picks it up. Examines it, puffing cigarette as he does so, turning the barrel to see if it is loaded, etc. He glances up the stairway. Then he knocks lightly on the table with the revolver. Waits a moment. Glances up stairway. Goes to stairway and knocks lightly on newel-post. Goes back to table, putting revolver on it and moves over near fire.*

DOROTHY *appears at the top of the stairway, much frightened, and looking fearfully about to see where the noise came from. After pausing a moment, she comes cautiously down the stairs, holding her hand tight against her left side as if the beating of her heart were painful. After a slight hesitation she reaches the floor. Just as she does so she sees* VOSBERG *and starts back with a stifled scream, clinging to the newel post for support.)*

DOROTHY. Oh—who's that!

VOSBERG. Hullo.

DOROTHY. Oh, Eddie! How you frightened me!

VOSBERG. Anything wrong?

DOROTHY. Wrong! What do you mean?

VOSBERG. I mean wrong. What's the matter with you?

DOROTHY. Why, you startled me so! I'd no idea you were here!

VOSBERG. Well, I am.—I'm here all right. (*Slight pause*) (*Indicating owl*) What's the matter with that?

DOROTHY. (*Slightly startled*) Oh—what?

VOSBERG. That bird I sent you. Was he cold?

DOROTHY. (*Not understanding*) Cold?

VOSBERG. Yes. You've covered him up, I see!

DOROTHY. Oh yes—we—we—

VOSBERG. Maybe you didn't like his looks!

DOROTHY. Why—you see, his eyes were so—so strange—

VOSBERG. (*With a slight grin*) Made you nervous, eh?

DOROTHY. A—a little.

(VOSBERG *sneers and turns away.*)

How did you get in? Did you open the window again?

VOSBERG. Of course.

DOROTHY. Oh! (*As if her feelings were hurt*) I asked you not to!

VOSBERG. Well—I knocked a long while and nobody heard. I couldn't camp out on the porch all night, could I?

(DOROTHY *goes to the electric button and turns on the lights.*)

VOSBERG. I've been waiting out there about ten minutes!

(DOROTHY *turns quickly and stands facing* VOSBERG.)

DOROTHY. Ten—ten minutes?

VOSBERG. Somewhere around there. It might be more —it might be less.

DOROTHY. At the—at the window?

VOSBERG. (*Nods ill-humoredly*) Yes! That one right there—in plain sight! And I saw a thing or two!

(VOSBERG *walks over to* DOROTHY *and stands close to her, looking into her face.*)

Say, you're not trying any little thing yourself, are you?

DOROTHY. (*Breathlessly*) I don't know what you mean!

VOSBERG. Don't you though!

DOROTHY. No!

VOSBERG. (*Turning away*) Oh, well—it's nothing special. Only if there was something I'd like to be in on the deal!

(DOROTHY *stands looking at him, not understanding.*)

DOROTHY. In on the deal?

(VOSBERG *strolls to small table and picks up the box of tablets.*)

VOSBERG. (*Carelessly*) Candy, I suppose?

DOROTHY. No—they're sleeping tablets. Dr. Ackerman gave them to us!

VOSBERG. (*With a gesture up the stairway*) Well, you gave them to him all right! (*Strolls back to table and tosses the box down on it*) You shoved in four or five —unless I saw crooked!

DOROTHY. Why, they're perfectly harmless—you know they are!

(VOSBERG *picks up the teacup and glances into it carelessly.*)

VOSBERG. Say, take a hint from me! You'd better rinse that out! (*He puts cup down again.*)

DOROTHY. He was very nervous and tired—it was absolutely necessary for him to sleep!

VOSBERG. Well, I don't want to disturb him, do I! I know well enough he doesn't want to see me!

DOROTHY. Oh, Eddie—(*Going to him*) if you could only see what a life you're leading—and how hard it is for Mary!

VOSBERG. (*Looks down a moment*) I see well enough! You don't have to tell me!

DOROTHY. (*Hand on his shoulder.*) That's what Herbert can't endure! He doesn't mind my helping you—really he doesn't.

VOSBERG. He doesn't mind, eh?

DOROTHY. No.

VOSBERG. Then I wish to God you'd help me now. It might mean a lot to Mary and me.

DOROTHY. What can I do? I haven't any—you know my allowance—

VOSBERG. (*Interrupting*) It isn't money. Dorrie—I see a chance to make a new deal all around!

(DOROTHY *looks at him.*)

I know what I am—and how I treat Mary and all. I want to pull up and reform the worst way! I don't suppose you'll believe me, but I do!

DOROTHY. Oh, I will believe you! And if you'll only reform and—and—

VOSBERG. Well, I can do it—if you'll help me a little! And it won't be any trouble for you either!

DOROTHY. (*Eagerly*) Tell me what it is!

VOSBERG. It's a chance to make enough money so I can leave the Street—and get quit of all the things that drag me down—all the boys—all the places that tempt me—and live a decent life.

DOROTHY. But what can I do?

VOSBERG. You can tell me something—that's all—tell me something I want to know! Will you *do* it?

DOROTHY. Why, of course I will—if I can!

VOSBERG. Well, you can all right!—He's got a lot of bonds here—you needn't be alarmed—I just happened to know about it—no one else does.

DOROTHY. Yes?

VOSBERG. They'll be thrown on the market tomorrow. If I could find out the dates and the numbers I could play the allied stocks before the slump and make enough to pull out on and never speculate again! If I can get hold of enough to make us comfortably off, I'll quit the whole game—upon my soul I will! Now don't answer me till you think of it! It's a thing he approves of and does himself!

DOROTHY. No—no! He doesn't!

VOSBERG. Yes, he does! I can prove it to you! He'll be in it himself for all he's worth in the morning! All I want to know are the dates and numbers on those bonds!

DOROTHY. But you ought to find this out from Herbert! He's the one to—

VOSBERG. (*Interrupting*) Now don't be foolish! You know I can't ask him! He wouldn't tell me anyway! It's such a little thing! You might do it for Mary if not for me! Here!—(*Suddenly recollecting*) This is a note from her asking you to. (*Hands her a note*) Just look it over! You'll see it means a lot to both of us!

(DOROTHY *takes the note and reads it. After looking at it she raises her eyes to* VOSBERG.)

DOROTHY. You want the dates and numbers on the—on the bonds?

VOSBERG. Yes. You can get a look at 'em, can't you?

DOROTHY. I can if he's asleep.

VOSBERG. Oh, he's asleep all right!

(DOROTHY *turns and slowly goes up the stairway. When a little way up she stops and turns to him.*)

DOROTHY. How many numbers are there?

VOSBERG. There ought to be about fifteen.

DOROTHY. But I can't remember as many as that!

VOSBERG. (*With assumed carelessness*) Oh—bring the bunch down then!

(DOROTHY *looks suddenly at him.*)

You needn't bring 'em here—just read 'em to me from the head of the stairs!

(DOROTHY *turns and goes up the stairway, disappearing at the top. Loud ticking of clock.*

VOSBERG *watches her until she disappears. Then he turns quickly back into the room and goes to the door left which he unlocks and opens and closes to see that it is ready for a hasty exit. Then he goes to the table and hastily examines the revolver again. Hearing*

DOROTHY *coming, he crosses and waits near foot of stairs.* DOROTHY *appears at top of the stairway with a large packet in her hand tied with heavy red tape, and sealed in several places. She comes down to the landing and looks at* VOSBERG.)

VOSBERG. Well? Aren't you going to tell me what they are?

DOROTHY. I can't find anything on the outside.

VOSBERG. They must be there! (*Moves a little nearer.*)

(DOROTHY *looks at the package again.*)

DOROTHY. You said dates, didn't you?

VOSBERG. Dates and numbers! I want 'em both!

DOROTHY. There's some figures here.

VOSBERG. But I want the dates! (*Moves a little nearer while she is looking at the papers.*)

DOROTHY. There aren't any!

VOSBERG. Hold it up and let me see!

(DOROTHY *holds the packet up so that* VOSBERG *may look at it. He is now quite near her.*)

(*As if trying to make out what is on the packet*) Why, there they are! (*Pointing to the packet.*)

DOROTHY. (*Looking quickly at packet again*) Where?

VOSBERG. (*Edging nearer*) Under that last line of figures!

DOROTHY. (*Coming down a step or two to get better light—looking intently at bonds*) The last line?

VOSBERG. Yes!—Here! You're looking in the wrong place! (*He suddenly springs up within reach and seizes the packet out of her hands with a quick wrench.*) Let me show you! (*He goes back down the stairs into the room.*)

DOROTHY. (*Instantly following after him with outstretched hands*) No—no—no!

VOSBERG. (*Moving away from her above the table*) Let me show you, I say! (*Pushes her off.*)

DOROTHY. (*Following* VOSBERG *and trying to get the*

*package away*) Give it back to me! Give it back to me!

VOSBERG. (*Backing away and throwing her off as she seizes his arms*) Keep away! I'll give it back in a minute!

DOROTHY. (*Following him madly and grasping at his arms or hands or the package.*) No, now! I want it now! What do you mean?

VOSBERG. (*Throwing her off roughly*) I mean I've got it and you'd better keep quiet! (*Stands scowling at her*)

(DOROTHY *stands suddenly motionless near stairway look- at him.*)

DOROTHY. (*After pause. Intensely but in low tone.*) Now I know what you are! (*After a slight pause*) Now I know you!

VOSBERG. (*Scowling at her*) You do, eh! (*Putting the packet securely in his overcoat pocket.*)

DOROTHY. Yes—I do! I knew you were a drunkard and a gambler—and a beat! I knew you neglected your wife and lived a life of shame and infamy! Now I know that you're a thief—and a robber—and a convict!

VOSBERG. Anything more?

DOROTHY. (*Coming down to chair right of table*) Nothing but this! If you give that back to me at once I'll debase myself so far as to say nothing! If you don't, I'll expose you!

VOSBERG. You won't expose me in a hurry, my dear!—Look at that stuff you gave him! You're hardly the one to speak!

DOROTHY. Well, I will speak! (*Moving back toward the stairway*) I'll call him this instant! (*She turns and starts toward the stairs as if to call.*)

VOSBERG. (*Not too loud*) Wait!

(DOROTHY *stops and turns.*)

One little thing before you do that! One little thing!

DOROTHY. (*Breathlessly*) What!

(VOSBERG *quietly picks up the revolver from table.*)

VOSBERG. This is loaded—*isn't* it!

DOROTHY. What if it is!

VOSBERG. Nothing. Only I thought I'd tell you—as it is loaded you'd better not call him, just now! Do you get the idea?

DOROTHY. You—you— (*A dazed motion toward the revolver.*)

VOSBERG. If he shows his head in this room he'll get a bullet in it!

(*Pause.*)

D'ye spose I'd stop for him with a couple o' millions at stake!

(*Pause.*)

You're not quite so anxious to call him, I see!

Well—(*Moving as if to cross to door down left and still keeping the revolver*) I haven't time to—

DOROTHY. (*With a sudden subdued scream*) Oh—(*Springs to door left and stands before it*) You shan't go!

(VOSBERG *pauses.*)

VOSBERG. You'd better be a little careful!

DOROTHY. You'll have to kill me first!

VOSBERG. I don't want to have any trouble with you!

DOROTHY. You will have trouble with me!

As long as I'm alive you shan't get out of this house—as long as I'm alive!

VOSBERG. (*Handling the revolver threateningly*) See here! I wouldn't stop for you either!

DOROTHY. Shoot me! Shoot me dead! I hope you will! At least he'll know I tried to stop you!

(*Instant's pause.*)

VOSBERG. Oh, here! (*Puts revolver in right hand overcoat pocket*) I guess I can handle a woman without that! (*Strides to her quickly and seizing her in a *rough grip, drags her back towards center. She struggles to hold him.*)

DOROTHY. You shan't! You shan't go!

VOSBERG. Let go!—Let go, I tell you!

DOROTHY. (*Clinging to him*) You shan't go! You shan't!

(VOSBERG *gets her to center and makes a sudden turn coming to left of her and trying to get away. She gives a sharp subdued cry and clings desperately to him, holding him back.*)

VOSBERG. (*Striking her arms and hands*) Let go! Let go or I'll hit you in the face! (*He suddenly throws her off, sending her against the table to which she clings half falling. He turns with an imprecation and starts towards the door at left. There is a loud knock at the door left.* VOSBERG *stops motionless.* DOROTHY *straightens up, slowly listening. Her face shows only blank surprise. It is too soon for hope.*)

VOSBERG. Who's that! (*Turning partly toward* DOROTHY.) Who'd be coming here now!

DOROTHY. (*Coming close to him quickly*) Whoever it is—whoever it is, I'll expose you—unless you give that back this instant!

VOSBERG. (*Taking out revolver*) Whoever it is I'll blow the head off him if he gets in my way!

(*A tremendous rapping on the door at* L. *as if it were struck with a heavy club.*

VOSBERG *stands with the revolver in his right hand pressed close to his right side so that it could not be seen from the door.*

DOROTHY *backs away from his a step or two coming against the table.*)

VOSBERG. (*Voice of loud bravado*) Come in!

(*Enter a* POLICEMAN *at the door left.*)

(*The three stand motionless an instant regarding each other.*)

POLICEMAN. I beg your pardon, ma'am—is everything all right here?

DOROTHY. A—all—right—?

POLICEMAN. Yes ma'am. We had a call down at the station.

DOROTHY. A—a call?

POLICEMAN. Yes, ma'am. I was the only one in except the Captain, so I came along to see what it was.

DOROTHY. Oh—I see. Yes.

(POLICEMAN *glances about the room.*)

VOSBERG. (*Who has quietly slipped the revolver into his right overcoat pocket on seeing the* POLICEMAN, *moves near* DOROTHY *and speaks to her in a quick aside*) Don't give me away! You can have that packet!

DOROTHY. (*Aside to* VOSBERG) When?

VOSBERG. As soon as I can get it out!

DOROTHY. You promise?

VOSBERG. Yes, yes! Send him away!

POLICEMAN. I daresay it's all right around here.

DOROTHY. Oh yes—it's all right!

POLICEMAN. No—no strangers in the house?

(DOROTHY *gives a quick glance back at* VOSBERG, *turning instantly to the* POLICEMAN *again.*)

DOROTHY. Oh, no! There's no—there's no trouble at all!

POLICEMAN. You didn't hear anybody at any of the windows?

DOROTHY. Hear anybody! Why, no!

(*The* POLICEMAN *watches* DOROTHY *closely.*)

Did you—did you—?

POLICEMAN. We heard there was a man getting in here.

DOROTHY. Why, who—who told you?

POLICEMAN. It was Mr. Travers, ma'am, J. B. Travers. He phoned us from his house.

DOROTHY. Phoned you?

POLICEMAN. Yes'm. He was on his way home in an auto, an' he thought he saw a man getting in here.

DOROTHY. Oh—Yes. Well, I—I'm very much obliged indeed!

POLICEMAN. You're the lady, I suppose? You live here?

DOROTHY. Yes—I'm Mrs. Brandt.

POLICEMAN. And—(*Indicating* VOSBERG.) Mr. Brandt, I suppose?

DOROTHY. No—Mr. Brandt is up-stairs asleep. This is my brother Mr. Vosberg.

(POLICEMAN *looks sharply at* VOSBERG.)

POLICEMAN. Oh, I see. Your brother.
Mr. Vosberg lives here, does he?

VOSBERG. (*Breaking in easily and naturally, and approaching a step or two toward the* POLICEMAN) No, I live in town—197 West 84th. I was only making a call.

POLICEMAN. You'll excuse my asking all this? I only want to make sure it's all right before I go.

VOSBERG & DOROTHY. Oh certainly!—Of course—Yes —we're very much obliged.

POLICEMAN. Not at all, ma'am—that's my business. And you're sure you didn't hear anyone at any of the windows?

DOROTHY & VOSBERG. (*With great certainty*) No!—Oh no!—No one at all!

(POLICEMAN *looks sharply at them.*)

POLICEMAN. Well, I think I'll just take a look about before I go—then we can rest easy. (*He starts as if to move up left. A glance of alarm from* VOSBERG.)

DOROTHY. (*With a movement toward* POLICEMAN) Oh, but I—I—

(POLICEMAN *stops and stands looking at her.*)

I hope you won't disturb my husband!

POLICEMAN. What's the matter with him? Is he sick?

DOROTHY. No—but he's very tired! Very tired indeed! It's the first sleep he's had for several nights!

POLICEMAN. Oh—that's the way it is!

DOROTHY. Yes—I'm really very anxious about him!

POLICEMAN. Well—of course it would be a pity to disturb him if he's tired—(*Glances up toward stairway*) He's up-stairs, you say—in that part of the house?

DOROTHY. Y—yes.

POLICEMAN. Well. I suppose it won't do any harm for me to have a look at this window? (*Indicating window up left.*)

DOROTHY. (*Doubtfully*) No.

POLICEMAN. (*Going to window*) Not if I do it as quiet as possible? (*He begins to examine the window.*)

DOROTHY. (*Quick aside to* VOSBERG) If you don't give it back I'll tell him!

VOSBERG. I'm going to! I'll put it on the stairs!

DOROTHY. Then do it!

(POLICEMAN *turns at window and looks at them.*)

POLICEMAN. There's someone been fooling with this window, ma'am.

DOROTHY. (*Turning quickly*) Fooling with it!

POLICEMAN. Yes, ma'am. They've pushed a knife or something up through and pried the bolt back.

VOSBERG. (*Coming center. Speaks in an easy jolly sort of way*) Oh, see here, Sergeant, I'll have to tell you—you're going so devilish far, you know! It was only a little joke of mine and we thought it was all right to keep quiet about it! The fact is I got in that window myself!

POLICEMAN. Oh—you got in there!

VOSBERG. Yes—you see I came up here late and they were both upstairs, and I couldn't make 'em hear, so I opened the window with my knife and came in. I did it more as a joke than anything else! Now I'm infernally ashamed it caused all this trouble—I am, upon my word—and I'd like to square it with you some way—(*Moves toward* POLICEMAN, *at the same time putting hand in his pocket for money.*) just to show there's no ill feeling!

POLICEMAN. (*Motioning* VOSBERG *back.*) Wait a minute.

(DOROTHY *is watching* VOSBERG *like a cat.*)

POLICEMAN. That's right, is it, ma'am?

(DOROTHY *does not answer. Her eyes are on* VOSBERG.)

(VOSBERG *looks round at her to see why she will not speak.*)

(*Repeating.*) He was right about coming in that window was he, ma'am?

VOSBERG. (*Pretending to be very indignant.*) Look here! I said I came in that window! Can't you take my word for it?

POLICEMAN. (*Good humoredly.*) Sure!—But I'd like the lady's word, too!

VOSBERG. (*Turning to* DOROTHY.) What's the matter? Aren't you going to tell him?

DOROTHY. (*Her eyes on* VOSBERG *meaningly.*) Yes. I'll tell him everything that occurred—if you wish me to!

VOSBERG. (*Quickly.*) You know I came in that way! Can't you tell him?

DOROTHY. Yes—I know he came in that way!

VOSBERG. (*To* POLICEMAN.) Of course she does! You want to be a little more careful about doubting a gentleman's word! You're getting entirely too officious—that's what you are!

(*The* POLICEMAN *stands watching him.*)

We don't need you any longer here—nobody's in the house that doesn't belong in it—and everything's perfectly safe!

POLICEMAN. See here, young man, what have you got that gun in your pocket for?

VOSBERG. (*After an instant's pause.*) Gun!

POLICEMAN. Yes. (*With a careless motion towards* VOSBERG'S *right hand overcoat pocket.*) There in your pocket. Take it out.

VOSBERG. (*As if suddenly remembering.*) Oh, this! (*He takes out revolver.*)

POLICEMAN. You ought not to carry those things around like that! What are you doing with it?

VOSBERG. Nothing at all! It was on that table when I came in and I picked it up and put it in my pocket just for a joke.

POLICEMAN. This must be your night for joking. Whose is it?

VOSBERG. Mr. Brandt's. (*Holding it toward the* POLICEMAN.) You can see his name on the plate.

POLICEMAN. Does that belong to your husband, Ma'am?

DOROTHY. Yes. It belongs to my husband.

POLICEMAN. (*To* VOSBERG.) And you found it on that table, you say?

VOSBERG. That's what I said!

POLICEMAN. Well, go and put it back on the table where you found it.

(VOSBERG *looks at* POLICEMAN *an instant and then goes slowly to the table and tosses the revolver down upon it carelessly.*)

POLICEMAN. Now move away a little.

VOSBERG. (*Looks at* POLICEMAN.) Move away?

POLICEMAN. Yes.

(VOSBERG *moves sullenly toward center.*)

A little further if you don't mind!

VOSBERG. (*Breaking out indignantly.*) What do you mean by giving me orders like this!

POLICEMAN. (*To* DOROTHY.) What was your husband doing with a revolver—out here on the table tonight?

(*Pause.*)

Was he cleaning it or repairing it?

DOROTHY. He was not.

POLICEMAN. Was he playing with it?

DOROTHY. No.

POLICEMAN. Well, what did he have it out for?

DOROTHY. For safety.

POLICEMAN. Safety!

DOROTHY. Yes. (*She looks at* VOSBERG.)

POLICEMAN. From what?

DOROTHY. From thieves or robbers.

POLICEMAN. Was he expecting anything like that?

DOROTHY. He was afraid they might come.

POLICEMAN. Why? Did he have money with him?

DOROTHY. He had a package of something—money or bonds—I'm not sure which—but so valuable that he sat up until half an hour ago guarding it.

POLICEMAN. What did he do then?

DOROTHY. He was so worn out that he finally went up stairs to get a little sleep.

POLICEMAN. Did he take the money with him?

(DOROTHY *looks at* VOSBERG. VOSBERG *has been standing motionless listening. He now slowly moves his arm as if to get something out of his inside overcoat pocket. While doing so he darts a sharp glance at the window*) Did he take the package of money with him, Mrs. Brandt?

(VOSBERG *tosses package of bonds quietly down on a lower step of the stairway.*)

DOROTHY. (*Watching* VOSBERG.) Yes—he took it with him.

(VOSBERG *cautiously gets the package again, endeavoring to slip it under his coat unobserved.*)

POLICEMAN. Is it up there now?

(*Pause.* DOROTHY *sees that* VOSBERG *has taken the package of bonds from the stairway.*)

DOROTHY. No—it is not up there now!

POLICEMAN. (*Quickly.*) Where is it?

(*Pause.* DOROTHY *looks at* VOSBERG.)

Where is that package now, Mrs. Brandt?

(DOROTHY *does not answer.*)

(POLICEMAN *after a second's pause, glances round at the door left, but instantly turns back again, keeping his eyes on* VOSBERG *and* DOROTHY. *He then quietly backs to the door and reaching behind him gets hold of the key out of the lock and puts it in his pocket. All this without taking his eyes from* VOSBERG *and* DOROTHY.)

POLICEMAN. Mr. Brandt's asleep upstairs, you say?

(DOROTHY *makes no reply.*)

(POLICEMAN *gets his whistle.*)

I'd better give him a call and see what he's got to say about this. (*Blows his whistle.*)

(*Pause.*)

Your husband seems to be a pretty sound sleeper, Mrs. Brandt. (*He blows his whistle again, this time making several short blasts in rapid succession.*)

(*Pause.*)

I'm sorry to inconvenience you, Mrs. Brandt, but I'll have to take a look up there. (*He walks to the foot of the stairs keeping his eyes on* VOSBERG *and* DOROTHY. *At the foot of the stairs he makes a quick turn about, swings round so that* VOSBERG *and the door are not out of his sight, and stands an instant glancing quickly from* VOSBERG *to* DOROTHY, *showing that he has them both in sight.*)

POLICEMAN. (*At foot of stairs.*) I'm only going half way up. I ought to be able to make him hear—if he's still alive!

DOROTHY. (*Quick gasp.*) Alive!

POLICEMAN. (*Turning to her almost on the word.*) He isn't dead, is he?

DOROTHY. No no!—you don't understand!

POLICEMAN. (*Moving up the stairway sidewise so that he keeps* VOSBERG *and* DOROTHY *in view.*) No—I don't understand, Mrs. Brandt—but I will in a minute!

(*With his eyes still on them he raps violently with his club on the balustrade. Slight pause. He taps again, making a terrific noise.*)

HERBERT. (*Off.*) What is it? What's the matter?

POLICEMAN. (*Loud voice.*) Is that you, Mr. Brandt?

HERBERT. Yes!

POLICEMAN. Come down here quick!

HERBERT. (*Loud cry.*) Here! It's gone! (*Coming nearer.*) Dorrie! —(*Close to entrance at top of stairway.*) Great God!

POLICEMAN. (*Turning his head an instant to speak to* HERBERT.) Don't stop to talk—if you—

(VOSBERG *makes a sudden rush and plunges through the window up* L. *taking the sash and glass with him in a loud crash. Instantly on the crash* DOROTHY *screams and seizing the revolver from the table darts across the room and plunges out through the window up left after* VOSBERG. *The* POLICEMAN *runs down the stairs and across to door left, taking the key out of his pocket as he does so, and shoving it quickly into keyhole, unlocks and opens door, raising his whistle at the same time.* HERBERT *enters at top of stairway as* POLICEMAN *runs across to the door, and comes down the stairway so that he is in plain sight on the landing as* POLICEMAN *pulls the door open to run out.*)

HERBERT. (*In loud voice.*) Stop! Stop, I say!

(POLICEMAN *turns hurriedly at the door.*)

What are you doing there?

POLICEMAN. They've got it! They've run with it!

HERBERT. Who?

POLICEMAN. Your wife and a crook! (*Turning as if to dash out at door.*)

HERBERT. (*Voice of thunder.*) You're a liar!

POLICEMAN. (*Turning back to* HERBERT.) Well, if it wasn't your wife, then there's a pair of 'em—and they've robbed you!

HERBERT. Robbed me! (*He comes down the stairs.*)

POLICEMAN. Didn't you have something? Tell me quick!

HERBERT. (*A wild glance about.*) My wife!

POLICEMAN. Then it was her! I'll just whistle up the roundsman!

HERBERT. No you won't!

(POLICEMAN *turns back to him.*)

Don't you dare blow that whistle!

POLICEMAN. (*Roughly.*) What do you mean?

HERBERT. Don't blow it—that's all!

POLICEMAN. Hasn't she got something of yours?

HERBERT. No!

POLICEMAN. I can't hold 'em unless you tell me! —Hasn't she run off with something?

HERBERT. Not a thing!

(POLICEMAN *stands nonplussed, looking at* HERBERT. HERBERT *turns away with a look of agony, puts his hand to his head as if half stupid. Sees the tea-cup on the table. Suddenly forgetting the* POLICEMAN *he goes to it quickly and picking it up looks eagerly in the bottom of it.*)

(*Half to himself.*) My God!

POLICEMAN. (*Instantly pointing to the cup.*) Ah ha—she doped you!

HERBERT. (*Quickly recovering himself.*) No!

POLICEMAN. (*Advancing toward* HERBERT *with quick stride.*) Give me that cup!

(HERBERT *dashes the cup violently to the floor. The* POLICEMAN *stands an instant looking at* HERBERT. *Suddenly he runs to the table and seizes the box of tablets.*)

What's this?

(HERBERT *knocks the box out of* POLICEMAN'S *hand before he can look at it, and it falls to the floor, breaking and spilling white tablets over the carpet.*)

POLICEMAN. (*Seeing the tablets on the floor.*) That's enough for me! (*He turns and runs to the door left putting whistle to his mouth as he reaches it. He pulls the door open and is about to whistle when two shots ring out in quick succession outside in distance. The* POLICEMAN *backs a step into the room and turns front listening.*) Worse than I thought! She had the gun—but he might a' got it away from her! (*Turns to* HERBERT.) You stay here—I'll see to this! (POLICE-

MAN *hurries off. An instant after his exit, his whistle for help is heard outside, several times.*
*There is a pause. Then the sound of quick light steps outside left. Enter* DOROTHY *at window torn and soiled—with the package in her hand. She staggers toward* HERBERT.)

DOROTHY. Herbert! Herbert!

HERBERT. Dorothy! (*He runs toward her and catches her in his arms.*) Dorothy—what is it!

DOROTHY. (*Holding out the packet blindly. Breathless. Gasping.*) I've got it! You see! . . . I've got it! Here it is! Here it is, Herbert! (*Falls into his arms.*)

HERBERT. My darling! (*Taking the packet, but still holding her close.*) You shot him!

DOROTHY. It was Eddie!

HERBERT. (*Astounded.*) What! (*Turning and looking off left at same instant.*)

DOROTHY. He snatched it away from me! He was running with it! What could I do!

HERBERT. My God! If you've killed him!

DOROTHY. (*Subdued cry of horror.*) Oh, no!

(*Both stand looking off to left.*)

(*Brief pause.*)

(*Enter the* POLICEMAN.)

HERBERT. (*Breathless.*) Well?

POLICEMAN. It's all right, sir—he's hardly hurt at all!

HERBERT. Thank heaven! (*Holds* DOROTHY *close.*)

DOROTHY. (*With a cry of relief.*) Oh! (*Buries her face on* HERBERT'*s breast.*)

POLICEMAN. But she stopped him nice—I will say that. It took him in the foot! You won't have any trouble about this—but I'll have to stay here till you explain how it is to the Captain.

HERBERT. Stay! I hope you'll stay all night, Sergeant!

POLICEMAN. Well, it's near that now!

DOROTHY. Herbert! Can you forgive me!

HERBERT. Forgive you! (*Folds her in his arms. As*

*he holds her he suddenly sees the owl.*) I'll forgive you all right—but I'll be hanged if I'll have that damned bird around here! (*He goes toward the Owl.*)

DOROTHY. (*Following him.*) Oh, no! Do get rid of it!

(HERBERT *throws the* OWL *into the fire. There is a flare of flame.* DOROTHY *falls into his arms again.*)

CURTAIN.

# THE RECTOR

COMEDY IN ONE ACT

## RACHEL CROTHERS

Rachel Crothers was born at Bloomington, Illinois, in 1878. We are told that when still in her teens she tried her hand at playwriting. She shortly joined an amateur dramatic club in her home city, and later taught elocution. She then joined a theatrical company and toured for some years. Her earliest plays, among which is "The Rector," were produced when she was an advanved student at a school of acting. Her first play was produced in New York City in 1903. "The Three of Us," one of her first significant plays, was produced in 1906. This was followed by "A Man's World," "He and She," "The Herfords" and "Young Wisdom." Among her best recent plays are "Old Lady 31," "Nice People," "Mary the Third" and "Expressing Willie."

Miss Crothers excels in the art of characterization. Like most women damatists she is at her best among the types she knows and understands. Her satirical works are skilful exhibitions of American life and character. "The Rector" is the best of Miss Crothers' short plays and has for several years been a favorite among amateurs.

Following is a list of Miss Crothers' published plays:

"He and She"; "A Man's World"; "The Three of Us"; "Mary the Third"; "Old Lady 31"; "A Little Journey"; "39 East"; "Nice People"; "The Rector"; "Expressing Willie."

# THE RECTOR*

## CHARACTERS

JOHN HERRESFORD
MARGARET NORTON
VICTORIA KNOX
MRS. LEMMINGWORTH
MRS. MUNSEY
MISS TRIMBALL
JANIE

SCENE: *Study in a Country parsonage.*

TIME: *The present.*

*A winter morning.*

*The study in a country parsonage. There is a bay window in flat* R., *showing the yard with fence and trees covered with snow.*

*The door at* L., *in flat, opens into a narrow hall—off of which the street door opens.*

*A door up left opens into the dining room, and one at* R., *into the Rector's sleeping room.*

*A large shabby desk is placed sidewise in the window with a rickety revolving chair before it.*

*The sofa and chairs, awkward and uncomfortable, are covered with horse-hair. There is an oval shaped marble topped table at* L. C., *with three chairs about it.*

*The table and several chairs are heaped with newspapers and books. The desk is strewn with writing materials, letters, books, etc. There is a half dead fire in the small fireplace down* L.*—and the general effect is shabby, neglected and desolate.*

---

*It is snowing without and as the characters enter the snow is seen on their clothing.*

JANIE *is the Rector's housemaid. Her little sunny face smiles upon him and the friends of whom she approves, but frowns with open displeasure upon those she suspects of designs upon the Rector and his household.*

*She wears a neat red calico dress, an apron much patched, and her hair, brushed as tightly back as possible, is braided and twisted into a large knot from the middle of which dangles a shoestring. On her forehead one small curl paper shows a small desire for beauty and improvement.*

*As the curtain rises she comes in from the hall, sniffing and shivering with the cold, with a bunch of letters in her hands which she examines curiously—then turning suddenly she rushes back into the hall, calling loudly from the street door.*

JANIE. Here; here! this isn't for us. What? No—Hilborn—Mrs. Hilborn. Oh! I know—she's visitin' the Smiths. Just come yesterday. She's not so much either if she is from New York. I saw 'er. What? Yes—make good sleighin'. Bur—r— (*Slamming the door and coming back into the room. She goes to the Rector's desk and examines the letters in a way which is curious but not sly. Her walk, her manner, her speech, are uncouth but lovable—utterly without training, and yet with an air of self-confidence that makes her always mistress of the situation.*) Stupid thing! Everything that begins with a "H" he brings here. (*Looking at letters again*) Um—um—I know that handwriting all right, all right. Miss Trimball again. 'Twon't do you any good, missy, writin' letters. If you think our dominie 'ud ever *look* at you. Hum! *I* know a thing 'er two. (*Dusting the desk*) There! he didn't mail these letters. Oh, such a man! (*Bell rings without.*) Now, who's that? What's going on to-day? (*She picks up a tablet of engagements, reads.*) Wednesday, ten a.m., committee for new carpet, Miss Norton, Miss Knox, Miss Trimball, Hump! much *she* knows about carpet. (*Reads.*) "Mrs. Munsey," *and* "Mrs. Lemmingworth." Lord save us! (*Bell rings again.*) Now, you can just wait, whoever you are—it won't hurt you. (*She gives a final rub to a chair, hides the dust cloth behind her back, and goes into the hall. Sound of outer door.*)

MRS. LEMMINGWORTH. (*Without.*) Good morning, good morning, Janie. I'll just leave my rubbers and umbrella right here in the hall. Mind they don't get mixed with anybody else's. (*Coming in.*) Mr. Herresford not in? (MRS. LEMMINGWORTH *speaks in a loud voice; her manner is dictatorial; her dress severe and old fashioned.*)

JANIE. No'p.

MRS. LEM. I came a little early: I wish to speak to him on a little matter of business before the others arrive. Will he—has he—been out long?

JANIE. (*Going on with her dusting.*) Oh! he'll be back in *time.*

MRS. LEM. (*Aside.*) Impudent thing! I wouldn't have her in my house a minute. (*To* JANIE.) You're a little late with your dusting, aren't you?

JANIE. Oh, I don't know! (*Shaking the dust cloth.*)

MRS. LEM. Good gracious, child! what do you mean? Don't you know better than to shake a rag in the house? That comes of not having a woman in the house. Poor man!

JANIE. "Poor man!" You needn't worry about *him. He's* all right! He won't have a woman here till he gets good an' ready, an' then it 'll be the *right* one. I can tell you *those.*

MRS. LEM. (*Aside.*) Now what does she mean by that? (*To* JANIE.) By the way—has he—has the—has he—(*Seeing the Rector as he passes the window.*) Here he is now. (*Rising.*) I just wanted to ask, has the mail come yet this morning?

JANIE. (*At hall door.*) Of course.

MRS. LEM. Well, has he had time to read it?

JANIE. No, he hasn't! (*Bell rings.*)

MRS. LEM. Wait a minute, just let me step into the parlor while he reads it, and then you can call me when he has finished. (*She hurries into the hall.*)

JANIE. Now what does she mean by that? (*She goes into hall to open outer door.*) (MR. HERRESFORD *whistles as he passes the bay window, and continues to do so softly as he enters. Taking off his gloves, coat and hat, he gives them to* JANIE, *who stands waiting for them.* MR. HERRESFORD *wears the clerical dress. He is thirty-two years old. Boyish and keenly alive to the happy side of the world—with a serious purpose, a hidden strength and a patient kindliness and tolerance.*)

MR. HERR. Thank you, Janie. Is anyone here? I have an uncomfortable feeling that I have forgotten something. (*Going to desk and taking up tablet.*) Why, of course, the carpet committee at ten.

JANIE. (*Aside.*) No wonder he felt uncomfortable. (*To* MR. HERRESFORD.) Mrs. Lemmingworth is here, sir.

MR. HERR. Is she?

JANIE. In the parlor. She's waitin' for you to read your mail.

MR. HERR. What?

JANIE. That's all I know. She said she didn't want to disturb you, and I was to call her when you are through.

MR. HERR. (*Laughing.*) Well, that's very kind of Mrs. Lemmingworth, I'm sure. (*He sits at desk and takes mail. Exit* JANIE L.) So little Hilda Martin (*Smiling as he reads.*) is going to have a wedding. (*Reading another letter.*) Oh! and a funeral for someone else. So runs the world away. (*Frowning as he reads another letter.*) Why does she write when she's coming anyway? Isn't she? (*Taking up tablet.*) Yes, here she is. (*Reads.*) "Just a line to tell you that you may depend upon my help and sympathy in the trying decision about the carpet. I shall be there at ten. Your every ready and willing friend, Aurelia Trimball." (*With a sigh and a smile he tears the letter and drops it into the basket.*) What atrocious writing. (*Taking up another letter.*) What? Oh, it can't be! It must be a joke. No it's too insulting for that. Oh, I—

JANIE. (*Re-entering.*) Shall I bring her in now?

MR. HERR. No! What? Oh, I suppose so. (*He crushes letter, then smooths it out and puts it in drawer, which he locks.*) Wait a minute. Bring her in and say that I'll come in a minute.

(*Exit* MR. HERRESFORD *at* R.)

JANIE. Now, what was that? Never saw him look so thunderin' mad in my life. Wonder why he locked it up. (*Going to hall door and calling.*) You can come in now.

MRS. LEM. (*Entering.*) Good morn—

JANIE. He'll be here in a minute. (*Aside as she goes out.*) She's too nosey.

MRS. LEM. (*Sitting* R. *of table* L. C.) I wonder—I hope I—Oh! I shall be so glad when everything is settled and running smoothly. The man doesn't know what's best for him, of course, and it's my duty to—Oh, good morning, Mr. Herresford.

MR. HERR. (*Entering.*) Good morning, Mrs. Lemmingworth. How are you this morning? (*Shaking hands with her.*) Ready for work?

MRS. LEM. Oh dear, yes! Dear, dear, yes! I've made some notes on the question, and I've brought some samples. I went in town yesterday, and I just made it a point to look at carpets too, and get an idea of color and design and durability; so that I could report and help things along. Here they are. (*Taking squares *of carpet out of the black silk bag with she carries.*) Now, you know—but of course you *don't* know, how could you, being a man, and alone at that—but it *is* a fact that *red*, in the long run, is more lasting and satisfactory on the whole than any other thing in the carpet line. Now, a good housekeeper knows the important thing—there it is again, a good housekeeper! What do *you* know about good housekeepers? And by the way, my dear boy, that reminds me. You know I look upon you very much as a mother would; for I know how lonely and helpless you are, and I'm going to speak from my heart. I know it isn't always possible for you to know just what is best for you, and how you stand in the community. Now I—I speak for your own good, you know,—I have heard of late many complaints, because you are so young *and* unmarried. (MR. HERRESFORD *walks away quickly, trying to conceal his irritation.*)

MR. HERR. My dear Madam—

MRS. LEM. Now, you know, my boy, there is nothing so helpful to a church and its pastor as a good helpful wife. Ahem! Now, there is *one* young woman in your congregation who will make you a *good* wife.

MR. HERR. I can't listen to this.

MRS. LEM. (*Drawing her chair forward and hurrying on breathlessly.*) A noble wife, pious, discreet, and economical.

MR. HERR. Mrs. Lemmingworth, I beg—

MRS. LEM. We *all think* so. It's the only thing necessary to make your success here complete. You must know who I mean of course.

MR. HERR. Mrs. Lemmingworth, you don't realize what you are saying.

MRS. LEM. Miss Trimball, of course.

MR. HERR. Mrs. Lemmingworth, think of the lady!

MRS. LEM. I *am* thinking of her—she's—

JANIE. (*Throwing open the hall door.*) Miss Trimball!

(MISS TRIMBALL *enters. She is tall and thin and has a cold. Her dress suggests a little attempt at being in the fashion. She speaks in a high voice and titters constantly. One toe is turned in slightly. She carries a small basket covered with a napkin.*)

MISS TRIMBALL (*Coughing and wiping her nose.*) Oh, good morning, Mrs. Lemmingworth, am I late? Good morning, Mr. Herresford. (*Offering her hand awkwardly.*) I've brought you some fresh doughnuts. I thought they'd be nice to munch on while you're writing your sermons.

MRS. LEM. (*With emphasis.*) A good idea!

MISS TRIMBALL. (*Giving the basket to* JANIE.) Keep them in a crock.

MRS. LEM. And put a damp cloth over them.

JANIE. (*As she marches out.*) Oh! we've had doughnuts before.

MISS TRIMBALL. (*Seeing the samples of carpet.*) Oh, how beautiful! You have some samples. Now isn't that just like Mrs. Lemmingworth, Mr. Herresford? So thoughtful. (*She crosses complacently to the sofa and sits with one foot persistently turned in.*)

MRS. LEM. I was just telling Mr. Herresford that all good housekeepers consider *red* the best investment in a carpet. (*The door bell rings.*) Now, you know what good housekeeping is, *don't* you, Miss Trimball?

MISS TRIMBALL. (*Tittering and looking at the ends of her shabby gloves.*) Oh, Mrs. Lemmingworth, how can you! Poor little me. Do you really think I do?

JANIE. (*Who has opened the street door, now appears with a broad smile of approval as she announces.*) It's Miss Margaret.

MR. HERR. (*Going forward eagerly to greet* MARGARET.) Good morning, Miss Margaret. It's awfully good of you to come out in this storm, and really it isn't necessary. It's snowing quite heavily, isn't it? (MARGARET *has the glow of health in her cheeks and a smile of kindness and strength in her eyes. Her gown is simple and becoming, and she brings with her fresh air and confidence.*)

MARGARET. (*Brushing the snow off her coat.*) Oh, the snow is glorious! and don't tell me I'm not necessary, that isn't nice. Good morning, Mrs. Lemmingworth. Good morning, Miss Trimball. No, thank you, Mr. Herresford, I won't take off my coat, I will just throw it back. Um, perhaps I had better. It does seem a little warm here after my walk. (MRS. LEMMINGWORTH *sniffs significantly and exchanges glances with* MISS TRIMBALL, *as* MR. HERRESFORD *takes off* MARGARET'S *coat and places it carefully over the back of her chair.*)

MARGARET. (*As she takes off her gloves.*) I pulled little Willie Green most of the way on his sled. You never *saw* such a happy child. He scarcely ever gets out you know. He can hardly walk at all now. I saw him in the yard trying to make snowballs and I asked him if he didn't want a ride; then I got the grocery boy to take him back again. He actually had a little color in his face.

MRS. LEM. Humph! I should think so—probably half frozen. That trifling careless mother of his never keeps him half dressed.

MARGARET. Oh! don't say that, Mrs. Lemmingworth. Poor woman, she's so busy sewing for other people she never has time to do anything for him. A shoemaker's children, you know—

MISS TRIMBALL. (*A little vaguely.*) Charity begins at *home.*

MR. HERR. Couldn't something be done for the little fellow? Couldn't his lameness be cured, or helped at least?

MARGARET. (*Quickly.*) Why, I think so. I was just going to ask at the aid society to-morrow if we couldn't possibly raise money enough to—

MRS. LEM. Pshaw! that's out of the question. The aid society has more than it can stand up under, *now.*

MISS TRIMBALL. (*Trying to be positive.*) Yes, I think so, too.

MRS. LEM. Besides I don't think she's a member of our church.

MARGARET. Oh, yes, she is.

MISS TRIMBALL. But she never comes.

MARGARET. I suppose she's too worn out to go when Sunday comes.

MRS. LEM. That's no excuse.

MARGARET. Well, what if she isn't a member of our church? Aren't we supposed to help everybody we can?

MRS. LEM. We've got to draw the line some place—and our church must help its *own* members.

MR. HERR. (*Quietly.*) "Our church," Mrs. Lemmingworth? What *is* "our" church?

MRS. LEM. Why, *the* church—*our* church. What do *you* think the church is?

MR. HERR. (*With a far-away look in his face.*) I think it's the hand of God reaching to earth. We *ought* to be the fingers, touching and blessing all we can. What are we without love, Mrs. Lemmingworth, universal love?

MARGARET. (*With a mist of tears in her eyes.*) It all seems so simple if we look at it that way.

MR. HERR. (*Going on—half to himself.*) Kindness, to help—help. Kindness—Love.

MISS TRIMBALL. (*Speaking quickly in a high voice.*) Yes, *I* think love is the greatest thing in the world. Have you ever read the essay, Mr. Herresford, "Love is the greatest thing in the world"? I'll lend it to you, if you haven't. But *I* think charity begins at home.

MARGARET. (*Laughing.*) If you keep on saying that, Miss Trimball, you may find a place that it fits. Oh, what beautiful samples!

MR. HERR. (*Who has taken out his note-book.*) Did

you say—— Oh! I beg your pardon——(*realizing he has interrupted.*) Did you say——is it the third house from the corner, Miss Margaret?

MARGARET. What? Oh, no, the second—the little brown one with the picket fence around it, you know.

MR. HERR. (*Writing.*) Yes, I know.

MARGARET. Now, what beautiful samples of carpet. Now, isn't this nice. How's the cold, Miss Trimball? We missed your solo, Sunday, awfully. (MARGARET *smiles brightly at* MISS TRIMBALL *who titters in spite of* MRS. LEMMINGWORTH'S *frown.*)

MISS TRIMBALL. Oh, thank you. I really ought not to have come out to-day but I never fail in my duty.

MARGARET. You set us all a beautiful example, I'm sure.

MRS. LEM. Mrs. Munsey is late, *of course.* I think we need not wait any longer for her.

MR. HERR. Oh, better give her a few minutes' grace, hadn't we? The snow, you know, makes it hard walking.

MRS. LEM. Very small things are hard for some people. Here's Miss Trimball oughtn't to be out of bed, yet *she* didn't find it hard to come.

MISS TRIMBALL. (*Coughing violently.*) Oh, Mrs. Lemmingworth, how can you! I'm sure it's only a pleasure to do my duty. (JANIE *crosses from the dining-room into the hall with a broom, and is seen sweeping the snow tracks in the hall.*)

MARGARET. (*Laughing.*) There's someone else too, isn't there, Mr. Herresford? Victoria, isn't she on the committee? (MARGARET *watches the instant disapproval which comes into* MRS. LEMMINGWORTH'S *face.*)

MR. HERR. Oh yes, to be sure. I believe she is. (*Referring to his tablet on his desk.*) Yes, yes, here she is.

MARGARET. We must wait for Victoria. We can't get on without her, can we? (*Still laughing.*)

MRS. LEM. (*Bristling.*) Oh, nonsense! That *is* a farce

—waiting for Victoria Knox. I have everything all settled, and it will only take a few minutes. (*The bell rings,* MARGARET *and* MR. HERRESFORD *both start toward the door.*)

MARGARET *and* HERR. There, there she is now.

MRS. MUNSEY. (*Without—stamping her feet.*) Oh dear, such a time! I do hope I haven't got my feet wet. (*She appears at the hall door.* JANIE *brushes the snow from her feet as* MRS. MUNSEY *shakes her skirts.*) Oh dear! do you think my feet are wet, Janie?

MR. HERR. Come right in, Mrs. Munsey. Come over to the fire and warm those feet. We were waiting for you and talking about you. (MRS. MUNSEY *is a pretty widow in black with coquettish touches of white. She rolls her big baby blue eyes and smiles constantly, as she speaks in a gushing manner—with over-emphasized words.*)

MRS. MUNSEY. (*Establishing herself in the armchair by the fire, as* MR. HERRESFORD *kneels to take off her rubbers.*) Oh, you *dear* Mr. Herresford! Did you hear that, ladies? Good morning, everybody. Don't let *me* interrupt you. I'm so sorry I'm late. Just let me sit over here, and don't mind *me*—go right on. Oh, *thank* you, *dear* Mr. Herresford, you're so kind. Do you know——

MRS. LEM. (*Knocking on the table.*) Then, ladies, if you will kindly come to order.

MRS. MUNSEY. (*Still smiling at* MR. HERRESFORD.) Do you know the snow isn't shoveled at all on our street?

MRS. LEM. (*Knocking again.*) If you will *kindly* come to order.

MR. HERR. I beg your pardon, Mrs. Lemmingworth.

MRS. MUNSEY. Oh, go right *on,* of course. Don't mind *me.* I'm late because I had to stop at the dressmaker's, and she took so long to fit the waist. Mrs. Green is always *so* particular about *my* dresses. She says I—

Oh, what do you think, she's making Hilda Martin's wedding dress, and it's—

MISS TRIMBALL. (*Starting up and crossing to* MRS. MUNSEY.) Oh! is Mrs. Green making Hilda Martin's wedding dress? What is it? Why *I* never knew Hilda had a dressmaker make anything.

MRS. LEM. Humph! she never *did.* Heaven knows where she'll get the money to pay for this.

MARGARET. Oh, but this is her wedding dress. Of course she'd have to have that made.

MISS TRIMBALL. What is it? What is it made out of, Mrs. Munsey?

MRS. MUNSEY. Why, it's blue cashmere. Now, of course, *some* people might like it, but it wouldn't be *my* taste. Now, when I was married—

MISS TRIMBALL. Is it light blue or dark blue? How is it made?

MARGARET. I'm sure Hilda would look very pretty in light blue—she's so fair.

MRS. LEM. I don't approve of her having any such non-sense about a wedding when she—(*The ladies discuss the possibilities of* HILDA's *wedding dress in a most animated way—all speaking at once, and no one listening to anyone else—much to* MR. HERRESFORD's *amusement, who picks up a book from his desk and waits for peace.*)

MRS. LEM. (*Waving her hands in the air.*) Ladies, ladies—if you will kindly come to order.

MARGARET. (*Laughing.*) Yes, we must get to work.

MRS. MUNSEY. Yes, of course. Don't mind *me.*

MISS TRIMBALL. (*As she goes back to the sofa.*) I think blue is funny though.

MRS. LEM. (*Seating herself at the head of the table.*) As the chairman of the committee, I have deemed it wise to obtain these samples of the material which may be procured for the price within our limit. Now, the short aisle, leading across the front of the church at the left, is never seen, and almost never used; and in considering the matter I have decided that it would be a useless and wasteful expenditure to put carpet on that.

MARGARET. Oh! but let's do it well—now that we really can have a new carpet at last.

MRS. LEM. Ahem! we take it for granted, of course, that this sum intrusted to us will be expended to the best advantage, and not uselessly or recklessly.

MARGARET. Yes, but just that little strip won't be much more, and it will spoil it all if we don't have it.

MISS TRIMBALL. I agree with Mrs. Lemmingworth—we mustn't waste the money.

MR. HERR. What do you think of this, Mrs. Munsey?

MRS. MUNSEY. (*Who has risen to look at herself in the mirror over the mantel.*) What? Oh! I—why, don't ask *me*. I don't know anything about business, you know. Whatever you say, of course, Mr. Herresford, will be all right. (MARGARET *and* MR. HERRESFORD *laugh—the others frown.*)

MRS. LEM. This is not a matter to be lightly considered —on the contrary it is a matter of *very* grave importance.

MRS. MUNSEY. Oh, I *know* it is. *Do* forgive me, my *dear* Mrs. Lemmingworth. But, you know, I really— you *will* excuse me, *won't* you, dear?

MRS. LEM. Am I to consider Mrs. Munsey's out of the matter, then?

MR. HERR. Oh, no, no! You must help us out, you know, Mrs. Munsey.

MARGARET. Oh, she will, of course.

MR. HERR. If we're going to vote about it, we'll have to wait for Miss——

MARGARET. For Victoria, yes, to be sure.

MRS. LEM. That is unnecessary, we have a majority here. We will now put the question to vote. Those in favor will signify by saying "aye."

MRS. MUNSEY. Aye, for what? Which is which?

MISS TRIMBALL. Oh dear!

MRS. LEM. Ahem! I will state the question once more, those in favor of carpeting the side aisle——

JANIE. (*Entering from the dining-room.*) Excuse me, Mr. Herresford, Maria wants to know if you forgot to get the butter.

MR. HERR. Why, Janie, I——

MARGARET. (*Smiling.*) Oh, you know you did, Mr. Herresford.

JANIE. I'll get it and be back in a jiffy.

MRS. MUNSEY. (*Rising.*) Why, you poor dear *man!* Haven't you any *butter? We* have lovely butter, and I'll send you some as soon as I go home.

MRS. LEM. You don't mean to tell me you don't have butter from one place regular. Why, old John Watts has been bringing me butter and fresh eggs for the last ten years every Saturday morning. But what can you expect?

MISS TRIMBALL. (*Rising excitedly and going to* MR. HERRESFORD.) I've churned myself this morning and I'll go right home and fetch you some.

MR. HERR. Ladies, I beg. Sit *down,* Miss Trimball, I couldn't think of letting you. Janie, get some—get *any*thing.

JANIE. Will I go to Hipsley's or Crocker's?

MARGARET. (*Still laughing.*) Mr. Hipsley has some nice fresh butter just in. I stopped there as I came along.

JANIE. (*From the dining-room.*) Maria, I'm going to get the butter. If the front door bell rings while I'm gone you'll have to go.

MRS. LEM. I will state the question once *more*—those in favor of carpeting the side aisle at a needless expense, will signify it by saying "Aye."

MR. HERR. Just a moment, please. I believe I'd better not vote. It really isn't a matter which concerns me at all, you know.

MRS. MUNSEY. *Oh,* Mr. Herresford! *No* fair! How will we know how to vote?

MARGARET. Yes, of course, you mustn't desert us.

MRS. LEM. I must ask for seriousness and respect.

MR. HERR. I beg your pardon, Mrs. Lemmingworth, I'm sure. I'm in favor of carpeting then.

MRS. MUNSEY. So am I! So am I!

MARGARET. Here too!

MRS. LEM. This is non-parliamentary, and I consider the decisions are given without due consideration.

MISS TRIMBALL. I vote *against* it.

MRS. LEM. That is useless now, You are quite overweighed, of course. However, now, if I may be allowed a *word of suggestion* on the matter, I present this as being the best thing in the market for the price.

MARGARET. (*Leaning forward to take the sample.*) Oh, that's lovely, Mrs. Lemmingworth! Isn't it, Mrs. Munsey? (*Aside to* MRS. MUNSEY.) Do say yes, and let it go without a fuss. This will do as well as anything.

MRS. MUNSEY. Oh, beautiful! Mrs. Lemmingworth has such good taste, hasn't she?

MARGARET. Why not leave the entire thing in Mrs. Lemmingworth's hands, now? We know it will be *well* done, and ask Miss Trimball to be a committee of one for advice and consultation.

MR. HERR. By all means. Don't refuse us, Mrs. Lemmingworth.

MRS. LEM. Well, I—

MARGARET. No, we won't take "no" for an answer. Make her say "yes," Miss Trimball.

MISS TRIMBALL. (*Simpering.*) Your duty, you know, Mrs. Lemmingworth.

MRS. MUNSEY. Yes, Mrs. Lemmingworth, remember your duty. (*Turning away her head to hide her smiles.*)

MRS. LEM. My duty! Yes, it is my duty alone which makes me consent—not that I like the position of—

MARGARET. Oh, no, we understand. It's very unselfish and kind of you to do it for us, I'm sure. Now, that's all, isn't it, this morning? (*Rising.*)

MRS. MUNSEY. Oh, is that all?

MISS TRIMBALL. (*As the others rise.*) May I speak to you a moment, Mr. Herresford?

MR. HERR. Certainly.

MRS. LEM. (*Drawing the others aside.*) Look at this closely and you'll see what a really superior thing it is.

MISS TRIMBALL. I want to ask you about my solo next Sunday. I want to sing something fitting and sympathetic with your sermon. I can sing so much better when I know I'm in harmony with your thoughts.

MR. HERR. I see. Well, anything simple and sweet will do. Your songs are always pleasing, Miss Trimball. We all appreciate them very much.

MISS TRIMBALL. Oh, do you? You are so good! I try *so* hard to please you.

MARGARET. Well, I must hurry. Good-bye, good-bye, everybody.

MR. HERR. (*Quickly.*) Oh! are you going?

MARGARET. Yes, good morning.

MR. HERR. Good morning. (*He indicates by pantomime that* MARGARET *is to wait in the parlor until the others are gone.*)

MISS TRIMBALL. (*Calling* MR. HERRESFORD *back as* MARGARET *goes into the hall.*) Then you can't suggest any special thing?

MR. HERR. No, I believe not.

MISS TRIMBALL. You couldn't let me *read* the sermon, so I could be sure of selecting the right thing?

MR. HERR. (*Embarrassed and annoyed, but trying to be kind.*) Oh—I—I'm afraid not—I really haven't it in shape, you know.

MRS. MUNSEY. (*Who has been adjusting her bonnet at the mirror.*) Why, has Margaret gone? I must go too, then. Good-bye. Good-bye, my *dear* Mr. Herresford, you've been *so* kind.

MR. HERR. (*Taking her hand.*) You're sure you're quite warm now, Mrs. Munsey?

MRS. MUNSEY. Oh, quite. Dear me! Now, isn't that just like me? I've forgotten my rubbers.

MR. HERR. Let me get them for you. Allow me, if you'll sit down.

MRS. MUNSEY. Oh! thank you, *thank* you. You're *so* good. It does seem nice to have a man do things for you. Mother says I'm spoiled. Dickie spoiled me. Poor dear Dick! (*Putting her handkerchief to her eyes.*)

MR. HERR. (*Rising.*) There.

MRS. MUNSEY. Oh, *thank* you! This heel doesn't seem quite on. (MR. HERRESFORD *kneels again.*) The snow makes them stick so. Oh! (*Losing her balance and putting her hand on* MR. HERRESFORD'S *shoulder.*) Mother says I ought to wear arctics but I can't *bear* them. They make your feet look so big, don't they, Miss Trimball? (*To* MR. HERR.) Don't forget you're coming to have a cup of tea with mother and me Tuesday at five, you know. We shall be so heartbroken if you do. Mother is *so* fond of you, you know. And dear me, dear me, how dreadful! I've forgotten, why, I never could have gone home without it—I've forgotten to give you mother's *love*, and she sent it *so* carefully. Do forgive me. I'm *so* sorry. I *meant* to of course. But I haven't much of a *mind*, you know, Mr. Herresford. Good morning, *good* morning.

MR. HERR. (*Following* MRS. MUNSEY *to the door.*) Good morning.

MISS TRIMBALL. (*Calling him back again.*) You will know whatever I sing, my heart is in it, won't you, Mr. Herresford?

MR. HERR. I'm sure your heart is always in your work, Miss Trimball. (MISS TRIMBALL *sighs conspicuously and goes up to* MRS. LEMMINGWORTH, *who can be seen struggling with her rubbers in the hall.*)

MISS TRIMBALL. Come, Mrs. Lemmingworth, are you ready?

MRS. LEM. I'm just putting on my rubbers. There now! Come on. Good-bye. I'll do the best I can in the matter.

MR. HERR. I'm sure you will.

MISS TRIMBALL. There isn't anything I can do for you? Anyone sick I can visit?

MR. HERR. Oh, nothing, nothing, thank you. Go home and take care of yourself. Good morning, ladies. Thank you very much for coming. (*As the outer door closes with a bang,* MR. HERRESFORD *comes back into room and listens.* MARGARET *comes cautiously across the hall.*)

MARGARET. (*At door.*) Are they all gone?

MR. HERR. All gone. I always feel like a conspirator when I'm with you.

MARGARET. (*Laughing.*) That's rather a doubtful speech.

MR. HERR. Because you're the only one in the whole place who understands *at all.*

MARGARET. (*Still laughing and turning away nervously.*) Poor Mrs. Lemmingworth. That was rather a master stroke of yours.

MR. HERR. Of *yours,* you mean. I'm always a coward where Mrs. Lemmingworth is concerned. I've given up long ago.

MARGARET. But we got the side aisle, didn't we?

MR. HERR. Yes, we got the side aisle—rather you did.

MARGARET. I notice you never give up anything but—something you don't want, anyway.

MR. HERR. (*Walking away, with a quick sigh.*) I don't know about that. (*Turning back to her.*) Margaret, Miss Margaret, you're very wise—if you're not gray-headed. Sit down. I so often wonder where it all came from—your strength and judgment. Every one turns to you intuitively for guidance, and I also wonder what you are going to do with it all; if you don't sometimes rebel at this little narrow life and want something freer, broader, where you can *use* that beautiful mind of yours. (MAGRARET *looks at him quickly then away.*) And I want to ask you something which I want you to answer very honestly. Do you think I had better go away?

MARGARET. (*After a pause.*) What do you mean?

MR. HERR. Haven't I made a mistake by coming at all? Haven't I failed dismally? There's something wrong —somewhere.

MARGARET. (*Recovering her composure.*) Yes, there *is* something wrong.

MR. HERR. (*Eagerly.*) You feel it?

MARGARET. But not with you. If you think the life seems little to me—what must it be for you? I've seen it all from the first—the prejudice because you did come from another world—the petty annoyances that have come to you in a thousand ways. I know there have been times when you have wanted to scream out from the house tops, "Let me alone! let me alone!" But you have gone on, bravely and patiently until— no, don't say you have failed—it isn't that: they *do* love you and believe in you.

MR. HERR. It puts new life into me to hear you say so. Are you sure—are you sure? (*Going to her.*)

MARGARET. (*Raising her eyes to him.*) I am *sure.*

MR. HERR. Thank you. And now—I—I'm going to show you something. (*He takes the letter from the desk and gives it to* MARGARET *who reads it slowly aloud.*)

MARGARET. (*Reading.*) "A silent friend warns you— you *must* marry Aurelia Trimball." (*After a pause.*)

I can't believe it! I can't *believe* it! Oh! I'm so sorry for you, and so ashamed—for *us.*

MR. HERR. (*Taking the letter and tearing it up.*) Never mind. Don't let it trouble you. Funny, isn't it?

MARGARET. Funny? It's disgraceful! What are you going to do?

MR. HERR. That's just it. That's what I want to ask you. Shall I go away, or shall I stay—and ask—some-one *else* to be my wife? (MARGARET *moves away.*) Don't think me a coward. It isn't myself—I'm thinking of *her;* and whether they'd make her miserable; and whether she'd be brave enough to face it—even if she *cared* for me.

MARGARET. (*Slowly.*) Why, of course, she would—if she cared.

MR. HERR. Even if she were—Victoria? (MARGARET *puts out her hand for a chair and sits quickly.*) Ah! you see, even you hesitate at Victoria.

MARGARET. (*With her face turned away.*) It *is* Victoria then?

MR. HERR. Yes, Victoria. Is it very strange? I suppose it does seem so—and yet to me it seems the most natural thing in the world. She—she—*needs* to be loved, you know. She is not like you—so strong and well poised. (MR. HERR. *goes to* MARGARET *and stands bending over her a little, as she sits with her back to him, her head resting on her hand, her elbow on the back of the chair.*) Do you know, Margaret, you don't mind my calling you Margaret, do you? I've wondered so many times what sort of a man you will marry. I've thought of all the men I've known—and know, and among them all I can't find one worthy of you. I can't imagine a man *daring* to woo you—or thinking for a moment he could satisfy you or make you happy. But I want you to be happy. I hope I may see the completion of your glorious womanhood.

MARGARET. (*With an effort.*) Thank you, Mr. Herresford.

MR. HERR. Do you mind telling me what you *really* think about Victoria—and me? Don't hesitate. If you think I'm a fool—say so. I want to know. It will help me.

MARGARET. (*Slowly, without moving.*) I think Victoria—the most lovable—the most irresistible girl I have ever known. With a mind far beyond what she is supposed to have, and a heart which, if touched in the right way—and by the right one, could lift her into great spiritual strength and sweetness.

MR. HERR. Do you? *Do* you? How good it is to hear you say it.

MARGARET. (*Without moving—going on in the same monotonous tone.*) I think a strong good man can make a woman what he wants her to be, if she loves him; and why shouldn't Victoria—love you? I don't know—it all seemed a little strange just now. I hadn't thought, of course. But don't be afraid, if you are *sure* that that is what your life and heart need. Don't fear that she can't realize your ideal of what your wife ought to be—to help—and *you* know. Love always touches the highest key in a woman's nature, and *through* it, and *because* of it, and *for* it (*Emphasizing her words with her tightly closed hands*) even the most commonplace of us may sometimes do things which at least we will not be ashamed to look back at, through the years that are to come. (*She fights back the tears.*)

MR. HERR. Then you *don't* hesitate, even at Victoria?

MARGARET. (*After a moment's pause—rising, smiling bravely and giving him her hand*) Not even at *Victoria.*

MR. HERR. (*Taking her hand in both his*) God bless you, Margaret! I hope love—*a great* love, will come to you.

MARGARET. Don't you think there are sometimes things *greater* than love?

MR. HERR. Only one thing. (*The bell rings.*)

MARGARET. And that is?

MR. HERR. Renunciation.

MARGARET. (*Slowly—drawing her hand away*) Yes—renunciation.

JANIE. (*Throwing open the hall door*) Here's Miss Victoria.

(*Enter* VICTORIA—*bright, gay, frivolous.*)

VICTORIA. Oh, here you are! Your mother said I'd probably find you here. Good morning, Mr. Herresford. Are you and Margaret *all* the committee? I was quite sure you wouldn't need me.

MARGARET. Oh! but we *did* need you. Indeed it all depends upon you, Victoria. Doesn't it, Mr. Herresford? The question remains for you to settle. I'm off—no, you can't come with me; I have a thousand things to do. Make her tell you, Mr. Herresford. Good-bye—good-bye, dear. (*Pushing* VICTORIA *back from the door, she rushes out laughing and waving her hand as she passes the window. There is a long pause after* MARGARET *goes out—then* VICTORIA, *smiling over her muff says*)

VICTORIA. I wonder if I could have a glass of water. I'm so thirsty.

MR. HERR. Why, of course. (*Going quickly to the door*) Janie, Janie! a glass of water, please. (*Another pause,* VICTORIA *goes to the window, looking out interestedly*).

VICTORIA. Isn't the snow pretty? (*Another pause*) Don't you like pretty things, Mr. Herresford? (*Stretching her head to see up the street.*)

MR. HERR. (*Significantly*) Yes. (JANIE *enters with the glass of water*) Thank you. Janie. *Thank* you, Janie. (JANIE *peers around him at* VICTORIA, *then exit.* MR. HERRESFORD *crosses to* VICTORIA *with the water, but stands staring at her and forgetting to give it to her*) Oh! (*Starting, as* VICTORIA *smiles at the glass which he holds.*)

VICTORIA. (*Just touching her lips to the glass*) Thank

you. That was so good. I was so thirsty. Well, I must go now. (*She drops her glove and they both stoop to pick it up.*)

MR. HERR. (*Holding on to the glove*) Oh, don't!

VICTORIA. (*Drawing it slowly away*) Oh, but I must!

MR. HERR. Why did you desert us?

VICTORIA. Why did you put me *on* the stupid thing? Don't you know by this time that I utterly abhor all that sort of stuff, and will not be bothered with it? A *carpet* committee! (*Laughing*) Why didn't you give Margaret Norton the money and send her to town to buy the carpet and be done with it? You know perfectly well she knows more about carpets than all the rest of the congregation put together. She's much more capable of running a church than *you* are. Now, isn't she?

MR. HERR. Yes, I believe she is. I don't know what I should do without her.

VICTORIA. Oh! (*Looking at him quickly and then crossing to fire.*)

MR. HERR. Are you cold?

VICTORIA. Oh, dear no, not at all.

MR. HERR. Let me put some more wood on the fire.

VICTORIA. No—no—no! not for me. I'm going this minute.

MR. HERR. Oh, don't—don't! not just yet.

VICTORIA. But I must. This is highly improper. What would Mrs. Lemmingworth say if she knew I was calling on the Rector?

MR. HERR. Oh, bother Mrs. Lem—

VICTORIA. What? That's rank heresy—positive sacrilege! What has come to you? (*Laughing she goes to the door.* MR. HERRESFORD *following, takes her hand and draws her back.*)

MR. HERR. Please, just a moment. I—I want to ask you something.

VICTORIA. Ask *me?* Why didn't you ask Margaret? I don't care whether you have a carpet at all or not.

MR. HERR. (*Turning away*) No, I know you don't. That's just it. I know my life—I mean the church life —but I—I—I—

VICTORIA. Do you? What is it you want me to say—whether it shall be red—green—or blue?

MR. HERR. Oh! it isn't the carpet at all. It's you.

VICTORIA. Me? (*Laughing*) I don't understand.

MR. HERR. And I can't tell you. It seems harder—more impossible than I thought.

VICTORIA. *I* am more impossible than you thought? Thank you. Oh! you want me to come to prayer meeting?

MR. HERR. Oh, don't! I—I love you. It's absurd I know—and you're laughing at me. I'm poor—a country minister, and you—you're a butterfly—utterly free, apart from duties and troubles of any kind. That's all. I'll go—and you'll forget. But I'm glad I said it. I love you. That's all.

VICTORIA. (*After a pause*) That's all?

MR. HERR. (*Holding the door open for her*) That's all. Good-bye.

VICTORIA. (*With her head bowed—going slowly to the door*) I'm sorry I won't do. I should have tried so hard. I—I think I could make even Mrs. Lemmingworth love me—if I *tried*—for *you.*

MR. HERR. Victoria! (*Springing toward her.*)

VICTORIA. (*Stepping back from him*) No—no! you didn't ask me.

MR. HERR. (*Catching her in his arms*) Will you?

VICTORIA. (*Lifting her head after a moment*) Shall I have to go to prayer meeting? (*He smiles at her*) No, I'm not laughing now. I shall always have a prayer in my heart that I may be worthy of you. But it frightens me a little.

MR. HERR. Margaret says love teaches us—and I believe it does. CURTAIN

# A FLOWER OF YEDDO

JAPANESE COMEDY IN ONE ACT

[*Adapted from the French*]

## VICTOR MAPES

Victor Mapes was born in New York City in 1870. After graduating from Columbia University he was Paris correspondent of the New York Sun. In 1897 he became stage manager of the Lyceum Theater in New York under Daniel Frohman. After a short term as dramatic critic of the New York World he assumed the duties of general stage manager of Daly's Theater. "A Flower of Yeddo" was one of his earliest successes. For the past twenty-five years he has written, either alone or in collaboration, a number of successful plays, among which the best known are "The New Henrietta" and "The Boomerang." "A Flower of Yeddo," though one of Mr. Mapes' first plays, is typical of his skill as a dramatic craftsman.

Following is a list of Mr. Mapes' published plays: "The Boomerang," "The Hottentot" (in collaboration), and "A Flower of Yeddo,"

# A FLOWER OF YEDDO*

## CHARACTERS

KAMI
SAINARA
MUSME (Sazhima)
TAIPHOON (Djouros)

The action takes place in a room of Kami's little country house, near Yeddo.

### DESCRIPTION OF CHARACTERS

The principal charm of the play is its quaintness and daintiness, and this observation applies especially to the leading character, KAMI. The part should be played with comical gestures, intonations, grimaces, and business of all kinds—at the same time being always quaint and dainty.

SAINARA and MUSME, are both, properly speaking, "soubrette" parts, SAINARA, however, should be more demure and modest in appearance than MUSME, and the part might be satisfactorily played by an ingenue.

TAIPHOON is a broad character part and should be played by a female comedian with great gusto and exaggeration so as to be comical in its fierceness.

### PRONUNCIATION OF NAMES

| | |
|---|---|
| Kami—Kam-mee, | Sazhima—Sá-zhee-má, |
| Sainara—Sá-ee-ná-ra, | Djouros—Djoor-os, |
| Musme—Moos-may, | Taiphoon—Ty-foon. |

---

[*Interior of Kami's little house—Night—At the rise of curtain,* KAMI *is seated on the floor, with his legs doubled under him, before a low table. He has a long pointed brush in his hand and a roll of parchment before him on the table.*]

KAMI (*with quaint enthusiasm, holding the brush up in the air*).

As numerous as waves that roll in from the sea
The verses from my brush's point flow gracefully.
(*Looking at manuscript*)
—That makes eight thousand, two hundred and forty-four— (*He pauses to reflect*)
I'll write, I think, about ten thousand verses more—
That's few? . . . Still, lengthy poems are sometimes not the best. . . .
There!——

(*He puts the brush on the table, and reaching with his hand up behind his ear, draws out a little fan which was folded up and stuck in the collar of his gown. He opens it with a snap and fans himself.*)

Now let's smoke a pipe and take a little rest.

(*He closes the fan with a snap, and places it in his belt. He rises. Then he takes from his belt a little pipe, made of silver, and a small tobacco-pouch. He fills the pipe and lights it at a tiny little stove* L.)

How thoughts affect the heart! I stifle, I declare!
(*Moving* C.)
Besides, 'tis warm.—Suppose I tempt the evening air?

(*He goes up stage and slides open the wooden curtain that closes the large bay window. Then he takes a few quick puffs of smoke and stands a moment contemplating the poetic landscape through the window.*)

Ah, stars, of gold! You flash and twinkle in the skies
(*Turning and coming down a little*)
With flits of flame—just like a witty maiden's eyes!

(*He takes a final puff or two, and replaces his pipe in his belt. Then he draws out his fan again, going back to his poem. He kneels down before the table again and closing up the fan taps the parchment-roll with it, unrolling five or six feet of manuscript. He then places the fan in his belt and picks up his brush from the table. Before writing a word, however, he glances up and exclaims contentedly:*)

In this secluded spot, far from the haunts of man,
I'm certainly the happiest person in Japan!

TAIPHOON R. SAINARA L. MUSME, *up* C.

Sweet Solitude!——

(*As he utters the word "Solitude" three pretty feminine heads appear simultaneously—one at the door* (*Right*), *another peeping through the hanging beads at the door* (*Left*), *and the third at the bay window* (*up Centre.*)

Sweet Silence, too!——

(*He is interrupted by three sudden bursts of laughter, and the three heads are withdrawn quickly. The poet, greatly surprised, turns round. He rises, and goes up a few steps toward bay-window. He comes back to table before speaking, and glances about to see where such strange noises could have come from. He sees nothing, but he smiles and nods his head knowingly.*)

Ah? Little birds!

(*He sits and continues his interrupted soliloquy*)

Each week, I come here, to describe in well-rhymed words
Dear Sainara, whom I love devotedly.
Yes, even I, Kami, dealer in bronzes and ivory,
While she treats me with scorn!—No matter! still I say
I'll keep on loving her until my dying day!
Constancy, at times, has vanquished unkind fate;
So, if I falter not, but sing her praise and wait,
. . . Who knows? . . . Once more to work! . . .

(*He glances over the poem with a look of satisfaction.*)

Yes, these thoughts of mine
Without exaggeration, are extremely fine!

(*He takes up manuscript*)

Sweet Sainara, here is what your lover true,

Although he is despised, thinks and says of you:

(*He reads.*)

When your dainty little feet
On the water's edge you place,
The jealous lilies can't compete
With their exquisite grace!

When your hands, so white and slim,
The mandolin chords are wooing,
They seem like birds upon a limb
A-billing and a-cooing!

Your smiling mouth is sweet and nice,
All tempting charms combining,
With teeth like wholesome grains of rice
In rich red sauce reclining!

The sparkling glimmer of your eye
Is like the new moon's light
Reflected for the passer-by
On a lake at night . . .

* * * * *

(*He stops and looks into space reflectively.*)

Let me see—is what I say there quite correct?
The surface of the lake, I'm certain, does reflect
The new moon charmingly—But does it sparkle so!
That's something that a truthful poet ought to know.

(MUSME's *head appears at the bay-window.*)

Perhaps, to be quite sure, I'd better go and look?

(*Rising and coming down left of table*)

The water of the lake is near my peaceful nook.
Yes! (*moving* R.) I'll go, at once (*pausing*), observe the lovely moon!

(*He puts on a pair of high sandals, like little benches, takes the hand-lantern, and opens door* R. *Before going out he gives a final glance at the room to assure himself that all is well. He goes out.* MUSME, *her hair dressed most elaborately, and a great amount of rouge on her cheeks, watches him mischievously till he goes out. She puts one leg very daintily over the window-sill. She puts the other leg over and sits on the sill. She wears the costume of a Japanese dancing-girl. She drops down inside. As soon as she gets in, she gives a hasty glance about, then, opening her fan, runs as rapidly as a little bird to the door* L. *and peers in through the bead curtain. Then she runs in the same rapid way across to door* R., *and listens a moment. Then she runs up above table, with a reassuring glance at the bay-window. Then she looks out to audience with a mischievous expression. She closes fan with a snap, kneels down above table, snatches up the brush and traces a few words rapidly, writing from top to bottom and from right to left. Then she pauses and looks up.*)

MUSME. My name is Sazhima, but here I'll sign Musme.
Sainara's wise—'twas she who chose this way
Of putting poet Kami to a triple test.
(*She puts brush down and rises*)
(*She comes down* R. *of table.*)
First, I come, attired thus at her request,
To see if he be true (*opening her fan moving a few steps* R. *with a toss of her head*), or fickle like most men!
I'll tempt him (*She makes a mischievous gesture of importance*) and we'll see!—If he resists (*She pauses a moment, then takes a few steps left and back again fanning herself and speaking rapidly*), why then
Sainara, I think, may feel a little pride
To know that such a man seeks her to be his bride!
(*Another gesture*)
Next (*she closes her fan with a snap*) Djouros, in warlike (*She struts left imitating a soldier's gait and stops below seat* L. C.) dress disguised, will see
What courage Kami has. For if he's cowardly
And fears to die for honor, Sainara's hand

He'll lose. (*She sits* L. C.) But if he's courage, he must still withstand
A final trial. Sainara here will come
To borrow, on some pretext, a colossal sum.
A merchant holds on fast to money, so they say,
But he must hand his out—and that without delay,
Or else no wedding, sir! (*She rises. She opens her fan and moves* C.) However, we shall see—
'Tis warm in here. . . . (*She looks about, catches sight of the tea things up* L., *closes her fan and runs up a few steps quickly toward them. Then she stops an instant, looks out at audience mischievously.*) I'll take a taste of Kami's tea! (*She goes to it and pours out a cup of tea. She stands* L. *of tea table, so the audience can see her pouring. Then she takes cup and saucer in her hand and runs down* C. *before drinking. She drinks it.*)
A vile concoction! (*She makes a wry face, runs back to tea table and sets cup down*) Bah! Never since the world began
Was tea worth drinking made in the house of a single man! (*She listens.*)
Hark! (*She runs across to door* R.) 'Tis he! He comes! I have no time to lose! (*She scurries across to door* L. *looks in, is afraid to go that way*)
Which way? (*She looks to bay-window again and runs to it. She climbs out over the window-sill, as she came in*) 'Tis not quite modest, but I couldn't choose!

KAMI. (*Coming* R. C.) I was quite correct—the point I settled soon—
In all I said about the sparkling of the moon.
(*He goes up, sets down his lantern and removes sandals. Then he comes down* R. C. *fanning himself.*)
I envy fish that swim in water, cool and clear!
Phew! (*Moves* L.) Yes, for such a night, I went too fast, I fear. (*He goes up* L. *toward tea—stops and looks out at audience.*)
A cup of tea refreshes one, although 'tis hot—

(*He goes toward the teapot. He attempts to pour tea—sets down teapot and takes off the lid and draws back in astonishment.*)

Ah! Oh, indeed! That's strange! (*He comes down a few steps looking into space.*) Who's emptied my teapot? (*He pauses an instant, then glances out through window.*)

Some spirit? Yes, perhaps—Or some nymph from the wood!

No harm. I'll heat more water. (*He takes tea-kettle from behind stove—looks in it to assure himself that it contains water and places it on stove.*) 'Twill be just as good. (*He pauses to look at it, then turns* C. *and thinks once more of his poem.*)

Now then, to work! (*He starts to go* C. *then pauses.*)

For my description's not yet done

Of Sainara's charms. In fact 'tis but begun. (*Takes a step or two* C. *then pauses again.*)

Next I must describe her dainty little nose

Which vibrates when she laughs! (*He moves up above table as he speaks.*) Let's see—what flower that grows

Does it resemble? (*Sits. He sees the words written by* MUSME.) Ah! what's this? Can it be true?

(*Kneeling down.*)

Some one has been here! Yes! and written "I LOVE YOU!"

"I love you"—and it's signed "Musme"? (*He looks up before speaking the word,* MUSME, *and utters it in a loud puzzled way. A knock is heard at the door* R.)

MUSME. (*Off* R.) Open the door!

KAMI. (*Rising and coming down* L. *of table.*) What's that?

KUSME. Open, I beg!

KAMI. (*He goes toward door* R. *then pauses.*) I'll wager it's some bore! (*He opens the door and falls back in amazement.*)

A woman! How strange!

(MUSME *enters pretending to be very much agitated. She*

*crosses* L. C. *fanning herself.* KAMI *comes down* R. C. *bows low, rubbing his knees and shins.* MUSME *makes a gesture, as if to speak. He interrupts her.*)

But, Madam—first be seated, pray!

MUSME. (L. C. *pretending to be embarrassed.*)

O sir, 'tis going to rain, and I have lost my way!

KAMI. (*Moving up above table* R. C. *astonished.*)

The sky is cloudless, madam,—the air is dry and warm.

MUSME. (*Giving him a very tender look, and speaking reproachfully.*) O Signor Kami—(*She scurries across to* R. C.)

KAMI. (*Coming down* L. C. *Aside, in amazement.*) My name!

MUSME. (R. C. *coquettishly and playfully, looking at him.*) I'm sure 'tis going to storm!

KAMI. Permit me! . . . (*He taps his forehead with the closed fan then taps the palm of his hand—a quaint and characteristic gesture.*)

I open my door, o'ercome with surprise—

A wind-tossed blossom drops in from the skies!

MUSME. (*Pretending to be tremendously pleased and flattered, she takes a few steps toward him. Making eyes at him bewitchingly.*) A compliment? (*She goes a little above him and curtsies, looking him tenderly in the eyes.*) My thanks!

KAMI. (*Moving a little* L. *Aside.*) What's this I feel? My heart

Palpitates! Her glances pierce me, like a dart!

MUSME. Sir, my name is Musme—

KAMI. (*Pointing to the poem.*) Musme!

(*Aside, fanning himself.*)

On my word,

This fluttering of my heart is really quite absurd!

MUSME. I'm Musme, sir—Musme, the dancer.

(*She pirouettes* R. *then looks at him coquettishly.*)

KAMI. (*Politely.*) A nymph, or elf

Beholding so much grace, I think would hate herself!
(*Fans himself.*)

MUSME. (*Coming toward him.*) Flatterer!

KAMI. (*Moving a little toward her.*) I speak the truth.

MUSME. My vanity
You please, of course, 'tis true, I do dance prettily
—All Yeddo is agreed on that. . . .

(*Pirouetting, she crosses him and stops* L., *more glances.*)

KAMI. (R. C. *aside.*) What can she mean?
Such saucy, tempting glances I have never seen.
(*Aloud.*)
Madam. . . .

MUSME, L. C. Oh, I am still a damsel.
—To-night
I strayed off by the lake—no one was in sight—
When suddenly a man sprang out—an armed man,
Frightful and fierce. I gave a scream—I turned and ran
Until I reached your door.

KAMI. Indeed you—

MUSME. (*She hides her face with her fan and moves* L. *as he speaks.*) My surprise—(*Turning to him.*)
My unexpected joy, I should say, you surmise,
When the unknown protector, to whose house I came
Proved to be that gifted poet—Kami, by name,
Whom Sainara has the bad taste to despise
(*With exaggerated modesty.*)
But who might . . . who has . . . in some one else's eyes
Won special favor. . . .

KAMI. (*Blushing.*) Madam! . . .

MUSME. (*Taking a step toward him, tenderly.*)
Won't you call me Musme?

KAMI. (*Embarrassed.*) Madam. . . .

MUSME. (*Another step. More tenderly.*) Musme!

KAMI. (*Moves* R. *a little, then turns.*) Well, to please you then, *Musme,*
Permit me to observe that you seem to me
To overstep the bounds of maiden modesty!

MUSME. (*Looking down.*) I'm a dancing girl, you know! (*She laughs, going toward him tenderly.*)
Come tell me why
To my tender advances you make such cold reply.

KAMI. Musme, an honest man . . .

MUSME. (*Looking right into his eyes.*) Well?

KAMI. (*Loses courage, moves a step* R. *and turns.*)
Only this I'll say,
My heart's true love I've vowed until my dying day,
To a young lady——

MUSME. (*Making eyes at him.*) I'm young too!
My eye is bright!

KAMI. Madam—

MUSME. (*Tenderly.*) Musme!

KAMI. Madam——

MUSME. (*Throwing herself almost in his arms, passionately.*) Musme!

KAMI. (*Crossing* L., *aside.*) Heavens, such light
As flashes from her beauteous eyes ne'er did I see!

MUSME. (*Following him a little.*) I love you!

KAMI. (*Aside.*) What temptation!

MUSME. I love you, Kami! (*She points to the poem.*)
The fond confession that I scribbled there for you—

KAMI. (*Resolutely.*) So be it, Madam! Yet to one name I'll be true,
And that name is—

MUSME. (*Expectantly.*) Well?

KAMI. (*Fanning himself energetically.*) Is Sainara!

(*When* KAMI *says* "SAINARA" MUSME *sees she has failed and snaps her fan open, moving away from him* C.)

(*Loud knocks are heard at the door* R., KAMI *runs up* C. *left of table.*)

TAIPHOON. (*Off right.*) Open, I say!

(MUSME *recognizes* TAIPHOON'S *voice. She gives a little laugh to herself then runs up on* KAMI'S L. *in pretended fright.*)

MUSME. (*Up* L. C. *Pretending to be terrified.*)
That voice! I'm lost! The man—He's come to drag me away!

KAMI. (*Up* C., *bravely.*) By Buddha, no! He shall not touch you! (*He moves left.*)
Enter here

(*She hangs back. He reassures her.*)
This way—Trust to a humble poet and have no fear
For while I live, know this—no man will pass that door!

(MUSME *crosses to door* L. *and stands with the curtain parted. The knock is repeated.* KAMI *starts to go* R. *and stops* C. MUSME *throws a kiss to him and disappears* L.)

TAIPHOON. (*Off* R.) Open I say, you clown! or by thunder, I'll have your gore!

KAMI. (C.) His voice is most unpleasant! (*He goes to door* R. *and stops to speak before opening it.*)
He called me a clown!

(*He goes* R. *and opens door.* TAIPHOON *enters wearing the costume of a Japanese noble. She has two large swords in her belt and fans herself as she enters.*)

TAIPHOON. (L. C. *crossing* L. *and fanning herself violently.*) How's this, pale friend? Did you want me to break the door down?
Would you like three inches of steel run in your breast?

KAMI. (R. C. *Bending low, rubbing his shins.*) Forgive me—I was dreaming—I had gone to my rest.

TAIPHOON. (*Sitting down* L. C.) You're dreaming still, sir!

KAMI. (R. C.) No, I'm now quite wide awake.
My guest I welcome. What refreshments will he take?
(*Moves up* C.)

TAIPHOON. That's better!

KAMI. (*Above table* C.) Permit me—

(*He taps his forehead and his palm with the fan—the characteristic gesture.*)

The arm-ed soldier enters the poet's bower,
Like a cannon ball meeting a fragile flower!

TAIPHOON. (*With a scornful gesture, rising.*) Humph! You're a rhymester, I perceive! (KAMI *pleased to be called a rhymester comes down* R. *of table and goes toward* TAIPHOON, *nodding his head pleasantly.*) So much the worse! (KAMI *gives a jump of surprise and disappointment.*)

There's nothing so contemptible as a dabbler in verse!
(*Moves* L.)
I love my swords, my horse and Musme, the dancer—you hear!
And I kill, for recreation, some fifty men a year!
(*Crossing him and going* R., *fanning herself majestically. Sits on cushions* R. C.)

KAMI. (*Aside.*) He's rude—ill-bred, I think, but still I'll be polite.
(*Aloud, graciously offering wine on tray.*)
This wine, most gracious sir, I hope you'll find just right.

TAIPHOON. Enough of that! (KAMI *runs back* L. *and sets down tray and flaggon.* TAIPHOON *rises.*) I've something else to think about!
Where did Musme go? That's what I would find out.
(*Coming* R. C.)

KAMI. (*Up* L. C., *pretending ignorance.*) Musme?

TAIPHOON. The dancing-girl I've honored with my love.

KAMI. Ah!

TAIPHOON. (*Crossing* L., *fanning herself.*) She adores me.

KAMI. (*Coming* C.) Ah!

TAIPHOON. But she's a playful sprite!
She slipped through my fingers just now—thanks to the night.
'Twas easy enough to follow her, by sniffing the air,

Which caught the perfume as it wafted from her hair.
(*Coming to him threateningly.*)
That is the reason, poet, I came and knocked at your door.

KAMI. (*On his dignity.*) Why, sir!
(*Aside.*) I'll be polite
(*Aloud.*) Kind sir, you astonish me truly.

TAIPHOON. Young man, don't dare to lie to me! (*Suddenly sniffing the air. She crosses* R.) I smell Patchouli! (*Turning on him.*)
The woman is here!

KAMI. Permit me, sir——

TAIPHOON. You lie, I say!

KAMI. (*His blood rising.*) Stranger of high rank, please not forget, I pray,
That you are in my house—and that I have no arm!

TAIPHOON. Where's Musme? Come, hand her over, and I'll do you no harm.

KAMI. That I'm but a humble poet, I'll not gainsay it—
But I know what honor is and try, sir, to obey it.
And though your murd'rous sword may slash me and cut me in two,
When you address me thus, I'll not reply to you!
(*He fans himself violently and moves* L.)

TAIPHOON. (*Closing his fan with a snap.*) My name's Taiphoon and, by the gods, you lie, I say!
(*Moves up* L. C.)
(*His eye lights on the poem, as if by chance.*)
Ah ha! Look here! These words of love are signed Musme!
(*He hits* KAMI *on the cheek with his fan.*)
There, coward! There—take that!
(*Walks majestically* R.)

KAMI. (*Stung by the insult, closing his fan furiously.*) O Buddha! He slapped my face!
(*He controls himself, overcome by the enormity of what has happened. Aside.*)
Kami, you're dishonored—nothing can erase
That insult.

(*Aloud.*) Sir, you're noble—I'm a common man,
I bow before your rank—the customs of Japan
Forbid my killing you——

TAIPHOON. (*Mockingly.*) Oh ho! We're very brave!

KAMI. No, I'm but a poet,
(*He bows.*) Your most unworthy slave.
I cannot avenge your blow, nor challenge you to strife,
To save my honor, then, I'll sacrifice my life.
The law permits it, and perhaps you'll cease to gloat,
When Kami, the poet (*Opening his fan and fanning himself*), has neatly cut his throat.

TAIPHOON. (*Ironically.*) Bah! That sounds all right—your talk is very brave;
You'll change your mind and keep on living like a knave!
(*Moves* R.)

KAMI. Come to-morrow, sir—now that you have heard—
Convince yourself that Kami never breaks his word.

TAIPHOON. (*Coming toward him.*) 'Tis well, my good young friend, I'll do as you have said,
I'll come at dawn and hope to see you stretched out dead
In a pool of oozing blood—but killed by this sharp blade!

KAMI. (*Losing patience.*) You've said enough, I think. I'll not require your aid
In seeking death.

TAIPHOON. (*Going to door* R.) We'll see! (*at door* R.) While looking for Musme
I'll choose a burying-ground for you, along the way.

KAMI. (*Bowing.*) I thank you in advance, sir.

TAIPHOON. (*Fiercely.*) Au revoir! (*He goes out* R.)

(KAMI *stands a moment* C. *without speaking, then closes door after him and comes back* C.)

KAMI. (*To himself.*) I see
I erred, just now, to boast of my tranquillity! (*He goes to door* L. *and parts the curtains.*) Madam. (*He perceives that the room is empty.*) She's gone! The

window's open—she's——fled that way. (*He comes back to* C.)
So spin the fates! And I have lived my final day!*
O Sainara, merry maid with lips so red,
'Twere sweet to die for you, but for another to shed
My youthful blood, when I might live so happily
Is rather sad, I think . (*He turns* L. *then turns back and moves up* C. *left of table.*) Time flies—alas, it forces me
To hurry with my poem. It must be found upon my breast,
All finished, when I lie in cold and clammy rest.
Fair Sainara, will that touching sight affect you?
You'll know that even in death your Kami (*fanning himself*) didn't neglect you.
Who will publish the manuscript, when I'm no more?
(*He sits down before the table and prepares to write. To his working instruments:*)
Good brush! and perfumed ink! Aid me, I implore
To fix my fleeting thoughts—to clothe my final dream
In rich and graceful rhymes. The hour is supreme!
I wish them such that Chinese poets in despair
With jealousy will bite their nails and tear their hair.
(*He holds up the brush.*)
To work, dear silent brush, the poet's one true friend,
Skim o'er the smooth and spotless paper—rise, descend
Carrying on your paint, like captured prey, each word
(*He makes a little gesture with the brush.*)
As o'er the shining lake a little bird
Skims swiftly, bearing in its beak a fly (*Sadly*),
To-morrow I'll be dead, and you, well you'll be dry!*
(*A knock is heard at door* L.)
Hello . . . . (*He rises.*)
Alas, poor poem, that knock, I fear, is your death knell.
My final moments these intruders steal away
And who will finish you? (*He opens the door* R., *looks*

* The lines included between asterisks may be omitted at performance.

*out, and comes back in astonishment.*) That's strange! (*The knocking is repeated at left door.*) Once more Musme! (*He crosses left and parts the beaded curtain.*)

Sainara! . . . . .

(SAINARA *enters. Her gown is modest and exquisitely harmonious*)

SAINARA. (*Crossing* C.) Yes.

KAMI. 'Tis quite beyond belief
That you who've scorned me so should come here—

SAINARA. (*Smiling.*) Like a thief! (KAMI *makes a polite gesture of reproach at such an idea.*)
Yes, through your open window!

KAMI. (*Smiling.*) You intend to twit me,
But thieves who come like you I'm glad to tempt. Permit me:
(*He makes the characteristic gesture with the fan.*)
She wafts in the window, for all her chaffing words,
Like perfume from the flowers, or like the song of birds!

SAINARA. (Softly.) Kami.

KAMI. (*In a transport of joy.*) Sainara, you, the fairest of the fair!
You here!

SAINARA. (*Crossing* L. *fanning herself.*) Enough of sugary words! I do not care
For them. If I have come alone at night, this way,
Please understand I've something serious to say . . .
Time flies.

KAMI. (C. *aside, with a sombre expression.*) Time flies! I was forgetting that to-night
Ends all. How short these minutes of supreme delight!

SAINARA. (*Astonished, taking a step towards him.*)
Poet, what's on your mind?
(*With modesty.*) You surely cannot think
Because you see me here, that I am on the brink
Of sentimental folly! No, I had another

Motive—in fact I treat you as a (*fans herself*) sort of brother!

KAMI. For two years I have known you scorned me as a mate,
Alas, the only feeling I inspired was one of hate!

SAINARA. (*Embarrassed, playing with her fan.*) Hate. Have I said it?

KAMI. Yes, you hate me, I know well.

SAINARA. (*Playing with her fan.*) I never said so——

KAMI. That may be. But actions tell
Better than words the feelings of the heart. I see it in your eyes.

SAINARA. (*Piqued.*) Well, since my eyes so skilfully
You read, read also there that I must go. 'Tis late.

(*Crosses* R.)

KAMI. (*Pleading.*) Sainara!

SAINARA. (R. C.) No, I'll take away my hate!

(*She makes a movement as if to go.*)

KAMI. (*On his knees.*) Stay! Sainara, stay!

SAINARA. (*Relenting.*) You wish it?

KAMI. Pity me!
Forgive my words, I beg, implore!

SAINARA. 'Tis well; I see
You're sorry. (*Crossing* L. C.) I'll remain, but henceforth have a care!

KAMI. (R. C., *overjoyed.*) You make me happier than e'er I've been, I swear! (*Rises from his knees.*)
Permit me: (*He makes the usual gesture.*)
A smile creeps in among my mournful tears,
As when, mid clouds, the sun's bright ray appears.

SAINARA. (*Seriously.*) I'll tell you why I came.

KAMI. My happiest of days!

SAINARA. Kami, let me speak.

KAMI. O let me sing your praise!
Permit me. (*He makes the usual gesture.*)
As I behold you here where just now all was gloom.
I say—a white camelia's blossomed in my room!

SAINARA. (*Half pleased.*) Always gallant, I see.

KAMI. I love you always, yes!
Have you forgotten?

SAINARA. (*Crossing* R. C.) No; that's why in my distress
I sought you out.

KAMI. (C.) How can I serve you? Speak, I pray.

SAINARA. Well, Kami, to-morrow——

KAMI. (*Aside.*) To-morrow!
(*Aloud.*) Pardon me—You say?

SAINARA. My uncle—uncle Shak—I think he's known to you?

KAMI. Hardly a pleasant man, I grieve to say.

SAINARA. That's true.
But uncle Shak, whom you dislike so heartily,
To-morrow will be ruined, unless you will agree
To help him——

KAMI. Speak, O flower of love, what can I do?

SAINARA. (R. C., *fanning herself.*) Lend him eight hundred and sixty-seven itzibou!

KAMI. Eight hundred and sixty-seven itzibou! Let's see—
That makes two hundred bags of rice!

SAINARA. (*Crossing* L.) Undoubtedly.
And he must have it before the dawn.

KAMI. A heavy sum!

SAINARA. (*Emphatically.*) So you refuse!

KAMI. One moment, please!

SAINARA. (*Speaking rapidly.*) I was wrong to come.
(*Crosses* R.)

KAMI. Sweet Sainara, listen——

SAINARA. (R.) No.

KAMI. 'Tis the last time
I'll e'er address you.

SAINARA. No; you'll make another rhyme
No doubt, and think to please me. So I'll say goodbye.

KAMI. My love!

SAINARA. (*Coming down* R. *putting her fan over her eyes and pretending to cry.*)

Poor uncle Shak, alas, he'll have to die!

KAMI. (C.) He'll live, my Sainara! I've tried to tell you twice,
Here in my house—I have two hundred bags of rice,
No, Sainara, no! You have no need to cry;
Those bags of rice I treasured up were meant to pay
For publishing my poem. I fondly hoped, some day,
That poem would honor you—your charms, described in rhyme,
I hoped to see adored by the universe, in time.
But now I'm willing to renounce all hope of fame!
A sacrifice for you is worth a glorious name!
All my itzibou your uncle's free to take.

(*Going toward door* L.)

Indeed, I feel I love him now, for your sweet sake!

(*Turning toward her.*)

All that I ask, my love, is that my memory
Henceforth, when I am gone, you'll cherish tenderly.

(*He looks at his manuscript.*)

Permit me: (*He makes the usual gesture.*)

A starving fox once near a stream lay down to die;
A kindly crane, whose nest was full of eggs, passed by;
She pitied him, and sacrificed to his distress
Her life, her eggs—all hope of future happiness!
Tis thus these verses, offspring of your lover's heart,
Will die, unpublished. Love them well; when I depart
This poem I leave to you, for with the rising sun
The life of poet Kami will have all been run.

SAINARA. (R. C., *smiling increduously.*) You? Die?

KAMI. You laugh? Believe me, 'tis no jest.
Even now grim death draws near to take me to my rest.

SAINARA. You, Kami, die? (*She laughs and crosses* L. *A knock is heard at door* R.)

KAMI. Ah, hark!

TAIPHOON. (*Off* R.) Come, dabbler in verse! Arise!

The golden light of dawn's already in the skies!
Now is the time to keep your word!

SAINARA. (L. C.) What do I hear?

KAMI. Politely he observes the dragon of day is near;
My hour of joy is over, I must end it now,
And welcome death.

SAINARA. You have to die?

KAMI. I made that vow.

(SAINARA *moves* L. *a little, then turns.*)

SAINARA. But if I wanted you to live?

KAMI. What, you confess
I'm dear to you? O Sainara, tell me——

SAINARA. Yes!
I love you, Kami.

KAMI (*Wringing his hands.*) O Heaven above,
What joy is mine! What miracle! She gives her love
To Kami, and he, alas, is——

SAINARA. Come, I know a place so nice;
So calm, secluded, beautiful, a paradise
For loving hearts. A lake there is and shady bowers
Where singing birds fly in and out, sweet scented flowers
Perfume the air. At night we'll sit and feast our love
With no companions save the moon and stars above—
Come . . . The dawn is near—Let's seek that blissful spot.
Come, Kami! Love!

TAIPHOON. (*Off right.*) Eh! Poet!

KAMI. (*Suddenly awakened to the situation.*)
Alas, no! You love me not!
That's plain. What you propose now cuts me like a knife—
You think I'd give up honor just to save my life?
You must despise me still. You'd better go. Goodbye.
The name of Kami I'll keep stainless, and I'll die
Precisely as I promised, before the sun appears!

(SAINARA *burst out laughing, moving* L.)

You laugh? (*She laughs again.*)

Go, madam, I beseech you, spare me your jeers!

(SAINARA *crosses* R. *and opens door* R.)

SAINARA. Come, Djouros! Sazhima! Come in!

(SAZHIMA (MUSME) *enters by the door, right, while* DJOUROS (TAIPHOON) *climbs over the window-sill up centre.* KAMI *sees* SAZHIMA *first.*)

KAMI. (*Greatly astonished.*) What's this? Musme?

MUSME. (*Graciously.*) I'm Sazhima.

KAMI. (*Shaking his head.*) Musme!

MUSME. Sazhima, I say!

(*He sees* DJOUROS (TAIPHOON), *who has come through window. She has taken off her head-gear but puts up the chin-piece with her hand.*)

KAMI. What, you here, too? Most noble sir, you've come too soon.

TAIPHOON. (*Taking down chin-piece and showing herself a girl. She crosses* C.) My name is Djouros, at your service.

KAMI. (L. C.) What! Taiphoon
Is Djouros—Musme's Sazhima! What means this jest?

SAINARA. These two are friends of mine who came at my request.

KAMI. (*In his polite manner, making a gesture with his fan.*) Such dainty flowers are usually asleep at night!

MUSME. (*Stepping forward and giving curtsey.*) Thank you.

TAIPHOON. (*Stepping forward and giving curtsey.*) Thank you.

SAINARA. (*Stepping forward and giving curtsey.*) Thank you.

MUSME. You are most polite.

SAINARA. My friends and I have put you to a test.

KAMI. It seems
To me that I've been living in a land of dreams!

SAINARA. Poor uncle Shak's a myth!

KAMI. (*To* TAIPHOON.) And with a bloody knife I need not cut my throat?

(TAIPHOON *and* MUSME *both turn and look at* SAINARA, *for an answer to this question.*)

SAINARA. (*Going to him coyly.*) You'll have to wed a wife!

(MUSME *and* TAIPHOON *move* R. *and hide their faces behind their fans.*)

Forgive me, Kami, for doubting you. I wanted to feel
Before I married, that my husband was ideal.
I wished him brave and faithful, generous as well—
Whether you had those qualities I could not tell
But you have proved it now before my eyes—
You've conquered in the battle of which my heart's the prize.

KAMI. (L. C.) (*on his knees before* SAINARA.)
My poem! My wife! 'Tis too much bliss! It dazzles me!

MUSME. (*Running down to footlights, with quick curtsey.*) So ends the comedy.

TAIPHOON. (*Running down beside her, with quick curtsey.*) We hope you like it.

(KAMI *rises and brings* SAINARA *down to footlights beside* MUSME—*as if presenting her to audience. She gives a quick curtsey and fans herself.*)

KAMI. (*To audience.*) Permit me!

(*He makes the usual gesture, then changes his mind and says simply, looking from one girl to another.*)

To finish properly
We'll first salute our friends, then drink a cup of tea.

(*The three girls scamper up stage quickly and sit on floor around little table.* MUSME *is above it*—TAIPHOON R. *of it—and* SAINARA L. *of it.* KAMI *goes to tea things up* L. *The girls look out at audience—then* MUSME *whispers something to them.*)

MUSME, SAINARA *and* TAIPHOON. (*Together, to*

*audience.*) Oy-a-sumi! . . . . Oy-a-sumi! . . . . Good-night! . . .

KAMI. Oy-a-sumi . . .

ALL. (*Together.*) Oy-a-sumi!

CURTAIN.

# DECEIVERS

**PLAY IN ONE ACT**

## WILLIAM C. DE MILLE

William C. De Mille was born at Washington, D. C., in 1878. His early education was received in Germany. Later he was a student at the American Academy of Dramatic Arts. His first important success was "Strongheart," produced in 1905. "The Warrens of Virginia," two years later, produced by David Belasco, is an atmosphere play such as this dramatist has often written, a particularly theatrical and well-buit play of American life and character. Though he was successful as a dramatist he has for the past few years devoted his energies entirely to the production of motion pictures. Several of Mr. De Mille's plays are in the one-act form; they are ingenious little dramas of situation. Of these one of the most interesting is "Deceivers."

Following is a list of Mr. De Mille's published plays:

"Strongheart"; "The Genius"; "In 1999"; "Food"; "Deceivers"; "Poor Old Jim"; "The Forest Ring"; "The Royal Mounted."

# DECEIVERS*

## CHARACTERS

AMOS LITTLE
FLORA LITTLE
PHIL, "THE MINK"

SCENE: *A Home in the Suburbs.*

TIME: *The Present.*

*A comfortably furnished living room—large windows back* C. *Door to bedroom* L. 2 E. *Door to hall* R. 1 E. *A piano is set diagonally in upper left corner. A small stand with practical electric lamp up* C. *in front of windows. Lamp is lit at rise. Library table* R. C. *with easy chair on each side—a lighted lamp on the table, also a telephone, books, magazines, box of cigarettes, ash tray, matches, etc. A small desk with papers, letters, etc. down* L. *in front of door. Curtain rises on empty stage. The 'phone is ringing—*AMOS *enters rather hurriedly from* R. *He is a rather small man of about 35 or 40—perhaps inclined to baldness. He wears a smoking jacket. He speaks over his shoulder out* R. *as he enters.*

AMOS. All right, dear, I'll answer it—finish your dessert —(*He picks up the 'phone and half sits on the table.*) Hello— Yes, this is Amos Little— Oh, that you Harry —Hold the wire—just a minute—(*He puts down the 'phone, goes over to* R. *door which he closes carefully— then comes back and picks up the 'phone again.*) Hello Harry—what, to-night? Oh, pshaw—I promised to



This play is also published separately, paper bound, at 30 cents a copy.

take my wife to the theatre— Five handed? Oh, I'll make six. Yes, but Flora—. What?—I think she's getting wise to this night work at the office— Oh, well I'll take a chance—I promised her to give up Poker— All right—sure you can count on me—what —is it—all Jacks? sure that's the best game— All right I'll be there in half an hour— Good-bye. (*As he hangs up the receiver the door* R. *opens and* FLORA *enters in evening dress.*)

FLORA. Hurry up, dear. You've just got time to change your clothes—(*Crossing* L. *to go to bedroom.*) What was the 'phone?

AMOS. The office——

(FLORA *stops dead and eyes him.*)

FLORA. (*Sarcastically.*) Oh—you've got to work to-night, I suppose?

AMOS. Yes— It's hard luck—I'd been *counting* on taking you to the theatre.

FLORA. (*Dryly.*) H'm—so had I.

AMOS. But business before pleasure—(*She eyes him intently—he gets uncomfortable.*) What are you looking at me like that for?

FLORA. This is the second time this week you've broken a theatre engagement with me.

AMOS. Do you think I *enjoy* slaving away at the office?

FLORA. Last Saturday, you were at "the office" till four o'clock Sunday morning. Tuesday night you came home from "the office" at three fifteen—This is Thursday——

AMOS. (*Trying to bluff.*) Look here, Flora, I don't like your tone.

FLORA. This is not the busy season——

AMOS. But I've told you—this war——

FLORA. (*Advancing a step.*) Amos, where are you spending your nights?

AMOS. (*Sinking into chair* L. *of table.*) Oh, Lord!

This is the thanks I get for working my hands to the bone for——

FLORA. How is it I can't get you on the 'phone when you're at "the office?"

AMOS. The girl's not at the switchboard and——

FLORA. (*Alert.*) Where is she then?

AMOS. At home and in bed——

FLORA. How do you know?

AMOS. I don't know—I——

FLORA. Then why—?

AMOS. Now for heaven's sake don't start that again— The idea—being jealous of a poor little 'phone girl——

FLORA. (*Tossing her head.*) H'm——

AMOS. Would it make you feel any better to come with me? Would you like to sit in an empty office while I work on the books? If so come along. (*Rising.*)

FLORA. Of course you'd stay while I was with you.

AMOS. Flora, I'm disappointed in you— You don't trust me any more— You're jealous.

FLORA. Why shouldn't I be? You're jealous enough of me—there's very little *I* can do that you don't want to know about.

AMOS. (*With dignity.*) That's very different.

FLORA. Well, it's going to be different from now on. I'm tired of being left alone night after night—

AMOS. (*Losing his temper.*) Well—what are you going to do about it?

FLORA. You'll see——

AMOS. Is that a threat?

FLORA. (*Facing him.*) Yes.

AMOS. (*With great dignity.*) Oh, very well. I shall change my coat and go to the office—perhaps when I return, you'll be yourself. (*He goes out* L. FLORA *sits in chair* L. *of table—The 'phone rings—* FLORA *answers it.*)

FLORA. Yes— This is Mrs. Little—who—? the Detec —wait a minute— Hold the wire—(*Goes to door* L.

*cautiously, closes it, then returns to the 'phone—speaking in lowered voice.*) Hello, now—tell me—what have you found out? Sh—don't speak so loud—I don't want my husband to know I've put a detective on him — No—he'd never forgive me—but I *must* know— What! You can't report over the 'phone? I see— But I don't know you—I've only seen your chief— Oh, yes—(AMOS *opens door* L.—*the door closes—he enters quietly—hears the following words and stops—then goes up to end of piano where he is invisible to her, but in full view of the audience*—FLORA *doesn't see him—her back is toward the* L.— *She continues.*) Well you'd better come here to-night— Yes—but be sure my husband doesn't see you— Yes, he'll be out—and I'll be alone— Yes it's better for you to come at night than in the daytime— The neighbors talk so—and a strange man coming here would make gossip, so I'd better *always* meet you at night—(AMOS' *face has changed from interest to amazement—from amazement to fury.*) Oh, we'll have plenty of time—My husband never comes back before two or three o'clock— Now listen—when he leaves the house, I'll put out the lamp in the back window— Be sure you don't come until you see the lamp go out— All right— I'll expect you— Good-bye——

(AMOS, *during the last few words, has gone out quietly, a picture of intense rage*—FLORA *hangs up the receiver and* AMOS *is heard singing in a very forced way— He re-enters* L. *making considerable noise.*)

AMOS. (*Restraining his wrath—and speaking with repression.*) Well, I'm off— What was the 'phone?

FLORA. Oh, nothing—a mistake.

AMOS. Flora, what did you mean when you said that you were tired of being left alone night after night?

FLORA. Never mind what I meant.

AMOS. But I *do* mind——

FLORA. All right—mind then— Good night. (*She exits* L.)

(AMOS *goes over to door* R.—*goes out*—*a door slams outside*— *He re-enters at once*—*cautiously goes up and conceals himself behind the piano*— *He can appear at either end of the piano and be seen by the audience.* FLORA *enters cautiously, looks down hall* R.—*then puts out light up* C.—*stage lights do not go down*— *She exits* L.—AMOS *comes from behind upper end of piano*—*goes back to window and tries to see out*—*sees something and conceals himself again*—PHIL, *the Mink, appears outside windows. He uses a jimmy to open the window softly and enters*—*goes to door* L.—*listens*—*then to door* R.—*then he examines drawers of desk* L. *He is a young, well set up chap, and doesn't look like a burglar*— *He is dressed in good business clothes*— *He makes himself at home*—*takes a cigarette from box on table and lights it*—AMOS *watching him from behind piano*—FLORA *enters*— *He hears her and turns*— *His hand goes to his pocket*— *He speaks quickly.*)

PHIL. Don't make a noise——

FLORA. (*Advancing.*) Oh, it's all right, my husband has gone——

PHIL. (*Surprised.*) Oh—has he indeed?

FLORA. I hope he didn't see you come in.

PHIL. I hope he didn't.

FLORA. Of course, I expected you—but my maid didn't tell me you had come— Did you 'phone from the drug store?

PHIL. Er— Yes—(PHIL *follows every move she makes with his eyes.*)

FLORA. (*Coming down and facing him.*) Well—

PHIL. Well——

FLORA. We'd better not delay— You must be gone when my husband returns.

PHIL. That suits me perfectly.

FLORA. Won't you sit down?

PHIL. Thank you—(*He waits for her to sit— She sits* R. *of table*—*he* L.)

FLORA. I'm afraid I'm rather embarrassed— You see I've never done anything like this before.

PHIL. (*Taking the cue.*) Of course not—but now that you have begun——

FLORA. Oh, I shall see it through— My husband's conduct has made this necessary.

PHIL. Oh—yes—yes, absolutely.

FLORA. I feel sure that he is deceiving me—otherwise I would never have asked you to—you understand.

PHIL. I don't blame you a bit— Excuse me— May I see your hand a moment—(*Rises and stands in front of table, leaning against it.*)

FLORA. My hand? Why what——

PHIL. Just a moment—I'll show you—(*He takes her hand and looks at it intently.*) Ah, these are very beautiful rings——

FLORA. (*Starting to draw away her hand.*) Yes—but—

PHIL. (*Holding the hand.*) Oh, it's a beautiful hand too——

FLORA. Really I——

PHIL. You know—I can see by your hand that I am going to acquire sudden wealth—(*Starting to take off her rings.*) Allow me——

FLORA. (*Pulling her hand but not releasing it.*) Look here—what do you mean? Let go my hand——

PHIL. A mere trifle I know—but they will remind me of you—please don't struggle.

FLORA. Oh, oh, I see— You're not the man I thought you were—you're a——

PHIL. Don't scream—(*He puts his hand over her mouth, holding her other hand—the struggle looks like an embrace—at this moment* AMOS *confronts them, a pistol in his hand.*)

AMOS. (*Covering them with his pistol.*) So— This is what you meant——

(PHIL *turns—sees he is covered and puts up his hands—* FLORA *rushes to* AMOS.)

FLORA. Oh, Amos—Amos—protect me.

AMOS. (*Casting her off.*) Protect you— Ha! This is a nice time to ask protection from me—(*To* PHIL, *who starts to lower his hands.*) Keep your hands up.

FLORA. I'll 'phone for the police.

AMOS. Why?

FLORA. To turn him over—he's a burglar——

AMOS. Ha— The old story—I wonder how many trusting husbands have been fooled by it——

FLORA. But I tell you——

AMOS. Oh, you act it well—if I didn't know better I'd believe you even now— But I heard you making the appointment with him over the 'phone—I heard you tell him to wait till your husband was out—I saw you meet him—heard you tell him he had to be gone when your husband returned and finally found you in his arms— Is that the way one receives a burglar?

FLORA. But—but—I——(*She is speechless.*)

AMOS. If you didn't expect this man—whom did you expect?

FLORA. No one—that is— Oh, I won't be questioned like this—it's absurd—(*Starts to leave.*)

AMOS. Stay here—(*She stops— To* PHIL.) Now—what have *you* got to say for yourself?

PHIL. Not a word—I'm in the hands of Providence.

AMOS. I suppose you don't claim to be a burglar?

PHIL. (*Airily.*) No, no, I make no claim whatever— There's evidently been a mistake made, so I'd better— (*Starts to go.*)

AMOS. Stop—(*He keeps* PHIL *covered with the pistol.*)

PHIL. Just as you like— Do you mind if I put my hands down?

AMOS. No—but don't make any quick movements.

(PHIL *puts his hands down.*)

FLORA. Amos, can't you trust me?

AMOS. Do you think I'm a fool?

PHIL. You don't have to answer that if you don't want to——

AMOS. (*To* PHIL.) Now, I am going to have the truth from you. How long have you been her lover?

PHIL. Now look here, old man, that's not a fair question.

FLORA. Amos I—(*To* PHIL.) Why don't you explain? Tell him you're a burglar——

AMOS. Do you think I'd believe him—now?

PHIL. (*To* FLORA.) You see he wouldn't believe me— Of course, I'd like to do anything I could—but——

AMOS. I suppose I ought to kill you in your tracks.

PHIL. (*Conciliatingly.*) Well, I don't know about that — In *my* opinion, you'd be making a great mistake.

AMOS. (*Dryly.*) Oh, you think so, eh?

PHIL. Yes, yes, I'm sure of it— What good would it do?

AMOS. (*Between his teeth.*) Wipe out the dishonor of my home.

FLORA. Amos, you're making a complete fool of yourself.

PHIL. (*Soothingly.*) Well, he's excited just now— He'll be all right in a few minutes.

AMOS. You can't get away with this and you can't bluff me—I must know how long this has been going on— If you'll confess—I may let you go alive—after all, if I killed you, it would only make scandal.

PHIL. Absolutely— It would be the worst thing in the world for all of us.

FLORA. (*To* PHIL.) Look here, Sir, I don't know your name, but you seem like a gentleman ,though you are a burglar.

AMOS. Yes—I've noticed that too, a little strange isn't it?

PHIL. Oh, not in these days.

FLORA. (*To* PHIL.) Then I appeal to you as a gentleman— Don't you see the position you put me in by your silence?

PHIL. Yes, it *is* extremely awkward,

AMOS. Yes, *extremely* awkward.

FLORA. Then why don't you confess that you're a burglar, I'll see that no harm comes to you?

AMOS. Oh, no you won't—(*To* PHIL.) If you stick to this burglar story of hers, you go to jail—understand?

PHIL. (*To* FLORA—*shrugging his shoulders.*) You see?

AMOS. Come—come— Choose— Tell me all that's passed between you and her, or I turn you over to the police.

PHIL. And if I tell you what you want me to— I'll get my head blown off—is that it?

AMOS. No—I'll give you your life—but I must know the truth.

FLORA. Oh, you idiot— How can he confess what isn't so?

AMOS. (*To* FLORA.) He doesn't need any prompting from you. (*To* PHIL.) Will you confess, or shall I —(*Reaches for 'phone.*)

PHIL. (*To* FLORA.) I'm afraid it's no use—I should like to protect your good name—but after all, he *saw* us didn't he? So we may as well own up——

FLORA. *We*—well of all the— Why I never saw you before——

AMOS. (*To* FLORA.) You keep still—I'm getting the truth at last.

FLORA. But I— Oh—(*Sits in utter desperation.*)

AMOS. (*To* PHIL.) Go on.

PHIL. There's nothing more to be said—I admit we love each other——

FLORA. Oh— You— You wretch— You miserable liar!

PHIL. Of course, she doesn't seem to love me much at this moment—but—well—you know how women change——

AMOS. (*Letting his head sink.*) Yes—I know—I—loved her myself—once.

PHIL. (*Very sympathetically.*) It's cruel, isn't it? I make no excuses—only—don't be too hard on her—

You know men and women can't always control their hearts——

AMOS. (*His rage changed into grief.*) I know—

FLORA. Oh! You—you cowardly thief. (*To* AMOS.) This has gone quite far enough— If you want to believe this man's lies—do so—but I'm going to call the police—(*Reaches for 'phone.*)

PHIL. Stop her, man— (AMOS *does so.*) If she tells the police this absurd story about my being a burglar —I shall have to let the whole world know the truth.

AMOS. Yes—you're right—(*Taking the 'phone from* FLORA.) Put that down— This is terrible enough without making it public.

FLORA. But, Amos, his pretending to be my lover proves that he is a burglar—can't you see?

AMOS. No, I can't.

PHIL. Gently, brother; the lady's point is well taken— You see if I really *were* her lover, I would admit being a burglar and go to jail to save her. On the other hand, if I really were a burglar, I would admit being her lover and save myself— It's very perplexing; I don't blame you a bit for being puzzled.

FLORA. There, Amos, he admits that he is a burglar.

PHIL. Oh, no, I don't. You were entirely too eager to give me to the police— The minute we were caught your one thought was to save yourself. You would have had me languish in a dungeon cell, while you went free. In that moment, you killed in me every spark of love— You wouldn't lift your hand to save me, so why should I save you?

FLORA. Oh, I give it up—believe what you please Amos, I won't deny anything—(*Sits again.*)

AMOS. (*To* PHIL.) Go on—tell me the rest.

PHIL. Say, look here, old man, why make me tell all the painful details? I've told you what you wanted—now let me go and I'll try to forget her. (*Starts to go.*)

AMOS. (*With pistol.*) Stop! (PHIL *stops.*) The story

doesn't end here— If I spare your wretched life, you've got to do the square thing by her— After the—the divorce, you must marry her.

FLORA. What!

PHIL. I shall be delighted.

AMOS. I have your word?

PHIL. If she wishes it— Yes.

AMOS. (*Pointing to door* R.) Then go— (*Pockets his pistol.*)

PHIL. Thank you—(*Starts to go*—FLORA *gets between him and the door.*)

FLORA. Stop— You—you can't leave me in this false position. If you go like this, he'll always believe—what he does now—(*To* AMOS.) I can't stand this, Amos, the man you heard me 'phoning to was a detective—I've had you shadowed—to find out the truth. The detective was to come here to-night—when I found this man in the room I thought it was the detective. There—now you know the truth—(*To* PHIL.) Oh, please, please, have the decency to save my reputation!

PHIL. (*Covering* AMOS *with a pistol which he takes from his pocket.*) Certainly, I never could resist beauty in distress— Keep quiet brother and don't make any sudden motions— The lady is perfectly right—I am a burglar.

AMOS. (*Turning to* FLORA.) And you put a detective on me, eh? You treated your own husband as if he were a criminal.

FLORA. (*Going to him.*) Forgive me, Amos, I was mad with jealousy—I didn't believe you spent the nights working at the office.

AMOS. And you are the woman who swore to love and honor me— You suspect me of lying to you— of deceiving you—when I am sitting night after night over my desk, working to give you comforts—working until my eyes close with fatigue and I sleep in my chair—working until—(*'Phone rings.*)

PHIL. Don't move please—(*Keeping them covered with the pistol he answers the 'phone from chair* R. *of table.*) Oh— Hello— Yes this is Mr. Little's house. Mr. Little can't come just now—I'll take the message— Oh, it's all right—I'm an intimate friend—I see— Yes— Yes, all right I'll tell him—Good-bye. (*Hangs up and turns to* AMOS.) Mr. Jack Evans says you are to hurry up and that Billy just held four aces.

FLORA. (*Recoiling from* AMOS.) Jack Evans! Four aces— So *that's* the way you work your fingers to the bone to give me comforts.

AMOS. But my dear——

FLORA. Bah— Don't speak to me—(*Starts to go.*)

PHIL. One moment—(*Keeping them both covered with the pistol.*) Kindly stand perfectly still—both of you. I'm glad I came to-night— You two people really love each other, but you are both absurdly jealous and each of you has been deceiving the other—(*Going to* FLORA.) Your rings, please.

FLORA. But——

PHIL. Please. (*Under compulsion from the pistol, she gives them to him.*) My dear children, love never thrives on deceit. Trust each other and you will be happy. Now the necklace—(*He gets it and turns to* AMOS.) You see, honesty is the best policy—(*While talking he goes through* AMOS's *pockets, taking pistol, watch, pin, pocketbook, fountain pen, knife, loose change, etc.*) You must have faith in each other. Let him play a game of poker occasionally. If he had played to-night he'd have lost less than he's losing now. (*To* AMOS.) But don't tell her you're working at the office — That's not honest—it's not fair to her—and Oh!— it's so old! That's all you've got to remember— Honesty—it's the thing that makes life worth living— An honest man fears nothing—he can look the world in the eyes—I'm going to leave you now—(*He takes the 'phone and jerks it loose, leaving it on the table. A ring is heard at the door bell* R.) There's your detective— If you will both wait in here, I'll let him in— But I'm sure you won't need him now. In here please—(*He puts them out* L.) I'll send him right in here— He can let you out—and remember—*Honesty*—(*He closes and locks the door* L., *leaves key on table. Ring repeated at bell* R. *He takes another cigarette from table, lights it*—AMOS *bangs on door* L. PHIL *calls to him.*) Tell the detective the key is on the table— Good-night——

(*Banging continues* L. *Ringing repeated* R. PHIL *exits jauntily* R.)

CURTAIN.

# THE GIRL

DRAMA IN ONE ACT

## EDWARD PEPLE

Edward H. Peple was born at Richmond, Virginia, in 1867. Mr. Peple was for several years in the railroad business, and entered the theatrical world at a comparatively late date in his career. "The Prince Chap" (produced in 1904) was his earliest play. This was followed by several other plays of which the most important are "The Littlest Rebel" and "A Pair of Sixes." Mr. Peple died in 1924.

Edward Peple possessed a very genuine gift for the theater. This, combined with his skill in dialogue, give to his best plays an air of actuality which is distinctly American. He wrote few one-act plays, but "The Girl," now published for the first time, was very successful in vaudeville, and reveals a knowledge of that particular technical facility without which the one-act play is merely an ineptitude.

Following is a list of Mr Peple's published plays; "A Pair of Sixes"; "The Prince Chap"; "The Littlest Rebel"; "The Girl"; "A Jury of Our Peers."

# THE GIRL

## CHARACTERS

FREDERICK CAWLEY
BOB CONNELL
KREBS

SCENE: *The Bachelor quarters of Cawley, New York.*

TIME: *The present.*

*The bachelor quarters of Frederick Cawley, New York City.*

*The furnishings are the kind that give an air of comfort and good taste. Main entrance at rear center. Door with practical transom over it giving out upon a small entrance hall. At right is a door leading into bed-room. Right of center is a table desk with shaded lamp and a few books and papers. Lounge to the left. At side of it a small table with telephone on it. Several easy-chairs scattered about. At rear against wall is a small writing desk with droplid. It is evening.*

KREBS, *an English valet, is discovered at the rise of the curtain; he is a man of conventional type, deadly serious, slender and frail of figure. He is lounging on the sofa, awaiting the arrival of his master, with an air of utter weariness. After rise of curtain, he yawns, rises slowly, crosses to side-board and takes a drink of whiskey from a small glass. In the act of swallowing it, he starts, glances at the door rear, chokes and con-*


This play is also published separately, at 50 cents a copy.

*ceals glass in his side pocket, as he crosses and opens the door.*

*Enter* FREDERICK CAWLEY, *a heavily-built, dominant man of thirty-five, in dinner coat and light overcoat. He glances quizzically at* KREBS *who is coughing.*

CAWLEY. Good evening, Krebs.

KREBS. (*Coughing.*) Er—good evenin', Mr. Cawley, sir. (*Advancing and coughing.*) Allow me, sir. Shall I take your 'at an' coat?

CAWLEY. Yes, thank you. (*As* KREBS *takes hat and coat.*) Catch cold?

KREBS. Er—arskin' your pardon, sir—er—no, sir.

CAWLEY. (*Smiling.*) Oh! Excuse. I thought you *had.* Judging by the remedy. (*As* KREBS *registers.*) And you'd better take that glass out of your pocket. You might fall down and hurt yourself.

KREBS. (*Rolling his eyes.*) Er—yes, sir. Very good, sir. (*Goes up stage with coat and hat.* CAWLEY *crosses to desk.*)

CAWLEY. Mail?

KREBS. No, sir.

CAWLEY. Callers?

KREBS. No, sir.

CAWLEY. Any one ring up?

KREBS. No, sir.

CAWLEY. U'm. All right. That's all.

KREBS. Yes, sir. Thank you, sir. (*Starts up stage.*)

CAWLEY. Oh! Wait. (*Crosses to him, takes a large envelope from pocket of overcoat which* KREBS *has taken from him, and tosses it on desk.*) Thanks. That's all. (*Exit* KREBS *into bed-room.* CAWLEY *seats himself at desk table on which is a picture of a girl in a large silver frame. He leans forward looking at it, then leans back as* KREBS *re-enters.*)

KREBS. Yes, sir.

CAWLEY. I am expecting a visitor this evening—at about eight-thirty. (*Looking at watch.*) By George! It's nearly that now. (*Unlocks table drawer and looks in it, though what he does with his hands is not seen by the audience.*)

Krebs. Very good, sir. (*While* CAWLEY *is engaged with table drawer,* KREBS *goes to rear and lets down lid of desk. As he does so an electric light inside the desk lights up. From desk drawer* KREBS *takes a hand glass, powder box, and starts to place them on desk.*)

Cawley. And, Krebs—while we are still alone, I want to —(*Stops suddenly, as* KREBS *has advanced with glass and box.*) Well? What are you doing with *those* things?

Krebs. Er—awskin' your pardon, sir, you said as 'ow you was expectin' a visitor, sir—an'—(*Pauses, looking from the hand-glass to the powder-box.*)

Cawley. Well, you put those things back. And get the whiskey.

Krebs. Eoh! (*Again glancing at glass, then turning to* CAWLEY.) Then—then it's a *gentleman* wot's comin', sir. (*Crosses to desk, putting up glass and box.*)

Cawley. Yes, Krebs. As it is neither a lady nor any other sort of female, your peculiarly active intelligence has alighted upon the masculine gender as a possible alternative.

Krebs. (*Not understanding.*) I beg pardon, sir?

Cawley. You may also bring the cigars.

Krebs. Yes, sir. Very good, sir. (*From a side-table he brings decanter, glasses, water and a box of cigars.*)

Cawley. (*Leaning back, puffing smoke and regarding him critically.*) Krebs—do you believe in the transmigration of souls?

Krebs. (*Blankly.*) Beg pardon, sir?

Cawley. No, I *see* you don't! The theory is this. We don't live on earth just *once*—but *many times.*

Krebs. (*Staring at him.*) Ew! Do we, sir?

Cawley. We do. If we live in accordance with normal

ethics, choosing, say decanters, instead of hand-glasses and powder puff-boxes, we progress—spiritually. (KREBS *puts hand to ear.*) If, on the other hand, we select a moral toboggan, as it were, we are apt to be reborn as a frog or a tom-cat, or—or something else equally depressing. Catch the idea?

KREBS. Yes, sir. Thank you, sir.

CAWLEY. I'm glad you digest it; because in your next existence, Krebs, you are going to be a damned old maid, with immoral tendencies, but without the courage to collect returns. (*Pours out a drink of whiskey, while* KREBS *rolls his eyes.*)

KREBS. Yes, sir. Certainly, sir. (*Starts away. Phone bell rings.*)

CAWLEY. Answer it.

KREBS. (*Crossing and taking up receiver.*) Hello! Mr. Cawley's *apartment*. Yes, sir. I'm not sure, sir, but I'll see. (*Turns, with hand on mouth piece.*)

CAWLEY. Who is it?

KREBS. (*In 'phone.*) Er—who is it, please? One moment. (*Turning.*) Mr. Connell, sir.

CAWLEY. Ah! Tell him to come up!

KREBS. (*In 'phone.*) Hello! Awsk the gentleman to come up, please. (*Hangs up receiver.*)

CAWLEY. Now, Krebs, listen to me—(*Crosses center.*) carefully. This is the visitor I was expecting. He doesn't love me any more than I love him; and in case of trouble I may want your assistance.

KREBS. (*Nervously.*) Er—awskin' your pardon, sir, but I should think you was big enough to 'andle 'im alone, sir.

CAWLEY. (*A little sharply.*) Don't be an idiot! I could pick him up and throw him out of the window—as easily as I could you.

KREBS. (*Backs away.*) Yes, sir, very likely, sir.

CAWLEY. Neither will be necessary.

KREBS. (*Sighing.*) Thank you, sir. (*Starts toward door.*)

CAWLEY. Wait! I might explain more fully; but in one event I'd rather you retained your convenient ignorance. So I want you to promise that no matter *what* happens in the next half-hour, you'll follow my directions—implicitly! Understand? Implicity!

KREBS. Yes, sir. Of course if—

CAWLEY. Cut it! There's no if about it. (*Door-bell rings.*) No, wait a minute. There's going to be one thing or the other. Do what I tell you, and I'll pay you—and pay you well. (*Stepping nearer and speaking sternly.*) Fall down in it, and so help me, I'll break every bone in your body. Now then! (*Pause. As door bell rings again,* KREBS *makes a nervous movement, and* CAWLEY *grips his shoulder.*) Hold on! You know *me*—and I don't threaten—as a bluff. Well?

KREBS. (*Nervously.*) I—I promise, sir. On me honor.

CAWLEY. (*Releasing him.*) All right. We'll see what it's worth. (*Sits down by table. Points to door and crosses to table, seating himself carelessly, while* KREBS *goes and opens door, bowing to* BOB CONNELL. *He is a young man of twenty-five, a trifle pale, and at present sullen in his manner.*)

KREBS. Good evenin', Mr. Connell.

BOB. Good evening.

CAWLEY. (*Cheerfully, and with apparent heartiness.*) Hello, Bob! Glad to see you. Come in! (*As* BOB *slowly turns his eyes on him.*) Let Krebs take your coat and hat. (KREBS *advances, but* BOB *waves him away.*)

BOB. I can only stay a few minutes. I have an appointment.

CAWLEY. Oh, I see. Why not 'phone to the lady? Tell her you are with *me*. It might relieve her mind to know you are in good company. (*As* BOB *shrugs and makes no reply,* CAWLEY *turns to* KREBS.) That's all for the present. When I want you, I'll ring. Remember what I said.

KREBS. Yes, sir. Very good sir.

(*Exits into adjoining room right, closing door, but eyeing the two men furtively as he goes.*)

(CAWLEY *comes down, looks at* BOB.)

BOB. (*After a slight pause, turns to* CAWLEY *who has been watching him.*) Well? You insisted on seeing me. Here I am. What is it?

CAWLEY. If you didn't *want* to come, why did you?

BOB. (*Sullenly.*) Well—we had just as well have it over now as any other time.

CAWLEY. Good! Won't you have a seat?

BOB. I'm doing very nicely as I am.

CAWLEY. Oh, hell, Bob! Even if we have to quarrel, we might just as well do it comfortably. Be sensible, sit down. (BOB *hesitates, then throws off his coat and hat, and drops into chair opposite* CAWLEY.) That's better. Have a cigar?

BOB. No.

CAWLEY. (*Pushing decanter over.*) Whiskey?

BOB. No.

CAWLEY. Sick? (BOB *makes impatient gesture.*) By Jove, what a difference it does make when little Mr. Cupid wounds a young man in the ribs. (*As* BOB *turns in his chair impatiently,* CAWLEY *laughs.*) Why, Bob, old chap, when I think of you in the old days—half shot —roaring a comic song—with a blonde chorus girl on one knee and a brunette on the other—

BOB. (*Sharply.*) Cut that out!

CAWLEY. Oh! Pardon me! I forgot about your moral Turkish bath. (*Smiling.*) My, how the angels must have rubbed you!

BOB. (*Turning on him.*) See here! You can leave my morals out of it. Fish or cut bait!

CAWLEY. (*Sits.*) All right we'll fish. (*Lights his cigar*

*and leans back in chair.*) Now as to our mutual friend, Miss——

BOB. (*Sharply.*) Leave her out of it, too!

CAWLEY. What! The very key-note of our discussion? Leave *her* out? Oh, my boy! My boy! (*Leans forward looking at picture on table.* BOB, *seeing it for the first time, rises angrily, facing* CAWLEY, *with clenched fists.* CAWLEY *still looks at picture.*) Rather a good likeness, isn't it? (*As* BOB *seizes picture in both hands and drops it face downward in a chair,* CAWLEY *rises angrily, and the two men face each other across table.*) Look here! What do you mean by that?

BOB. I'm telling you something you ought to know.

CAWLEY. What?

BOB. That putting the picture of any respectable woman on your table is a greater insult to her than you can possibly offer me.

CAWLEY. (*Rises slowly, after slight pause.*) Bob—you almost make me lose my temper. (*Sits down again.*) To preserve a temporary truce, we'll eliminate the girl —as far as possible. (*Waves hand toward chair and* BOB *sits.*) We'll take *you!* Do you think you've been exactly square with *me?*

BOB. I do.

CAWLEY. Well, I don't! I introduced you—took you to her home—in a purely friendly spirit. What's the result? You go quietly, systematically to work—and undermine my interests.

BOB. You never told *me* you *had* any interests.

CAWLEY. Naturally. A man can't post a keep-off-the-grass sign in a lady's drawing-room. I relied somewhat upon your sense of gentlemanly discernment. (BOB *glances at him, rises, takes a thoughtful turn and faces him.*)

BOB. See here, Cawley! If you think I haven't acted fairly, I'm sorry. I've done absolutely nothing to undermine your interests; but I *have* done everything

I could to advance mine. You seem to forget that a woman has a right to her own choice.

CAWLEY. Granted. What else?

BOB. And if she chooses *me*, it's your misfortune, not my fault. She—well, she *liked* me—from the first; and helped me to despise the sort of man I *was*—and *you* still *are*.

CAWLEY. Thank you prettily.

BOB. You asked me to be honest, didn't you? And now I'll be a little more so. (*Stepping toward table.*) I'm going to marry her.

CAWLEY. Are you? H'm! What income can you offer her?

BOB. (*Turns on him.*) None of your damned business!

CAWLEY. Thank you. Just what I wanted to know. Had the income been large, you would have stated the figure—to prove your point. Since it is small, it proves mine. Now then! Do you think—honestly—that, say, eighteen hundred a year is any sort of income to offer any sort of respectable life partner?

BOB. It depends upon the partner.

CAWLEY. Exactly! The wife! The poor, trusting girl, who, because of a temporary aberration, wrecks her prospects and ties herself, body and soul, to an equally insane young pauper. Good Lord, Bob! Think of her! You can't even afford sugar—for your lemonade.

BOB. Maybe she prefers my society to your money.

CAWLEY. Very possibly. But it isn't a question now of *her* preference; but mine.

BOB. Yours!

CAWLEY. And *yours!* You haven't saved anything—not a dollar—and you won't! Saddle yourself with a wife and further, with a family—and you'll live and die a stoop-shouldered, spindle-legged clerk. Bright prospect, isn't it? Let me offer you something better. You are nothing in this town. Skip out to another one, and start in business—for yourself.

BOB. (*Contemptuously.*) With what?

CAWLEY. (*Rises.*) With this. (*Rises and takes up package from table, opening it.*) Two thousand—cash! Now don't blow up! Take it as a loan. If you never pay it back, it will be worth the amount to have you start right—once. Well?

BOB. H'm! And what of *her?*

CAWLEY. (*Stepping around edge of table.*) You will leave *her*—and a clear field—to *me.* (*Pause. They stand looking each other in the eye.*) Well? What's the answer?

BOB. This! (*He swings straight at* CAWLEY'S *face with his fist.* CAWLEY *catches his wrist.* BOB *strikes with his left; this is also caught,* CAWLEY *holding both wrists and looking closely into his face.*)

CAWLEY. A pretty weak answer, Bob. (*Flinging him back into chair and standing over him.*) You infernal little worm! Try that again and you'll regret it. (*Swings* BOB *to him.*)

BOB. Well, go ahead. But when it comes to a show-down, what will you gain? You are big enough and strong enough to hammer me to a pulp—yes! But will you get the girl? You won't! Go ahead and smash me! Take advantage of your brute strength, just as you try it with your money! But before I'd accept your dirty proposition, I'll *take* the licking.

CAWLEY. All right. You may have that chance, too. (*Opening table drawer and taking out two revolvers.*) This town isn't big enough to hold us both, and one of us has got to go. Candidly, I'm not particular which. (*Strikes bell on table. Enter* KREBS. *He sees revolvers in* CAWLEY'S *hands and looks at him in horror.*)

CAWLEY. (*To* BOB.) Take one!

BOB. What do you mean?

CAWLEY. That I'll stand over here. You there. Krebs will hold a handkerchief, and when he drops it—

KREBS. (*Stepping back trembling.*) Me, sir? *Me?*

CAWLEY. Shut up! And do as I tell you. (*Turning to* BOB *and holding out revolvers.*) Well? Take one!

BOB. I won't do it! It isn't fair! I know nothing about those things, and you've been handling them all your life!

CAWLEY. That's your misfortune—not my fault!

BOB. Well, I won't!

CAWLEY. You little fool, I'm giving you a chance. Not only a chance with me . . . but a chance for *her*. If you're not a coward, as *well* as a fool, you'll take it! (BOB *looks at him in hesitation, then clenches his hands, compresses his lips, takes up one revolver which* CAWLEY *pushes toward him.*)

CAWLEY. Now, Krebs, pick up that handkerchief! (*As* KREBS *obeys, he points up-stage.*) Stand over there. (*As the trembling valet hesitates.*) Do you hear me? Stand there!—(*As* KREBS *obeys,* CAWLEY *takes position opposite* BOB, *but speaks to* KREBS.) Now listen to me —carefully. You'll count slowly. Then drop the handkerchief at any number between four and ten. Understand?

KREBS. Y-yes, sir.

CAWLEY. Then do it! Go ahead.

KREBS. One—two—three—

BOB. (*Steps toward them.*) Hold on! I won't have that! You've arranged the signals between you. You——

KREBS. But honest, Mr. Connell, sir. I swear it on me soul, sir—I——

CAWLEY. Tut! (*To* BOB.) Arrange your *own* signals. *I* don't care. Go ahead!

BOB. All right. I will. (*To* KREBS.) Use the letters of the alphabet. Start with G. And drop the thing whenever you like. Understand?

KREBS. (*Trembling.*) G—very good, sir.

BOB. Then go on—and get it over. (*As* KREBS *stands in hesitation and terror, looking from one to the other,*

BOB *speaks to* CAWLEY, *nervously, intensely. Turns.*) You know what you're doing, don't you? It's murder, that's what it is—and I hope you'll swing for it!

CAWLEY. You'd better watch the handkerchief. Go on, Krebs.

KREBS. Yes, sir. (BOB *steps back, holding handkerchief and speaking in gasps.*) G—haich—hi—J—K—*hell!* (*Stops.*)

CAWLEY. (*Sharply.*) Well, what's the matter with you? Why don't you drop it?

KREBS. I—I cawn't sir. Me—me fingers won't turn loost.

CAWLEY. They will if I tickle 'em with a bullet! (KREBS *cries out, and starts back.*) Now then! Start again—and this time—*drop it!* (*Turning.*) Ready, Bob!

KREBS. Y-yes, sir. Very good, sir! (*Speaking as before, but with increased terror.*) G—haich—hi—J—K—hell—hem—hen—ho—P—Q. (*He drops handkerchief, turns his back, and covers eyes with his hands.*)

(BOB *raises revolver quickly and fires.* CAWLEY *starts, spins once round and pitches forward, his pistol exploding as he falls.*

CAWLEY *lies on his face,* BOB *stands staring at him.* KREBS *turns slowly, looking at* CAWLEY, *his hands going to his cheeks.*)

KREBS. Oh, my Gawd! My Gawd! My Gawd! (*He sinks to his knees, repeating over and over in a whisper, till only his lips are seen to move.*

BOB *takes a step toward* CAWLEY. *He stops, looks at the revolver in his hand, starts and drops it. He runs his hand over his eyes then goes forward and kneels by* CAWLEY.)

BOB. Cawley! Cawley! (*Pauses. He moves back, then rises, looking about him as if bewildered.*)

KREBS. My Gawd! My Gawd! My Gawd!

BOB. Stop it, Krebs! Stop it! (*Going to him.*) Stop

it! (*Lifting him to his feet, holding his shoulders and looking into his face.*) Listen to me! Can you hear me?

KREBS. Y—yes, sir!

BOB. (*Also speaking in a whisper.*) All right! I'll want you—for a witness—that I did it—in self-defense. *You saw it!*

KREBS. (*In terror.*) But they won't believe us, sir. They'll say—*we* done it! You, sir! An' me! (*Trying to release himself from* BOB'S *hold.*) I got to get out of here! I got to go!

BOB. (*Holding him.*) Wait! Wait! So have I, Krebs! (*Glancing at* CAWLEY.) He *wanted* me to go! Tried to force me! And now I've *got* to. I've got to! (*Nervously, as he looks about, breathing rapidly.*)

KREBS. (*Snatching up coat and holding it for him.*) 'Ere, sir! But 'urry! 'Urry! We'll 'ave to go!

BOB. Yes, Krebs, I know. I've got to! I've got to! (*Looking at* CAWLEY, *moving toward table and repeating over and over in a whisper.*) I've got to! I've got to! Before they find out! I've got to! (*His hand goes out to the money on table, grips it and slips it into his coat pocket.*) I've got to! I've got to! (*To* KREBS, *who sees him take money.*) He wanted to pay me, Krebs—to get out of town! And now I've got to! I've got to! (*Looks down at* CAWLEY, *shudders and turns away.*) All right, Krebs. I'm ready. Come on!

KREBS. (*Who has entered room at the right for an instant and returned with hat and coat.*) Yes, sir. Yes, sir.

BOB. (*Crossing to door at rear, and turning.*) Turn off the light.

KREBS. Yes sir, yes sir. (*Crosses to switch.*)

BOB. Wait! (*Comes back, takes up the picture in silver frame and starts up-stage.*) I'll keep *her* out of it—anyway. Now turn it off—and come on.

KREBS. (*Switching off the light.*) Yes, sir. Yes, sir.

(*The stage is now in darkness. As the two men open the door, their silhouettes are seen on the back-ground of light in the hall. They close the door, and the lock is heard to click.*)

(*The curtain is lowered for an instant, to denote lapse of six hours.*)

*The stage is in darkness except for the pale light which can be seen through the transom over the door in rear. There is a slight scuffling noise outside, and the transom opens slowly.* KREBS *climbs through and drops down into the room. For an instant there is silence. Then* KREBS *can be heard as he moves slowly, uttering short ejaculations, as if in cold terror.*)

KREBS. Oh! Oh! Oh! (*Slight pause.*) If 'e *was* to set up and *look* at me! Oh, my Gawd!

(*There is another slight pause.* KREBS *strikes a match, and by its light his face can be seen as he looks at the empty floor. He shows wonder and fear, that* CAWLEY'S *body is not there, and holds his open-mouthed, tense attitude till the match burns down to his fingers. As the match goes out the electric lights are turned on, and* CAWLEY, *in a dressing gown, enters and looks at* KREBS *with a smile.* KREBS *gives a choked cry, then slowly backs away until he is stopped by the wall.*)

CAWLEY. Good morning, Krebs How are you? Scared pretty stiff, aren't you? Well, as I'm not a ghost, you can limber up. Come here! (*As* KREBS *holds position,* CAWLEY *speaks sharply.*) Come here! (KREBS *advances slowly, standing before* CAWLEY *who looks him up and down critically.*) What are you doing back again?

KREBS. (*With a frightened, apologetic manner.*) I—well, awskin' your pardon, sir—I—took the liberty of returnin' for—for a few trifles, sir.

CAWLEY. Yours—or mine? However, that's a detail. ~~Why the transom?~~

KREBS. I—left me latch key be'ind, sir.

Cawley. Oh, I see. Well, I'm rather glad you're here. I want some information. But first I'll give *you* some. (*Sitting on edge of table.*) You don't think for a minute, Krebs, that I was ass enough to let that young idiot shoot at me with a real bullet, do you?

Krebs. (*In amazement, looking at the smashed lamp.*) But, sir the broken lamp, sir—

Cawley. Exactly. That was *my* bullet. I didn't want too much light on my dying countenance. *His* shells were blanks. (*Takes up pistol from table, and throws out shells.*) Observe?

Krebrs. Oh!

Cawley. That's it. Oh! I wanted to get him out of town. Offered to buy him, but he wouldn't sell; so I had to get him out the other way. (*As* krebs *stares at him.*) Now then! You can give *me* some information. (*Looking at corner of table.*) First, I notice that he took my money. (*As* krebs *makes no answer.*) You needn't hesitate, for I saw him—out of the corner of my dead eye. Well?

Krebs. Er—yes, sir.

Cawley. And gave you a part of it to keep your mouth shut?

Krebs. Er—yes, sir.

Cawley. How much?

Krebs. Er—one thousand, sir.

Cawley. Ten per cent, eh? Well, I'm glad to save that much, anyhow. Shell out. (*Holds out his hand.* krebs *takes roll of money from his trousers pocket and ruefully hands it over.*) Thank you. It's worth the other nine to have him off the field. By the way, you are quite certain he has gone?

Krebs. Oh, yes, sir. I was with 'im till 'e took the train.

Cawley. Good! (*Pouring whiskey into glass.*) Have a drink, Krebs. You need it.

Krebs. Me, sir? Thank you, sir!

Cawley. Don't mention it. (*Pouring a drink for him-*

*self and turning with a happy smile.*) And now just one more thing. (*Holding whiskey glass in his hand.*) Did he—er—did he tell the girl?

KREBS. The girl? Oh, yes, sir. *She's* gone *with* him! (CAWLEY *looks at* KREBS *in amazement, his mouth going slowly open. He drops the glass from his hand and sinks into chair.* KREBS *drinks.*)

CURTAIN

# PEACE MANŒUVRES

DRAMA IN ONE ACT

## RICHARD HARDING DAVIS

Richard Harding Davis was born in 1864. His early training was received as a newspaper man, especially as war correspondent in the Balkans, in Cuba and in South Africa. His best known books are his novels and the volumes describing his experiences as a correspondent.

His first experiment as a dramatist was "The Littlest Girl," produced in 1895. His plays were more or less by-products, but the best of them are characterized by a certain freshness of treatment, in particular the one-act plays, "Miss Civilization," "The Zone Police," and "Peace Manœuvres."

Following is a list of Richard Harding Davis' published plays: "The Galloper," "Miss Civilization," "Peace Manœuvres," "The Zone Police," "The Dictator," and "The Orator of Zapata City."

# PEACE MANŒUVRES*

## CHARACTERS

HENRY HAMMOND *of Squadron A, New York Militia.*
"BUCK" MILEY } *Gunmen.*
"IKEY" SCHWAB }
POLLY WARREN.

SCENE: *A country road near New Haven.*

TIME: *The present.*

*A lonely and unfrequented spot on a country road near New Haven, Conn. Halfway up stage a board fence stretches left and right. The fence posts are three feet six inches high. Between them are four boards six inches wide, six inches apart, the lowest board resting on the ground cloth. In center of fence, two square gate posts, practical gate on hinges with latch. On left gate post a rural delivery letter box; the opening for letters is towards the audience. Gate and fence painted white. Fence is supposed to run parallel and close to a road.*

*Down stage on left a set piece representing a stone wall about three feet high, and with the end in view unfinished and dismantled. It projects upon the stage a distance of ten feet. It is covered with ivy; and behind it appear the tops of three small evergreen trees. The stone fence and the trees are supposed to be on the side of the road opposite to the white fence. Between the board fence and the line of the stone fence the ground cloth is painted to represent a road; back of each fence it is painted to represent grass, except*


This play is also published separately, in paper, at 30 cents a copy.

*where a path comes down from upper right to the gate, passes under it and is merged in the road. The back drop represents a closely grown wood. The borders hang low and show leaves and branches of trees.*

*The time is summer, but the light is shaded to suggest a place shut in by trees.*

(BUCK *stands at stone wall with back to audience peering off left through evergreens. His movements are those of a man anxious not to be seen. He hears a noise off left, in alarm looks left.* IKEY *enters left carrying over his shoulder, by the barrels, two rifles; in his left hand are two uniforms of khaki tied up in bundles. On top of each bundle is a campaign hat with a broad band of light blue.* IKEY *moves heavily as though weighed down by the rifles,* BUCK *vehemently motions him to join him behind the stone wall.*)

BUCK. (*In loud whisper.*) Hist! Keep down! Keep out of sight of the house. Come here! (IKE *comes below stone wall. Drops bundles. With sigh of relief, lowers butts of rifles to the ground; rubs his right shoulder.*) You got 'em, hey? Good! Any trouble?

IKE. (*Contemptuously.*) Trouble? I coulda lifted a *hundred* uniforms. The *whole* regiment was in swimming.

BUCK. (*Kneels and opens bundles.*) I told you so. Who did you get *these* from?

IKE. Two sentries. I say if they wanted to go in swimming, too, I'd guard their clothes for them. I'm still guarding 'em. (*Pause.*) There's no use your going through the pockets; I done that. They're empty. (*Indignantly.*) And the cartridges in these guns—they're empty, too. They're *blanks!*

BUCK. 'Course, they're blanks. This ain't no *real* war. It's a practice war. The New York Militia is the Red Army, it's defending New York. The Connecticut Militia is the Blue Army, they're trying to get into

New York. (*Points to blue bands on hat.*) You and me are going to join the *Blue* Army.

IKE. There's no army big enough to get *me* into New York. Not if the bulls see me first. It's all foolishness, anyway! For why should men run through the woods shooting off blank cartridges? What good does that do?

BUCK. It does *us* a lot of good! If we went near that house—(*Points off upper right.*) looking like this, they'd sick the dog on us, wouldn't they? (IKE *remains sullenly silent.*) *Wouldn't* they?

IKE. You *know* they would! They done it already. (*Rubs his leg.*)

BUCK. But when we get into these uniforms, we can go where we please. Aren't all these farmers shouting "Rah for the Blues!" "Rah for the Reds!" Aren't they all saying, "Come in, Mr. Soldier. Have a piece of pie, Mr. Soldier. Sit down." Haven't you heard 'em? (IKE *remains silent.*) Haven't you heard 'em?

IKE. Yes.

BUCK. Have you heard 'em ask *you* to sit down?

IKE. No!

BUCK. But when they mistake you for a soldier they will. They'll be crazy about us.

IKE. Any man what would mistake me for a soldier would be crazy.

BUCK. Then see you don't give yourself away. Do what I do. I've *been* a soldier.

IKE. (*With disgust.*) Yah! how long were you a soldier?

BUCK. Till I deserted.

IKE. I thought so!

BUCK. But I've been all through these manœuvres. Now understand, you're a soldier of the Blue Army, and if you see a soldier of the *Red* Army——

IKE. (*Impatiently.*) I know! I run!

BUCK. You do not run! You take him prisoner.

IKE. (*Furious.*) For what do I want with a prisoner?

BUCK. If you don't take *him* prisoner, he'll take you.

IKE. (*In lower tone.*) How can we break into that house with a *prisoner* tagging at our heels?

BUCK. That's right! Maybe you'd better *shoot* him—*dead.*

IKE. Shoot him! With blank cartridges, eh?

BUCK. You only *pretend* to shoot him, you bone-head, and *he* pretends to die. Then, he must go back to his own army and report himself dead.

IKE. (*With disgust.*) Oh! what foolishness!

BUCK. Don't you see; it's the only way to get rid of him. If we pretend we're soldiers we've got to follow the rules of this war game.

IKE. For why do we play a game we don't know? For why do we dress like soldiers? We have a chance now to get into that house. Everybody has gone to see the battles—*except* that girl with them pearls. *Our* game is to *get them pearls*—not to go to no fancy dress ball.

BUCK. (*Threatening him.*) You'll do as I tell you, or I'll—(BUCK *looking off right, shows concern.*) Damn!

IKE. What is wrong, hey? (IKE *turns and looks off right.* BUCK *passes above him, and halts center, looking right.*)

BUCK. It's that young fellow who was on guard here yesterday. We've got to get rid of *him.* Go behind those bushes—(*Points lower left.*) and get into your uniform.

IKE. I will not!

BUCK. You *will!* We're two to one. We'll take him prisoner, and order him to his headquarters. That's the *only way* we can lose him.

(IKE *shifts rifles to left hand; with his right draws from his hip pocket a revolver.*)

IKE. No, it ain't. There's no blanks in *this.* And I want that necklace!

BUCK. (*Savagely.*) Cut that out! Do you want to

make a noise, and bring the whole army here? We'll get rid of this fellow, quiet and regular, and *then* you can go after the necklace anyway you damn please.

(IKE *looking past* BUCK, *and with excitement points up right.*)

IKE. Look! There's the girl now! And the necklace! Now's our time! (IKE *starts right.* BUCK *pushes him left.*)

BUCK. Get back, you fool! He'll see you. Behind those bushes! Quick!

(*Reluctantly* IKE *runs off left,* BUCK *picking up the bundles, follows him.* POLLY *enters upper right carrying letters. Comes down slowly sorting and examining letters, passes through gate which swings shut behind her. One by one she drops the letters into the opening of the letter box. Her face is turned left.* HENRY *enters right. He carries his Krag at the "ready." As though seeking the enemy, he glances in every direction.*)

HENRY. (*In brisk military tone.*) Pardon me!

POLLY. (*Startled.*) Oh! (*She turns.*)

HENRY. Have any of the Blue *Army* passed this way? (POLLY *recognizes* HENRY *and exclaims indignantly.*)

POLLY. Oh!

HENRY. I'm sorry. Did I frighten you?

(*There is a pause in which* POLLY *looks at him angrily. He pretends not to observe this and continues to peer about warily.*)

POLLY. (*With disdain.*) No, you did not frighten me. You surprised me, you disappoint me.

HENRY. (*Innocently.*) Have you seen any of the Blue Army this morning?

POLLY. (*Ignoring his question.*) You disappoint me because I thought when you gave your word—you would *keep* it! I told you all is over between us. I told you I did not want to see you again, and you *promised* you would not try to see me, nor write me, nor telephone me for *twelve months*. That was *yesterday*. And here you *are*—back again.

HENRY. But, I was ordered back—by my *Colonel*. I'm on *duty*. (*In hurt tones.*) You forget, I'm a scout.

POLLY. You have the whole state of Connecticut to scout in. You needn't scout in front of my house.

HENRY. Your house is on the chief line of communication between the Blue Army and the Red Army. If you don't want me here you must send the army down another road—or move the house.

POLLY. The road is five miles long—you don't have to stand at my gate.

HENRY. (*Smiling.*) Well, I don't wish to appear rude, but neither do *you*.

POLLY. Thank you, I don't intend to! (*Pushes open gate, and bangs it.*)

HENRY. Polly, please! (POLLY *halts inside gate.*) What I meant was *you* have a *house* to go to; I haven't. *I* haven't been inside a house in four days; been sleeping in the road, sleeping under bushes; haven't had a square meal in four days, either. If you had a *heart*—which I have frequently told you you *have not*—you'd invite me inside—you'd do as much as *that*, for a tramp—and give me something to eat. (*Pause. He looks appealingly at* POLLY, *she remains stern.*) Or, even a drink? (*Looks at her, hopefully.*) Or, one of your father's cigars. God knows, that's not asking *much!*

POLLY. (*Indignant.*) You see! You're not serious. You never *are* serious. That's why I can't take you seriously.

HENRY. Polly, dear, I don't care *how* you take me, so long as you *take me*. (POLLY *starts up.*) Don't go! It's like this. When I'm with you, I'm too happy to be serious. When I'm not with you, I'm miserable. *You* tell me that my love for you bores you. What do you think it's doing to *me?* It's killing *me*. Can't sleep, can't eat. I'm a wreck. I'm a skeleton. Look at me! I ask you, look at me!

POLLY. (*Coldly.*) I *am* looking at you, and I never saw you looking better—and you know it. And you know that that uniform is particularly becoming. (*Indignantly.*) I believe you came here just to show it to me.

HENRY. (*Regarding himself approvingly.*) It *is* rather nice, isn't it? I thought you would like to see me in it. That's why I brought on this war. (*Briskly.*) And now, as I've had nothing to eat in four days, I will *accept* your very kind invitation to come to lunch, and —(*Moves towards gate.* POLLY *places hands on top of gate and bars his progress.*)

POLLY. You will NOT come to lunch.

HENRY. Very well. If you want to see a man die of starvation at your very gate, watch *me.*

POLLY. If you'll only promise *to go away* from this gate, I'll bring you anything we have in the house.

HENRY. The only thing in that house I want—is *you.*

POLLY. (*Haughtily.*) Do you intend to drive me away from my own door, or will you go?

HENRY. All right! I'll go. No one can take a *hint* quicker than I can. (*Slings rifle over shoulder, starts left, halts, and turns.*) And, when you've made up your mind, I'll come back.

POLLY. (*Indignantly.*) I *have* made up my mind!

HENRY. Then, I'll come back when you've changed it. (BUCK *and* IKE *creep on lower left and hide behind stone wall. They are in uniform and carry rifles.* HENRY *starts left, pretends to reconsider, and again turns.*) No! it's not *right.* I *can't* go!

(BUCK *and* IKE *show concern.*)

POLLY. (*In dismay.*) What?

HENRY. (*Firmly.*) I see my duty. It is to stay here, and protect *you.*

POLLY. Protect *me?* From what?

HENRY. Oh, tramps and camp followers. And there's

a lot of professional crooks up here from New York trailing our army and robbing the farm houses.

(BUCK *and* IKE *show concern.*)

POLLY. Your duty to the state——

HENRY. My duty to the state is to guard this road; and I can guard you and the road at the same time. Now, don't talk to the sentry. He's on duty. (*Shoulders rifle, takes three paces left, then "about faces" and takes three paces right.*)

POLLY. I don't *want* you to guard me.

HENRY. Well, if not you, then the house and the family jewels. (IKE *nudges* BUCK *excitedly.*) Think of yourself alone in a house *filled* with jewels and entirely surrounded by armies. (*Mysteriously.*) And what's more, these woods——

POLLY. (*Alarmed.*) Yes?

HENRY. These woods are infested with wild rabbits.

POLLY. Oh! you are intolerable!

HENRY. They are! I saw two this morning; *big* fellows.

POLLY. (*Vindictively.*) I wish the Blues would take you.

HENRY. Take me *where?*

POLLY. Anywhere, away from me! (HENRY *laughs, and turns left. By a gesture of surprise* POLLY *shows she has discovered* BUCK *and* IKEY. *She puts her finger to her lips to warn them to be careful. She smiles triumphantly.* HENRY *turns and marches right.*) Aren't you *afraid?*

HENRY. Afraid of rabbits? No; a rabbit doesn't bite you unless he's wounded.

POLLY. I mean afraid the Blues might creep up on you and make you prisoner.

HENRY. (*With burlesque sentiment.*) A pair of blue eyes made me prisoner many——

POLLY. (*Angrily.*) For the last time—will you go, or——

HENRY. Or stay? I'll stay, thank you. (*His back is turned to* BUCK *and* IKEY. *They stand up.*)

POLLY. (*Triumphantly.*) Then, you won't stay long. (*To* BUCK *and* IKE.) *Take him!*

(BUCK *and* IKEY *point their rifles at* HENRY.)

BUCK. Hands up! You're my prisoner! (*At the sound of* BUCK'S *voice,* HENRY *turns toward him, raising his rifle.*) Drop that gun! (*He backs across the stage right.* IKEY *remains behind stone wall left.* HENRY *looks at the two pointed rifles, and turns his head toward* POLLY.)

HENRY. Did you know they were there?

POLLY. I did.

HENRY. You *must* want to get rid of me! (*To* BUCK.) See here, boys, you can't get away with this. I have a dozen men up that road.

BUCK. You have *not.* There's no more *Reds* within a mile. Come, now. You know the rules. Gimme that gun, and report to our Colonel.

HENRY. (*Trying to gain time.*) Colonel? Where *is* your Colonel?

IKE. (*Eagerly warning him left.*) Just up that road. About two miles. You can't miss him.

HENRY. (*Surprised.*) Aren't you going to *take* me there?

IKE. (*Roughly.*) We got no time! Take yourself there. Tell him you be a prisoner.

HENRY. (*Indignantly.*) Tell him nothing! I'm no prisoner unless you *keep* me prisoner. (*Shoulders his rifle.*)

POLLY. (*To* BUCK.) Oh sergeant, please take him away! I wouldn't have let you capture him, if I hadn't thought you'd take him away at once!

BUCK. Why don't you go when the lady wants you to?

HENRY. I'm not taking orders from that lady— not *yet.* My orders from my *captain* are to stay here. If I'm a prisoner you can take me away, if I'm not a prisoner ——

IKE. (*To* BUCK, *with conviction.*) I tell you, it is better that we shoot him! (*Points rifle.* POLLY *screams and dodges.* HENRY *smiles upon* IKEY *and shakes his head.*)

HENRY. You can't shoot me.

IKE. Why can't I?

HENRY. You can't shoot a prisoner. It's against the rules. (*To* BUCK.) Isn't that right, Sergeant?

BUCK. (*Nods gloomily.*) Yes. (*To* IKEY.) We should've shot him soon's we saw him.

HENRY. Yes, *that* would have been all right. But it's too late, now. I'm sorry; you should have thought of that sooner.

POLLY. (*To* BUCK, *eagerly.*) Sergeant, you can do it THIS way. You *can* shoot a prisoner, if he tries to *escape.*

HENRY. (*Hastily.*) Ah! but I *haven't* tried to escape. *Have* I, boys?

BUCK. (*Persuasively.*) Naw, but why don't you? Be nice, now. A prisoner—he's a nuisance—but a dead man's no bother to nobody.

IKE. Yes, Mr. Soldier, *please* be dead!

POLLY. Yes, please be dead.

HENRY. I'd no idea I was so popular! Well, I can take a *hint* as quick as anybody. (*Hangs rifle over shoulder.*)

BUCK. You see, if you're dead, you can stay in camp all day and get rested, and eat all you want.

HENRY. You make death sound most attractive. All right! Now, I'll pretend to escape, and you shoot me. I fall dead. Then, I *report* myself dead to my captain.

POLLY. (*With relief.*) At last!

IKE. Good!

BUCK. Thank you, Bo!

HENRY. Oh, that's all right; always willing to oblige. (*To* POLLY.) "Hail Cæsar! I, who am about to die, salute thee!" And my last words are: "Had I a *thousand* lives to give, I'd give them all to——"

POLLY. (*Haughtily.*) They're waiting to shoot you.

HENRY. I'd give them all to the State of New York. (*To* BUCK.) Wait! Who shot me?

IKE. We do!

HENRY. Well, who are "we?" What *regiment* do you belong to?

IKE. That's MY business!

HENRY. Well, it's my business, too. I got to tell my Captain who shot me.

BUCK. Third Connecticut.

HENRY. (*Puzzled.*) Third Con—— Why, there's no— (*To* IKEY.) Third *what;* infantry, Cavalry?

IKE. (*Roughly.*) How should *I* know!

HENRY. How should *you* know? You're a *fine* soldier! Don't you know whether you walk, or ride a horse? What's your Colonel's name?

BUCK. (*Fiercely.*) Don't tell him!

IKE. I'm not going to tell him.

HENRY. Don't you know the name of your Colonel? (*Studies* IKEY *closely, then advances suspiciously.*) *Where are your collar ornaments?* (*To* BUCK.) What have you done with your insignia?

BUCK. (*Insolently.*) We're scouts. We don't *have* to wear 'em!

(HENRY *crosses to* BUCK *threateningly. He leaves* POLLY, *who is inside the gate at his upper left.*)

HENRY. You do! (*Accusingly.*) Where did you *get* these uniforms?

(BUCK *retreats right.*)

BUCK. (*Shouting to* IKEY.) He's escaping! Shoot him!

(IKEY *drops rifle against stone wall, from hip pocket draws automatic, aims at* HENRY'S *back. The wall and evergreens hide his actions from* POLLY.)

HENRY. (*Savagely.*) No, I'm not escaping—not *now! What right* have you to that uniform?

BUCK. He's escaping! Shoot him!

(IKEY *fires.* HENRY *throws up his arms, sinks to his knees, then falls forward, his head towards the right.* BUCK *looks down at him in dismay and anger.* POLLY *remains unmoved.* IKEY, *his eyes on* POLLY, *creeps around end of wall, and goes up to left of* POLLY. *She is looking at* HENRY, *at first smiling, then as he remains motionless, with alarm. Opens gate and comes down.*)

POLLY. (*To* BUCK.) Why doesn't he get up? *Tell* him to get up. (*Calls.*) Henry! Henry! don't *do* that! You frighten me. *Speak* to me! My God, he's hurt! (*To* BUCK.) Help me! Quick! get some water. (*To* IKEY.) Take him to the house, *please*.

IKE. (*Menacingly.*) No, take *me* to the house!

POLLY. (*Confused.*) What?

IKE. Take me to them jewels!

POLLY. Jewels!

IKE. He said the house is full of jewels. I want them!

POLLY. I have no jewels. I'll give you *money* if you'll help me. (*Appealingly.*) He's hurt, he's wounded——

IKE. No, he's not; he's croaked. And I'll croak *you*, if you——

POLLY. (*Screaming.*) Sergeant! Help!

(BUCK *runs to her right side. He hides* HENRY *from* IKEY. HENRY *raises his head cautiously and reached back to his hip for his automatic.*)

BUCK. (*Fiercely, close to* POLLY.) Stop that noise! We want that necklace. Take it off, or we'll *choke* it off you.

POLLY. (*With horror.*) You thieves! You killed him —for *this!* (*Hands to necklace.*)

IKE. Yes, I killed him, and I'll kill you——

(HENRY *rises on one knee, points automatic.*)

HENRY. No, you *missed* him! but he won't miss *you!* (*Fires;* IKEY *clasps his left shoulder.*) Hands up, you crooks! (IKEY *raises left arm still with his right hand clasping his left shoulder.* BUCK *raises both arms. With his left hand* HENRY *motions* POLLY *towards gate.*) Keep back, Polly.

BUCK. (*To* IKEY.) Your gat! Quick! He's only *one* man!

HENRY. (*Mocking him.*) No; he's a dozen men! (*Shouts over right shoulder.*) Corporal of the Guard! Post number one! Corporal of the Guard! Post number one! (*Off right* VOICES, *at varying distances, repeat three times "Corporal of the Guard, post number one."* HENRY *glances over right shoulder.*) Hurry, boys, hurry! (*Takes step towards* VOICES. POLLY, *thinking he is going to them, in alarm, springs to his side.*)

POLLY. Henry! Don't leave me! (*He gives her his left hand. She clings to it.*) Oh promise me you'll *never*, never leave me again!

(HENRY *puts his left arm around her.*)

HENRY. You *bet* I'll never leave you! (*He draws* POLLY *close to him. On tiptoe* BUCK *and* IKEY *attempt to back off left.*) Halt! (*They halt.*) 'Bout face! (*They turn their backs.*) Hands up! (*They raise their arms. Still covering them with his gun, he promptly kisses* POLLY.)

CURTAIN.

# MOONSHINE

DRAMA IN ONE ACT

## ARTHUR HOPKINS

Arthur Hopkins was born at Cleveland, Ohio, in 1878. For some years a journalist, he first became known as the producer of Eleanor Gates' "The Poor Little Rich Girl," in 1912. He has since that time established himself as one of the few thoroughly competent artistic managers in the theatrical world.

Though Hopkins is not a regular professional dramatist, he has shown extraordinary skill in the development of plot and character in "Moonshine." This is the only one of his plays that has been published.

# MOONSHINE*

## CHARACTERS

LUKE HAZY, *Moonshiner*
A REVENUE OFFICER

SCENE: *Moonshiner's Hut.*

TIME: *The Present.*

*Hut of a moonshiner in the mountain wilds of North Carolina. Door back left. Window back right center. Old deal table right center. Kitchen chair at either side of the table, not close to it. Old cupboard in left corner. Rude stone fireplace left side. On back wall near door is a rough pencil sketch of a man hanging from a tree.*

*At rise of curtain a commotion is heard outside of hut.*

LUKE. (*Off stage.*) It's all right, boys. . . . Jist leave him to me. . . . Git in there, Mister Revenue. (REVENUE, *a Northerner in city attire, without hat, clothes dusty, is pushed through doorway.* LUKE, *a lanky, ill-dressed Southerner, following, closes door.* REVENUE'S *hands are tied behind him.*) You must excuse the boys for makin' a demonstration over you, Mr. Revenue, but you see they don't come across you fellows very frequent, and they allas gits excited.

REVENUE. I appreciate that I'm welcome.

LUKE. Deed you is, and I'm just a-goin' to untie your hands long nuff fer you to take a sociable drink. (*Goes to stranger, feels in all pockets for weapons.*) Reckon


This play is also published separately, in paper, at 35 cents a copy.

yer travelin' peaceable. (*Unties hands.*) Won't yer sit down?

REVENUE. (*Drawing over chair and sitting.*) Thank you. (*Rubs wrists to get back circulation.*)

LUKE. (*Going over to cupboard and taking out jug.*) Yessa, Mister, the boys ain't seen one o' you fellers fer near two years. Began to think you wus goin' to neglect us. I wus hopin' you might be Jim Dunn. Have a drink?

REVENUE. (*Starts slightly at mention of* JIM DUNN.) No, thank you, your make is too strong for me.

LUKE. It hain't no luck to drink alone when you got company. Better have some.

REVENUE. Very well, my friend, I suffer willingly. (*Drinks a little and chokes.*)

LUKE. (*Draining cup.*) I reckon ye all don't like the flavor of liquor that hain't been stamped.

REVENUE. It's not so bad.

LUKE. The last Revenue that sit in that chair got drunk on my make.

REVENUE. That wouldn't be difficult.

LUKE. No, but it wuz awkward.

REVENUE. Why?

LUKE. I had to wait till he sobered up before I give him his ticket. I didn't feel like sendin' him to Heaven drunk. He'd 'a' found it awkward climbin' that golden ladder.

REVENUE. Thoughtful executioner.

LUKE. So you see mebbe you kin delay things a little by dallyin' with the licker.

REVENUE. (*Picking up cup, getting it as far as his lips, slowly puts it down.*) The price is too great.

LUKE. I'm mighty sorry you ain't Jim Dunn. But I reckon you ain't. You don't answer his likeness.

REVENUE. Who's Jim Dunn?

LUKE. You ought to know who Jim Dunn is. He's just about the worst one of your revenue critters that ever hit these parts. He's got four of the boys in jail. We got a little reception all ready for him. See that? (*Pointing to sketch on back wall.*)

REVENUE. (*Looking at sketch.*) Yes.

LUKE. That's Jim Dunn.

REVENUE. (*Rising, examining picture.*) Doesn't look much like anyone.

LUKE. Well, that's what Jim Dunn'll look like when we git 'im. I'm mighty sorry you hain't Jim Dunn.

REVENUE. I'm sorry to disappoint you.

LUKE. (*Turning to cupboard and filling pipe.*) Oh, it's all right. I reckon one Revenue's about as good as another, after all.

REVENUE. Are you sure I'm a revenue officer?

LUKE. (*Rising.*) Well, since we ketched ye climin' trees an' snoopin' round the stills, I reckon we won't take no chances that you hain't.

REVENUE. Oh.

LUKE. Say, mebbe you'd like a seggar. Here's one I been savin' fer quite a spell back, thinkin' mebbe I'd have company some day. (*Brings out dried-up cigar, hands it to him.*)

REVENUE. No, thank you.

LUKE. It hain't no luck to smoke alone when ye got company. (*Striking match and holding it to* REVENUE.) Ye better smoke. (REVENUE *bites off end and mouth is filled with dust, spits out dust.* LUKE *holds match to cigar. With difficulty* REVENUE *lights it.*) That's as good a five-cent cigar as ye can git in Henderson.

REVENUE. (*After two puffs, makes wry face, throws cigar on table.*) You make death very easy, Mister.

LUKE. Luke's my name. Yer kin call me Luke. Make you feel as though you had a friend near you at the end—Luke Hazy.

REVENUE. (*Starting as though interested, rising.*) Not the Luke Hazy that cleaned out the Crosby family?

LUKE. (*Startled.*) How'd you hear about it?

REVENUE. Hear about it? Why, your name's been in every newspaper in the United States. Every time you killed another Crosby the whole feud was told all over again. Why, I've seen your picture in the papers twenty times.

LUKE. Hain't never had one took.

REVENUE. That don't stop them from printing it. Don't you ever read the newspapers?

LUKE. Me read? I hain't read nothin' fer thirty years. Reckon I couldn't read two lines in a hour.

REVENUE. You've missed a lot of information about yourself.

LUKE. How many Crosbys did they say I killed?

REVENUE. I think the last report said you had just removed the twelfth.

LUKE. It's a lie! I only killed six . . . that's all they wuz—growed up. I'm a-waitin' fer one now that's only thirteen.

REVENUE. When'll he be ripe?

LUKE. Jes as soon as he comes a-lookin' fer me.

REVENUE. Will he come?

LUKE. He'll come if he's a Crosby.

REVENUE. A brave family?

LUKE. They don't make 'em any braver—they'd be first-rate folks if they wuzn't Crosbys.

REVENUE. If you feel that way why did you start fighting them?

LUKE. I never started no fight. My grandad had some misunderstandin' with their grandad. I don't know jes what it wuz about, but I reckon my grandad wuz right, and I'll see it through.

REVENUE. You must think a lot of your grandfather.

LUKE. Never seen 'im, but it ain't no luck goin' again yer own kin. Won't ye have a drink?

REVENUE. No—no—thank you.

LUKE. Well, Mr. Revenue, I reckon we might as well have this over.

REVENUE. What?

LUKE. Well, you won't get drunk, and I can't be put to the trouble o' having somebody guard you.

REVENUE. That'll not be necessary.

LUKE. Oh, I know yer like this yer place now, but this evenin' you might take it into yer head to walk out.

REVENUE. I'll not walk out unless you make me.

LUKE. 'Tain't like I'll let yer, but I wouldn't blame yer none if yu tried.

REVENUE. But I'll not.

LUKE. (*Rising.*) Say, Mistah Revenue, I wonder if you know what you're up against?

REVENUE. What do you mean?

LUKE. I mean I gotta kill you.

REVENUE. (*Rising, pauses.*) Well, that lets me out.

LUKE. What do yu mean?

REVENUE. I mean that I've been trying to commit suicide for the last two months, but I haven't had the nerve.

LUKE. (*Startled.*) Suicide?

REVENUE. Yes. Now that you're willing to kill me, the problem is solved.

LUKE. Why, what d'ye want to commit suicide fer?

REVENUE. I just want to stop living, that's all.

LUKE. Well, yu must have a reason.

REVENUE. No special reason—I find life dull and I'd like to get out of it.

LUKE. Dull?

REVENUE. Yes—I hate to go to bed—I hate to get up—I don't care for food—I can't drink liquor—I find people either malicious or dull—I see by the fate of my acquaintances, both men and women, that love is a farce. I have seen fame and preference come to those who least deserved them, while the whole world kicked and cuffed the worthy ones. The craftiest schemer gets the most money and glory, while the fair-minded dealer is humiliated in the bankruptcy court. In the name of the law every crime is committed; in the name of religion every vice is indulged; in the name of education the greatest ignorance is rampant.

Luke. I don't git all of that, but I reckon you're some put out.

Revenue. I am. The world's a failure. . . . what's more, it's a farce. I don't like it but I can't change it, so I'm just aching for a chance to get out of it. . . . (*Approaching* luke.) And you, my dear friend, are going to present me the opportunity.

Luke. Yes, I reckon you'll get your wish now.

Revenue. Good . . . if you only knew how I've tried to get killed.

Luke. Well, why didn't you kill yerself?

Revenue. I was afraid.

Luke. Afreed o' what—hurtin' yourself?

Revenue. No, afraid of the consequences.

Luke. Whad d'ye mean?

Revenue. Do you believe in another life after this one?

Luke. I kan't say ez I ever give it much thought.

Revenue. Well, don't—because if you do you'll never kill another Crosby . . . not even a revenue officer.

Luke. 'Taint that bad, is it?

Revenue. Worse. Twenty times I've had a revolver to my head—crazy to die—and then as my finger pressed the trigger I'd get a terrible dread—a dread that I was plunging into worse terrors than this world ever knew. If killing were the end it would be easy, but what if it's only the beginning of something worse?

Luke. Well, you gotta take some chances.

Revenue. I'll not take that one. You know Mr. Luke, life was given to us by someone who probably never intended that we should take it, and that someone has something ready for people who destroy his property. That's what frightens me.

Luke. You do too much worryin' to be a regular suicide.

Revenue. Yes, I do. That's why I changed my plan.

Luke. What plan?

REVENUE. My plan for dying.

LUKE. Oh, then you didn't give up the idea?

REVENUE. No, indeed—I'm still determined to die, but I'm going to make someone else responsible.

LUKE. Oh—so you hain't willing to pay fer yer own funeral music?

REVENUE. No, sir—I'll furnish the passenger, but someone else must buy the ticket. You see when I finally decided I'd be killed I immediately exposed myself to every danger I knew.

LUKE. How?

REVENUE. In a thousand ways. . . . (*Pause.*) Did you ever see an automobile?

LUKE. No.

REVENUE. They go faster than steam engines, and they don't *stay* on tracks. Did you ever hear of Fifth Avenue, New York?

LUKE. No.

REVENUE. Fifth Avenue is jammed with automobiles, eight deep all day long. People being killed every day. I crossed Fifth Avenue a thousand times a day, every day for weeks, never once trying to get out of the way, and always praying I'd be hit.

LUKE. And couldn't yu git hit?

REVENUE. (*In disgust.*) No. Automobiles only hit people who try to get out of the way. (*Pause.*) When that failed I frequented the lowest dives on the Bowery, flashing a roll of money and wearing diamonds, hoping they'd kill me for them. They stole the money and diamonds, but never touched me.

LUKE. Couldn't you pick a fight?

REVENUE. I'm coming to that. You know up North they believe that a man can be killed in the South for calling another man a liar.

LUKE. That's right.

REVENUE. It is, it is? Well, I've called men liars from

Washington to Atlanta, and I'm here to tell you about it.

Luke. They must a-took pity on ye.

Revenue. Do you know Two Gun Jake that keeps the dive down in Henderson?

Luke. I should think I do. . . . Jake's killed enough of 'em.

Revenue. He's a bad man, ain't he?

Luke. He's no trifler.

Revenue. I wound up in Jake's place two nights ago, pretending to be drunk. Jake was cursing niggers.

Luke. He's allus doin' that.

Revenue. So I elbowed my way up to the bar and announced that I was an expert in the discovery of nigger blood . . . could tell a nigger who was 63-64th white.

Luke. Ye kin?

Revenue. No, I can't, but I made them believe it. I then offered to look them over and tell them if they had any nigger blood in them. A few of them sneaked away, but the rest stood for it. I passed them all until I got to Two Gun Jake. I examined his eyeballs, looked at his finger-nails, and said, "You're a nigger."

Luke. An' what did Jake do?

Revenue. He turned pale, took me into the back room, and said: "Honest to God, Mister, can ye see nigger blood in me?" I said: "Yes." "There's no mistake about it?" "Not a bit," I answered. "Good God," he said, "I always suspected it." Then he pulled out his gun. . . .

Luke. Eh . . . eh?

Revenue. And shot *himself*.

Luke. Jake shot hisself! . . . is he dead?

Revenue. I don't know—I was too disgusted to wait. I wandered around until I thought of you moonshiners . . . scrambled around in the mountains until I found your still. I *sat* on it and waited until you boys showed up, and here I am, and you're going to kill me.

LUKE. (*Pause.*) Ah, so ye want us to do yer killin' fer ye, do ye?

REVENUE. You're my last hope. If I fail this time I may as well give it up.

LUKE. (*Takes out revolver, turns sidewise and secretly removes cartridges from chamber. Rises.*) What wuz that noise? (*Lays revolver on table and steps outside of door.* REVENUE *looks at revolver apparently without interest.* LUKE *cautiously enters doorway and expresses surprise at seeing* REVENUE *making no attempt to secure revolver. Feigning excitement goes to table, picks up gun.*)

LUKE. I reckon I'm gettin' careless, leavin' a gun layin' around here that-a-way. Didn't you see it?

REVENUE. Yes.

LUKE. Well, why didn't ye grab it?

REVENUE. What for?

LUKE. To git the drop on me.

REVENUE. Can't you understand what I've been telling you, Mister? I don't *want* the drop on you.

LUKE. Well, doggone if I don't believe yer tellin' me the truth. Thought I'd just see what ye'd do. Ye see, I emptied it first. (*Opens up gun.*)

REVENUE. That wasn't necessary.

LUKE. Well, I reckon ye better git along out o' here, Mister.

REVENUE. You don't mean you're weakening?

LUKE. I ain't got no call to do your killin' fer you. If ye hain't sport enough to do it yerself, I reckon ye kin go on sufferin'.

REVENUE. But I told you why I don't want to do it. One murder more or less means nothing to you. You don't care anything about the hereafter.

LUKE. Mebbe I don't, but there ain't no use my takin' any more chances than I have to. And what's more,

Mister, from what you been tellin' me I reckon there's a charm on you, and I ain't goin' to take no chances goin' agin charms.

REVENUE. So *you're* going to go back on me?

LUKE. Yes, sirree.

REVENUE. Well, maybe some of the other boys will be willing. I'll wait till they come.

LUKE. The other boys ain't goin' to see you. You're a-leavin' this yer place right now—now! It won't do no good. You may as well go peaceable, ye ain't got no right to expect us to bear yer burdens.

REVENUE. Damn it all! I've spoiled it again.

LUKE. I reckon you better make up yer mind to go on livin'.

REVENUE. That looks like the only way out.

LUKE. Come on, I'll let you ride my horse to town. It's the only one we got, so yu can leave it at Two Gun Jake's, and one o' the boys'll go git it, or I reckon I'll go over myself and see if Jake made a job of it.

REVENUE. I suppose it's no use arguing with you.

LUKE. Not a bit. Come on, you.

REVENUE. Well, I'd like to leave my address so if you ever come to New York you can look me up.

LUKE. 'Taint likely I'll ever come to New York.

REVENUE. Well, I'll leave it, anyhow. Have you a piece of paper?

LUKE. Paper what you write on? Never had none, Mister.

REVENUE. (*Looking about room, sees Jim Dunn's picture on wall, goes to it, takes it down.*) If you don't mind, I'll put it on the back of Jim Dunn's picture. (*Placing picture on table, begins to print.*) I'll print it for you, so it'll be easy to read. My address is here, so if you change your mind you can send for me.

LUKE. 'Taint likely—come on. (*Both go to doorway* —LUKE *extends hand,* REVENUE *takes it.*) Good-bye, Mister—cheer up . . . there's the horse.

REVENUE. Good-bye. (*Shaking* LUKE's *hand.*)

LUKE. Don't be so glum, Mister. Lemme hear you laff jist once before yu go. (REVENUE *begins to laugh weakly.*) Aw, come on, laff out with it hearty. (REVENUE *laughs louder.*) Heartier yit. (REVENUE *is now shouting his laughter, and is heard laughing until hoof beats of his horse die down in the distance.* LUKE *watches for a moment, then returns to table—takes a drink—picks up picture—turns it around several times before getting it right—then begins to study. In attempting to make out the name he slowly traces in the air with his index finger a capital "J"—then mutters "J-J-J," then describes a letter "I"—mutters "I-I-I," then a letter "M"—muttering "M-M-M, J-I-M—J-I-M—J-I-M." In the same way describes and mutters "D-U-N-N."*)

LUKE. Jim Dunn! By God! (*He rushes to corner, grabs shot-gun, runs to doorway, raises gun in direction stranger has gone—looks intently—then slowly lets gun fall to his side, and scans the distance with his hand shadowing his eyes—steps inside—slowly puts gun in corner—seats himself at table.*) Jim Dunn! —and he begged me to kill 'im!!

CURTAIN.

# THE DYING WIFE

## LAURETTE TAYLOR

Laurette Taylor was born in New York City in 1887. At an early age she made her début as an actress. She made her first appearance on the New York Stage at the age of sixteen. After some years in stock she returned to New York in 1909. Her first substantial success was in the part of Rose Lane in "Alias Jimmy Valentine" during the season of 1910. But it was in "Peg O' My Heart" (1912). written by her husband, J. Hartley Manners, that she achieved one of the greatest triumphs in her career.

Laurette Taylor has since appeared in the following plays by Mr. Manners: "The Harp of Life," "Out There," "The Wooing of Eve," "Happiness," "One Night in Rome," and "The National Anthem."—"The Dying Wife" is the only play written by Laurette Taylor.

# THE DYING WIFE*

CHARACTERS

MAURICE FITZ-MAURICE
ARABELLA, *His Wife*

SCENE: *A Boudoir.*

TIME: *The Present.*

*The action takes place in a charmingly-furnished boudoir. A flickering fire is sputtering in the grate, throwing fitful shadows across the darkened room.*

ARABELLA, *a fair, impressionable young woman of perhaps twenty-four or possibly twenty-five is lying on a luxurious couch covered by a Liberty wrapper. But neither the luxury of the couch nor the delicate texture of the wrapper bring her comfort. She is writhing in pain, evidently of an internal nature.*

*Moving slowly about the room, glancing ever and anon at a porcelain banjo-clock, gnawing a somewhat stubby moustache, and occasionally throwing an interrogative and impatient look at the sufferer on the couch, is* MAURICE FITZ-MAURICE. *He is a tall, uncertain man of middle age. He is evidently under considerable strain which he betrays by his sudden, impulsive movements, noiseless ejaculations and genuine irritation.*

ARABELLA. (*After groaning audibly and breathing heavily for several seconds, calls.*) Maurice! (*Waits; then, louder.*) Morry!

FITZ-MAURICE. (*Goes to her.*) I am here.

---



*(The author wishes to express her indebtedness to the Jugo-Slav homily "Knowledge is death when the wronged are instructed thereof.")

ARABELLA. (*Groping for him.*) Where?

FITZ-MAURICE. Beside you.

ARABELLA. It's so dark. I can't feel your hand. (*Clutching his hand.*)

FITZ-MAURICE. (*Eagerly.*) Can't you? Is your sense of touch going?

ARABELLA. I don't think so. This *is* your hand?

FITZ-MAURICE. Take care. You're crushing it. (*Takes his hand away, wrings it, examines it and then puts it carefully inside his vest.*)

ARABELLA. What time is it?

FITZ-MAURICE. (*Triumphantly.*) Eight minutes to eight.

ARABELLA. Why doesn't the doctor come? Why doesn't he come? Why doesn't he——?

FITZ-MAURICE. (*Glowering down at her.*) He will not come.

ARABELLA. Why won't he? Why won't the doctor come?

FITZ-MAURICE. You will not need him.

ARABELLA. But I do need him. I need him terribly. I need him——

FITZ-MAURICE. His coming now would be totally unnecessary.

ARABELLA. Unnecessary! Morry! I'm going to get well. That's why he won't come. I'm going to——

FITZ-MAURICE. You are going to die in seven minutes.

ARABELLA. Die! Die! (*With a loud cry.*) I can't die in seven minutes.

FITZ-MAURICE. When the hour-hand touches eight on the dial of that clock you will breathe for the last time, Arabella.

ARABELLA. (*Cries in fear and pain.*) I can't. Why should I? I'm not ready to die. You won't let me die, will you, Morry?

FITZ-MAURICE. Neither human power nor mine can save you, Arabella. (ARABELLA *moans and sobs.*) Is there anything you wish to say before your spirit passes?

ARABELLA. I can't believe it. I'm too young. Too—too——

FITZ-MAURICE. Too—*what*, Arabella?

ARABELLA. We've been so happy together. So happy. Haven't we, Morry?

FITZ-MAURICE. *You* have been happy, I *hope*.

ARABELLA. We have been so much to each other.

FITZ-MAURICE. You have been to me.

ARABELLA. (*Gasping.*) I can hardly breathe. Can it really be that I——?

FITZ-MAURICE. In five minutes, Arabella.

ARABELLA. There is one thing I must confess. Confess to you as I would to a priest. You must give me absolution, Morry. You must forgive and absolve me.

FITZ-MAURICE. Confess, Arabella.

ARABELLA. (*Gasping as her breathing shortens.*) In Switzerland. Geneva. You remember? You would not climb the Jung-Frau. I wanted to, and I did. I *did* climb it. I *did. Indeed* I did.

FITZ-MAURICE. Go on. Only four minutes.

ARABELLA. It won't *take* four minutes. Four minutes! All the rest of my life telling you of my shame! The man who climbed with me—I did really climb the Jung-Frau, Morry! *Really* I did. The man—Silvanus Saxon. I was excited. Everything was so—so—exalted! I felt so—so—above the earth—so spiritual.—And I—he—and he—. We were like children, Morry. Two little children up and up on the Jung-Frau! Alone in the world. And I forgot everything. The cold seemed like fire. The snow melted at the touch as rose-leaves. Rose leaves!! In my hair and in my brain. And I—And he—Oh, Morry!! We betrayed you! (*Cries; waits.*) You say nothing. How you must love me! You don't reproach me! You don't even seem surprised that your own Arabella could have——

FITZ-MAURICE. I am not surprised.

ARABELLA. You are not? Morry! . . . Surely you did not think me capable of deceiving you?

FITZ-MAURICE. I knew you had.

ARABELLA. You knew I had deceived you?

FITZ-MAURICE. Yes, my darling. *That's why I put poison in your coffee.*

(*The clock strikes eight. On the last stroke* ARABELLA *sinks back on her luxurious couch.* MAURICE FITZ-MAURICE *frowns down on her, gnawing his extremely stubby moustache. Suddenly he breaks into fiendish laughter.*)

CURTAIN.

# THE LITTLE FATHER OF THE WILDERNESS

COMEDY IN ONE ACT

## AUSTIN STRONG

Austin Strong was born at San Francisco, California, in 1881. He was educated in New Zealand and was for some time a landscape architect. During the past twenty years he has written several plays, some of them, like "The Little Father of the Wilderness," written in collaboration with Lloyd Osbourne. Of recent plays, "Three Wise Fools" has been the most successful, though for many years his one-acters, "The Drums of Oude" and "The Little Father of the Wilderness" have been played with great success.

"The Little Father of the Wilderness" is a very effective and dramatic stage play. It was for some years acted by Francis Wilson.

Following is a list of Mr. Strong's published plays: "Three Wise Fools"; "The Toymaker of Nuremberg"; "The Little Father of the Wilderness."

# THE LITTLE FATHER OF WILDERNESS*

## CHARACTERS

PÈRE MARLOTTE, *an heroic Jesuit priest.*
FRÈRE GRÉGOIRE, *Franciscan friar.* MARLOTTE'S *friend.*
CAPTAIN CHEVILLON, *of the King's Guard.*
MLLE. HENRIETTE, *Louis' favorite of the hour.*
LOUIS XV.
CHEVALIER DE FRONTENAC, *Governor of New France.*
DUKE DE ST. ALBERT.
*Extras for Ladies of Court and Suite.*

SCENE: *An antechamber of the Palace of Versailles.*

TIME: *Mid-eighteenth century.*

SCENE: *An antechamber in the palace of Versailles. Throne-like seat to* L. *front. Two huge French windows at* L. *rear, looking out on the great gardens of Versailles. Grand double-door entrance at* R. *rear. Between windows and doors at rear is a table, upon which is a decanter encircled by wine-glasses. Fireplace at* R., *with lighted logs. Enormous chandelier hangs from the ceiling.*

TIME: *Eleven-thirty in the morning.*

*Curtain rises on empty stage. Pause. Enter* CAPTAIN CHEVILLON *of the King's Guard. Young, soldierly, swaggering, handsome man, in steel breast-plate, lace collar, boots, etc. He enters angrily, and gives a com-*

---

*prehensive glance about the room. Shakes the fire up. Then goes back to entrance, and beckons contemptuously to someone without.*

CAPTAIN CHEVILLON. (*Coming down stage.*) This way, you two! Come on, come on! (*Crosses* L.)

(*Enter* PÈRE MARLOTTE *and* FRÈRE GRÉGOIRE. *They stand on the threshold of the door and timidly look, awe-stricken, at the gorgeousness of the room.* PÈRE MARLOTTE *is a little Jesuit priest, timid and white-haired. He carries in his arms a large wooden cage containing an American coon, his shovel hat, a large green umbrella, and a bandanna handkerchief.* FRÈRE GRÉGOIRE *is a little Franciscan friar in the conventional garb of his order—sandals, scapula, etc. He is the adoring and simple-minded comrade of* PÈRE MARLOTTE. *He is from* PÈRE MARLOTTE'S *native town, Bourron, and has never before been outside its narrow limits.*)

CAPTAIN CHEVILLON. (*From front to them at rear.*) Don't stand there—come *here!* (*Indicates a spot on the carpet in front of him. The two little priests enter on a run, and carefully look on the ground, and stand on the actual spot, looking up at the Captain with trepidation. Crosses to* L. C. *Gruffly.*) Are you sure there is no mistake about this? Where are you from?

PÈRE MARLOTTE. (R. C. *Gabbling inarticulately with fright.*) P-p-please, M-m-monsieur le Capitaine——

CAPTAIN CHEVILLON. (*Shouting.*) Can't you speak? Where are you from?

PÈRE MARLOTTE. (*In terror.*) From the village of Bourron, may it please your Excellency, Monsieur le Capitaine!

FRÈRE GRÉGOIRE. (*Ingratiatingly.*) Bourron, Monsieur le Capitaine!

CAPTAIN. Bourron! Never heard of it! Where's your order to see the King? (PÈRE MARLOTTE *first carefully puts down the caged coon on one side; then his umbrella on the other side; then his shovel-hat and hand-*

*kerchief in front of him; all the while never moving from the spot indicated by the* CAPTAIN. *He unbuttons his cassock at the bosom, and produces an enormous document, two feet long, heavily attached with seals, and hands it trembling to the* CAPTAIN. *After reading the document.*) The King commands your presence here—Père Marlotte—! Are you Père Marlotte?

PÈRE MARLOTTE. May it please Your Excellency, Monsieur le Captaine, yes, I am Père Marlotte.

CAPTAIN. Thirty thousand pigs! What does His Majesty want to see you for?

PÈRE MARLOTTE. I do not know, Monsieur le Capitaine!

FRÈRE GRÉGOIRE. (R.) He does not know, Monsieur le Capitaine!

CAPTAIN CHEVILLON. (L. C.) Thunder of Man, you do not know!

PÈRE MARLOTTE. (*Bewildered.*) No—I—no——

FRÈRE GRÉGOIRE. (*Crosses to* C. *Confidentially.*) The good father, Your Excellency, is over-modest! His Majesty the King has doubtless sent for him to reward and honor the greatest missionary of America!

PÈRE MARLOTTE. (R. C. *Deprecatingly.*) Please, my dear Grégoire—my dear friend—no, it could not be possible His Majesty has heard of my poor work!

FRÈRE GRÉGOIRE. (*Valiantly.*) Not heard of the man who, single-handed, with no other weapon than his intrepid courage, his chalice and his crucifix, has won for his king a country greater tenfold than the size of France! Not heard of the man who, undeterred by sickness, wounds, starvation and torture, has carried the Agnus Dei—(*Both cross themselves.*)—to the uttermost limits of that unknown and terrible country! Not heard of the hero of Wis-con-sing, who saved Frontenac and his entire army! Not heard——

CAPTAIN. (*Stops* FRÈRE GRÉGOIRE *by tapping him on the head with the immense document.*) Tut, tut, tut, mon brave! Save that for the pulpit and the flock.

(*Crosses to* PÈRE MARLOTTE *and hands him the document.*) Here! The King will see you presently. Wait here! (*Goes toward door* B. R. C. *and then halts at the sight of the cage.*) What is that thing? (*Points.*)

PÈRE MARLOTTE. (R.) May it please Your Excellency —(*Ingratiatingly.*)—I brought it all the way myself from the Mes-cha-sippi! It is what is called a raccoon!

CAPTAIN. (B. R. C.) Thirty thousand pigs! What's it doing here?

PÈRE MARLOTTE. (*With the first touch of pride.*) I have brought it as a present from Père Marlotte to His Majesty!

CAPTAIN. (*Laughing boisterously.*) Ha, ha, ma foi— that's good! Ha, ha, ha! (*Exit, convulsed with derisive laughter. The two little priests stare after him in silence. A pause.*)

PÈRE MARLOTTE. (*Turning his face to* GRÉGOIRE.) Why does he laugh, Frère Grégoire?

FRÈRE GRÉGOIRE. (*Shaking his head bewilderedly.*) I do not know, Père Marlotte.

PÈRE MARLOTTE. (*Wiping his forehead with handkerchief.*) Ah, good friend, no Sioux Indian at Quebec was ever more out of place than I here! (*Crosses to* L. C. B.)

FRÈRE GRÉGOIRE. (*Not listening, but gaping, head in air, at the gorgeousness of the room.*) O—oh—'tis magnificent, is it not! The Holy Father Himself would not be ashamed of such a room as this. 'Tis gorgeous —— (*Goes about fingering the walls, furniture, etc.*) Superb——

PÈRE MARLOTTE. (*Serenely looking after him.*) Ah, good Grégoire, if you had lived for years under the sky and stars, the very thought of walls would stifle you! (*Then overcome at his own presumption.*) Oh, but I am such a barbarian!

FRÈRE GRÉGOIRE. Père Marlotte, you are trembling!

PÈRE MARLOTTE. (*With a frightened laugh.*) *Am* I?

When—when I think that in a moment His Most Christian Majesty will enter that door to speak to *me*—to me—— I—I—— Oh, Grégoire, what shall we do—what is correct? Shall we kneel—shall we kiss his hand—— (*Looks at throne.*)

FRÈRE GRÉGOIRE. Oh, surely, yes!

PÈRE MARLOTTE. Come, good Grégoire, seat yourself there. (*Indicates throne.*) You be the King, and let us see how I acquit myself!

FRÈRE GRÉGOIRE. (*Staggered.*) I in His Majesty's throne!

PÈRE MARLOTTE. Yes, please, my dear Grégoire—my good Grégoire! For *my* sake! (PÈRE MARLOTTE *pushes the reluctant* GRÉGOIRE *onto the King's throne; then tiptoes to the doorway and looks out into the corridor. Reassures himself that no one is coming. Then, picking up the caged coon, walks with solemn dignity and pomp to the throne, and kneels at* GRÉGOIRE's *feet. After kissing* GRÉGOIRE's *hand.*) Your Most Christian Majesty, I am here in obedience to your royal command—— (*Kisses* GRÉGOIRE's *hand.*) Now tell me to rise, Grégoire.

GRÉGOIRE. (*With a kingly air.*) Rise Père Marlotte! (*Then stands embarrassed, not knowing what to say next.*)

PÈRE MARLOTTE. (*Picks up cage and offers it to the* FRÈRE.) Now you say—"What is that, Père Marlotte?" (*Implying cage.*)

FRÈRE GRÉGOIRE. (*In exactly the same voice.*) What is that, Père Marlotte?

PÈRE MARLOTTE. (*With winning voice.*) A present from Père Marlotte to Your Majesty! (*As he hands cage to* GRÉGOIRE.) An American raccoon, Your Majesty!

FRÈRE GRÉGOIRE. (*As he holds the cage awkwardly and looks around it at* PÈRE MARLOTTE. *Sits on throne with raccoon on lap.*) As Sovereign Lord of France we welcome you, Père Marlotte, to our palace at Versailles! We have sent for you, Père Marlotte, to offer you your well-deserved reward! (*Addressing an imaginary cardinal.*) My Lord Cardinal—(*Business.*)—forthwith make Père Marlotte a bishop!

PÈRE MARLOTTE. (*Overcome at the thought.*) A bishop —— O-oh——! Frère Grégoire! (*Beams.*) It is wrong to be ambitious.

(*A roll of drums and a fanfare of trumpets are heard without in the gardens.* GRÉGOIRE *skips off the throne, and they both hold onto each other in terror. They wait in silence. Nothing happens. They regain their courage.*)

FRÈRE GRÉGOIRE. (*Puts down cage.*) Now you be king, Père Marlotte, and let me try! (*Crosses to* L. C. PÈRE MARLOTTE, *with great pomp, marches to the throne, and seats himself with mighty dignity.*)

PÈRE MARLOTTE. Yes! I'll be King. (FRÈRE GRÉGOIRE *approaches humbly, and kneels. As the King.*) Père Marlotte—we have sent for you——(*Then anxiously.*) See if there is anyone outside the door, Grégoire! (FRÈRE GRÉGOIRE *looks out, and then, reassured, returns with pomp and kneels again at* MARLOTTE's *feet.*)

PÈRE MARLOTTE. (*As the King.*) Père Marlotte, we have sent for you—we—we—— (*He falls on throne with a groan.*) Grégoire!

FRÈRE GRÉGOIRE. (*Not noticing anything wrong.*) Your Majesty—— (*Then.*) What is the matter—good father? Speak to me—you're ill! (PÈRE MARLOTTE *rises, assisted by* GRÉGOIRE.)

PÈRE MARLOTTE. (*Painfully, and pressing his closed fist to his breast in agony.*) Grégoire, the heart can forgive, but the body never forgets. (*With a gasp of pain.*) Ah!

FRÈRE GRÉGOIRE. What is it, Father? What is the matter?

PÈRE MARLOTTE. My wounds! The Indians! It was only their play! They know not what they did!

FRÈRE GRÉGOIRE. (*Angrily.*) Only their play—'twas torture—torture!

PÈRE MARLOTTE. (*Still gasping with pain, yet with pride.*) But they didn't get away from Père Marlotte! I baptized every one of them within the year!

FRÈRE GRÉGOIRE. The pitiless savages!

PÈRE MARLOTTE. Oh, no, no, good Grégoire. (*A pause.*)

FRÈRE GRÉGOIRE. You are better now, dear Father?

PÈRE MARLOTTE. (*Down* L. C., *still half supported by* GRÉGOIRE. *Cheerfully.*) It—it has passed. Ah, ah, Grégoire—I ought to be grateful indeed that my children spared me my eyes.

FRÈRE GRÉGOIRE. *Deo gratia!*

(*Sudden roll of drums and fanfare of trumpets from without. Both cross themselves. They cling to each other and listen.*)

PÈRE MARLOTTE. His Majesty!

FRÈRE GRÉGOIRE. At last! (*Both run and carefully seek the spot indicated by* CAPTAIN CHEVILLON. *They stare restlessly at the doorway. No one appears.*)

FRÈRE GRÉGOIRE. (R. C.) His Majesty does not seem to be coming.

PÈRE MARLOTTE. (*Turns to audience, and gives a great sigh of relief, agitation, fear and regret.*) His Majesty doesn't seem to be coming.

FRÈRE GRÉGOIRE. Go and look down the hall, Père Marlotte.

PÈRE MARLOTTE. (*Terrified.*) N-n-no—you go!

FRÈRE GRÉGOIRE. (*More terrified.*) No—no— please! *You* go!

PÈRE MARLOTTE. (*Putting his arm through* GRÉGOIRE'S.) We'll *both* go! (*The two little priests gingerly tiptoe to the great doorway, and twitteringly peep out into corridor toward* R. *They come back to* L. C. *on a run, and cling to each other in terror.*)

FRÈRE GRÉGOIRE. (*In a hoarse whisper.*) Did you see it?

PÈRE MARLOTTE. (*In the same tone.*) Yes, I saw it—— It's a woman!

FRÈRE GRÉGOIRE. Pray Saint Anthony she won't come here! (*A girl's voice is heard gaily singing and drawing nearer.*) She's coming here——! (*Panicstricken.*) What shall we do, Père Marlotte?

PÈRE MARLOTTE. (*More panicstricken.*) What shall we do, Grégoire?

(*Enter* MLLE. HENRIETTE *in a rush, still singing gaily. She is young, pretty and vivacious. She stops in the middle of her song, and stares in astonishment at the two little priests, who stare back at her in terror.*)

HENRIETTE. (R. *With a short laugh.*) Who are you?

PÈRE MARLOTTE. (*Backing* L.) Père Marlotte, and Frère Grégoire, Y-y-your Highness!

HENRIETTE. (R. C.) What are you doing here?

PÈRE MARLOTTE. I—I—we—we—— Oh, Grégoire, what are we doing here?

FRÈRE GRÉGOIRE. (*Bowing timidly.*) Mademoiselle— His Majesty the King has deigned to command the presence of the famous American missionary, Père Marlotte!

HENRIETTE. (*Curiously.*) That little man? Famous ——?

PÈRE MARLOTTE. (*Deprecatingly.*) Ah, Mademoiselle, my—my good friend here—is too—is too—

HENRIETTE. (*Crosses to* C. *Interrupting.*) The King doesn't want to see you—he's playing tennis with St. Albret!

PÈRE MARLOTTE. (*With timid triumph, pulling out the great document.*) Mademoiselle is mistaken. If Mademoiselle will graciously glance at this——(*Opens and presents the King's order for her to read.*)

HENRIETTE. (*Laughs, and knocks it up.*) Then he has forgotten all about you—— (*Crosses to* R.)

PÈRE MARLOTTE. (C., *turning bewilderedly to* GRÉGOIRE.) Forgotten?

FRÈRE GRÉGOIRE. (*Stoutly.*) It is not possible, Mademoiselle!

HENRIETTE. (B. L. C.) Possible——! At Versailles——! Oh, you little innocents, possible! (*Poignantly, as she presses her hand to her breast.*) Who can be sure that the King *won't* forget one tomorrow?

PÈRE MARLOTTE. (B. C.) The King has forgotten us, Grégoire!

HENRIETTE. (*Crosses to* MARLOTTE, *touched and indignant.*) Poor little man, it's a shame! He's always doing this—— But you won't have to wait long. Stay here. (*Crosses to door* B. R. C.) I'll bring him—I'll *drag* him here by the ear! (*Flies out with her head in the air. The two little men stare solemnly at each other.*)

PÈRE MARLOTTE. (L. C.) Could he indeed have forgotten me, Grégoire?

FRÈRE GRÉGOIRE. (*In warm denial.*) Oh, my dear Père Marlotte——

PÈRE MARLOTTE. But still—Grégoire! (*Looks at* GRÉGOIRE *worriedly.*)

FRÈRE GRÉGOIRE. The excellent Mademoiselle will surely bring him.

PÈRE MARLOTTE. (*Looking with awe at* GRÉGOIRE.) She said, Grégoire, she'd drag His Majesty here by the ear! (*Glances nervously toward entrance.*)

FRÈRE GRÉGOIRE. (*Significantly, in a hoarse whisper.*) She must be Mademoiselle Henriette—— (*Behind his hand.*)—the lady of the hour!

PÈRE MARLOTTE. (*Shocked, and with sudden sternness.*) Grégoire!

FRÈRE GRÉGOIRE. (*Collapsing.*) I mean—Père Marlotte—I think——

PÈRE MARLOTTE. (*Thundering.*) Silence——! Defame not him—— (*Points heavenward.*)—who is God's an-

*eyebrows.*) Have we heard anything of this man's work?

PÈRE MARLOTTE. In Canada, Sire, amongst the Indians —the American Indians.

LOUIS. (*With contracting brows.*) Canada——Canada —— Ah, yes—I remember now—a priest from Canada! What for? What for? What did I send for vou for? Let me think! Canada!—Priest——! (LOUIS *puts his right hand to his mouth, and looks at the floor, and thinks. Silence. Suspense.* PÈRE MARLOTTE *turns a white face to* GRÉGOIRE.)

LOUIS. (*Turning, puzzled, and scratching his head.*) Henriette, do you know why I sent for this little man?

HENRIETTE. (L. C. *Sadly.*) I haven't the remotest idea! (*There are tears in her voice.*)

LOUIS. Oh, I have it! Of course——! Look here! (*Runs to entrance like a boy, talking excitedly.*) Don't you remember—Henriette! Isabelle! Louise! (*To* CAPTAIN.) Get St. Albret! (*Exit* CAPTAIN CHEVILLON. LOUIS *standing in the doorway and shouting.*) St. Albret! Here, St. Albret! (*Then laughs.*) Ha, ha! Now you'll see if I wasn't right now—now you'll see —I said I was right—I know I was right——(*Calling.*) St. Albret! St. Albret! (*Rubbing his hands delightedly and smiling at the ladies.*) Fifty louis, Mesdames! Fifty louis!

HENRIETTE. (*Coldly.*) Wasn't it sixty?

LOUIS. Ha, ha! You're right—sixty! All the better! Sixty! Hurry, St. Albret! Hurry, St. Albret!

(*Enter the* DUKE DE ST. ALBRET, *an empty-headed, foppish young courtier, with a blatant voice and manner. He addresses the* KING *with a mixture of deference and boon companionship.*)

ST. ALBRET. You sent for me, Sire?

LOUIS. (*Convulsed with laughter, as he takes* ST. ALBRET *by the lapel of his coat and brings his face close to his own.*) Ha, ha! Now, rash young man! Ha, ha! You'll set up your popinjay opinion against royal France! (*Strikes his breast.*) Got sixty louis?

St. Albret. (L. C. *Puzzled.*) Pardon, Sire——?

Louis. (*Turning, and pointing front to the priests.*) Look—what I have brought you!

St. Albret. (*In a guffaw.*) What, the missionary from Canada—you sent for him! (*Then with eager excitement.*) Now you'll see if I'm not right! (*With significance.*) Have *you* got sixty louis?

Louis. (*Laughing.*) Have I! (*Calling.*) Henriette—come here—now you hold the stakes!

(HENRIETTE *holds her skirts up in front of her like an apron.*)

St. Albret. (*Pouring money out of his purse into her lap.*) I wish I'd made it six hundred now!

Louis. (*Searching each of his pockets carefully and finding nothing.*) Why—why—it seems that I haven't any money!

St. Albret. (*Shouting.*) No, you don't, Sire! Put up your money! I want to see money!

Louis. Cruel—cruel St. Albret—before the ladies, too—the poor ladies—ahem—— (*Crosses to ladies of court circle to* C. *again*—ST. ALBRET *follows.*)—but I must ask the ladies—for, for—a little assistance. Have any of you got sixty louis? (*Passes his hat playfully about. They all shake their heads and turn their backs saucily on him.*)

Henriette. Give him nothing—His Majesty still owes me a hundred pistoles!

Louis. (*As he passes his hat.*) Pity a poor King. (*They remain adamant. He turns helplessly toward* ST. ALBRET.)

St. Albret. (R. C. *Unmoved.*) Money up, Your Majesty!

Louis. (*Trying to carry it off.*) It's all right, mon cher. I'm going to win. There's no need of all this!

St. Albret. (*Stolidly.*) Money up, Your Majesty!

(LOUIS, *sighing, as he draws off ring from his finger and drops it into* HENRIETTE's *lap.*)

LOUIS. (*To* PÈRE MARLOTTE.) Little man—what's your name again?

PÈRE MARLOTTE. (*Picking up hope.*) Marlotte, Sire, Père Marlotte! (LOUIS *crosses to* MARLOTTE.)

LOUIS. Marlotte—yes—that's it. Now what we want to know is—— (*With a change of voice.*) Wait a moment—St. Albret, let's get this right. I said three miles, didn't I?

ST. ALBRET. No, you don't, Sire. Four miles—four miles. Henriette, didn't His Majesty say four miles?

HENRIETTE. (*Regarding the priest sadly.*) Yes—he did!

LOUIS. Well—four miles, then!

ST. ALBRET. (*To* PÈRE MARLOTTE.) Now, listen, you priest——

LOUIS. (*Stopping him.*) No, let me put it to him——!

ST. ALBRET. Your Majesty, wait—now, look here, priest——! (*Crosses to priest.*) Answer truthfully. His Majesty being His Majesty mustn't make any difference—understand? (PÈRE MARLOTTE *bewilderedly nods assent.*)

LOUIS. (L.C. *Laughing.*) Ha, ha! That's all right, St. Albret—— A cat may be right when a King is wrong.

ST. ALBRET. The cat *is* right this time, Your Majesty! (*All laugh.*)

LOUIS. (*Crosses to* MARLOTTE.) Now you, Père Marlotte, it's absolutely true you've been in America?

PÈRE MARLOTTE. Ah—— (*Pressing his hands to his breast.*) Ah, Your Majesty, yes.

LOUIS. I have sent for you, Père Marlotte, all the way from your village——

PÈRE MARLOTTE. (*Pleadingly.*) Pardon—one moment, Sire! (*Leaves the King astonished as he rushes up front, takes up the huge cage, and running back with it, forces it into the King's arm. Breathlessly.)* A present from Père Marlotte to Your Majesty—an American coon, Sire! (*The ladies giggle.*)

LOUIS. (*Angrily.*) Tut, tut, tut! (*Hands the cage to* CAPTAIN CHEVILLON, *who has come up for that purpose, purple with rage.*) Listen to what I'm saying——! I have sent for you——

PÈRE MARLOTTE. (*Eagerly.*) Yes, Your Majesty!

LOUIS. To decide a bet!

PÈRE MARLOTTE. (*Stunned.*) A bet, Sire!

LOUIS. Yes, yes, a bet! *I* say that the Falls of Niagara are four miles high; and St. Albret here insists that they are not. Now, who is right?

PÈRE MARLOTTE. (*Helplessly looking at the King.*) A bet, Sire!

LOUIS. Yes, yes. (*Petulantly.*) Can't you speak! Answer! Which of us is right?

PÈRE MARLOTTE. (*Turning a white face to the audience.*) Your—Your Majesty is *wrong!*

ST. ALBRET. (*With a yell of triumph.*) Yah, I've won! (*Crosses room.*) I *knew* I was right!

LOUIS. (*Sternly.*) Little man, do you tell the truth? Are you sure you've been there? Have you seen these Falls of Nia-gára?

PÈRE MARLOTTE. Yes, Sire, I said the first Mass there.

LOUIS. (*Giving* MARLOTTE *his hand carelessly to kiss as a sign of dismissal; and as* PÈRE MARLOTTE *falls on his knees, he turns to the others, talking at the top of his voice.*) Now I don't care—somebody told me they were four miles high. I'd like to know who it was—four miles high—he said four miles high—I know somebody said it was four miles high——

(*All talk at once, as the King goes rear* L. *and is surrounded by the ladies.* PÈRE MARLOTTE, *left on his knees, tries vainly to rise to his feet. Is helped up by the faithful* GRÉGOIRE, *who picks up for him and hands him his umbrella, his great shovel hat, and his bandanna handkerchief. The two little men give one farewell look at the group, forlornly turn their backs to the audience, and start toward the doorway.)*

ST. ALBRET. (*Running excitedly up to the two and forcing a handful of louis into* PÈRE MARLOTTE'S *hand—boisterously.*) Good for you, little priest! Take this for your trouble. (*Runs back and rejoins the others.*)

(PÈRE MARLOTTE *looks helplessly at the money in his hand, unheeding the coins that drop to the floor.* GRÉGOIRE *makes a motion to go forward.*)

CAPTAIN. (*Coming up angrily, and forcing the large cage into* PÈRE MARLOTTE'S *arms.*) Here, take this away! (*He half pushes and shoos them toward door.*)

HENRIETTE. (*Who has been watching the little priest throughout with compassion.*) Stay, Captain Chevillon. (*Crosses to* MARLOTTE. *Exit* CAPTAIN C. *She takes the caged raccoon from* PÈRE MARLOTTE *and puts it on the floor, and then regards the priest. In a tender voice.*) There are tears in your eyes, good father—you're as pale as death. Come, let me give you a glass of wine before you go. (*She puts an arm about him, and leads him, together with* FRÈRE GRÉGOIRE, *into the window recess at rear, and pours them both out some wine.*)

(*Fanfare of trumpets.*)

LOUIS. (*Petulantly.*) Now what's that? Have I got to see anybody else this morning?

CAPTAIN. (*Entering, and coming up close to the King, with a salute.*) Sire!

LOUIS. (*Crossly.*) Well?

CAPTAIN. Chevalier de Frontenac, Governor and Lieutenant-General of Your Majesty's American Dominions, awaits with his suite Your Majesty's royal pleasure.

LOUIS. (*Delighted, and clapping his hands.*) Ah, Frontenac! Bring him, Chevillon, bring him! (*Exit* CHE-

VILLON.) Ah, the good news! Ladies, St. Albret—Frontenac is here! In France! (*Rubbing his hands.*) My brave Frontenac! We must receive him properly! (*Goes up to his throne and seats himself, while the others group themselves about him.* ST. ALBRET *kneels, and places the footstool for him.*)

CAPTAIN. (*Entering and announcing.*) The Governor and Lieutenant-General of Your Majesty's American dominions, Chevalier de Frontenac!

(*Trumpet—Drums.*)

(*Pause.*) MARLOTTE *is seen at rear to start and stare wildly.* HENRIETTE *is astonished by his action, and puts her arm protectingly around him.* FRÈRE GRÉGOIRE *stands behind* MARLOTTE. *Enter* CHEVALIER DE FRONTENAC, *a magnificent old soldier, in steel breast-plate, with scarlet ribbon to which hangs an order. His rugged face is deeply bronzed. His moustache and imperial are snow white. His suite follow. Their magnificent uniforms, faded and battle-worn, are eked out with moccasins, buckskin, etc. Amongst them two Indian chiefs, almost naked, with feather head-dresses. The suite all follow* FRONTENAC *as he falls on one knee before the King's throne.*)

LOUIS. Rise, Messieurs! (*They rise.* LOUIS *rises himself. His voice becomes noble, kingly and sincere, in marked contrast to his previous frivolity.*) Chevalier de Frontenac, and these valiant gentlemen, it gives me great pleasure to welcome you home to France! For the last six years we have followed with admiration and approval every step of your undaunted career! From Quebec to Wis-con-sing, from Mackinaw to the Mes-cha-sippi, your King has ever been with you, sharing your hardships, your perils, your heroism, and your triumphs! Ah, Chevalier de Frontenac, and you, messieurs, you have ever had a loyal supporter in your King. Let history do me the justice to say that, however much I may have fallen short myself, my reign has been illumined and made glorious by such names as yours! Gentlemen, from my heart I welcome you!

CHEVALIER DE FRONTENAC. Your Majesty, would that we had the words to give voice to what is so inarticulate here! (*Strikes his breastplate with his gauntletted fist.*) Let our deeds instead speak for us, and accept our gratitude in an Empire.

LOUIS. (*Descending from his throne and shaking hands warmly with* FRONTENAC, *throwing ceremony aside.*) Welcome, my good friend—thou wast not more eager to see France than I thee! (*Turning to the ladies.*) But there are others also! Henriette—! (*The crowd parts so that a lane is opened, showing* HENRIETTE *at rear beside* PÈRE MARLOTTE.)

LOUIS. Ah, Henriette, come and add your greeting to these noble gentlemen!

CHEVALIER. (*Perceiving* PÈRE MARLOTTE.) What, is it possible—— Père Marlotte!

THE AMERICAN SUITE. Père Marlotte! Père Marlotte! The Little Father of the Wilderness!

PÈRE MARLOTTE. (*Advancing tremulously, with both hands raised.*) My children! (*The* CHEVALIER, *his suite, and the two Indian chiefs kneel like one man at the feet of the little priest. The Indians kiss the hem of his cassock.* PÈRE MARLOTTE *puts his hands tremblingly on his breast, and stares at the King, terrified at being so honored before him.*)

CHEVALIER. (*Turning to the King, but still on his knees.*) Your Majesty has deigned to praise us for our deeds in America—but here stands the greatest of us all, Père Marlotte!

LOUIS. Père Marlotte!

LADIES. Père Marlotte!

FRONTENAC. (*Still on his knees.*) Sire, my conquests in the New World have left little, I fear, but whitened bones, while the victories of this little priest, victories of peace, of love, of savage hearts won and kept, will endure forever. The Lilies of France would have perished in those dark and savage forests had it not been for the blood and the tortured body of Père Marlotte! Ah, Your Majesty, France owes a tribute indeed to the Little Father of the Wilderness!

LOUIS. (*Coming up to* PÈRE MARLOTTE—FRONTENAC *makes a movement to rise*—LOUIS *raises his hand.*) Stay, Frontenac! (LOUIS *halts in front of* PÈRE MARLOTTE *and regards him in silence. A pause.*) The Sovereign of France stands before you, Père Marlotte, ashamed; and he, with his Court, kneels to ask the blessing of the Archbishop of Toulouse!

(*Then* LOUIS, *with all his Court, kneels at the feet of* PÈRE MARLOTTE, *and the curtain goes down as the little priest, trembling, raises his hand and silently blesses them with the sign of the cross.*)

CURTAIN

# THE ROBBERY

COMEDY IN ONE ACT

## CLARE KUMMER

Clare Kummer's success as a playright came comparatively late in her career. She was for several years known only as a writer of songs. Though her first venture into the theater (a play written in collaboration with Sydney Rosenfeld) dates from 1912, it was not until 1916 that she revealed her true talents: "Good Gracious Annabelle!" was immediately recognized and appreciated as a delicate and subtle—if very light—comedy, original in conception and deft in execution. "A Successful Calamity," produced not long after by William Gillette, proved that the dramatist could handle a plot as well as she could dialogue and character. The best of Miss Kummer's recent comedies are "Rollo's Wild Oat," and "Be Calm Camilla!" The four published one-act plays are made notable by the same qualities of good humor and satire that characterize the best of the full-length plays.

Following is a list of Miss Kummer's published plays: "A Successful Calamity," "Good Gracious, Annabelle!" "Rollo's Wild Oat," "Be Calm, Camilla!" "The Rescuing Angel," "The Robbery," "Chinese Love," "The Choir Rehearsal," and "Bridges."

# THE ROBBERY*

## CHARACTERS

JOHN UPTON, *A Father*
MARGARET UPTON, *A Mother*
EDIE UPTON, *A Daughter*
ROBERT HAMILTON, *A Son*
FIELDING, *A Butler*

SCENE: *Sitting-room of the Uptons' house, New York.*

TIME: *The Present.*

SCENE.—*The sitting-room of the* UPTONS' *house on Seventy-second Street. A door* L.U.E. *leading into hall and sleeping rooms, and window and window-seat below. Another door* R.U.E. *leading into hall and downstairs. It is an English basement house and the sitting-room is on the second floor.*

*It is summer and the furniture is covered with linen.*

*On rise the clock is striking twelve.* FIELDING *enters stealthily* L.U.E. *with case containing silver. He extinguishes the light which is burning dimly. As he goes to pick up the suit case, his foot upsets it, making a light crash. He picks it up and hurriedly exits.*

*Enter* EDIE *almost immediately. She wears a negligee and slippers. She peers into the room, runs to door* R.U.E., *looks out, comes back, rings bell and runs to the window, opens it and calls out.*

EDIE. Help! Help! (*Looking in greatly frightened.*) Oh, dear—what shall I do, if someone comes! (*Bell rings.* EDIE *again looks out.*) Who is it? Are you a policeman? Yes, I'm afraid something is the matter—


This play is also published separately, in paper, at 50 cents a copy.

but I can't let you in unless you're a policeman—I'm all alone in the house, and I think there's a burglar! Wait! (*She switches on the lights. By this time* HAMILTON *is coming through the window. He is a little dishevelled, but very serious and polite. He wears a dinner coat and carries a soft hat. This he lays on chair almost immediately.*)

BOB. I thought I'd better come right in—you see, I don't know any policemen around here—yet.

EDIE. Oh, mercy!

BOB. Don't be frightened. I live just across the street.

EDIE. Are you sure?

BOB. Yes—really. My mother's in the country, but my father's there—he's bought the house and gone to bed—and I was just sitting on the front steps asleep when I heard you call "Help!"

EDIE. Sitting on the front steps asleep!

BOB. Yes. My father has my key. He doesn't like my being out nights. So I either have to go to a Turkish bath or sit on the steps all night.

EDIE. But it's only twelve o'clock.

BOB. Splendid of you to say so. My father likes to have the lights out at ten. You see, I'm going to be his partner some day, so he wants me to be down bright and early to sweep out the office—— What was it that frightened you?

EDIE. I heard things!

BOB. *Really?* What sort of things?

EDIE. I don't know. Then there was a crash—and I ran out and saw a man disappearing down the stairs.

BOB. Oh—you did!

EDIE. Then I rang for Fielding, and there was no answer—and then I opened the window and called for help.

BOB. Fielding?

EDIE. The butler.

BOB. There's no one else in the house?

EDIE. Well, mother's maid is supposed to be here, but she isn't.

BOB. I see.

EDIE. I let her go to her sister's down on Long Island, because poor Maggie's husband has broken his leg, and Maggie wanted to come to town and see him—she has so little pleasure—so I let Ellen go to look after Maggie's children.

BOB. I see.

EDIE. Do you suppose Fielding is dead?

BOB. Probably a sound sleeper.

EDIE. Father has the bell in the servants' room specially hung—he could never sleep through it.

BOB. Well, it wasn't long ago. Maybe he's dressing. If butlers ever take off their clothes—I don't know whether they do or not. Shall I go and look for him?

EDIE. No—I'll ring again. But I'm sure there's no one alive in the house. Don't you have that feeling? (*She rings again.*)

BOB. Well, no, I must say it's awfully cheerful and pleasant after the front steps.

EDIE. (*Hesitating prettily.*) Won't you sit down—while we're waiting? (*She sits at one end of couch.*)

BOB. Thanks. Excuse my collar, won't you? I'd have taken more care of it at the banquet if I'd known I was coming.

EDIE. Oh—you've been to a banquet?

BOB. (*He sits* L. *end of couch.*) Yes. It was jolly, but it lasted a little too long. Our class is going to the boat race to-morrow and one of the fellows unfortunately had a birthday.

EDIE. I see. Well, do you think we ought to telephone for the police?

BOB. Why, not on my account. Are you afraid now?

EDIE. No, not now. But——

BOB. I'll stay till the butler gets dressed. I'm sure he's not dead. They always live to be awfully old.

EDIE. I wonder what it could have been that made that dreadful crash. It sounded as if all the chandeliers in the house were falling.

BOB. They don't usually take those.

EDIE. (*Darting forward, picking up salt spoon.*) Oh, look——

BOB. What is it?

EDIE. It's one of the little silver salt spoons!

BOB. Oh—he was after the silver!

EDIE. Yes—but you don't understand—this is one of Aunt Abingdon's salt spoons.

BOB. Does that make it better or worse?

EDIE. Oh, it makes it dreadful—for he must have taken it all! The whole case!

BOB. (*Taking the spoon.*) Well—we've got this much left of it—anyway.

EDIE. It was in father's room—wait—I shall look and see if it's gone. But I'm sure it is—aren't you?

BOB. Oh, absolutely. Let me go first. . . .

EDIE. It's the room across the hall. Wait! You'd better take the poker—but I don't believe there's anyone in there—now. (*They go up to door* L. EDIE *holds the door open.* BOB *looks in door across hall.* EDIE *closes her eyes.*) Do you see anybody?

BOB. No.

EDIE. Is there a suit-case lying on the couch at the foot of the bed?

BOB. No.

EDIE. Then it's gone. (*They come back.*) He did take it! How terrible!

BOB. Is it? Can't you get some more?

EDIE. Not like this. . . . It's been in the family for years. (*Replaces poker.*) Sit down and let me tell you—— (*They sit on the couch, a space between them.*) Father and mother were taking it to Rochester to-night to Aunt Abingdon's wedding. No one ever thought she would marry, you see—and *she* didn't think so—so she let father keep the silver for me in his safe deposit vault——

BOB. (*Rousing himself.*) I see!

EDIE. Then she suddenly decided to marry—and sent for it, and father and mother started with it—they took the midnight train. But there were so many suit-cases that father evidently left the wrong one—and I saw it lying on the couch at the foot of the bed in his room after they'd gone—— (*During this recital* BOB *falls asleep.*) Why, he's asleep. (*Takes* BOB's *hand.*)

BOB. (*Singing cheerfully.*) Cheer, cheer, the gang's all here! (*Opening his eyes.*) I beg your pardon——

EDIE. I'm awfully sorry to wake you up—but I was telling you about the silver.

BOB. I know it—I remember perfectly—it's gone. Do you feel very badly about it?

EDIE. Well, it would have been terribly nice to have it. The tea-pot was so cunning.

BOB. Well, I'll tell you. You can have mine. I have a lot of silver coming to me and I don't care anything about it, at all. There ought to have been a girl to have it, but there wasn't. It's marked with an E. What's your name?

EDIE. My name is Edie—isn't that wonderful? But of course I couldn't take it——

BOB. Oh—you couldn't?

EDIE. No—because those things descend in families, you know. There's a regular form that has to be gone through.

BOB. I see. Well, can't we go through it? Anyhow, there's nothing very regular about the way yours has descended. It may not even have the right initials for the burglar's family.

EDIE. I know—and doesn't it seem dreadful for all the little burglars to be eating with Aunt Abingdon's spoons?

BOB. Sorry I made you think of that.

EDIE. You know I ought not to keep you here—but there's no one I could telephone to come and stay with me—everyone is out of town.—We're out of town, too, if it hadn't been for the wedding.

BOB. Lucky for me that Aunt Abbie decided to get married. I'd go, but I really don't think I ought to leave you—do you? If you send me away there's nothing but the cold steps across the street.

EDIE. Wouldn't they really let you in?

BOB. Here I am.

EDIE. I'm surprised you didn't go to a hotel!

BOB. Well, it takes quite a lot of time and courage to get home. And somehow, after you get home you haven't the heart to go anywhere else. It seems as though the least they could do is to let you in.

EDIE. I should think so. You're sleepy—if only you could stay until it gets just the least little bit light.

BOB. (*Rises.*) Certainly I will. I'll stay—and I'll try to stay awake. And you go and get some sleep—there's nothing for you to worry about any more. There's a man in the house.

EDIE. (*Rising.*) I wish I could make you more comfortable.

BOB. Oh, I'm all right.

EDIE. No, you're not. I think it's your collar.

BOB. I know it is.

EDIE. I know—you shall put on father's dressing-gown—then you can lie down—if you find you can't sit up. (*She hurries to door* R.U.E.) Of course if you could keep awake until it's just a little bit light, it would be better. (*Exit.*)

BOB. I'll keep awake—here's how I'll do it! (*Starts Victrola, which is already wound. It plays "The Brook."* BOB *goes to couch and sits on the arm for a moment. Blinks his eyes, goes back to Victrola. Closes it. Places one arm on top, his head in his hand. Enter* EDIE. *She has the dressing-gown.*)

EDIE. (*Laying the dressing-gown on the table.*) Oh, what a splendid idea!

BOB. Isn't it? But I think a waltz or a fox-trot would be more effective.

EDIE. Oh, but haven't you ever waltzed to this? I have. It's heavenly!

BOB. Is it? (*They dance. After a few steps.*) Why, it *is* heavenly!

EDIE. It's "The Brook," you know.

BOB. (*As they dance.*) "The Brook?" Does it go on forever? I hope it does. It's wonderful—so dreamy . . .

EDIE. Dreamy—yes—perhaps we'd better stop.

BOB. (*Stopping the Victrola.* EDIE *sits on arm of couch.*) Every time I go to sleep I'll just wake up and start the music. I guess Fielding is dead—or he'd be here by this time. By Jove—I've an idea! Have you had him long?

EDIE. No—not very.

BOB. Maybe he took the silver!

EDIE. Oh—do you think he did?

BOB. If it makes you feel any better, I'm sure he did.

EDIE. Well, if he did I'm sure he won't come back. At least I shouldn't think he would. So I shouldn't be in danger any more and perhaps I ought to let you go.

BOB. Please don't. Anyway—you can't be sure with a man like that. Even if he's taken the silver—he might decide to bring it back.

EDIE. It's the idea of being alone in the house, that's sort of terrifying——

BOB. Of course. I shouldn't think of allowing it. I've taken charge of things now—and I order you to talk to me for just a few minutes more, then go to bed. (*He puts on the dressing-gown; it is a soft silk one and slips on easily over his coat.* EDIE *sits on the couch.*)

EDIE. What sort of things are you interested in? Do you like going to college?

BOB. Oh, I'm all through college—yes—didn't I tell you

I'm going into business? I'm interested in electricity and motor boats and girls.

EDIE. Don't you care for anything else?

BOB. (*Sitting beside her. A little nearer this time.*) Oh, yes. I'm awfully fond of my mother.

EDIE. Do you know what I want to do? I want to raise violets. I simply adore them—sweet ones, I mean.

BOB. So do I. Let's raise them.

EDIE. You never can buy them any more, you know—they're not the least bit sweet. And it's a pity to let such an exquisite fragrance die out of the world?

BOB. Why, it's terrible. Is it dying really? No one ever told me.

EDIE. Girls can't, you know. They can't say, "The violets you sent me were perfectly horrid." But they always are. Because they're not raised right. They're hurried, and chilled and dead. Just dead violets with a ribbon round them.

BOB. Where's my handkerchief!—Can we do anything about it to-night?

EDIE. No—but I'm going to have violet frames under my window in the country. Father says I may. Won't that be heavenly? Then if I make a success of them I'll send them in to shops. Just so that people can buy them and not be disappointed.

BOB. You must let me buy the first bunch—and send it to you.

EDIE. (*Wishing to inject a little formality into the conversation.*) What have you been reading lately?

BOB. Why—the last thing I read was the newspaper. Don't feel that you have to talk to me, Edie.

EDIE. Oh, I love it.

BOB. But aren't you sleepy?

EDIE. Oh, no, it's only that I got up awfully early to come to town, so I could go to the wedding. And then mother decided it was too much for me. To be on the train all night.

BOB. I'm so glad. Tell me—would you like to have a dog?

EDIE. I have two, but I'd *love* to have another.

BOB. I've got a lovely dog—he's just a pup.

EDIE. But don't you want him?

BOB. Yes, but I'm going into business. And he's a bird dog and he's awfully unhappy in the back yard.

EDIE. I'll take him up to the country—to-morrow.

BOB. All right. He's a thorough-bred—very good—but he's just the age where he needs a lot of care. His ears don't stand up quite right.

EDIE. And what do you do about them?

BOB. Well, when I'm reading I sit and hold them forward and up a little—he likes it.

EDIE. The darling. I'll remember to do it.

BOB. He doesn't know much, but he'll be a fine watch dog for the violets. You know, that idea about the violets is immense. I can't wait for the great day when the first fragrant violet in years hits New York. Why not call it "violet day," and have a holiday?

EDIE. (*Laughing a little.*) Wouldn't that be lovely? (*The tiniest yawn. She glances hastily to see if it was observed. It was not.*) You know, I can't understand Mother's letting Father forget the silver.

BOB. Maybe Father let Mother forget.

EDIE. Oh, no—Mother never forgets.

BOB. Mothers are wonderful.

EDIE. Aren't they? Fathers are nice, too.

BOB. Yes, sometimes. But they can't keep it up like mothers.

EDIE. Oh, no, of course not. You couldn't expect that. (*A tiny yawn. She puts her finger on her mouth and looks very serious.*)

BOB. No, anyone that expects to be like a mother has got to *be* one, that's all. . . . I'm going to tell you something—when I sat there on those steps a little while ago—— What I thought about life—well, it wouldn't do at all for a little girl like you to hear. But I was wrong, I don't care what anyone says, it's all right. And we ought to realize when we're unhappy, that any time, a little thing like a robbery can make it beautiful.

EDIE. (*Sleepily.*) I think life is beautiful.

BOB. I know it is.

EDIE. I don't understand people who are unhappy—Aunt Abbie was always unhappy.

BOB. Because she wasn't married, I suppose.

EDIE. I suppose so. And now she'll be unhappy because she is.

BOB. (*A little sleepy.*) When would you like to get married? I mean do you believe in early marriage or do you think it's better to wait?

EDIE. Well, I think it depends.

BOB. So do I. But why wait? I mean if a thing's worth doing, it's worth doing well—I mean—quick. After all, love is just love, isn't it? If it's going to last it is—if it doesn't, it isn't. I mean if it isn't, it doesn't. So it's not going to make things any better as far as I can see, to wait.

EDIE. No. Not in the least. (EDIE *goes to sleep.*)

BOB. Dear little thing, she's gone to sleep. Thank goodness, she won't have to worry any more about my keeping awake. Edie, are you asleep? (*Very softly.*) She is. Now how am I going to tell when it gets the least little bit light? (EDIE'S *head droops against his shoulder. A little disturbed he uncrosses his knees carefully, then deciding not to wake her, re-crosses them. He goes to sleep. He gently, in his sleep, puts his arm around her. His head rests against hers.*)

(*After a few moments Voices off.*)

MARGARET. Well, I know her better than you do, dear. You'd have had a very cold reception without the silver, I can tell you.

JOHN. All right, all right. You know best about your own relatives—but I must say if it weren't for Edie's future I wouldn't go a step—not a step.

MARGARET. Don't wake Edie talking so loud. Just slip in and get it, and come right out again.

(JOHN *enters, followed by* MARGARET. JOHN's *eyes rest on the sleeping pair.*)

JOHN. (*Horrified.*) Margaret!—Margaret!

MARGARET. John?

JOHN. (*Hardly able to speak.*) Will you—will you look on the couch? Edie! And a strange young man—— (*Peering at them.*) Yes—in my dressing-gown!

MARGARET. (*Greatly interested.*) Why, John! Who do you suppose it is! I never saw him before in my life!

JOHN. Margaret, I have told you all along that your ideas about bringing Edie up would result in disaster. Now you see for yourself.

MARGARET. See? See what? I don't see any particular disaster about it yet. Of course I don't understand it, but the boy is a very nice-looking, in fact quite a distinguished-looking boy. . . .

JOHN. And he's here in my house asleep in my dressing-gown, with my daughter in his arms! That's all right, I suppose. Quite all right if one is modern enough to think so.

MARGARET. John, do lower your voice and don't talk about *your* house and *your* dressing-gown and *your* daughter. The house is ours and the dressing-gown I gave you for Christmas and Edie is certainly mine. . . .

JOHN. (*Gloomily.*) I fear the worst.

MARGARET. I don't. I have perfect confidence in my child. I don't know anything about your ancestors, John, but mine alone would prevent any scandal occurring in the family.

JOHN. She said going to Rochester would be too much for her—but she's killed her father—that's what she's done!

MARGARET. John, don't be ridiculous—why don't you wake him up and ask him what he's doing here?

JOHN. I don't need to ask him. But I will. . . . (*He leaps upon* BOB. *They fight.*)

BOB. It's Fielding! So you're back, are you, after that salt spoon?—you avaricious old thief!

EDIE. Stop! Mercy!

BOB. Don't be worried—I can handle him.

EDIE. Don't! That's my father!

MARGARET. Stop him, Edie!

BOB. Oh, I beg your pardon—I thought you were the butler!

JOHN. And who are you, if I may ask?

EDIE. Father, don't—don't tremble so!

JOHN. I'm not trembling—or if I am it's not with fear.

EDIE. Of course not, dear. I didn't mean that.

JOHN. To come into my house at this hour and find a perfect stranger and in my dressing-gown——

BOB. I'll take it off——(*Does so.*)

MARGARET. Edie, who is he?

EDIE. His name is—I forget—but he lives across the street.

JOHN. Then what is he doing here—if he lives across the street?

EDIE. Father, you don't understand. . . .

JOHN. No—I don't. Why isn't he across the street where he belongs?

BOB. I was. But I heard a call for help and I came in and found your daughter alone in the house——

JOHN. I should hope so——

BOB. I couldn't leave her alone in the house——

JOHN. Why couldn't you?

EDIE. Father, listen to me—don't you realize that the house has been robbed? All Aunt Abingdon's silver and I don't know what besides—you know you left it.

MARGARET. Where did you leave it, John?

JOHN. I didn't leave it at all—you left it.

MARGARET. Why, I didn't—you said in the cab it was somewhere.

EDIE. Well, it isn't anywhere now—and we think Fielding has taken it—for he doesn't answer the bell—either that or Fielding is dead—but we don't think he is—for we turned the Victrola on and still he didn't come. (JOHN *goes to bell. Rings, exits.*)

MARGARET. Isn't even Ellen here?

EDIE. No, darling—she's gone down to Maggie's house. But it's all right, Mother. This is Robert Hamilton—I remember now. He was sitting on the steps of his house when I called for help.

BOB. I suppose you think that's very strange, Mrs. Upton?

MARGARET. Why, not any stranger than anything else.

BOB. I was locked out, you see. My father is—well—he's a little like Mr. Upton.

(MR. UPTON *returns.*)

JOHN. The silver is gone—and Fielding is not in his room. Well, I never liked his face. I said he had a shifty eye.

MARGARET. But only one—the other was very nice—and he told me the shifty one was hit by a boy with a bean-shooter.

JOHN. You will engage the servants, in spite of any protests from me. Well, we won't go to Rochester without that silver. At least I won't. (*Telephone.*) Now who's that?

MARGARET. Maybe it's Fielding!—To say he's sorry!

JOHN. (*At the phone.*) Yes—that's very likely. (*Into phone.*) Who is it? Fielding? Yes, yes! Where are you? At the station? With the silver? Well, my good man—you have made us all a great deal of trouble . . . Of course we won't go tonight. No, Mrs. Upton is too upset. Bring the silver back, here to the house.

MARGARET. (*To* EDIE.) Isn't it wonderful how your father is always wrong about everything?

BOB. I suppose I'd better go.

JOHN. Indeed you'll not go. I want an explanation of how you come to be here and who you are.

BOB. My name is Hamilton. Robert Hamilton. My father has just bought the house across the street.

JOHN. Edie, have you ever met this young man before?

EDIE. No, Father.

JOHN. And—and—I find you asleep in his arms?

EDIE. Father, was I? How dreadful! (*Turning to her mother.*)

MARGARET. (*Putting her arms around* EDIE.) John, you shouldn't have told her.

BOB. It wasn't dreadful. She went to sleep and I didn't like to wake her up. She's nothing but a tired child—if you scold her I—I have my opinion of you.

JOHN. Indeed! And your name is Hamilton. Where do you live?

BOB. Just where I did before, across the street.

JOHN. That's easily verified. (*Going to phone.*) Hamilton.

BOB. The phone is 4664 River, but I wouldn't advise you to call him.

JOHN. Indeed . . . (*At phone.*) 4664 River.

BOB. He's a brave man.

EDIE. I'm so sorry!

JOHN. (*In phone.*) Is this Mr. Hamilton? Well, I'm sure—— Wait—— But I—why, you——This is Mr. Upton speaking. Your son—your son—your son! (*His voice increasing in volume. Retreats from phone, defeated.*)

BOB. (*Going to the rescue.*) Allow me—— (*At phone.*) Hello, Dad—I had to save a girl's life across the street. A robbery. . . . Yes, sir, case of silver. But it's been returned now and I can come home. That's what made me late. I'm there now—I mean here. I knew you wouldn't let me in. All right, sir—all right. (*Picks up his hat.*)

EDIE. Are you going?

JOHN. My boy, you put my dressing-gown right on again and stay. I wouldn't go home at all—if I were you.

BOB. Oh, it's all right—he says he'll open the door. Good night. . . .

(BOB *goes.* JOHN *goes with him.*)

EDIE. Oh—he'll never come again—father acted so dreadfully.

MARGARET. Well, he won't come to see your father certainly. (*Sits on couch.* EDIE *sits beside her.*)

EDIE. He was so nice. He'd been to a banquet, Mother, and he was terribly tired—and still, he was nice.

MARGARET. I really think he was, and I loved the way he fought with your father. And I thought your father fought very well.

EDIE. I should say so—especially after they stopped. Oh, dear! I liked him so much and he was going to give me a dog, and now it's all over!

(BOB *off stage whistles a bar of "The Brook."* EDIE *runs to the window, she turns and smiles at her mother.* MARGARET *goes a few steps toward her.*)

EDIE. (*Looking out.*) Father's going across the street with him. Father's gone in——(*Runs to her mother, taking her hands.*) Oh, Mother—now we know the Hamiltons! (*Embracing her mother.*)

CURTAIN

# SUCH A CHARMING YOUNG MAN

COMEDY IN ONE ACT

## ZOE AKINS

Zoe Akins was born in 1886. Her first experience as a writer was gained in connection with Reedy's Mirror in St. Louis, to which she contributed verse and criticism. In 1911 she published her first book, a collection of poems. Her comedy, "Papa," was produced the same year. Her subsequent plays were two or three one-acters produced by the Washington Square Players and other groups. It was in 1919 that she first became known to the theatre-going public. "Déclassée," in which Ethel Barrymore played the principal role, was one of the important plays of that season. This was followed by a number of others, the best of which are "Daddy's Gone a-Hunting," and "Greatness."

Miss Akins, in her short plays, as in the more ambitious work, is revealed as a clever satirist with an ingratiating gift for dialogue and the finer shades of character. "Such a Charming Young Man" is her best short play, and a thoroughly characteristic sample of her methods.

Following is a list of Miss Akins' published plays: "Déclassée," "Daddy's Gone a-Hunting," "Greatness," "Papa," "The Magical City," and "Such a Charming Young Man."

# SUCH A CHARMING YOUNG MAN*

## CHARACTERS

LEONTINE
MARGARET
HUBERT
A WONDERFUL-LOOKING WOMAN
GERALD
PHILANDER HICKS
JONES
A WAITER
A PAGE

SCENE: *A Restaurant.*

TIME: *The Present.*

*The stage is set to represent a shallow balcony overlooking the main floor of a fashionable restaurant. Two tables are placed, a little distance from each other, near the railing. Beyond is the lighted abyss over the restaurant below, and farther off the opposite wall. Music is playing softly in the distance.*

MARGARET, LEONTINE *and* HUBERT *are finishing their coffee at a table laid for four; they are all smoking as they casually watch the people below. All three are very fashionable, well gotten-up young people with attractive voices and engagingly bad manners. Now and then a benign waiter flits about, but they are practically alone, so secluded is their table.*

---

LEONTINE. (*Looking over the balcony.*) I say! Isn't that my husband?

MARGARET. Where?

LEONTINE. Over there.

HUBERT. I don't see.

LEONTINE. Do you see the very blonde person rising to go?

HUBERT. Being tenderly put into her sables by the waiter? Yes . . .

MARGARET. Oh yes!

LEONTINE. Wait until she moves. . . . Now. . . . Isn't that Ned? With a very pretty girl?

HUBERT. In brown? Yes.

MARGARET. Yes, that is Ned.

LEONTINE. So I thought. One may forget the color of one's husband's eyes, but one always knows the back of his head. (LEONTINE *puts up her lorgnette and stares attentively. There is the merest pause.*) What a very pretty girl! I wonder who she is? They're going.

MARGARET. Ned sees you. You always put him out by staring when you meet him anywhere, Leontine; why do you do it?

LEONTINE. I love to stare. I always stare. (*There is another bare pause.* LEONTINE *follows the invisible pair with her eyes. Again she speaks, very coolly, but with an audible sigh as she glances downward at herself.*) But he doesn't dress her very well, either.

MARGARET. (*Looking off.*) Do you see that wonderful-looking person?

LEONTINE. Where?

HUBERT. I see her—trying to find a table.

MARGARET. They are trying to find one for her, you mean; she wouldn't have one in the middle.

LEONTINE. How thrilling she looks! Now why can't Ned pick out that sort?

MARGARET. You know you'd be jealous!

LEONTINE. I might, of the clothes. But I love being jealous. I love to be made unhappy. I love sensations.

HUBERT. Ever go to a dentist?

LEONTINE. I know what you mean—the drilly grindy thing. I don't mind it; but what I do mind is having anyone look into my mouth. It seems an impertinence. I wish Gerald would come. He is such a charming young man. (*The orchestra begins to play a tango.*)

HUBERT. I can't keep still. Come on, Margaret. (HUBERT *rises, moving his arms to the rhythm of the music.*)

MARGARET. No, thanks.

HUBERT. Want to try it, Leo?

LEONTINE. Not now; did Gerald say he'd be here?

HUBERT. At one-thirty. . . . It's twenty minutes after three; want to wait?

MARGARET. (*With a touch of indignation at the question.*) Of course!

LEONTINE. Gerald is never on time.

MARGARET. He always has an excuse.

LEONTINE. Yes, Gerald's excuses are wonderful. I love imagination.

HUBERT. Gerald mixes you up so. You always refuse to believe him, and then you find out that he has told the truth.

LEONTINE. (*Touching* MARGARET'S *arm.*) My dear! There's that wonderful-looking creature!

MARGARET. They're giving her the next table!

(*The waiter appears, leading the way for a very strange and romantic looking* YOUNG WOMAN, *magnificently dressed. Her manner is that of one used to attracting attention and quite indifferent to it. She sits, and murmurs to the waiter as he bends over her, taking her order. Her table is prepared for three. Left alone, she waits, her face in the palm of one hand, as she stares dreamily and sadly at nothing.*)

LEONTINE. (*Lowering her voice only very slightly.*) Very, very good; her things, you know.

MARGARET. Do you suppose those are real pearls? They look fabulous.

LEONTINE. Why is it that people are willing to wear imitations if they have real ones locked up some place? That seems to make them feel perfectly honest about it.

HUBERT. What a face! What eyes! What dignity! It *is* dignity—isn't it?

LEONTINE. I should call it that. After all, it is rather nice to look like a princess, even if they don't look like themselves—at least not often. . . . I wonder who she is?

HUBERT. She must be French.

MARGARET. More Italian—or Spanish.

LEONTINE. No—Russian. . . . I'd love talking to her.

MARGARET. Here's Gerald!

(GERALD *enters,—a charming young man. He is delighted at having got here; he is so delighted that he does not see the wonderful-looking woman at the next table. He sits with his back to her.*)

GERALD. Hello! Maggie—Leo—Hubert!

MARGARET, LEO *and* HUBERT. (*Speaking almost together, accusingly.*) Why are you so late?

GERALD. (*Guilelessly, blithely, charmingly.*) I'm so sorry. Such extraordinary things happened.

LEONTINE. Now, let us prepare for romance!

GERALD. But really,—now you won't believe me——?

LEONTINE. Go on.

GERALD. My valet died.

HUBERT. Good!

LEONTINE. Yes, that is an excuse. I'll have my maid go off with apoplexy some time.

GERALD. But really,—the old fellow didn't come when I rang—and—it sort of does me up to talk about it—but he was dead, on the floor, by the window, with a pair of my trousers in his hand . . . and a smile on his lips,—I had to stop, of course, to attend to things. It was apoplexy, Leo.

LEONTINE. I'm glad that my suggestion proved available. (HUBERT *laughs heartily;* MARGARET *smiles indulgently,* LEONTINE *wickedly.*)

MARGARET. Is it really true—?

GERALD. I assure you that it is. (*He seems sincere, but his happy triumphant manner does not go very well with sad news.*)

LEONTINE. Did that make you two hours late? You were more considerate of the dead than the living, I should say.

GERALD. Oh, some other things happened too. I sent for the doctor, and got the janitor up,—he was the one who assured me that it was apoplexy, and telephoned my office boy to come up and take charge. Jim's a clever lad—thoroughly competent, you know; buys wedding presents, takes my mother to the boat, goes to the bank for me,—and all that. So I left things with him and started here. Then I got chased by bears.

MARGARET. Bears!

LEONTINE. Ripping!

HUBERT. Wall Street or the zoo?

GERALD. But really,—this actually happened. I was coming along and I saw a girl I know turn into the stage entrance of a vaudeville theatre. She's a nice little thing,—her mother was killed by a taxi-cab last week; I'd just heard about it, so I thought I would follow her and have a word with her—just tell her how sorry I was; but you know what traffic laws are—so by the time my man had driven around five or six blocks and stopped at the door I'd seen her going into, she naturally wasn't in sight any longer. But I didn't see anyone to stop me so I went in too, to look for her. "This is funny," I said to myself, "There's no one about to give a dollar to." Everything was quiet and dark; for the matinee had already begun, and an act was on; I kept waiting for a man to turn up to take my card, but no one came. I heard the applause from the front and I thought I'd take a look at the stage. It was bears. Now I don't know how it happened, but suddenly there was a lot of yelling from everywhere,—and three bears were rushing towards the open door, and me; and a wild dago-looking woman in a red and gold short dress, like a brass-band uniform was screaming and swearing, and flourishing a whip, first at me and then at the bears—and I got out! I tore through the door, but one big brown fellow came after me. I was a little bit annoyed. My taxi had moved on, so I couldn't find it, and there wasn't a policeman around to arrest the bear. Consequently I ran. Then I got out of breath and at the same time I began to worry because I was taking the bear away from the dago-lady. Bears cost money, you know. I figured out that if I would turn around and run the other way, and it would keep on following me, I could run back to the theater, and I might find my taxi. I turned, and heaven knows why I did it—but I took off my hat and bowed—just bowed—like this—to the bear! And what do you think that bear did? (*There is a pause as* GERALD'S *thrilling tale remains suspended; the others ask with one breath of interest and merriment.*)

LEONTINE, MARGARET *and* HUBERT. (*Speaking together.*) What?

GERALD. (*Triumphantly.*) It bowed back! And then it came, just as nicely as you please, and took my arm, and we returned to the theater together, with the crowd at our heels. The dago-lady was so pleased at having Teddy back that she stopped having hysterics and forgave me for leaving the door open in the first place—it seems you mustn't do that because when bears smell the fresh air they want to bolt; at least that's what she said—and actually I couldn't keep her from kissing me. Would you believe it?

LEONTINE. No, I wouldn't. But it was exciting; and then you looked at your watch and found it twenty minutes after three?

GERALD. No—my dear Leo, no! But I did look at my watch, and found that it had stopped. And then I looked around again for my taxi. And then a queer old chap, a Wild West sort, you know,—only mild and sweet and tame,—came up and asked to shake hands with me. He'd watched me come back with the bear. He was perfectly absurd about it, really,—and said that he didn't suppose I'd take a drink with him? I said that I would be delighted if he knew where to get one that wasn't poison. He knew, all right—even if he was a stranger in town. So we had several—back and forth. And what do you imagine this splendid old chap did?

LEONTINE. You imagine for us.

GERALD. But really,—it's extraordinary! He found out all about me. Before I knew it I was telling him how much money I owed—and all that sort of thing—and then this dear old chap insisted upon giving me an interest in a big gold mine that is going to make him and an old friend of his—and me—all rich!

LEONTINE. And then you looked at your watch.

GERALD. But really,—no! He looked at his, and said that he had to meet this old friend in five minutes at a cigar store on a corner where there used to be a little saloon when they were both newsboys. It was quite romantic. They had come over from England in the steerage together, to grow up and be president, you know—and all that. But the other boy got homesick and went back to England while my chap went West and grew up with the country; but in time the one who went to England came back to America—and now—after many many years they are going to meet again today!

LEONTINE. (*With mock interest and enthusiasm.*) No!

GERALD. (*Directing his attention solely at her, and continuing mischievously.*) Yes! (*Then to the three of them he explains earnestly.*) The other old fellow has a daughter who's rich and she's already lent my friend twenty thousand dollars. Not much, but it was enough to buy spades with; so that he could start the mine working, and go ahead and sell some stock—and get more money to get the gold out with. Anyone want to buy any shares? Where's the waiter? I'm hungry.

HUBERT. He's been hovering about. There he is. (*The waiter comes at a signal.* HUBERT *turns to* GERALD.) What'll you have?

LEONTINE. After your adventure with big game?

MARGARET. (*Looking at the card.*) Bear-steak?

GERALD. I couldn't, really. That bear and I parted such friends that I'd feel like a cannibal. Let's see.

THE WAITER. (*Helpfully.*) Something light for breakfast, Mr. Gerald?

GERALD. (*Gratefully.*) Thanks, Alphonse. Fix me up.

THE WAITER. Very good, sir. (*He goes away importantly.*)

MARGARET. All the waiters and policemen know you, don't they, Gerald?

LEONTINE. I wonder why it is so impressive?

GERALD. Will your father let me marry you when my gold mine makes me rich, Maggie?

LEONTINE. Haven't you got rather a long waiting-list, Gerald,—of the girls you are going to marry when you get rich?

GERALD. No longer than yours, Leo—of the men you're going to marry when you get divorced.

LEONTINE. Well, they're perfectly safe,—all of them, on both our lists.

MARGARET. I don't want to be safe. I want to marry Gerald.

GERALD. That's right. . . . We'd elope today if I were as rich as Hubert. I say, Hubert,—you've got a lot of money. Why don't you put some in our mine? It's a great opportunity. We've millions in the ground; and I get a commission besides on all the stock I sell. Want to take a chance?

HUBERT. What is your wild-westerner's name?

GERALD. I've got all the details right here. Just wait. (*He takes out of a pocket the daintiest of note-books, bound in gold. With some difficulty he finds the right place.*) Hicks. Philander Hicks. He said I could call him Uncle Phil.

HUBERT. (*Indulgently, as if playing a game.*) What's the name of the mine?

GERALD. The Bessie Jones. It's named after the old friend's daughter who gave Uncle Phil the $20,000 to get it going.

HUBERT. Where is it?

GERALD. Now! Isn't that careless of me? I forgot to ask. But it's somewhere out West. Where there are bears. A bear tried to kill Uncle Phil once. That was why he was so drawn to me. (*The waiter comes and sets a pot of coffee and some rolls before* GERALD.) Very good, Alphonse!

THE WAITER. Thank you, sir. Your 'am omelet will be right along, sir.

GERALD. (*To the others, as the waiter disappears.*) Waiters have wonderful memories, haven't they? I think they ought to be actors. Or diplomats. Now, on the stage, Alphonse would do aristocratic old roués or archbishops to perfection. And he'd make a more tactful, impressive ambassador than Colonel George Harvey—say.

(*He is pouring his coffee as he talks.* MARGARET *has pulled off two red petals from a rose in a vase on the table and holds them in her mouth so that they look like the lips of a Japanese woman. She draws up her eyes, slant-wise, with her fingers, and leans in front of* GERALD *who has begun to eat.*)

MARGARET. Look! (*She turns to* HUBERT *and* LEONTINE *in turn. The effect is amusing.*)

HUBERT. Adorable, Maggie!

GERALD. Very, very fetching!

LEONTINE. You've done that trick so often, dear. But it is quaint. (*Again the orchestra plays. The music is alluring and languorous, and is an almost irresistable invitation to a dance.* HUBERT *sways in his chair and then rises.*)

HUBERT. (*Pleadingly.*) Please, Leo. . . .

LEONTINE. If you insist.

(*They move to and fro in the small space doing a very delicate, stately tango. They are graceful and lazy as they glide through the steps, and with their eyes they show their interest in each other. Presently they see an acquaintance in the distance, stop dancing, and hurry away—apparently to speak to the person to whom they have just bowed. The wonderful-looking woman has become impatient and signals to the waiter. He seems to assure her that no one has asked for her. She decides to be served at once.* GERALD *eats hungrily. The rose-petals come loose from* MARGARET'S *lips and she blows them away. She says nothing, but her face grows stern, her attitude rigid.* GERALD *at last feels this, and looks up.*)

GERALD. What's the matter, Maggie? Cross?

MARGARET. (*With sudden feeling.*) I should say so! Our engagement is broken.

GERALD. You're cross with me, really?

MARGARET. Yes.

GERALD. Why? . . . Being late? . . . But really,—

MARGARET. I'm cross about a lot of things I'm cross because you are trivial and erratic and unscrupulous.

GERALD. (*Apologetically, but quite at a loss.*) I'm so sorry.

MARGARET. You don't want to marry me, anyway.

GERALD. I'd love to—but—(*He stops to take one more

*bite; then he is done with his food. He looks at her, seriously, with troubled eyes; then he proceeds generously.*) But—you're half right. I'm really no good.

MARGARET. (*Slightly touched.*) You are amusing, and you are a dear.

GERALD. But I can't let you marry me because I am amusing and a dear, can I? It wouldn't be right.

MARGARET. Right or wrong, I've decided not to do it.

GERALD. I am charming. I am attractive. People like me. I am generous. I am sympathetic. I am lucky. But those are not things that I can go and tell your father, are they?

MARGARET. It's because you don't really love me——

GERALD. I do! Don't accuse yourself of not being loved by me, Maggie.

MARGARET. If you did you'd understand how I feel about things.

GERALD. But it isn't my fault that your father won't let me come to his house, is it? And was I to blame because your mother and my mother had a quarrel at the dog-show? And now they hate each other, and I wouldn't even get my allowance if I went and married you, would I? But that's no reason why you should not stay engaged to me.

MARGARET. Very well; we won't talk about it. Of course there's no money; and no chance of our having any; so it's silly to keep on like this, isn't it?

GERALD. But I'm going to make money, Maggie. Just wait!

MARGARET. I'm afraid I'm not the sort to "just wait" all my life. I'm tired already. You make me too unhappy. You don't keep your engagements, and when I want to see you I have to telephone for hours, and when we do plan something you spoil it by not coming, or being late; and I have to pretend to every one that I don't mind . . . and, of course, you make love to every other woman. . . .

GERALD. That's all perfectly true, my darling. I am spoiled; I admit that. But I have never told any other woman that I love her. I make them think it, but I never come out and say so—like I do to you,—like this—(*He takes her hands and speaks solemnly and tenderly.*) "Maggie, I love you; and I don't love anyone else, and I never have, and I never shall." . . . There! Isn't that enough? What more can any woman want?

MARGARET. (*Wistfully.*) That would be quite enough, my dear, if it meant anything to you. I think that I'd wait for you forever if you'd only try—just a little—not to always disappoint me, and if you'd work.

GERALD. Work? I do work!

MARGARET. You go to an office for an hour, now and then——

GERALD. Women don't know anything about business. . . . I've mentioned half a dozen good things to Old Bagby, but he never takes my advice. An investment company that won't invest makes me tired. I get embarrassed when I tell him what to do and he continues to pay no attention. Now just to show you how hard I work, I'll tell you what happened on my way here. I saw Old Bagby come out of the subway. I had just left Uncle Philander Hicks. "By George," I said to myself, "Old Bagby ought to invest in our mine!" Uncle Phil is such a convincing old chap that I thought I'd let him do the talking, so I got out of the taxi and stopped Old Bagby, and picked him up and took him back to where I'd left Uncle Phil waiting for his old friend. Of course that made me a little later still—getting here, but I didn't mention it a while ago because I was afraid Leontine might think I was laying it on a bit thick. But anyway I left them together, Uncle Phil and Old Bagby, both looking at each other suspiciously, which means that they'll get on. You see, I get ten percent commission on all the stock I sell, beside the interest that Uncle Phil is going to give me. Now just suppose that the Bagby Investment company buys one hundred thousand dollars' worth of stock—Old Bagby wouldn't go into anything for less—I get ten thousand. And when I get twenty-five thousand ahead—that I've made myself—we'll be married, tout de suite, my darling!

MARGARET. (*Wearily.*) I'm a little tired of nonsense at serious moments, Gerald. I care more for you than I hope I'll ever care for any human being again,—*but*—I'm going to marry someone else.

GERALD. (*Suddenly grave.*) What's that, Maggie?

MARGARET. I said to myself this morning, quite firmly; "You've been out four years. You know that you are tired of quarreling with your family about Gerald; you are tired of pretending to people that you aren't ready to marry yet, and you're getting a little tired of him. You are a fool if you don't do something about it. You are a fool if you don't marry Howard Dillon." . . . Just then the telephone rang. Hubert said you'd asked us to luncheon with you . . . at half-past one, promptly. Then I called you up to ask if you could not make it earlier or later because I had a fitting at one. You said no; and that you wanted me to be half an hour early, so that we could talk before the others came. You asked me, particularly, to wear the flowers that you were sending. Of course they never came. That didn't make any difference. But I was half an hour early. I was giving you your last chance. Now I'm going to marry Howard.

GERALD. (*At a loss for words; sincerely bothered.*) I—I—can't seem to say anything—(*He breaks off; there is a little pause, tense for both of them. Then he begins in a relieved tone of voice at finding something else to speak of.*) It's funny about those flowers. He said he might not get his fresh orchids much before noon, and of course I wanted fresh ones, for you,—particularly. So I told him to send them here if he couldn't get them to your house before half-past twelve. I'll tell him——

MARGARET. (*Interrupting, a little coldly.*) The flowers didn't matter. I'm sorry I mentioned them.

GERALD. Then you're done with me?

MARGARET. Yes.

GERALD. You won't wait?

MARGARET. It's hopeless to wait.

GERALD. There's my gold mine!

MARGARET. How absurd!

GERALD. You know you are the one woman in the world that I never expected to have throw me down.

MARGARET. Not even if you gave every other one the chance?

GERALD. (*Evading her thrust.*) Howard Dillon is nothing but a lucky, red-faced——

MARGARET. We won't talk about him.

GERALD. I never did like him. . . . Anyway, Maggie, I did try to get here at one. You know I did! I told you what extraordinary things happened. Now, just because my valet died, and I got chased by that bear, and had the good luck to run into Uncle Philander—you throw me over. It isn't fair.

MARGARET. How ridiculous—to bring up those impossible tales at a moment like this!

GERALD. But they are true! Really, darling.

MARGARET. You don't mean to insult my intelligence by expecting me to believe you,—do you, Gerald?

GERALD. (*Drooping.*) I suppose they do sound fishy. But if I could prove——

MARGARET. (*Interrupting him, her voice suddenly tender.*) Gerald—I don't believe a word you say, ever; but I do love you; I love you so much that I'll wait another month—if you want me to—before I tell Howard that I'll marry him.

GERALD. Will you, really, my darling? (*He takes her hands impetuously.*)

MARGARET. If you will keep just half of our engagements, on time, telephone every morning before twelve, and go to your office for at least three hours a day.

GERALD. (*At once wryly and happily.*) You don't ask me to stop smoking and drinking, too, do you?

MARGARET. (*Hurt.*) Of course, if don't want to——

GERALD. But I do. I promise, oh, I promise, all right! Now let's dance just as far as that table and back, so I can hug you. We've been awfully serious.

(*They rise, a little dreamily; and dreamily, happily, move away in the dance. Almost instantly the music stops; but they dance on, obliviously—as if to music of their own; even the wonderful-looking woman at the next table becomes interested in them, and smiles; the waiter, bringing the ham omelet, smiles. Then* LEONTINE *and* HUBERT *return, walking to their places at the table. Their presence brings* GERALD *and* MARGARET *to earth, and back to the table.*)

MARGARET. There—there's your omelet, Gerald. . . .

(*But* LEONTINE *and* HUBERT *are not thinking of* GERALD *and* MARGARET. *They are watching the wonderful-looking woman, whom a waiter is now serving.*)

LEONTINE. She's decided not to wait.

HUBERT. Do you know, I believe I'm in love with her.

GERALD. Whom are you talking about?

LEONTINE. That wonderful-looking woman at the next table.

GERALD. Where?

(*He turns sharply, about to look. The woman gives him a swift radiant smile and bow. He bows to her, dazed. The others are interested.*) (*Turning around again.*) Now where did I meet her?

LEONTINE. Introduce us.

HUBERT. Ask her to join us.

MARGARET. (*With something like jealousy.*) You know her?

GERALD. She seems to know me—and I'm sure I've seen her before—but I have no idea . . .

HUBERT. Oh come, one does not forget a face like that!

LEONTINE. She is certainly somebody.

(*The wonderful-looking woman begins to eat—with her knife! The effect is dramatic as, again and again she puts her knife into her mouth.*)

MARGARET. (*A little maliciously.*) Evidently . . . she's eating with her knife.

LEONTINE. Then she is certainly somebody or nobody; barbaric nobility, perhaps.

HUBERT. From the Balkans, probably.

MARGARET. Can't you remember where you met her, Gerald? (*Again the woman smiles at* GERALD, *glowingly, invitingly.*)

GERALD. By George! Pardon me a minute. I've got to get this thing settled. (*He rises, leaves his friends, and approaches with a bow the wonderful-looking woman.*) How do you do? May I sit down a minute?

THE WOMAN. (*In a hearty deep voice without a trace of foreign accent, unless it is cockney.*) Sure! If you don't mind me eating. I don't take any lunch until after my act. (*She proceeds with her food though now that she has company she uses her fork instead of her knife with much care and some regret.* GERALD *is still at sea and curious regarding her identity. She continues to talk with great good-will.*) Say, you certainly was a sport! To bring my bear back. I thought I'd lost old Brownie for good. (*A glad light dawns on* GERALD'S *face.*)

GERALD. My dear Madame—? (*He pauses as if asking her name.*)

THE WOMAN. (*Correcting him.*) COUNTESS; I still go by the name of my husband before last. Countess Sitkawa.

GERALD. My dear Countess, I want to ask if I may introduce my friends?

THE WOMAN. (*Heartily.*) Sure! (GERALD *rises just in time to meet two rather old men who timidly approach, directed by the waiter.*)

GERALD. Great Scott, Jones! Aren't you dead?

JONES. (*Humbly.*) So they thought, Mr. Gerald—begging your pardon for putting you out, sir; but the doctor fixed me up all right, sir; it was only a little fainting spell, at hearing from an old friend, sir.

GERALD. And my Uncle Phil! By George, I've got it! You're Uncle Phil's old friend, Jones! And our partner in the gold mine! Do you know the Countess Sitkawa? (*He has seen them glancing at the wonderful-looking woman.*)

JONES. She's my daughter, sir.

THE WOMAN. (*Calling.*) Come and sit down, Poppa.

JONES. Yes, Bessie.

GERALD. (*With delight, as they move toward the Countess Sitkawa's table.*) She's the Bessie Jones!

HICKS. (*Looking at* GERALD *fondly, speaking to* JONES.) This is the young gentleman who I met with the bear.

JONES. I thought it must be him when you told me, Hicks.

GERALD. And it was your daughter's bear, Jones! Just Think!

JONES. We're very much honored, sir.

THE WOMAN. Sit down, all of you; let's eat. (JONES *doesn't know whether or not it's the proper thing for him to do.*)

GERALD. (*With tact, as he sits.*) Sit down, my dear partners. (*They sit.*)

JONES. (*Murmuring to* GERALD.) Begging your pardon, sir.

THE WOMAN. Well, what about your gold mine, Uncle Phil?

HICKS. You don't have to put up any more money, Bessie. We're going to begin to pay right now. This young gentleman introduced me to a rich man not more than an hour ago, who's just bought a fourth interest. He wanted more but I told him that one fourth belonged to you and your papa, because you'd put your money in on my sayso, at the start; and I was holding on to a half, for this young gentleman and myself—being as I had taken a great fancy to him, and meant to do him a good turn. It come out that this rich fellow's company knew the mine already, and had been trying to locate the owner for weeks. So when I proved that was me, he took your poppa and I right along to a hotel which he was on his way to, to eat dinner with his lawyer. We settled everything right there, quick, and here's his check. (*He takes a check out of his pocket-book and hands it to* GERALD.)

GERALD. Two hundred and fifty thousand! Old Bagby's check for two hundred and fifty thousand!

HICKS. Sight of money, ain't it? You get twenty-five thousand out of this today, young man—commission. We're much obliged.

GERALD. Wait a minute, Uncle Phil. (*With the check in his hand he goes to the other table.*) (*In a subdued, almost frightened voice.*) Maggie, come here. (*She rises.* LEONTINE *and* HUBERT *look up curiously.*)

LEONTINE. Who is she? Did you find out?

GERALD. (*Triumphantly.*) My friend, the Countess Sitkawa.

LEONTINE. Bring her to tea, will you, some time?

GERALD. Perhaps. (*He walks* MARGARET *a little distance away; they come to a halt, about mid-way between the two tables.* GERALD *draws her hand through his arm and takes on the air of a man who is about to confide an important secret.* LEONTINE *and* HUBERT, *left alone, lean toward each other and proceed with an engrossing flirtation. Neither looks up again. The Countess Sitkawa proceeds to eat heartily and silently as the waiter consults with* JONES *and* HICKS.)

GERALD. (*A little breathlessly.*) I can prove it all, now, darling—that's Uncle Phil, over there—and that's Jones, my dead valet—and she's the dago-bear-woman—and Jones' daughter! Just think! And look at this! I told you I left Uncle Phil and Old Bagby eyeing each other suspiciously.

MARGARET. (*Trying to read the check.*) But—

GERALD. (*Explaining it.*) This is old Bagby's check for two hundred and fifty thousand dollars. He bought a fourth interest in our gold mine. And I get twenty-five thousand out of this—tout de suite—my commission. I told you I'd marry you when I had made twenty-five thousand, didn't I? But you must promise never, never to doubt me again! (MARGARET'S *look tries to tell him that he is the most wonderful man in the world—although she is a little bewildered. A Page enters, crying out a perfectly unintelligible name. He is very small and has a tray in his hand, and one or two other things under his arm. Both* GERALD *and* MARGARET *feel him as an interruption as, again looking at them suspiciously, he shouts a name that no one could possibly understand.* GERALD *flags him.*)

GERALD. Boy! Did you say Sitkawa or Jones? (*The lad grins at the joke, and holds out a box to* GERALD.) (*Triumphantly.*) And here are your orchids, darling. (MARGARET *and the* PAGE *both stare at* GERALD, *reverently—as, happily, carelessly, he tosses the latter his last twenty dollar bill, and—*)

THE CURTAIN FALLS.

# JUDGE LYNCH

DRAMA IN ONE ACT

## J. W. ROGERS, JR.

John William Rogers, Jr., was born at Dallas, Texas, in 1894. He graduated from Dartmouth College in 1916. He was for some time in the publishing business, and is at present engaged in newspaper work in his native city.

"Judge Lynch," his only produced play—a work of particular dramatic merit and considerable theatrical effect—won the David Belasco cup in the 1924 National Little Theatre Tournament.

# JUDGE LYNCH*

## CHARACTERS

Mrs. Joplin
Ella, *her daughter-in-law*
Ed Joplin, *Ella's Husband*
A Stranger

Scene: *The back porch of the Joplin farmhouse somewhere in the South just after dusk.*

Time: *The present.*

Scene: *Looking into the back porch of an unpretentious Southern farmhouse. A door in the center, with a window on each side, opens on the porch from the interior of the house. Against the left window is silhouetted a shelf built between two of the plain, unpainted posts that support the roof of the porch. On the shelf stands a water-bucket with a dipper in it, and a tin basin. A rumpled towel is fastened to one of the posts beside it, and at the right from the eaves hangs a necklace-like string of red peppers drying. A large flat stone on the ground in front of the center of the porch serves for a step into the strip of yard between the porch and the audience. At the right in the yard lies a disordered heap of logs sawed into lengths for stovewood. A few of these are split and the axe stands driven into one of them. A cane-bottom chair is on the porch, just by the step. In it is a pan with two knives, and beside it on the floor is a basket of apples.*

---


The play is published separately at 50 cents a copy.

*As the curtain rises,* MRS. JOPLIN *opens the door and steps out of the lighted door onto the porch, carrying a tea-kettle which she proceeds to fill from the water-bucket with the dipper. She is a tall, plainly dressed country woman about fifty-five. Hard work has left its mark, but she has an unconscious dignity of manner which in spite of her lack of education commands respect. The monotonous years of trivialities and grinding daily tasks have never succeeded in killing an extraordinary emotional capacity.*

*While she is filling the pitcher, she stops abruptly, sets it down on the shelf and listens for something intently. The noise of someone moving a stove-lid inside the house disturbs her.*

MRS. JOPLIN. (*Irritable in her excitement.*) Stop rattling that stove and be quiet a moment, will you? (*The noise stops and as she listens once more, her daughter-in-law,* ELLA, *appears at the door holding a lantern.* ELLA *is still rather pretty in a commonplace, colorless sort of way, but is without distinction—an everyday, unimaginative country girl.*)

ELLA. (*Coming out on the porch with the lantern.*) What's the matter?

MRS. JOPLIN. I heard them hounds. Listen!

ELLA. (*After listening.*) I don't hear nothing. You couldn't hear them this far.

MRS. JOPLIN. Yes, you could. When the wind's this way. It carries off them hills like a soundboard. Maybe they've tracked him down the road trying to get away, anyhow.

ELLA. (*Beginning to be alarmed.*) Suppose he 'ould come here. He'd be desperate, I reckon. I don't think Ed ought to be stayin' off from home this time er night with a nigger like that loose in the woods.

MRS. JOPLIN. (*Cautiously.*) Where's that gun?

ELLA. In yonder by the mantelpiece.

MRS. JOPLIN. Better bring it out here. I'll take that.

(*She takes the lantern and hangs it on a nail in the right center post of the porch. Then she steps into the yard and listens intently until* ELLA *returns.*)

ELLA. (*Coming back.*) Did you hear them again?

MRS. JOPLIN. (*Starting back on the porch and stopping before the chair.*) Not yet . . . Here, take this knife. We might just as well finish these apples now. (MRS. JOPLIN *takes the gun from her, stands it against the right post, and hands her a knife; then seats herself in the chair, the pan of apples in her lap, and begins to peel.*) I'm shore I heard them hounds.

ELLA. I don't think Ed ought to leave us like this.

MRS. JOPLIN. Now, Ella, don't begin that again. You know Ed 'ull be back as soon as he can. . . . Reach me that wash-pan for the peels and you can have this one. (ELLA *does so and seats herself on the edge of the porch, above the step.*) We've got Pa's gun if anybody should come botherin' us. (*Moved.*) They'll get that nigger, though. They always do. It'll be a terrible death he'll die, but he's brought it on himself. . . . It does look like niggers would learn, but I reckon they wouldn't be niggers if they did.

ELLA. I guess that nigger would do anything now. I wish Ed would hurry back.

MRS. JOPLIN. Ed's just out doing his duty with the rest.

ELLA. If there's a lynching, I don't suppose you can blame Ed for wanting to see it. He said there ain't been a lynching in this county for ten years. Not since they took that young nigger down at Dugger's Mills, and Ed warn't there that time.

MRS. JOPLIN. How men have got the heart, I never could tell. It don't seem right, but I guess there ain't no other way. Every now and then it looks like niggers is just obliged to have an awful warning to make 'em fitten to live in a Christian land.

ELLA. What do you reckon they'll do with him?

MRS. JOPLIN. Hang him, I reckon.

ELLA. You don't suppose they'll burn him. I seen in the paper where they burnt two down in Arkansas last month.

MRS. JOPLIN. Oh, pray God they don't do that.

ELLA. Maybe they'll ask Mrs. Tatum what *she* wants done with him. With Squire Tatum lying there dead in his own blood, she might not be so particular about it. If a nigger was to slip up behind Ed and hit him with an axe-handle, wouldn't you——

MRS. JOPLIN. Ella, don't——

ELLA. Well, if a nigger slipped up behind my husband in the barn and murdered him, I wouldn't care what they done to the nigger.

MRS. JOPLIN. Pore Mrs. Tatum—it was a terrible thing for her—coming on her husband like that, all unexpected—and her going down to the barn to look for hen-nests. If her brother hadn't been ploughin' down in the fields and come running when he heard her screaming there ain't any telling what the pore thing would have done.

ELLA. They say her brother knowed right away it was the Jacks nigger who done it.

MRS. JOPLIN. I knowed that Jacks nigger when he was a tenant on Cousin Etty's place. I never would have suspected him of nothing like this. He always seemed a hard-workin' hand, and perlite and respectful as a body could want. Kinder timid-like too.

ELLA. Well, they knowed it was him, all right—if Squire Tatum had words with the nigger yesterday and cussed him and give him until Saturday to get moved off the farm with his family——

MRS. JOPLIN. Squire Tatum did have a terrible temper.

ELLA. Yes, the last time I was up home, I heard Uncle Jimmie talking about it. He wouldn't stand nothin' from no white man, let alone a nigger. Uncle Jimmie said he saw him at the store one day when a crowd was playing dominoes around the stove. A tobacco drummer that come in said something he didn't like, and before anybody knowed what was happening Squire Tatum had run at the man and pushed him clean onto the stove. He knocked the stove plum over, fire and all. And the stove-pipe came down, throwing soot all over the place. Uncle Jimmy said the man hadn't really said nothin' to him, neither.

MRS. JOPLIN. Yes, I always heard what a terrible tricky temper he had. But he was a good man as he saw it, and folks thought a heap of him when they come to know him. Look at that watch the Odd Fellows give him two Christmases back.

ELLA. I reckon that was the watch they say the nigger stole out of his pocket. Nigger was a fool to take that watch—everybody knows that watch. Remember, they had a picture of it in the paper when it was give to him. I saw the watch myself one Sunday when he was a-showin' it before church.

MRS. JOPLIN. (*Resting her hands in her lap.*) Well, I reckon I must have been mistaken about them hounds, and we ain't doing no good here. Ed'll be in soon, wantin' to know whatever's the matter with supper. (*Rising.*) I'll take them apples. (*Pointing to woodpile.*) You better bring in a armful of wood. Here, before you do it, put these peelin's along of yours and throw them over the fence where the pigs can get 'em in the morning.

(ELLA *comes down the step into the yard with the pan of peelings and starts toward the left. She gets almost to the side of the stage and is in the act of throwing them out, when she screams suddenly—frightened. She peers anxiously a moment into the darkness and then turns about, almost running to the porch.*)

ELLA. Ma, there's somebody over there. I seen 'em move.

MRS. JOPLIN. (*Catching her alarm and coming into the yard—reaching for the gun by the post as she does so.*) Where?

ELLA. (*Pointing, now thoroughly frightened.*) Yonder.

MRS. JOPLIN. (*In a gruff voice, born of fear, halfway pointing the gun to have it ready.*) Who's that out there? What do you want?

ELLA. (*After a tense moment, almost screaming.*) He's there, all right! See—he's moving! (*The two women draw away across the stage as the stranger enters slowly.*)

MRS. JOPLIN. (*With relief.*) Why, it's a white man. (*She relaxes the gun and puts its against the post, stepping back onto the porch as he speaks.*)

(*At first glance the stranger suggests a tramp, but a longer scrutiny reveals that he may more probably be a respectable workman, disheveled and travel-stained from an indefinite journey. Over his shoulder is slung a battered brown satchel.*)

STRANGER. Good evening, folks. Hope I ain't scared you? Could you spare a passing traveler a bit of water to drink?

MRS. JOPLIN. (*Hospitably offering him the dipper.*) Why, surely, here's some fresh drawed. (*She hands him the dipper. He drinks with a show of gratefulness.*)

STRANGER. My, that's fine water, lady. It's a fact—you've got a good well there.

MRS. JOPLIN. We likes it. The water always comes up good and cold. (*He hands back the dipper.*) Will you have some more?

STRANGER. No, much obliged. It's getting late, I guess I'll start on the road again. (*He looks hard at* ELLA, *makes a false start at going, then turns as if on sudden impulse. He speaks to* ELLA.) Pardon my speakin' of it, Ma'arm, but do you know I had quite a start when I first looked at you. You're that like my wife. I thought I was dreaming when I got a good sight of your face.

ELLA. (*Completely credulous.*) Aw, really?

STRANGER. That's a fact, and say, my wife's one fine-looking woman. I wouldn't be down in this part of the world tonight if my wife hadn't sent me. I wanted her to come in my place this year, but she says to me: "You go. Folks wouldn't believe the truth if they saw me now, and I was to tell them." Well, say, when I think of her four years ago, I know she's right. It just seems like a miracle, that's all, a plain out and out miracle.

ELLA. (*Interested.*) What happened four years ago?

STRANGER. (*Coming closer to her.*) Lady, have you seen one of these here sickly women that gets all pulled down and don't nothin' do no more good. Up in the morning, back in bed before 'leven. Backache, headache—can't eat nothin,' can't do nothin,' weak as a fly. Payin' out enough money in doctors and drugstore stuff to build a new barn. Always swallowing pills and making faces at a tablespoon. If I say it who shouldn't, that was a life-size picture of my wife. (*During this speech* MRS. JOPLIN *steps down from the side of the porch at the left and comes around down the stage to the box, where she seats herself during the stranger's next long speech. Both women listen to him with interest.*)

MRS. JOPLIN. Pore thing!

ELLA. Sounds like Mrs. Pittard up on Dry Creek, don't it, Ma? Don't nothin' seem to do her any good at all.

MRS. JOPLIN. (*Laughing softly.*) It shore do.

STRANGER. Well, folks, it run on until I just got plum discouraged. We kep' throwing our money to the drug trusts—and I guess we'd still be doing it today if my wife hadn't happened to hear of Nakomis and Korno. (*He pauses dramatically.*)

ELLA. (*Interested.*) Who's them?

STRANGER. I'm glad you asked me that, lady. Korno is just about the most wonderful thing I ever heard of, and you'll agree with me. Some day the women of America is going to build a monument to Korno and old Nakomis. Korno, that's the greatest boon known to woman. Nakomis was the old Indian squaw that give my wife the secret. Look here—(*He opens the satchel and takes out two bottles of red liquid which he stands on the water shelf.*) You've always heard how the Indians made the women do all the work. Folks, the Indians didn't make them—they couldn't keep 'em from it. Every Indian woman knowed about Korno. They took Korno and it kept them strong—they'd rather do the work themselves than fool with the men. Look at it, folks. (*He holds another bottle up so that it catches the light of the lamp.*) Look how it sparkles with health. Korno, the great Indian secret. That's what put my wife on her feet again. That's what makes her able to do a week's washing and start out smilin' after supper to a church social. How do I happen to be here tonight? Listen. It all came to my wife in a dream. One night an Indian woman appeared to her in a vision holding up a bottle of Korno, and the next day she says to me: George, we've got to give the women of America a chance to know about Korno. I'll look after the farm, you go and tell them. Well, folks, here I am. (*He takes four bottles out of his satchel and stands them in a row on the water shelf.*) If I was a drug trust, I'd charge you five dollars a bottle. After you've taken one bottle, you wouldn't be without a bottle if you had to pay fifty. But I ain't no profiteer. Now I'm goin' to let you have these six bottles—

ELLA. (*Bursting out suddenly.*) Ma, here's Ed!

(*The stranger's spell is broken by the entrance of* ED JOPLIN. *He is a healthy, smooth-faced farmer about thirty-three—dressed in everyday working clothes and carrying a shotgun. He has inherited some of the emotional capacity of his mother and is deeply moved by what he has just witnessed—so deeply, he tries to appear indifferent with only partial success. From the moment he comes on, the women forget all about the existence of Korno. They crowd about* ED *in their in-*

*terest while the stranger stands apart on the right listening.* ED *is too full of his news to notice him.*)

ED. (*After entering.*) Well, we got him. (*He walks to the center of stage and leans his gun against the left post.*)

ELLA. What did you do with him?

ED. (*To stranger as he puts down gun.*) Howdy.

STRANGER. Howdy.

ED. (*Still struggling to appear unmoved and stepping onto porch, where he washes his hands in wash basin.*) If they ain't cut him down yet, I guess he's still hanging to one of them trees in Squire Tatum's upper pasture. He won't never bother nobody else. I didn't count 'em, but I reckon there's fifty bullet holes in him. Let alone buckshot.

ELLA. How'd you ketch him?

(MRS. JOPLIN *follows* ED *onto the porch and stands in the doorway, handing him the towel as he turns to reach for it. He finishes, wipes his hands and throwing the towel back to his mother, steps down into the yard, giving his recital of the lynching in the center of the stage.* MRS. JOPLIN *stands listening by the water shelf, but as* ED *talks, in her intensity she steps down from side of porch and comes to stand by* ELLA *in the yard.*)

ED. That warn't hard. I got over to the Squire's place about the same time as Sim Butler. He had picked up Brother Williams and the Willard boys. Mrs. Tatum's brother met us and told us how the Squire had words with the nigger yesterday and how they found the Squire lying murdered in the hall of the barn.

MRS. JOPLIN. It must have been an awful thing.

ED. (*Coming into the yard again.*) While he was talking, they come bringing the nigger's wife up from her cabin. She let on she didn't know nothin.' She said the nigger took his gun after dinner and said he was going squirrel hunting up on the hill. Sim Butler grabs her by the arm. He shows her a big black-snake whip and tells her if she's lying—we wouldn't leave an inch of skin on her brown body. But she takes on and swears she didn't know nothin' 'tall. 'Bout fifty of us there then. Looked like the whole north end of Dry Creek County had got there while we was talkin'!

MRS. JOPLIN. It don't take long for news of that kind to draw a crowd.

ED. Sim Butler sort of took charge of things. Well, he says, it don't look like there's but one thing to do—find the nigger. We scattered out and we come on him down in the thick woods. The Williams boys just ahead of me seen him first and hollered to him to stop. We figured, havin' a gun, he was goin' to make fight and we was ready for him to start, but he was a foxy devil. He just stop and answer back perlite like. He let on he didn't know nothin' 'bout nothin' and he'd shot a squirrel, pretending to be really out hunting. But Yancy Williams walks up to him and grabs his gun out of his hand. Gimme that gun, you black—(*Turning to stranger*)—and Yancy shore did cuss him. "Where the hell do you think you're running away to?" and he let his fist go up against the nigger's head.

ELLA. Where was the others?

ED. We hollered 'em up and they come running . . . . I never before seen a nigger so near the color of ashes. At first he kept sayin' he didn't know nothing at all about it. He'd beg and cry and call on God as witness.

Some of them was for stopping his blasphemy with a rope right away. But Sim kept cool and held them back. "Men," he says, "I'm for law and order and justice. There's times when God-fearing, law-abiding citizens don't need no courts to help them do their duty. Squire Tatum lies down yonder murdered. We all know he had words with this nigger yesterday. And it don't take much to see who done the deed. But we ain't going to be hasty. There warn't any witnesses, so we're going to give this low down black scoundrel a chance to tell the truth and confess his crime before we send his soul to hell—if the scrimey ape's got a soul." With that Walter Williams hauls off and knocks the nigger down, shoutin,' "Confess, you black baboon, or we'll burn you alive." Sim kept Walter from hitting him again, but half a dozen of them began to yell. "Burn him—build a fire——" The nigger was on his knees cryin' and pleadin.' For a minute I thought they was going to burn him, in spite of everything, but Sim didn't lose his head. "Wait a minute, men, hold steady. I agree with you, he don't deserve no consideration, but we'll be generous. We'll give him a chance. If he'll confess, we'll only hang him. If he don't— Well, boys, we'll give him a minute to make up his mind how he's going to die before we start gathering the wood." Then Sim turns to the nigger who was down on his knees hollerin' and beggin.' "Stand up," shouts Sim. Two or three that was closest grabs him by the collar and pulls him up. His eye was swelling where Walter had hit him, and he couldn't no more have stood than a tadpole, if they hadn't held him. He kept moanin' he hadn't done it, until at last Sim gets out of patience and shouts, "All right boys, 'tain't no use wastin' no more time. Git your fire ready . . ." Look like it took about half a minute for it to get through that nigger's head who was goin' to be burned. Then all of a sudden, it come to him. I thought he was takin' on before. He hadn't started. "Don't burn me, oh Lawdy, don't burn me. Oh boss, I don't know what it is, but if you say I done it, I done it, just don't burn me. I done it all."

STRANGER. (*Who has been listening to the recital much moved, breaking out surprised in spite of himself.*) He confessed!

ED. (*Turning with a sort of scorn that it should be doubted.*) He did that, and it wasn't three minutes before he was hanging from a tree, fuller bullets as a rake is full er teeth. (ED *sits down on edge of porch and slips off shoes, standing up again in his sock feet.*)

ELLA. I reckon he would confess.

ED. I reckon he did. Mighty little good it would have done him, not confessing. Everybody knows he slipped up behind Squire Tatum in his own barn and murdered him with an axe handle. (*The* STRANGER *involuntarily turns away—on his face is written genuine horror and surprise. He tries to get hold of himself, but with difficulty.*)

ELLA. When are they goin' to have the Squire's buryin'?

ED. That warn't settled when I left. Sim said he'd stop by and let us know. He's going back tonight and set up with the corpse.

ELLA. Did they find the Squire's watch the nigger stole?

ED. No. Just before they put the rope around his neck, somebody thought of that and they stopped long enough to search for it. Sim tried to make him tell what he done with it, but shucks, that nigger was so scared, he didn't know his name.

ELLA. Hid it, I reckon. Maybe his wife's got it. (*The* STRANGER *looks about, anxious to go, but he is afraid to leave abruptly for fear of causing suspicion. The battle between flight and boldness is plain.*)

MRS. JOPLIN. Pore Mrs. Tatum, how was she?

ED. I didn't see her. Mrs. Williams and some of the women folks that come over when they heard the news was alookin' after her. They say she kept moanin' over and over, if the Squire only hadn't had such a terrible temper. She knowed all along something terrible would come of it some day. She knowed it was coming.

ELLA. He did have a powerful mean temper. (*The* STRANGER'S *face becomes dark and his fists clench slightly as though he remembered an insult.*)

ED. (*Picking up shoes and gun.*) He had a nasty way with strangers, but when you got to know him, he was all right . . . I'll just put up this gun. There's four mules and a passle of pigs that's got to be fed. I heard them pigs squealin' clean down on the road as I come up. (*He goes into the house followed by* ELLA. *The* STRANGER *stands eyeing* MRS. JOPLIN *irresolutely. His gaze shifts from her to the six bottles of Korno and he walks toward the shelf. She steps on to the porch and turns to him. He is not sure how to make the break of going.*)

MRS. JOPLIN. (*Interpreting his agitation.*) I saw how you took it when Ed was a-tellin' it.

STRANGER. (*Alarmed.*) Why, I don't know anything at all about it. I . . . . .

MRS. JOPLIN. Oh, I reckon I can understand how you feel, all right. *You* come from far off yonder where they don't have niggers. You can't make out how Christian men can do what you heard tell tonight.

STRANGER. (*Quickly.*) I don't blame anybody.

MRS. JOPLIN. Well, I could see how you took it. Strangers always feel that way.

STRANGER. (*Anxious to have done and leave.*) He confessed, he said he did it.

MRS. JOPLIN. I reckon there ain't any doubt about that.

STRANGER. (*Looks at her quickly and seeing that she is in earnest, is relieved.*) No.

MRS. JOPLIN. You can't make out how my Ed and the rest of them could do what they done today. How they could hunt a human being and kill him like a wild animal.

STRANGER. (*Beginning to be out of patience.*) I told you, lady, I don't blame nobody. (*He starts slowly to put the bottles on the shelf back into his kit.*) I guess I'll be getting along. It's late.

MRS. JOPLIN. (*Walking to the edge of the porch and resting against the post.*) You needn't keep pretendin.' Maybe you're just sensitive like and easily affected. It's easy to read it on your face. (*He stops putting away the bottles and turns toward her.*) But the right and wrong of it ain't as simple as you might think. I ain't never read it in no book and my Ed and the rest'll not admit it if you ask them, but it was being afraid that drove 'em to do what they done today. When the niggers were brought from that there African wilderness—they brung something along with them that folks didn't know was coming. Something that belongs to the wilderness—that ain't got no place in a white man's land, and never will. Niggers has got used to Christian clothes, they don't put rings in their noses no more, and some of them's ironed most of the kink out of their hair. But they ain't never got rid of that other thing, and civilization and laws ain't no good for it. Mostly it's asleep now, but you can't never tell when it's going to wake up—when it's going to lie waiting for you like one of them African animals they has in cages at the circus would. When it is awake, it don't know any language except what them animals knows. That's why no white woman dares go down a lonely road, or cross a field after dark. That's why Ed don't like to ride at night without his gun. It's fighting that wild thing, men are, when they do what they did today. Just like Ed hangs up a dead crow in a field.

STRANGER. (*Who has been fiercely occupied with his own thoughts.*) He had a terrible temper. They said just now he couldn't be civil to strangers.

MRS. JOPLIN. (*Bewildered.*) What?

STRANGER. Him—the one—the nigger—*killed.*

MRS. JOPLIN. Squire Tatum?

STRANGER. His wife knew. She understood. She said he'd bring an end like that. Maybe he only got what was coming to him. ( MRS. JOPLIN *stares at the* STRANGER, *unable to follow his words.* ELLA'S *voice comes from inside the house.*)

ELLA. Ma, come here a minute . . . Ma, did you move Ed's other shoes when you were cleanin' up this—(*Lost to audience.* MRS. JOPLIN *goes into the house. As she disappears, the* STRANGER *swiftly puts the last bottle into his satchel. He hesitates a moment, then as he walks toward the wood pile he draws something from his pocket in a fashion that gets the audience's sharp attention, and stands examining it darkly six counts, when* ELLA'S *voice is heard inside.)* All right, I'll tell him.

(*The* STRANGER *looks up guiltily and starts forward at the sound. He stumbles over the wood and drops the thing in his hand down among the lengths of wood. His first impulse is to get it back, but he hears the voice of* ELLA *coming back and realizes he hasn't time. With sudden decision, he makes a bolt and exits swiftly to* R.)

ELLA. (*After four counts, coming from inside the house.*) Mister—we don't want—where—why, he isn't here. (*Calling.*) Ma, he's done gone. He ain't here nowhere and he's took the bottles. (*Looking for him down in the yard.*)

MRS. JOPLIN. (*Entering from the house and following* ELLA *into the yard to look, then stepping back on the edge of the porch.*) That's queer. Medicine men ain't usually so quick to go without having a sight of your pocket book. He seemed kinder upset by what Ed said—yankee, I reckon. Aw, Ella just bring in an arm of that wood while you're out there and pick up a few of them little tiny pipe splinters for in the morning. (*She holds the lantern up for* ELLA *to see and* ELLA, *who has been peering left into the darkness to see if she can discover the departing* STRANGER, *comes slowly over to the wood and picks up several sticks which she lays across her arm. Then she catches sight of something shining—the thing the* STRANGER *had thrown there. As she picks it up, she lets the wood slip from her arm in surprise.*)

NOTE. *If it is easier for the actors, the* STRANGER *may on sudden impulse hide the watch in the woodpile, when he hears* ELLA'*s voice inside the house, instead of dropping it down among the wood.*)

MRS. JOPLIN. What's the matter? (*Brings lantern to yard to meet her.*)

ELLA. (*Bringing the thing over to the light.*) Ma—Ma—here's a watch. (*Very slowly in her amazement.*) It was lying down there among the wood, Ma—(*She pauses to examine it by the lamp—then looks at* MRS. JOPLIN. *Each word very slowly as her mind gradually grasps the full implication.*) It's Squire Tatum's watch. (*With sudden comprehension but slowly, with intensity.*) That nigger was here this afternoon. I told you Ed ought not to leave us alone. (*The two women stand staring at one another in horror at what they are both thinking.*)

CURTAIN.

# THE WIDOW OF WASDALE HEAD

A FANTASY IN ONE ACT

## SIR ARTHUR WING PINERO

Sir Arthur Wing Pinero was born at London in 1855. His earliest plays were written in the 70's while he was an actor in Sir Henry Irving's company at the Lyceum Theater. By all accounts he was not a great actor, but the five years training he received on the stage was undoubtedly of great assistance to him in his subsequent career. Although Pinero was one of the important figures in the so-called "Renascence of the English Drama," and wrote many interesting and amusing long plays, he has occasionally, of late years, turned his hand to the one-act form. "Playgoers," "A Seat in the Park," and "The Widow of Wasdale Head" are proof of his skill in handling a single situation in a thoroughly masterful fashion.

Following is a list of the published plays of Sir Arthur Wing Pinero: "The Magistrate;" "The Schoolmistress;" "The Hobby-Horse;" "Sweet Lavender;" "The Weaker Sex;" "The Profligate;" "The Cabinet Minister;" "Lady Bountiful;" "The Times;" "The Amazons;" "The Second Mrs. Tanqueray;" "The Notorious Mrs. Ebbsmith;" "The Gay Lord Quex;" "Iris;" "Letty;" "A Wife Without a Smile;" "His House in Order;" "The Thunderbolt;" "Mid-Channel;" "Preserving Mr. Panmure;" "The 'Mind-the-Paint' Girl;" "The Big Drum;" "The Enchanted Cottage;" "The Freaks;" "The Benefit of the Doubt;" "Trelawney of the 'Wells';" "The Money-Spinner;" "The Squire;" "The Rocket;" "In Chancery;" "Hester's Mystery;" "The Princess and the Butterfly;" "Playgoers;" "A Seat in the Park;" "The Widow of Wasdale Head."

References: A. E. Morgan, "Tendencies of Modern English Drama"; T. H. Dickinson, "The Contemporary Drama of England"; Barrett H. Clark, "A Study of the Modern Drama."

# THE WIDOW OF WASDALE HEAD*

## CHARACTERS

Sir John Hunslet
Mr. Edward Fane
Tubal (*A servant at the inn*)
Reuben (*Sir John's man*)
The Visitor
Mrs. Jesmond

Scene: *A room in an inn at Wasdale Head in Cumberland*

Time: *In the reign of George the Third.*

*A gloomy, ancient room, partly panelled in oak, of the time of Henry the Eighth. Its ceiling, heavy with massive beams, is blackened by age; and altogether the apartment, which bears the appearance of having once belonged to a private mansion, is fallen considerably into decay. In the wall on the right there is a cavernous fireplace; facing the spectator is a deep baywindow, heavily shuttered and barred; on the left of the window, against the farther wall, a steep staircase mounts to a landing from which a door opens into a narrow passage; and under the landing, in the left-hand wall and on the level of the floor, there is another door, also admitting to a passage.*

*In the middle of the room there is a round table with a chair on its right and left. A decanter of red wine and some glasses, a jar of tobacco and a tray of clay pipes, and a candlestick of two branches are on the table. Against the wall on the left, a chair on each side of it, is an escritoire, and on the top of the escritoire is a standish; and against the staircase, concealing the space beneath, there is an oaken dresser bright with crockery ware, pewter dishes and plates, and utensils. In the bay of the window are a small table and stool. A riding-cloak is thrown over the stool, and lying upon the table are a hat, a riding-whip, a pair of gauntlets, and two pistols in their holster-cases. A capacious arm-chair stands before the fireplace, and within the fire-place, at the farther side, there is a chimney-seat. A clock and a chest filled with logs occupy spaces against the right-hand wall; and on the wall against which runs the flight of stairs a number of hunting trophies are arranged, including a hunting-horn hanging by a cord from a nail.*

*The room is lighted by the candle on the round table and by candles in sconces attached to the wall on the left. A fire is burning.* (*Note*: *Throughout, "right" and "left" are the spectators' right and left, not the actor's.*)

*Seated at the round table, the one smoking and drinking, the other deep in thought, are* SIR JOHN HUNSLET *and* EDWARD FANE TUBAL *is engaged at the dresser. The wind is moaning.*

SIR JOHN. (*A gallant-looking gentleman of eight-and-twenty, accoutred in a handsome riding-dress and a periwig—on the left of the table.*) Ned, my dear fellow, you don't drink!

EDWARD. (*A grave young man of twenty-five, richly but soberly attired and wearing his own dark hair—rousing himself and filling his glass.*) A thousand pardons, Jack! (*Drinking.*) Welcome! (TUBAL, *bearing a pair of snuffers upon a dish, advances to the round table and trims the candles. The moaning of the wind rises to a howl.*)

SIR JOHN. (*To* TUBAL.) A wild night, my friend.

TUBAL. (*A venerable, wizen figure, half groom, half

*waiter.*) Aye, an' 'tis like t' be warser afwore mworn. Theer'll be sleats lowsed an' fleein' this neet, depend on't. Heav'n send th' chimley-stacks do hod oot!

SIR JOHN. Amen! (TUBAL *replaces the snuffers upon the dresser. There is a sharp, shrill sound from without, resembling the cry of a bird.*) What is that?

EDWARD. The sign of the house. 'Twill creak in that fashion, in the wind, for hours.

SIR JOHN. 'Gad, an aggreeable prospect! (TUBAL, *carrying a tray upon which are some remnants of a meal, goes out at the door under the landing.* SIR JOHN, *glancing over his shoulder, assures himself that he and* EDWARD *are alone.*) At last! (*Rekindling his pipe at the flame of one of the candles.*) I thought that ancient servitor would never leave us. (EDWARD *rises and walking away, stands gazing into the fire.*) And now, my dear Ned—my very dear Ned—*in amicitiâ autem nihil fictum,* as we learned to say at school—let me inform you without further delay of the cause of this intrusion.

EDWARD. 'Tis no intrusion; and, to be candid, I have guessed the object of your visit already.

SIR JOHN. Indeed? That being the case——

EDWARD. Confound you, Jack, you don't suppose I attribute your sudden and unlooked-for appearance to mere inclination for a gossip over a bottle! A man—Jack Hunslet least of all—does not quit town at this time of the year, journeying three hundred miles into the bargain, without an urgent reason. (*Facing* SIR JOHN.) Confess you are upon a mission.

SIR JOHN. (*Smiling.*) Since you press me——

EDWARD. You are sent by my mother.

SIR JOHN. The poor fond lady is vastly concerned at your absence.

EDWARD. In the name of patience, why? Her letters plague me to death, Jack.

SIR JOHN. My good Ned, do, I entreat, reflect. With your usual perspicacity you have just observed that it must be a strong inducement that draws a town man into the country at this season. And yet——

EDWARD. Such an inducement was mine. I came into Cumberland in fulfilment of a pledge to Sir Roger Boultwood—a pledge of long standing——

SIR JOHN. To be his guest at Hawkshead Priory. Your stay at Hawkshead ended two months ago.

EDWARD. In the meantime I had become bitten by the romantic beauty of the district. By the Lord, Jack, 'tis a lovely locality, in spite of flood and tempest!

SIR JOHN. Ah, I am forgetting you are a poet, and a monstrous pretty one to boot!

EDWARD. Pshaw! Pray don't roast me for my follies.

SIR JOHN. (*Laying his pipe aside.*) My dear fellow, if our follies ceased with the scribbling of verses, we should be warranted in esteeming ourselves wise. (*Rising.*) And so 'tis solely the beauty of the district that detains you, hey, Ned?

EDWARD. Chance directed me to this particular spot; and my nag falling lame almost at the door here——

SIR JOHN. (*Approaching* EDWARD.) You determined to cultivate the muse, and to seek inspiration, by this sombre lake; (*producing his snuff-box*) putting up at a bare inn, (*significantly*) and dispatching your servant back to Kensington within a fortnight.

EDWARD. (*Embarrassed.*) Why, as for that, I—I found I had little need of Gregory. He did but kick his heels about the place discontentedly.

SIR JOHN. (*Taking snuff.*) The sublimity of the scene proving less attractive to him than to his master. (*Closing his snuff-box.*) Well?

EDWARD. W-well?

SIR JOHN. And when I have made my compliments at Hawkshead and, with your aid, explored this enchanting neighborhood, do we travel home in company? (*There is a moment's hesitation on* EDWARD's *part, and then he moves to the middle of the room without speaking.* SIR JOHN *looks after him inquiringly.*) Ned!

EDWARD. (*Hanging his head.*) Forgive me, Jack. I declare again 'tis the most beautiful district in the kingdom; nevertheless, I am deceiving you, Jack, woefully. (*The door under the landing opens and* MRS. JESMOND *enters followed by* TUBAL, *the latter carrying a bowl of steaming punch, and instantly the wind increases in force and the sign-board resumes its squeaking. The loud slamming of a distant door is also heard.* MRS. JESMOND *is an elegant, girlish young lady, charmingly but simply dressed. She curtsies to* SIR JOHN *and to* EDWARD *and then takes the bowl from* TUBAL *and places it upon the round table.*)

MRS. JESMOND. (*To* TUBAL.) Secure the doors of the buttery, Tubal; 'tis they that are banging. (TUBAL *shuffles out and* MRS. JESMOND *addresses* SIR JOHN, *who is regarding her with respectful amazement. The wind lulls.*) I am sorry I was not by to receive you, sir. Late as it was, I was at my farm at Burnthwaite where I am in trouble with some sick beasts. I hear you have rid from Ulverston to-day, which is a weary road.

SIR JOHN. (*Stammering.*) Why, yes, I—I——

EDWARD. (*Presenting* SIR JOHN.) This gentleman is my friend Sir John Hunslet——

MRS. JESMOND. (*Curtseying again.*) Nay, if I had not been apprised of his arrival, there would be no necessity to name him. (*Advancing to* SIR JOHN.) I saw Sir John once, when I was a child, driving his curricle in Hyde Park, and am never likely to forget the fine show he made.

SIR JOHN. (*Bowing low.*) Madam, I—I—I am vastly honoured by your recollection of the circumstances.

MRS. JESMOND. Mr. Fane is heartily glad to see you here, Sir John; of that I am assured. Wasdale Head is but a stern and solitary spot at all times, and March our dreariest month.

Sir John. 'Faith, ma'am, Mr. Fane is no more rejoiced to see me than I him. We were *condiscipuli* at Winchester College and I hold him in great affection. (*Bowing again profoundly.*) And suffer me to add that it increases my happiness in no inconsiderable degree——

Mrs. Jesmond. (*Turning to* edward *merrily.*) La! I fear Sir John doth not even yet apprehend who and what I am. Pray enlighten him.

Edward. (*On the left.*) Mrs. Jesmond, Jack, is mistress of this inn and tenant also of lands adjacent to it. (*Another bow from* sir john, *whose wonderment increases.*) 'Twill make you better acquainted with her when I tell you that she was Miss Woodroffe—Miss Elizabeth Woodroffe of Appleby.

Sir John. One of the Woodroffes of Appleby! (*Seizing* mrs. jesmond's *hand.*) My dear madam!

Mrs. Jesmond. (*Withdrawing her hand.*) Nay, sir; my family and I are at enmity. (*Mournfully.*) Widow of Mr. Henry Jesmond of Egremont; I prefer that description.

Sir John. A widow, ma'am!

Mrs. Jesmond. (*Dropping another curtsey.*) Two years a widow, and a humble taverner and farmer; and at your service. (*To* edward.) I have brought you a bowl of punch, Mr. Fane, thinking it will be grateful to your friend after his long journey. (*To* sir john.) 'Tis of my mixing, and I beg your indulgence for the widow's offering.

Sir John. 'Gad madam, I swear you shall join us! (*To* edward, *who goes to the dresser.*) A third glass Ned!

Mrs. Jesmond. (*Hastening to the staircase.*) Oh, mercy, Sir John——!

Sir John. (*Following her and regaining possession of her hand.*) I insist! (*Leading her to the round table.*) On my knees——!

MRS. JESMOND. (*Laughing.*) Ha, ha, ha!

(*The wind howls again and the sign-board creaks.* EDWARD *carries three glasses to the table, and* MRS. JESMOND *fills two of the glasses to the brim and hands them to the gentlemen who stand one on each side of her. As she ladles a little of the punch into the third glass, the wind abates.*)

SIR JOHN. (*At the right of the table.*) Come, ma'am; bumpers! Ah, but that's not fair! Bumpers! (*The men drink, and* MRS. JESMOND *touches her lips with her glass.*) 'Pon my soul, 'tis delicious! 'Tis nectar! *Ille facit dites animos deus*, Ned; you remember! (*To* MRS. JESMOND.) Permit me to compliment you on your skill, ma'am.

MRS. JESMOND. (*Replenishing the men's glasses, modestly.*) The credit is none of mine, Sir John. (*In a sad voice.*) 'Twas my dear Harry that taught me.

SIR JOHN. (*Coughing sympathetically.*) Ahem! Ahem! (*Abruptly.*) A toast! I call a toast, Ned! (*Raising his glass and looking at* MRS. JESMOND *with admiration.*) I give you——

MRS. JESMOND. (*Quickly, raising her glass.*) The King!

SIR JOHN. Why, certainly ma'am; and I am obleeged to you for the reminder. His Most Gracious Majesty King George!

EDWARD. (*Drinking.*) The King!

SIR JOHN. (*Drinking.*) God bless him! (*Looking at* MRS. JESMOND *again.*) Another!

MRS. JESMOND. Nay; spare me!

SIR JOHN. Ned! (*Raising his glass.*) To the Lady of Wasdale!

MRS. JESMOND. The Lady of Wasdale!

(*The wind gives a sudden roar as the men drink the toast, and then subsides.*)

MRS. JESMOND. (*Curtseying once more.*) The widow thanks you, gentlemen, for your amiability; and with a full heart. (*With a change of manner.*) And now, if you will excuse me, I will go to your bedchambers and see that your beds are properly prepared.

SIR JOHN. (*Seizing the candlestick from the round table.*) Allow me to light you, ma'am.

MRS. JESMOND. (*Running up the stairs.*) 'Tis not necessary; a lantern hangs in the corridor.

(*She makes a final curtsey on the landing and withdraws, leaving* SIR JOHN *half-way up the stairs where he remains for a while as if rooted.* EDWARD *walks over to the fireplace and again gazes down into the burning logs.*)

SIR JOHN. (*After a silence.*) As I live, an adorable creature! (*He descends the stairs softly, replaces the candlestick, and stands contemplating* EDWARD.) Ned!

EDWARD. Jack?

SIR JOHN. 'Pon my conscience, you are right; Wasdale is the most beautiful district in the kingdom!

EDWARD. (*Turning to him.*) Ah, Jack, 'tis no matter for jesting.

SIR JOHN. Jesting! I swear I am all seriousness.

EDWARD. (*Ardently.*) Nay, then, if you are in earnest, is she not charming?

SIR JOHN. Charming? A divinity! (*Walking about animatedly.*) 'Gad, you may well describe this as a romantic locality! A Woodroffe of Appleby the mistress of a house of public entertainment! Prodigious! (*Sitting in the chair on the left of the round table.*) How the devil——!

EDWARD. (*Coming to the right of the table.*) 'Tis a simple story. Young Mr. Henry Jesmond of Egremont, having squandered the greater part of his patrimony, established himself here, with what remained of his fortune, as farmer and innkeeper. A short time previously, he had met Miss Elizabeth Woodroffe at the Hunt Assembly at Kendal, and they had become desperately taken with each other. Her parents discovered the undesirable attachment, intercepted communication between the lovers and confined their child within doors. Vain precautions! Elizabeth forced an escape, ran off with the object of her girlish infatuation, and married him.

SIR JOHN. 'Faith, since she hath been two years a widow, he must have carried her to church in a go-cart!

EDWARD. She was indeed but fifteen. She is little over seventeen now.

SIR JOHN. The deuce! 'Twas a brief wedded life.

EDWARD. A month.

SIR JOHN. Good Lud!

EDWARD. Riding homeward on a dark night with some boon companions from the hunt at Muncaster, Mr. Jesmond was thrown and mortally hurt. He breathed long enough, so the tale is told, to take his pistol from its holster and to shoot his poor mare, who had broken a leg; and then he laid his head upon her warm ribs and stirred no more.

SIR JOHN. (*Shocked.*) My dear Ned! (*Fastidiously.*) Leaving this delicately-bred young lady, estranged from her family, to brew punch, and to till the soil, for her subsistence!

EDWARD. (*Sitting at the right of the table.*) Why, Jack, there's the wonder of it! Mrs. Jesmond's aptitude is amazing. Among the farmers hereabouts—statesmen, they term them in Cumberland—there's not one can match her in knowledge of crops and cattle. (*The wind murmurs gently, almost musically.*) I have seen the oldest and wisest of them approach her, hat in hand, to ask her counsel in a difficulty, and her reply is always the same.

SIR JOHN. The same?

EDWARD. "Come back to me," she will say, "as soon as you please after Friday, and you shall have my advice."

SIR JOHN. Friday?

EDWARD. (*Checking himself and then nodding uneasily.*) Er—'tis on a Friday night, when her household is abed and the inn is silent, that she sits here alone and reads her farming-manuals, and makes up her books of accounts, and puts on her considering-cap, as she phrases it. (*Looking around.*) We are in her parlour, Jack.

SIR JOHN. (*Listening.*) How the wind sings! It hath a voice in it, positively! (*To* EDWARD.) Her parlour?

EDWARD. (*Nodding again.*) Aye; the principal guest-chambers are shut throughout the winter, and so she hath placed her room at my disposal. Every Friday night, at the stroke of ten, I leave her here, preparing for her vigil. (*Suddenly.*) What is to-day?

SIR JOHN. Friday.

(*The wind utters a loud wail and the sign-board creaks.*)

EDWARD. (*Rising and glancing at the clock.*) And look; 'tis close on ten now.

(*He resumes his former position at the fireplace and the wind its tuneful murmuring.*)

SIR JOHN. (*After another silence.*) Well, I own I am mightily relieved, Ned. (*Rising.*) 'Tis precisely as I suspected—that you had become entangled in a petticoat; (*going to the punch-bowl and helping himself to punch*) but a Woodroffe of Appleby is naught to be ashamed of, though 'twill be the tittle-tattle of the clubs and tea-tables that your mistress hath kept a mug-house. (*Drinking.*) Have you declared yourself yet?

EDWARD. (*Still staring into the fire.*) No.

SIR JOHN. (*Smacking his lips.*) 'Pon my honour, she is vastly genteel; she hath the *bel air* completely! I wager many of our town misses and madams—(*He breaks off, regarding* EDWARD *with surprise. The wind ceases.*) Why, man, what ails you? If Mrs. Jesmond had declined your suit, you could hardly be more glum.

EDWARD. (*Confronting* SIR JOHN.) Jack!

SIR JOHN. (*Staring at* EDWARD's *aspect.*) Ned?

EDWARD. Oh, Jack, I must confide in you! I am in torture!

SIR JOHN. Torture?

EDWARD. Terrible, grinding torment!

SIR JOHN. (*Joining* EDWARD.) Odds life, what's this! Have you discovered that the widow wears a false curl or two?

EDWARD. For mercy's sake, don't take me lightly! (*In a whisper.*) Jack, there is a mystery in this house.

SIR JOHN. Confusion!

EDWARD. A hideous mystery. (*Passing* SIR JOHN *and pacing the room on the left.*) And 'tis torturing me—driving me to destruction; and yet I lack the courage to attempt to unravel it.

SIR JOHN. (*Coming to the round table.*) Explain, Ned!

EDWARD. Oh, Jack, 'tis true that I leave Mrs. Jesmond here, and alone, every Friday night; (*halting*) but—Heaven forgive me for doubting her!—(*laughing mirthlessly*) ha, ha, ha, ha!—I feel she doesn't remain alone, Jack.

SIR JOHN. The devil!

EDWARD. (*Gripping the back of the chair at the left of the round table.*) Hell fury, no; unless she hath the habit of talking to herself, her vigil is no solitary one!

SIR JOHN. Talking to herself!

EDWARD. (*Sitting and putting his elbows on the table and digging his fingers into his hair.*) Ha, ha, ha, ha! (*Groaning.*) Oh, Jack, Jack!

(*Again there is a pause.* SIR JOHN *slowly produces his snuff-box.*)

SIR JOHN. Humph! (*Tapping the box.*) 'Gad, you disappoint me, Ned; you do really! Who would have thought it of her? (*Taking snuff.*) Pish! The jades; they are all of a pattern! (*To* EDWARD.) When——? (*The wind revives.*)

EDWARD. (*Raising his head.*) 'Twas the Friday night in the second week of my lodging here, and I had retired to my bedchamber carrying with me the delightful vision of her graceful, slender form as she sat, in this chair, bending over her books and papers. Some time after reaching my apartment, I recollected that I had left a letter from my mother lying upon the escritoire yonder; and I ordered my servant to fetch it. Presently the man reappeared, saying that, hearing Mrs. Jesmond's voice apparently in conversation, he had deemed it prudent not to risk incurring her displeasure by disturbing her.

SIR JOHN. In conversation?

EDWARD. I dismissed Gregory and stood for a while at my window, viewing the thick clouds scudding across the Pikes. Suddenly the idea possessed me to return, myself, to this room and recover my letter. Ha! The letter contained nothing of a private nature. I perceive now that 'twas merely a feeling of jealous surprise that impelled me.

SIR JOHN. (*His foot upon the rail of the chair on the right of the round table.*) You returned?

EDWARD. Yes. My ear was at the door, and I was wavering whether I should rap, when I was arrested by a sound behind me; and there was my servant, sheltered in an angle of the corridor, watching me curiously. I made an idle remark and again retired to my room; and the next morning I packed the fellow off to London, lest, his suspicions being aroused, he should play the spy on his own account.

SIR JOHN. What had you heard while listening at the door?

EDWARD. The low muttering of a voice, or of voices. I could distinguish nothing clearly, save that there was talking. (*Glancing at the door on the landing.*) The door is stout and, as you see, distant.

SIR JOHN. And since then?

EDWARD. Every Friday night 'tis the same. I steal to the door, hear the same whisperings, and slink back irresolutely to my bedchamber. Stay! Twice or thrice I have heard a soft, wailful note, as if from an instrument, proceeding from this room.

SIR JOHN. (*Bringing himself erect.*) A signal!

EDWARD. 'Sdeath, the thought hath crossed my mind! (*He rises and, ascending the stairs, removes the hunting-horn from its nail.*) 'Tis such an instrument as this that would produce the sound.

SIR JOHN. (*Following* EDWARD *and standing by the dresser.*) A hunting-horn.

EDWARD. 'Twas the property of the late Mr. Jesmond, I suspect. (*Doubtfully.*) But 'tis dull for want of use.

SIR JOHN. Nay, 'tis you that are dull. Look if its mouth is bright.

EDWARD. (*Examining the mouth of the horn.*) Why, yes; the metal here shines like a guinea!

SIR JOHN. Ha! I lay five to four that is not the only mouth pressed by those lips of hers! (EDWARD *replaces the horn and decends the stairs.*) My poor dear Ned, 'tis as plain as noonday; the widow's weekly vigil is but a ruse for entertaining her amoret at her ease. The trull! *Fronti nulla fides!* But you shall expose her, and to-night. (*Looking at the door on the landing and then pointing to the fire.*) Quick; some ashes from the hearth! I'll fill the lock with 'em and stop her turning the key.

EDWARD. (*Who is again at the fireplace gazing into the logs.*) There is no lock on either door. They are bolted from without.

SIR JOHN. Strange! The widow is somewhat incautious. However, 'twill make your task the easier. (EDWARD *faces* SIR JOHN *with a gesture of protest.*) Come, man, away with your scruples! We will leave the pretty witch to her pretence of poring over her damnable books; and then you shall return and walk boldly in, and interrupt her at her devotions.

EDWARD. By what right, Jack?

SIR JOHN. Pshaw! Do you imagine she isn't aware that you are honestly enamoured of her, though no word hath yet been spoke? *There* is title sufficient for you.

(*Sharply.*) Is your sword hanging in your bedchamber?

EDWARD. Yes.

SIR JOHN. Put it up at your side.

EDWARD. Why, would you have me a murderer as well as an eavesdropper?

SIR JOHN. 'Faith, I'd have you ready to defend yourself. A young lady of *ton* would scarcely dally with one of the clods of this beautiful district. (*Going to the table in the bay of the window and examining the pistols.*) 'Tis to a gentleman of the road, probably—a cut-throat highwayman—that she extends her hospitality. (*Taking up his hat, whip, and gauntlets, and carefully laying his cloak over the pistols.*) These pistols are well primed. I'll warn Reuben not to remove them.

EDWARD. (*Bursting out.*) Oh, Jack, Jack, 'tis impossible!

SIR JOHN. Impossible?

EDWARD. (*Walking across the room.*) 'Tis impossible that she should be frail. I'll not believe it. She hath the look and the bearing of an angel. Her eyes, Jack! Did you observe her eyes?

SIR JOHN. (*Standing with his back to the fire.*) Hang 'em, they *are* brilliant!

EDWARD. Nay, they're not brilliant. They resemble the blue of a summer morning ere the mist is dispelled. (*Pacing up and down.*) Her voice, too! Her voice!

SIR JOHN. 'Tis most musical, I admit.

EDWARD. Her voice hath the quality of the harp in it, when its strings are half muffled. (*Fiercely.*) Mark me, Jack, if I find her no better then she should be, I'll never trust woman again!

SIR JOHN. (*Taking snuff.*) Ned——

EDWARD. Never! Never!

SIR JOHN. Ned, I protest you recall Mr. Garrick to me, as the blackamoor in Shakespeare's play.

Edward. Ah——!

Sir John. When the great little man quits the stage ,you shall fill his place, my dear Ned; I vow you shall.

(*The wind swells for a moment as* mrs. jesmond *enters at the door under the landing, followed by* tubal, *with a lantern, and by* reuben *who is carrying two lighted candles in candlesticks.* tubal *goes to the window and, raising the lantern above his head, passes his hand over the bars of the shutters.*)

Mrs. Jesmond. (*To* edward, *sweetly but gravely.*) 'Tis past ten o'clock. (*Glancing at* sir john.) You have told Sir John?

Sir John. (*Advancing a few steps.*) Why, yes, ma'am; and, to say the truth, I shall not be sorry to find myself in a soft bed, and between a pair of sweet-smelling sheets, at an earlier hour than is customable with me.

Reuben. (*A bluff, burly fellow—standing by the table.*) Nor I either, sir. For of all the clattering, gusty places I've ever laid in, this Wasdale is the gustiest and the clatteringest—(*to* mrs. jesmond) saving your presence, Ma'am.

Sir John. Silence, Reuben! (*To* mrs. jesmond, *with a wave of the hand towards* reuben.) A good, faithful animal, Mrs. Jesmond, but plaguily rough-tongued.

Reuben. Well, sir, my tongue can't be rougher than the Cumberland weather; that's one comfort. (*Going to* edward *and presenting him with a candlestick as* mrs. jesmond *crosses to* sir john.) You'd best shield it with your hand, Mr. Fane——

Mrs. Jesmond. (*To* sir john.) Good-night, Sir John. (*Curtseying.*) 'Tis mighty civil of you to profess your willingness to be sent to bed like a bad child. (*Giving him her hand.*) You must dream you are in London, sir, and card-playing *en petit comité* with some choice cronies.

Sir John. (*Bending over her hand.*) Nay, madam, my dreams shall be of a far more interesting sort, I promise you. (*She curtsies to him again and returns to* EDWARD *who is watching her narrowly.* TUBAL *is now at the fireside, and* REUBEN *at the table in the bay window.*)

MRS. JESMOND. (*Giving her hand to* EDWARD, *a note of tenderness in her voice.*) Good-night, Mr. Fane.

EDWARD. (*With downcast eyes.*) Good-night.

(*He moves away and* MRS. JESMOND *goes to the escritoire and opens it with a key which dangles with others from her waist. Seeing that* REUBEN *is taking up the riding-cloak and the pistols,* SIR JOHN *hastens to him on tiptoe.*)

SIR JOHN. (*Under his breath, to* REUBEN.) No!

REUBEN. (*Astonished.*) Sir!

SIR JOHN. (*His fingers to his lips.*) Ssst! (*He motions to* REUBEN *to replace the pistols and riding-cloak.* REUBEN *does it.*) And now, my dear Ned—(*taking his candle from* REUBEN *and yawning demonstratively*) ah-h-h-h!—I declare I am as sleepy as the veriest owl. (*He signs to* EDWARD *to precede him, but* EDWARD *yields him the* pas.) My dear fellow! (*He ascends the stairs,* EDWARD *following him, as* MRS. JESMOND *carries some books to the round table and deposits them there.* SIR JOHN *makes her a grand bow from the landing,* EDWARD *a lesser one.*) My dear Madam! (MRS. JESMOND *curtsies to them deeply and returns to the escritoire.* SIR JOHN *and* EDWARD *retire.* TUBAL *shuffles across the room on his way to the door under the landing.*)

REUBEN. (*In a low voice, clapping* TUBAL *on the back.*) Good-night, old buck! (TUBAL *has a fit of coughing.*) Why, a man of your kidney should be in London. You'd turn all the girl's heads in London within a week. (*To* MRS. JESMOND, *as he goes up the stairs.*) Good-night, ma'am.

MRS. JESMOND. (*Bringing more books and some papers to the table.*) Good-night, friend.

(REUBEN *withdraws, closing the door.*)

TUBAL. (*At the door under the landing, to* MRS. JESMOND.) Be theer owt else I can do fer'ee?

MRS. JESMOND. No, I thank you, Tubal. Are the maids in their beds?

TUBAL. Aye, an' deid asleeap, I reckon, t'hussies! Good-neet, mistress.

MRS. JESMOND. Good-night.

(TUBAL *disappears, closing the door, and the wind again becomes violent and the sign-board squeals as if in pain.* MRS. JESMOND *remains quite still for a while; then, deliberately and methodically, and with an altered look on her face, she clears the table of the punch-bowl, the decanter and glasses, and the pipes and tobacco—carrying them to the dresser—and fetches the standish from the escritoire.*

*Having neatly set out her books and papers and the standish upon the table, she goes to the lower door, opens it a few inches and, after peeping along the passage, shuts the door silently. She repeats this proceeding at the door on the landing and finally, apparently satisfied, comes half-way down the stairs and unhooks the hunting-horn from the wall and blows a long, faint blast upon it; whereupon the wind gives a thundering bellow, the flames of the candles flicker, and for a moment there is almost total darkness. Then a bluish light pervades the room and the* GHOST *of a young man in hunting-dress and a bob-wig is seen, standing in an easy attitude with its back to the fire. There is another loud gust, followed by the crash of falling slates.*)

MRS. JESMOND. (*Regarding the* GHOST *with a tender expression and speaking in soft, caressing tones.*) That's the slates of the old lean-to in the stable-yard.

GHOST. (*In a calm, matter-of-fact manner.*) Well, you mun ha' 'em put on again, Betty. Gi'th' job to Hobbs at Ulverston. I'm sick o' Finch of Gosforth; leastways I *was*, before I met wi' my accident.

(MRS. JESMOND *replaces the hunting-horn and descends the stairs. Gradually the wind drops.*)

MRS. JESMOND. 'Tis a terrible night for you to be abroad, Hal. I had almost hoped you wouldn't obey my summons.

GHOST. (*Pulling off its filmy gloves.*) Eh, there you go, lass! How oft have I told thee th' weather makes no difference to me! (*Gloomily.*) All weather's one t' a ghost.

MRS. JESMOND. (*With a sigh.*) Yes, I forgot. (*Looking down at her books and papers.*) Shall we get to work?

GHOST. Aye, sit thee doon. (*She seats herself at the left of the table and chooses a pen from the standish.*) An' hark ye! If these winds continue t' blow, thou'dst best thing th' ewe flock off th' fells into th' lowlands. D'ye hear?

MRS. JESMOND. I hear, my dear.

GHOST. (*Taking out a spectral snuff-box and making a pretence of snuffing.*) Is there aught amiss this week here or at th' farms?

MRS. JESMOND. Four of the shorthorn bullocks at Burthwaite are lame from kibe. What am I to do for 'em?

GHOST. Kibe! Why, I gave thee a remedy for kibe a year since.

MRS. JESMOND. (*Pointing.*) I know you did, Hal; but I failed to note it.

GHOST. (*Dusting its neckcloth with the phantom of a pocket-handkerchief.*) I'm sorely afeared you've no head, Betty; thou'rt but a heedless, gay-hearted wench. What ha' you an' th' lads been doing for 't?

MRS. JESMOND. Rubbing tallow-fat betwixt the claws of the poor brutes.

GHOST. Tallow-fat!

MRS. JESMOND. Y-y-y-yes.

GHOST. Zounds, I marvel you ha'n't rubbed in some o'

th' sweet pomade thou hast sent thee from Lunnon for thy ringlets!

MRS. JESMOND. (*Sheepishly.*) He, he, he, he!

GHOST. Ods-bobs, you may well grin! 'Twould vastly tickle me, were I alive. Come, dip pen in th' ink! (*Dictating.*) "Kibe."

MRS. JESMOND. (*Writing in a book.*) "Kibe——"

GHOST. "Anoint wi' blue vitriol an' hog's lard——"

MRS. JESMOND. "Blue vitriol——"

GHOST. Williams at St. Bridget's will sell thee blue vitriol. (*She goes on writing.*) Mix th' stuff half-an'-half, an' within a fortnight th' beasts will be sound-footed.

MRS. JESMOND. (*Sanding her writing.*) Thank you, dear Harry.

GHOST. What's the next item, Bet?

MRS. JESMOND. (*Rummaging among her papers.*) The next—? (*Breaking off and gazing at the apparition wistfully.*) Hal——

GHOST. Hey?

MRS. JESMOND. (*In a voice full of yearning.*) Sit in thy chair to-night, yonder, while I am questioning thee, wilt thou?

GHOST. (*With an air of patronage.*) Certainly I will, child, if it will afford thee any gratification. (*Seating itself in the arm-chair.*) 'Tis all th' same t' a ghost whether he be sitting or standing or lying.

MRS. JESMOND. Yes, but it seems more domestic to see thee ensconced in what was thy accustomed seat.

GHOST. (*Throwing one leg over the other and sticking its thumbs in the armholds of its waistcoat.*) Which posture d'ye most fancy, Bet—this——?

MRS. JESMOND. (*Nodding.*) I remember thee in it constantly.

GHOST. (*Extending its legs and resting its fists on its hips.*) Or this?

MRS. JESMOND. That was your position when you were

engaged in argument. I had rather the other. (*The* GHOST *resumes its previous attitude.*) Oh! Oh, that I might fill thy pipe, and light it for thee at the candle, and slip the scarlet end of it into thy poor mouth, as I used to do!

GHOST. Nay, lass, that's talking sheer nonsense. (*She presses her eyes with the back of her hand.*) Come, 'tis no good whimpering; whimpering won't mend matters. Get on wi' thy work.

MRS. JESMOND. (*Leaning back in her chair and beating her clenched hands on the table.*) Oh! Oh, how cold you are! How cold you are!

GHOST. (*Annoyed.*) Cold! 'Pon my soul, that's monstrously inconsiderate an' unkind!

MRS. JESMOND. Ah, have I hurt thee?

GHOST. *Hurt* me!

MRS. JESMOND. I ask your pardon, Hal.

MRS. JESMOND. I ask your pardon, Hal.

GHOST. Nay, 'tis all very fine! (*Rising.*) Thou know'st 'tis not in my power to console thee.

MRS. JESMOND. (*Snatching at her pen.*) Ah, you're not vanishing. You'll not vanish so soon! Harry! (*The* GHOST *wags its head sulkily.*) Harry! Harry!

GHOST. I'll not if thou'lt be reasonable an' polite, an' I can sarve thee.

MRS. JESMOND. I will be reasonable; I will be. Oh, 'tis as hard on you as on me that, being a shade, you cannot take me to your breast; and 'twas cruel of me to complain! I swear I won't offend again, Hal.

GHOST. (*Loftily, repeating its performance with the snuff-box.*) Proceed, then.

MRS. JESMOND. Thank you, my dear. (*Drying her eyes hurriedly and referring to a paper.*) Andrew Todd of Mickle Gill hath begged me to test an example of oats that he hath brought me. The germination of his oat-seed last season greatly discontented him.

GHOST. (*Curling its lip.*) Zooks, but Andrew was ever a fool!

Mrs. Jesmond. (*Humbly.*) Nay, I am worse; for I am even more ignorant than Andrew how to make the test.

Ghost. I'll tell 'ee. Tear two strips from thine old flannel-petticoat an' lay th' seed between 'em an' float 'em in a crock full o'water. (*She again writes in her book.*) Stand th' vessel in thy sunniest window, an' in less than three days thou'lt be able to show Todd how many of his oats are speared. (*With a hollow, vain laugh.*) Ha, ha, Maister Todd!

Mrs. Jesmond. (*Throwing down her pen suddenly and leaning her head upon her hands.*) Oh, Hal, Hal!

Ghost. Why, what's wrong wi' thee now?

Mrs. Jesmond. Alas, and alas, I am but an impostor!

Ghost. Impostor?

Mrs. Jesmond. (*Starting up and walking about.*) A cheat! I despise myself for fobbing off these dalesmen with the belief that 'tis I that helps them in their difficulties.

Ghost. Why, 'tis you that do it, Betty, in sober truth.

Mrs. Jesmond. (*Reprovingly.*) Harry!

Ghost. I say 'tis so. An' were I alive, I should be consumedly proud of you, Bet; I should, b'George, though I do upbraid thee on occasions when thou dost desarve it.

Mrs. Jesmond. Thou wert never logical, Harry! Were you alive, 'twould be known that the cleverness is all thine. (*Leaning upon the dresser.*) Oh, 'twould relieve my conscience of a heavy burden, could I but reveal that you visit me in this manner!

Ghost. An' scare th' folks for miles around! Th' inn an' th' farms 'un be shunned, an' thou'd be reduced to beggary.

Mrs. Jesmond. (*Dejectedly.*) Oh! Oh!

Ghost. Nay, you need ha' no qualms on that score, lass. 'Tis lucky, I confess, that I had a bent for farming as well as for dicing an' cock-fighting; but husband an' wife are one, an' so, I take it, are a widow an' her husband's ghost, till she falls in love wi' another chap. (*Drawing itself up.*) There's logic for thee! (*The wind is heard again, and a whistle from the sign-board. The* GHOST'S *expression changes.*) 'Egad, but that reminds me, Bet——!

MRS. JESMOND. Of what, Hal?

GHOST. (*Scowling.*) Speaking o' falling in love, th' young gentleman that quartered himself here two months ago is still under thy roof. (*Her body slowly stiffens.*) Thou didst mention his name an' quality to me once——

MRS. JESMOND. (*Turning to the* GHOST, *but avoiding its eyes.*) Mr. Edward Fane? He resides with his mother, who is wealthy, at Kensington in London.

GHOST. (*With a sneer.*) That's him; a handsome, black young man, in 's own hair.

MRS. JESMOND. (*Advancing frigidly.*) Why, indeed, Mr. Fane wears neither wig nor powder; but, for the rest, I have scarce observed his looks.

GHOST. 'Faith, he hath obsarved thine! I've seen him through th' shutters, as I've rid past thy window on my grey mare, an' he hath been sitting opposite thee at table an' gazing at thee most fixedly.

MRS. JESMOND. (*Shrugging her shoulders.*) 'Tis when Mr. Fane and I have been playing a game of backgammon together that you must have remarked us.

GHOST. Eh, so you play backgammon wi' him, do 'ee, Betty?

MRS. JESMOND. To while away his evenings. (*Fingering the back of the chair on the left of the round table.*) Wasdale hath few attractions for a man of fashion; and this one is so excellent a customer that 'tis worth taking some pains to divert him.

GHOST. Nay, I wager he finds no lack of divarsion at Wasdale, or he'd not linger as he does. (*Lowering at her.*) He's sweet on thee, lass, to a certainty.

MRS. JESMOND. (*Indignantly.*) Hal!

GHOST. Aye, an' I warn thee, thou'lt be losing thy heart to *him,* if thou'rt not careful.

MRS. JESMOND. Harry!

GHOST. (*Bitterly.*) An' then I shall hear th' blast o' th' horn no more o' Friday nights, in spite of all thy oaths an' tears an' protestations; an' thou'lt cast me aside, an' out o' thy thoughts, like thy worn padesoy!

MRS. JESMOND. Oh! Oh! As if I could ever be inconstant to thee, my first and last love! Shame on you, poor grisly thing that thou art, for thinking it of me!

GHOST. Dang it, there you go again! Grisly!

MRS. JESMOND. (*Moving about the room, in a heat.*) Oh! Oh! I'll play no more backgammon with Mr. Fane from this time forth, I do assure you, nor with any other living man! Oh!

GHOST. 'Twas not backgammon you were playing when I last espied you both, Betty. Mr. Fane had a paper in 's hand an' appeared to be reciting to thee.

MRS. JESMOND. (*Halting.*) Ah, yes; he hath a taste for writing poetry, and was reading one of his compositions. (*Returning to the table, eagerly.*) That is the reason Mr. Fane lingers at Wasdale, Harry; the grandeur of the district elevates his mind, he declares. Immediately he reined up at this door, two months back, and I went out to greet him, he looked at me and said, "Why, madam, this is the very spot I have been searching for in my dreams!"

GHOST. (*Giving another hollow laugh.*) Ha, ha, ha, ha!

MRS. JESMOND. (*Reproachfully.*) Oh, Hal, thou wert never bookish; you never knew aught of poets and their ways!

GHOST. Not I. An' what's his poetry like, lass? I warrant 'tis all "love" an' "dove," an' that sort o' muck.

MRS. JESMOND. Nay, 'tis somewhat better than muck; though of no great merit perhaps.

GHOST. The piece he was reading when I watched thee ——?

MRS. JESMOND. 'Twas called—how was it styled?—"To Aminta——"

GHOST. Aminta?

MRS. JESMOND. "Aminta" is a fanciful conceit; she is no real person. 'Tis modish in a poet to inscribe his rhymes to Julia, or Chloe, or—or Aminta. Pshaw! Thou shalt judge how harmless the verses are. (*Disdainfully.*) "To Aminta, a Lady Dwelling in the Country."

GHOST. (*Suspiciously.*) A lady dwelling i' the' country?

MRS. JESMOND. (*Reciting, at first with a show of indifference, then with genuine fervour.*)

Belov'd Aminta, shall thy lone retreat
Hold thee for ever in his close embrace,
Whilst the vast waters stretching at thy feet
Capture the sole reflection of thy face?
Nay, let the lordly hill, the softer glen,
In Nature's sempiternal gifts secure,
Suffer thy charms t' illume the haunts of men,
Purge the vile Town and make the City pure!

(*She stands absorbed, looking into space. After a short silence, the sign-board creaks again gently.*)

GHOST. Ha, ha, ha, ha! (*She starts.*) Why, thou hast learned every syllable of it!

MRS. JESMOND. (*Guiltily.*) Oh, 'its but simple stuff, and readily committed to memory.

GHOST. A lady dwelling i' th' country! 'Tis thee, o' course!

MRS. JESMOND. La, there are hundreds of ladies that dwell in solitude in the country, Hal!

GHOST. "Whilst the vast water stretching at thy feet—"! 'Tis our lake o' Wastwater!

MRS. JESMOND. (*Resuming her seat at the table and

*handling her papers in a flutter.*) Nay, I am weary of talking about this Mr. Fane——

GHOST. An' he'd bear thee off t' Lunnon, would he, t'th' haunts o' men, th'—!

MRS. JESMOND. (*Picking up a paper hastily.*) I've a question to ask thee concerning the crooked field below Buckbarrow——

GHOST. Ha, ha, ha, ha!

MRS. JESMOND. Harry——! (*There is a sharp knocking at the upper door, followed by the click of the latch.*) Oh! (*Again the wind thunders, and again the candle-flames flicker and the room is momentarily in semi-darkness. Then the room brightens and* EDWARD *is seen upon the landing. The* GHOST *has disappeared.*) Who's there? (EDWARD *shuts the door at which he has entered and, staring about him wildly, rapidly descends the stairs. The wind moderates.*)

EDWARD. 'Tis I. (*Running his eyes around the room.*) Forgive me, madam.

MRS. JESMOND. (*Composedly, as though engrossed in work.*) Indeed, sir, you might have waited till I bade you come in.

EDWARD. (*Bewildered.*) M-m-may I have a word with you?

MRS. JESMOND. If you will remember that I am at my books and papers, and that even an innkeeper is not always at the beck-and-call of a guest.

EDWARD. (*Bowing.*) Nay, ma'am, I have apologized for my fault. (*Looking keenly in the direction of the lower door and the space under the staircase.*) The fact is that, hearing voices, I had less compunction in breaking in upon you than I should otherwise have had.

MRS. JESMOND. (*With assumed surprise.*) Voices?

EDWARD. The sounds of talking and laughing.

MRS. JESMOND. Why, Mr. Fane, 'tis not improbable that I chatter to myself while I am calculating my figures.

EDWARD. And laugh!

MRS. JESMOND. And laugh. (*Rising and moving to the fireplace.*) The farmer—man or woman—that attempts to cultivate this grudging valley may well laugh, sir, though the laugh be on the wrong side o' the mouth.

EDWARD. Oh, but this is evasion! Mrs. Jesmond——!

MRS. JESMOND. Evasion!

EDWARD. Is there anybody concealed here?

MRS. JESMOND. Concealed?

EDWARD. (*Peering into the space beneath the staircase and then returning and confronting her.*) Nay, then, he must have left the room as I entered it, and by this door!

MRS. JESMOND. Mr. Fane!

EDWARD. (*Going to her.*) I swear I heard more than one voice, and that a man's! By Heaven, you are deceiving me!

MRS. JESMOND. Deceiving you, sir! (*Haughtily.*) Why, what am I to you, or you to me, that I should deceive you, or enlighten you, on any affair that doth not concern your abode at this inn? So that your bed is clean, and your food wholesome, and my charges are just and fairly reckoned, and you acquit them promptly, what obligations, pray, are we under to each other? (*Stamping her foot.*) Withdraw from my room, Mr. Fane, and suffer me to resume my work! Stand aside, sir! (*He allows her to pass him but, as she does so, he catches her by the arms.*) Unhand me!

EDWARD. (*Passionately.*) Mrs. Jesmond——!

MRS. JESMOND. (*Releases herself and facing him.*) Oh, 'tis cowardly of you; and when my servants are abed, and I am unprotected! (*He retreats a step or two.*) Oh! You that have writ such tender poems, and delivered them with so much sensibility!

EDWARD. (*With dignity.*) Nay, madam, you misinterpret my action. Believe me, you have nothing to fear from my violence. (*Drawing himself erect.*) And yet you are right; I am a coward, and an arrant one.

MRS. JESMOND. Mr. Fane!

EDWARD. A coward. What else am I when I have hesitated so long to free myself from the malign spell your beauty has cast upon me——!

MRS. JESMOND. (*Faintly.*) Malign——!

EDWARD. When, suspecting you to be false and unworthy—as I have for many weeks past, and as I have to-night proved you to be—I have foolishly persuaded myself, against my innermost convictions, of your probity and virtue!

MRS. JESMOND. False and unworthy! You are mad, sir! False to whom?

EDWARD. To me.

MRS. JESMOND. To—to you!

EDWARD. Why, madam, you know that I have loved you —(*She puts her hand to her heart with a quick motion.*) *Do* love you!

MRS. JESMOND. (*Tremblingly.*) Indeed, and indeed, Mr. Fane——!

EDWARD. (*Sternly.*) Hush! To deny it is a lie! (*She makes a movement, as if to escape, and again he detains her.*) Stay! You *shall* hear me! (*She sinks into the chair at the right of the round table.*) I have loved you from the first moment I saw you, when, on that evil day on which accident brought me to this inn, and I checked my bridle at the porch, you stood with your hands resting on my horse's shoulder and your eyes drooped before mine. I have loved you from that moment, I repeat; (*accusingly*) while you, with the quick instinct that wakes intelligence in a woman's brain, if not response within her bosom, have divined my feelings and cruelly allowed me to foster them!

MRS. JESMOND. (*Weakly.*) I have oft been struck with the idea that you are exceeding well-disposed toward me——

EDWARD. Well-disposed! Ah, do not prevaricate!

Mrs. Jesmond. But you have never spoken a word of love to me, I do protest.

Edward. Not expressly, for 'twas on the night previous to the day on which I had intended to throw myself at your feet that, returning from my bedchamber to fetch a letter, I was startled by mysterious murmurs issuing from this room.

Mrs. Jesmond. (*Raising her head.*) Ah!

Edward. Since then (*pointing to the door on the landing*) I have listened there every Friday night——.

Mrs. Jesmond. Listened!

Edward (*abashed.*) I confess it—listened with my head upon the latch, lacking the courage to enter and perhaps confirm the dreadful doubts that assailed me.

Mrs. Jesmond. (*Scornfully.*) You do yourself scant justice, Mr. Fane. You are full of courage to-night, sir, at any rate!

Edward. Because I have to-night heard what I have not hitherto clearly detected—the sound of a man's voice; and have convinced myself that, aided by a specious but illcontrived stratagem, you are receiving a visitor clandestinely. (*She rises, standing before him with her head averted. The wind swells again.*) Mrs. Jesmond, I set out for London to-morrow, carrying with me recollections that will remain with me till death—recollections of the hours we have spent together in this apartment; hours of bliss, before I mistrusted thee, and afterwards when your charms have lulled me into the belief that the possessor of so fair an exterior must be the most innocent, as you are assuredly the most captivating, of your sex; hours of anguish, when doubt hath gained supremacy and I have endured the torments of the damned. Farewell! Did I desire retaliation, 'twould be in the thought that at some future time you will reproach yourself for having shaken beyond repair the faith of one who would have crowned you with his honor and esteem, adored you with his body, defended you with his sword, and given you a heart to lean upon that hath been touched by no other women. (*Bowing low.*) Madam——!

MRS. JESMOND. (*With a deep curtsey.*) Farewell, sir. (*He goes towards the staircase. Suddenly, with a gasp, she runs to the foot of the stairs and intercepts him.*) Ah, no! Mr. Fane——!

EDWARD. (*Drawing back.*) Mrs. Jesmond!

MRS. JESMOND. Mr. Fane, I cannot bear that we should part thus. Edward! 'Tis true; I *am* false and unworthy, as you have accused me of being. But 'tis my—my secret visitor that I am false to, and not to thee. (*Coming closer to him.*) Edward——!

EDWARD. (*Repelling her with a gesture.*) Ah——!

MRS. JESMOND. Nay, don't put me from thee, for this once. (*Simply.*) Edward, I *have* known of thy love for me; I have known it from the beginning. And, oh—Heaven pardon me, my dear—(*laying her head against him*)—I have *loved* that thou shouldst love me!

EDWARD. (*After a struggle.*) Betty——! (*He folds her in his arms. The wind roars and the sign-board screeches.*)

MRS. JESMOND. (*Feebly.*) And now—enough. (*Looking up at him.*) Only I beg thee to glance up at my window as you ride away tomorrow. Thou wilt do that for me, Edward?

EDWARD. (*In sudden fury.*) Oh——! (*He catches up the riding-cloak from the table in the bay of the window, flings it aside, and seizes one of the pistols.*)

MRS. JESMOND. Pistols!

EDWARD. (*Examining the lock of the pistol.*) They are Sir John Hunslet's. (*Grimly.*) He left them lying here, lest I should encounter the wretch that hath obtained such a pernicious influence over thee.

MRS. JESMOND. (*Laughing wildly.*) Ha, ha, ha, ha!

EDWARD. (*Grasping the pistol tightly.*) The villain—he that visits thee—where is he hid?

MRS. JESMOND. Ha, ha, ha, ha! Thy bullet cannot harm

him. 'Twould but whistle through him and strike the wall.

EDWARD. (*Gripping her wrist.*) Collect thyself; thou art out of thy senses!

MRS. JESMOND. (*Desperately.*) Am I! Thou shalt see! (*Pointing to the hunting-horn.*) Unhook that horn from its nail and bring it to me.

EDWARD. The signal!

MRS. JESMOND. What, hast thou heard that also! (*Hurriedly he takes down the hunting-horn and hands it to her. Again she blows upon it, and again the wind gives a mighty bellow, the candles flicker, and the bluish light suffuses the room.*) Look! (*Following the direction of her eyes, he turns and finds the* GHOST *at his elbow.*)

EDWARD. (*Under his breath.*) Merciful Powers! (*The pistol drops from his relaxed fingers and rattles on the stones of the floor. Slowly, with measured tread and with its head bent, the* GHOST *walks to the fireplace and stands there, gazing into the fire. The force of the wind decreases.*) A ghost! A ghost! A ghost!

MRS. JESMOND. (*Placing the horn upon the round table and addressing* EDWARD *in a hushed, steady voice.*) 'Tis my husband's spirit, Mr. Fane. My grief called it to me in the young days of my bereavement, and it hath visited me since every week, and guided me in the conduct of my land and property; (*with a slight shiver*) and 'tis my resolve to remain constant to this shadow as though 'twas blood and bone. (*Moving a little toward* EDWARD.) You have been pleased to take a kind interest in me, sir; and you will be glad, I am sure, when you quit Wasdale, to reflect that the poor widow that hath done her best for your comfort and entertainment is not entirely alone. (*Curtseying again.*) Good night. (*Speechless,* EDWARD *backs away from her and goes out at the door under the landing. She sees that the door is closed and then advances timorously.*

*The* GHOST *does not stir.*) Er—I hope thou'rt not angry Hal. 'Twas Mr. Fane that interrupted us. He returned to this room for some purpose, and our talk and laughter reached him as he was opening the door. 'Twas indiscreet in us to speak so loud. (*Coming to the round table.*) But, la, 'tis no matter; he is a person to be trusted! (*Lightly, toying with her books and papers.*) Beside—ha,ha!—it hath afforded me the opportunity of hinting to my gentleman that, should he ever revisit Wasdale Head, 'twould be useless for him to pursue thy Betty with his attentions, were he so minded. (*Seating herself at the table again.*) He doth depart to-morrow, I thank the Lord. (*Sorting her letters.*) What was it I was about to ask thee? (*Picking up a paper.*) Ah, yes, the crooked field by Buckbarrow—! (*The* GHOST *slowly turns and faces her and she stares at it agape. Its form and features have become less distinct.*) Why—how dim you are, Harry!

GHOST. (*Harshly, but in fainter tones than before.*) Dim! 'Egad, I should think so! Thou know'st that I owe this ghostly existence o' mine only to thy love for me.

MRS. JESMOND. W-w-well?

GHOST. Well! Ha, ha! I marvel, after witnessing what hath passed 'twixt you and Mr. Fane, that thou canst discern me at all, Betty.

MRS. JESMOND. (*Aghast.*) Witnessing——!

GHOST. Aye. Did'ee imagine I was out of eye-an'-earshot?

MRS. JESMOND. Y-y-y-yes.

GHOST. Not I. I've been wi' thee th' whole while. Ho, ho, ho, ho! (*There is a pause, and then* MRS. JESMOND, *pressing her temples, falls back in her chair with a groan.*) Nay, lass, 'tis I that should be making a fuss; an', b' George, I would too, but that thou hast diminished me to that degree that I'm scarce capable of it!

MRS. JESMOND. (*Raising herself.*) Oh! Oh! (*Dropping

*her outstretched arms upon the table and laying her head upon them.*) Oh-h-h-h! (*The wind gives a sigh and the sign-board creaks sympathetically.*)

GHOST. (*Wagging its head shakily.*) Ah, Bet, Bet, I own I've never suspected you would sell me i' this fashion. (*With a low cry, she rises and throws herself at the* GHOST's *feet.*) That thou shouldst prove such a smooth-tongued, double-faced hyprocrite! Dang it, that beats me, that had such a vast knowledge o' women!

MRS. JESMOND. Oh, hush, hush! Were I a hyprocrite, and merely feigning love for thee, there would be nothing of thee visible, Harry; not a vestige. (*Piteously.*) Ah, I've told thee already to-night, logic was never thy strong point!

GHOST. (*Meditatively.*) Zounds, I suppose 'tis possible for a woman to love a live man an' yet ha' a softish feeling for a dead one——!

MRS. JESMOND. (*Grovelling and weeping.*) Oh! Oh!

GHOST. But 'tis plain, Betty, that thy love for Fane is uppermost——

MRS. JESMOND. Oh! Oh!

GHOST. An' so, to presarve a morsel o' dignity, 'twould be prudent o' me to bid thee good-bye before I fade from thee completely.

MRS. JESMOND. No, no, Hal! Listen! (*Sitting up and clasping her hands supplicatingly.*) Oh, listen! (*The wind sighs again and the sign-board creaks.*) Hal—Hal, when the grave closed over thee, I did indeed believe that I was done with love for ever, and that my heart was but a dry and withered plant; but, oh, there are seasons when it will persist in putting forth green shoots, and when I find strange hopes and joys quickening within me that are unbefitting a woman that is devoted to the memory of her dead husband! Alas, Harry, 'twas at such a time that Mr. Fane came upon me! Though 'twas in January that he alighted at my door, the sun was shining in the valley, and our robins were chirping, and there was a tremble of Spring in the air; and 'twas then, when he had crossed my threshold and I filled him a cup of wine, and faced him while he drank—'twas then that I felt those green shoots in my breast burst and spread their leaves (*Wildly.*) But, oh, my dear, he is going, as you are informed—he is going! —and 'tis not likely that he will come my way again —nor that another young man of his rank and character will ever resort to this lonely inn. And so you must pardon me this one stumble; and by all that I hold most sacred, Hal——!

GHOST. (*Mournfully.*) Nay, nay, thou shalt make no more promises. Thou hast perjured thyself enough as it is.

MRS. JESMOND. Perjured myself! Ah, yes! (*Laying her head in abasement upon the chair at the right of the table.*) Oh, Hal, Hal, Hal!

GHOST. Ah, I perceive now—an' so dost thou, Bet—'tis a sad mistake for a widow in th' first flood of her grief to call her susband back from his tomb. What we do in heat we repent in cold. An' if 'tis so wi' widows in general, 'tis especially so wi' thee, that are still but a girl. (*She sobs.*) Zooks, 'tis my fault for having answered thy cry! I should ha' had more brains; an' would ha' had, but that I lost some in my accident. (*She sobs again.*) So, come, dry thine eyes. I tell 'ee I don't blame thee, nor bear thee malice; no, nor him. (*Attempting, with small success to repeat his pretense of snuffing.*) 'Tis th' way th' world. Ods-bobs, who is missed in't! (*Philosophically, flourishing his phantom pocket-handkerchief.*) Why, I recollect losing my dog Pincher when I was a bachelor, that died o' jaundice. How I raved about 'un, an' stamped up an' down' th' stable where he lay stiff! But a week or two later I was buying a couple o' pups at Gosforth fair, an' was in love wi' *them*, an' forgot Pincher; an' th' following week I met thee, and fell in love wi' *thee*, an' forgot the pups. (*Producing its gloves and speaking in the tone of a person preparing to depart.*) Well, lass—!

MRS. JESMOND. Ah! (*Turning swiftly, with a hoarse scream.*) Ah-h-h-h!

GHOST. (*Drawing on a glove.*) Perhaps 'tis all for th' best, though 't has been a sore blow to my pride. (*Hopefully.*) 'Egad, as I shall ride out no more, maybe 'twill settle th' question o' my future, one way or tother!

MRS. JESMOND. (*Frantically.*) Harry! Harry——!

GHOST. Th' grey mare too! She did but blunder once in her life; 'tis rough on her, poor slut, to have had her rest broke for a single slip. (*The wind roars again furiously, and the room darkens as the* GHOST *glides towards the window. Struggling to her feet,* MRS. JESMOND *staggers after the* GHOST *and tries to catch it.*)

MRS. JESMOND. Harry! No, no! Hal! Ah, I can't hold thee! I can't hold thee! Oh!

GHOST. (*Softly.*) Coom, mare, coom! Coom, coom, coom!

MRS. JESMOND. Wait! Wait—! (*The* GHOST *vanishes.*) A-h-h-h! Come back! Harry! My husband! (*She rushes, still crying out, to the stairs and gropes for the hunting-horn; then remembering that it is upon the round table, she flies to the table and seizes it.*) Oh! Harry! Harry! I love thee! I swear I love thee! (*She blows the horn and instantly the shutters disappear and the* GHOST *is seen upon the grey mare, the wild country beyond. Again the wind bellows.*) Oh! Wait! Ah-h-h! (*Holding the reins in its left hand, the* GHOST *waves its right hand in adieu; and then, with a hollow whoop, it claps its spurs to the mare's sides, and horse and rider plunge into the murk. The shutters reappear and the room is bright once more.*) Oh, no! Thou'rt not gone! Harry! (*She puts the horn to her mouth again and blows a loud blast. Then she runs about the room, searching and calling.*) Harry! Harry! I want thee! Where are you? (*Looking into the space under the staircase.*) Are you there, Hal? (*In the bay of the *window.*) Hal, I've something to ask thee! 'Tis important! (*At the fireplace.*) Harry! Oh, Harry—! (*Suddenly, throwing the horn from her.*) Ah-h-h-h! He's gone! He's gone! (*The door on the landing opens and* EDWARD *and* SIR JOHN HUNSLET *appear.*)

EDWARD. Mrs. Jesmond——!

MRS. JESMOND. He's gone! (*To* EDWARD.) You have driven him away! I hate you! I—! Harry—! (*She topples to the ground.* EDWARD *and* SIR JOHN *descend the stairs rapidly and* EDWARD, *kneeling beside* MRS. JESMOND, *lifts her into his arms. The wind lessens.*)

EDWARD. Mrs. Jesmond! Betty! Betty! (*To* SIR JOHN, *in alarm.*) Oh, Jack——! (SIR JOHN *takes the candlestick from the round table and bends over* MRS. JESMOND.)

SIR JOHN. (*Quietly.*) 'Tis only a swoon. (*Carrying the candlestick, he moves to the lower door.*) I'll go and rouse one of her women. (*The sign-board creaks.*)

THE END

# DOLLY'S LITTLE BILLS

COMEDY IN ONE ACT

## HENRY ARTHUR JONES

Henry Arthur Jones was born at Grandborough, Bucks, England, in 1851. His first play, an unimportant one-acter, was performed in 1878. Four years later he produced "The Silver King," one of the most popular melodramas of modern times. During the late 80's and early 90's, Jones wrote several serious plays, at the same time appealing vigorously to the public on behalf of the drama he went so far to develop. Until a few years ago he continued to put forth social comedies and plays of a more serious character, the best of which were recognized as masterpieces of the modern English stage.

Like Pinero, Jones has written a few one-act plays for the music hall. Of these the most amusing is "Dolly's Little Bills," a slightly adapted version of the famous "bill scene" in the longer comedy. "Dolly Reforming Herself." It is here published for the first time.

Following is a list of Henry Arthur Jones' published plays: "Harmony;" "Elopement;" "Hearts of Oak;" "A Clerical Error;" "An Old Master;" "A Bed of Roses;" "The Deacon;" "Sweet Will;" "Joseph Entangled;" "The Silver King;" "The Dancing Girl;" "The Hypocrites;" "Mrs. Dane's Defence;" "The Case of Rebellious Susan;" "The Liars;" "The Masqueraders;" "The Tempter;" "Dolly Reforming Herself;" "The Manœuvres of Jane;" "Judah;" "The Physician;" "Whitewashing Julia;" "The Rogue's Comedy;" "The Triumph of the Philistines;" "Mary Goes First;" "The Crusaders;" "Michael and His Lost Angel;" "Carnac Sahib;" "The Divine Gift;" "The Lie;" "The Goal"; "Her Tongue;" "Grace Mary;" "Dolly's Little Bills."

References: T. H. Dickinson, "The Contemporary Drama of England"; A. E. Morgan, "Tendencies of Modern English Drama"; Barrett H. Clark, "A Study of the Modern Drama."

# DOLLY'S LITTLE BILLS*

## CHARACTERS

HARRY TELFER, *Dolly's Husband*
MATT BARRON, *Dolly's Father*
MRS. HARRY TELFER, *Dolly*

SCENE: *The Drawing Room at Harry Telfer's.*

TIME: *January 1907 and 1908.*

*Drawing Room at Harry Telfer's, The Gables, Crookbury Green, Surrey. A well-furnished room in a modern red-brick country house.*

*At the back, a little to the right, is a door leading into the hall with backing of a door.*

*All along the right side is a glass partition, showing a conservatory, which is entered by glass doors, one up stage, one down.*

*On the left side is a large fireplace.*

*At the back, in the center, is a handsome writing desk with a shutdown flap lid.*

*Above the fireplace, facing the audience, is a large sofa, and below it in the left center of the room, is a small table, and near to it an easy chair.*

*Right center, down stage, is a larger table.*

TIME: *The afternoon of January 1st, 1907.*

(DOLLY TELFER, *a bright little woman about thirty;* MATT BARRON, *a pleasant-looking, easy-going cynic of sixty;* HARRY TELFER, DOLLY'S *husband, an ordinary, good-natured weakish, impulsive Englishman, about thirty-five, discovered.*)

HARRY. Now, my darling, we'll go into your bills—

(MATT, *who has been seated reading, suddenly rises, shutting his book.*)

MATT. And I'll get off to bed. (*Stretches his arms and yawns.*)

DOLLY. Don't you think, Harry, we might put off the bills till the morning?

HARRY. No, my darling, you put them off this morning, you put them off this afternoon, you put them off after tea. I'm thoroughly resolved to go thoroughly into them, and see how we stand before we go to bed to-night. (DOLLY *is pouting,* MATT *looks at her and pulls a long face.*)

MATT. What's the matter, Doll? You don't owe such a very alarming amount, do you?

DOLLY. Oh, no! Oh, no! And if Harry will only help me as he promised—(*Glancing beseechingly at* HARRY.)

HARRY. Yes—well, I'll see about it. In fact, I did mean to give you a pleasant little Christmas surprise and pay off all your debts.

DOLLY. Oh, you angel! But why didn't you do it?

HARRY. I've done it so often. You remember the last time?

DOLLY. (*Making a wry face.*) Yes, I remember the last time.

HARRY. And here we are again—

DOLLY. Oh, don't talk like a clown!

HARRY. But, my dear Dolly, here we are again—

DOLLY. Well, I haven't got the money sense—I simply haven't got it. I was born without it—wasn't I, Dad?

MATT. You were, my dear. She simply hasn't got the money sense, Harry; so, if I were you, Harry, I should put off the bills till to-morrow.

HARRY. (*Very firmly.*) No, to-night—at once.

MATT. Oh, very well. (*To* DOLLY.) Good night. Harry —(*Shaking hands.*)

HARRY. Good night, Mr. Barron.

MATT. (*To* DOLLY.) Night-night, dear.

DOLLY. Night-night, Dad. (*Kissing him.*) (*As* MATT *is going off he sees the collecting box which is now on the top of the writing desk.*)

MATT. Oh—oh—Harry, I forgot. (*Takes up the box.*) The Vicar left this box for you when you were out this afternoon. He said you'd know what it was for.

HARRY. Oh yes, that's all right. I know what it's for.

MATT. May I be so curious as to inquire what it's for?

DOLLY. Yes—you know Jobling the auctioneer? He used to have a lot of bad habits, such as taking a glass too much, and sometimes swearing at his wife. Well, last Christmas the Vicar sent him a box like that and made him promise to put in a shilling every time he used a bad word.

MATT. But Harry doesn't use bad language to you?

DOLLY. Not very often. But he gets into dreadful fits of temper, and the Vicar has made him promise to put in a shilling for the Blanket Club every time he forgets himself.

MATT. Oh, I see! Well, Harry—(*Tapping the box on the writing desk.*) There's the box. (*Exit.*)

DOLLY. Yes, there's the box. (*Bringing it down triumphantly to* HARRY *and holding it under his nose.*)

HARRY. Yes, never mind about that thing. We'll get on to your bills, if you please. Do you hear, my darling? Put the box down.

DOLLY. Very well. So long as you don't forget.

HARRY. I shan't forget. (*She puts the box on the table.*)

DOLLY. Harry, dear, my head will be so much clearer in the morning.

HARRY. My darling, remember what the Vicar said about procrastination in his New Year's sermon. And remember our good resolutions last night. If we break them on the first night of the year, where shall we be on the thirty-first of December?

DOLLY. I'm horribly fagged.

HARRY. Conquer it! Think how delightful it will be to

put your head on the pillow to-night without a single anxiety, without a single thought——

DOLLY. Except my gratitude to you!

HARRY. Come, dear, no time like the present.

DOLLY. (*Jumps up very briskly.*) No time like the present! (*Looking at him with great admiration.*) Oh, Harry, what a dear, kind, good husband you've always been to me!

HARRY. Have I, my darling? (*Modestly.*) I've done my best——

DOLLY. How I must have tried you!

HARRY. No, dear—at least, a little sometimes.

DOLLY. When I think what patience you've had with me, and never reproached me—

HARRY. Well, not often. We've had our little tiffs—that day at Goodwood—eh?

DOLLY. Don't speak of it. I was to blame—

HARRY. No, dear. I can't let you accuse yourself. I was quite in the wrong.

DOLLY. No, dear, it was my fault entirely.

HARRY. Well, we won't quarrel about that. Now, these bills—

DOLLY. And what good pals we've been!

HARRY. And always shall be. (*Kisses her.*)

DOLLY. (*Hugging him.*) Oh, you dear!

HARRY. Now, business, business!

DOLLY. (*Going up to writing desk.*) What a lucky woman I am!

HARRY. (*Seated at table.*) Bring them all. (DOLLY *goes to desk.*)

DOLLY. (*Has opened desk and taken up some bills—she looks round dubiously at* HARRY.) What a splendid thing it must be to be a husband, and have it in your power to make your wife *adore* you, by simply paying a few bills.

HARRY. Yes—bring them all. (*She comes down left of*

*him, with a bundle of about fifteen, hands them to him.*) Is this all?

DOLLY. All, of any importance.

HARRY. I want to see them all.

DOLLY. So you shall, but we'll go through these first, because if you want to ask any questions we can settle them on the spot, can't we?

HARRY. (*Reading from the bill.*) Maison Récamier, Court and artistic millinery. By Jove! (*Looks up.*)

DOLLY. What!

HARRY. One, two, three, four, five, six, seven, eight, nine —nine hats!

DOLLY. Different kinds of hats.

HARRY. Yedda straw hat four guineas, ostrich feather ruffle, twelve pounds ten—

DOLLY. That was the one—you remember—when I came into the room you said, "Stay there! Just as you are! I must kiss you!"

HARRY. Yes, but twelve pounds ten!—Moss green chip hat, four, fourteen, six. Heliotrope velvet toque——

DOLLY. That's the dear little toque you admire so much!

HARRY. Do I? Six guineas! Dear little toque! Hat in white Tegal, with plumes of Nattier Bleu—fifteen guineas—Fifteen guineas!

DOLLY. With plumes! Of Nattier Bleu!

HARRY. But fifteen guineas!

DOLLY. Oh, the woman's a fearful swindler! But what are you to do with such people?

HARRY. (*With bill.*) Total, sixty-four, seven, six. And I get only one silk topper a year, at a guinea, and three and six for doing it up. Total for me, one, four, six. Total for you—

DOLLY. My dear, Harry, don't make absurd comparisons!

HARRY. (*Takes another bill.*) John Spearman, artistic gown maker—ball gowns, reception gowns, race gowns —Good heavens!

DOLLY. What's the matter?

HARRY. Total, five hundred and fifty-six pounds—that can't be right!

DOLLY. (*Frightened.*) No, it can't be! Add it up!

HARRY. (*Reading.*) Tea gown of chiffon taffeta—

DOLLY. The one I took to Folkestone, you remember? (*With a little attempt at a kiss.*)

HARRY. (*Gently repulsing her.*) No, I don't. (*She puts her arms round his neck: he gently pushes her aside.*) Business first, please. (*Reads.*) Gown of white cloth with Postilion coat of Rose du Barri silk, motifs of silver, forty-five guineas——

DOLLY. You won't grumble at that, for when I first put it on, you stood and looked at me and said, "I want to know how it is, Doll, that the moment a dress gets on to your shoulders, it seems to brisk up, and be as cocky and proud of itself——" (*Again attempting to embrace him.*)

HARRY. (*Again repulsing her.*) Yes, well, now I do know! Jolly proud and cocky your dresses ought to feel at this price! (*Reads.*) "Evening cloak of strawberry satin charmeuse, trimmed silk passementerie, motifs and fringed stoles of dull gold embroidery, thirty-five guineas." What's a motif?

DOLLY. It's a trimming—a lot of little touches—a sort of a—a—a (*making a little descriptive gesture*) a suggestion—a motif—

HARRY. And Mr. John Spearman's motif is that I should pay him five hundred and fifty-six pounds. Well, I don't like Mr. John Spearman's motifs, and I'm not going to fall in with them. (*Puts the bill on the table rather angrily, takes up another, reads.*) "Artistic lingerie!" I wonder why all these people call themselves artists! "Underwear of daintiness and distinction."

DOLLY. Well, you've always praised—

HARRY. Yes. In future, I'm going to be very careful.

what articles of your dress I praise. "Three pairs of blue silk garters, forty-five shillings." (*She has settled herself in the armchair, looking a little sulky and obstinate, leaning back and pettishly swinging one leg over the other.*) What have you got so say to that?

DOLLY. Garters are necessary.

HARRY. Yes, but why three? and why blue silk? Why don't you speak?

DOLLY. The garters can speak for themselves!

HARRY. Very well. Garters that can speak for themselves can pay for themselves! (*Dashes the bill on the table, takes up another.*) (*Reading.*) Three bottles Coeur de Janette—three bottles Souffle de Marguerite—fifteen pounds for scent—and I have to smoke sixpenny cigars! And sometimes only fourpenny!

DOLLY. Well, if you will smoke those horrid strong things you can't wonder I have to disinfect the house for you.

HARRY. Disinfect the house *for* me! You'll very soon disinfect the house *of* me! (*Glances through the remaining bills, groans, puts them on the table, and walks about in despair.*) (DOLLY *rises and is going off.*) Where are you going?

DOLLY. To bed.

HARRY. (*Stopping her.*) No! Now we've begun, we'll go through to the bitter end, if you please. I want you to explain——

DOLLY. My dear Harry, it will be quite useless for me to explain in your present state——

HARRY. (*Getting furious.*) In my present state——

DOLLY. Dancing about the room and shouting!—

HARRY. I'm not shouting!

DOLLY. You're not shouting?

HARRY. No, and if I am, isn't it enough to make a man shout when his wife——(MATT *appears at the door in his dressing gown and slippers.*)

MATT. Excuse my interrupting. But you know my room

is just above this, and if you could manage to pitch your voices in rather a softer key——

HARRY. By Jove, I'd forgotten! We were getting a little noisy. I'm awfully sorry.

MATT. Don't mention it! The Professor gave me rather a stiff go of his Pableine, and I fancy it hasn't agreed with me (*tapping his chest*) for I can't get a wink of sleep. Is there a spoonful of whiskey about?

HARRY. On the sideboard in the dining-room.

MATT. Thankee. (*Tapping his chest.*) Harry, when you get over fifty, don't change your nightcap, or any of your other bad habits. (*Exit.*)

HARRY. Now, my darling, we shall best arrive at an understanding if we avoid all temper, and discuss it in a calm businesslike way.

DOLLY. (*A little frightened.*) Ye—es——

HARRY. Very well then, bring up your chair, and let us go into it, figure by figure, item by item, and see how we stand.

DOLLY. Ye—es. (*Bringing a chair a little way.*) Harry, you aren't going to be as business-like as all that?

HARRY. As all what?

DOLLY. I can't discuss it while you keep me at a distance. (*Suddenly rushes at him, seats herself on his knee, puts her arm around his waist, kisses him.*) There! now I feel I can discuss it thoroughly.

HARRY. Very well. (*Kisses her.*) So long as we do discuss it thoroughly.

DOLLY. I began to get quite frightened of you, Mr. Jobling.

HARRY. Jobling?

DOLLY. The Vicar had to get a money-box for him because he swore at his wife!

HARRY. Oh, yes.

DOLLY. You got so angry—and shouted—

HARRY. Well, there was no reason for that, especially as

getting out of temper is *the* one thing I'm quite resolved to conquer this New Year——

DOLLY. (*Kissing him.*) Don't forget that!

HARRY. (*Kisses her.*) Now, business, business! (*Takes up a bill.*) What have we here? Carchet Gantier et bonnetier, artiste——Hillo, here's another artist! In stockings this time. (*Suddenly.*) I say!

DOLLY. (*Frightened.*) Eh?

HARRY. (*Points to an item in bill.*) Come now, Dolly—this is really too bad—this really is too bad!

DOLLY. (*Frightened.*) What?

HARRY. One dozen pairs best black silk hose, with clocks——

DOLLY. Yes—how much does that come to?

HARRY. Eleven pounds two——

DOLLY. It does seem rather a high price, but——(*Drawing up her dress and showing an inch or two of silk stockings.*)

HARRY. You're wearing them about the house?

DOLLY. I can't go about the house without stockings. And I put them on for your especial benefit. (*He utters a contemptuous exclamation.*) They're a lovely quality—(*Drawing up her dress an inch or two higher.*)

HARRY. I daresay. (*Turning away.*) I'm not going to admire your stockings, or your ostrich ruffles, or your blue silk garters, or your motifs, or anything that is yours. It's too expensive.

DOLLY. (*Dress an inch higher, looking down at her stockings.*) It's the clocks you have to pay for—

HARRY. I beg your pardon, it's the clocks I haven't got to pay for! And don't mean to—if I can help it. Idiotic thing to go and put clocks on stockings—(*muttering*) damned silly idiotic——

DOLLY. Ah! (*Goes to table, brings the hospital box and puts it in front of him.*) Double fine this time.

HARRY. What for?

DOLLY. Naughty swear word and getting out of temper.

HARRY. Oh well—(*Fumbling in his pocket.*) I did say d——, but I didn't get out of temper!

DOLLY. You didn't get out of temper?

HARRY. Not at all. I'm quite calm. (*Sulkily puts shilling in the box.*) There! Now we'll go quietly and methodically through the remainder——(*Taking up a bill, looks at it, exclaims.*) Good heavens!

DOLLY. Good heavens what?

HARRY. (*In a low exhausted tone with groans.*) Good heavens! Good heavens! It's absolutely useless—Good heavens!

DOLLY. But what is it?

HARRY. (*Points to bill.*) Four more hats! Nine on the other bill—four more here. Thirteen hats.

DOLLY. No, one was a toque.

HARRY. But can you explain?

DOLLY. Yes. You said yourself that Madame Récamier was horribly expensive, so I left her and went to Jacquelin's—just to save your pocket——

HARRY. Never save my pocket again, please.

DOLLY. Very well, I won't.

HARRY. No, I daresay you won't, but I shall draw the strings very tightly in the future. Save my pocket! (*He is walking about distractedly.*) Save my pocket! (*Groans.*)

DOLLY. Now, Harry, it's useless to take it in this way —you knew when you married me that I hadn't got the money sense——

HARRY. (*Groans.*) *I* hadn't got any sense at all!

DOLLY. Very likely not. But try and have a little now. What have I done? Run a little into debt, solely to please you.

HARRY. Yes; well, now run out of it, and I shall be better pleased still.

DOLLY. After all, running into debt is a positive virtue beside the things that some wives do!

HARRY. Oh, it's a positive virtue, is it?

DOLLY. A husband is very lucky when his wife spends most of her time running up a few bills! It keeps her out of mischief. I'm sure you ought to feel very glad that I am a little extravagant!

HARRY. Oh, I am! I am! I'm delighted!

(*He sits at table, takes out a pencil, hurriedly puts down the amounts of the various bills.*)

DOLLY. What are you doing?

HARRY. I'm totting up to see how lucky I am! Forty-one, one, six. (*Groans.*) Ninety-four——(*Groans.*)

DOLLY. (*Has crept up behind him, puts her arms round his neck.*) Now, Harry, will you take my advice——?

HARRY. No.

DOLLY. It's past eleven. (*Trying to take the pencil out of his hand.*)

HARRY. (*Disengaging her arms, speaking very sternly.*) Will you have the goodness to let me have all your bills, so that I may know what help I shall need from my banker?

DOLLY. Harry, you don't mean that? Oh, that's absurd with our income!

HARRY. Will you have the goodness to do as I say, and at once, please? (*He is jotting down figures. She stands still in the middle of the room.*) Did you hear me?

(*She bursts into tears. He turns round and shows symptoms of relenting towards her, but steels himself and turns to the bills. She bursts into renewed tears. He goes on figuring.*)

DOLLY. (*Piteously.*) Harry! Harry! Harry!

HARRY. Well?

(*He turns and looks at her, is about to yield, but resists, turns away from her, settles resolutely to his figures.*)

DOLLY. And on the first night of the New Year, too! Just as we were going to be so happy! Harry! (*Holds out her arms appealingly.*) Harry! (HARRY *sud-*

*denly turns round and clasps her.*) How could you be so unkind to me?

HARRY. Was I? I didn't mean to be. Now! Dry your tears and help me to reckon this up——

DOLLY. Ye-es.

HARRY. But first of all let me have the remainder of the bills.

DOLLY. Yes.

HARRY. At once, my darling—it's getting late.

DOLLY. Yes. (*Goes up to desk.*) You won't reproach me?

HARRY. Of course I won't.

DOLLY. I can bear anything except your reproaches. Promise me you won't reproach me.

HARRY. I won't, unless——

DOLLY. Unless what?

HARRY. It's something too awful.

DOLLY. Oh, it isn't. Not at all. Not at all. (*Goes up to desk with great affected cheerfulness.*) There! You see, it's nothing!

HARRY. (*Hastily looking at the totals.*) Nothing. You call these nothing?!

DOLLY. Nothing to speak about—nothing awful!

HARRY. Good heavens! How any woman with the least care for her husband, or her home—(*looking at one total after another.*) how any woman with the least self-respect—(DOLLY *goes to him, puts her arms round him, tries to embrace—he repulses her.*) No, please. I've had enough of that old dodge.

DOLLY. Dodge!

HARRY. I remember that last two hundred pounds and how you sweedled me out of it!

DOLLY. Sweedled?

HARRY. Yes! Sweedled!

DOLLY. There's no such word!

HARRY. No, but there's the thing! As most husbands know. (*Referring to one bill after another, picking out items.*) Lace coat, hand-made. En-tout-cas, studded cabochons of lapis lazuli—studded cabochons—studded cabochons!

DOLLY. (*Has quietly seated herself, and is looking at the ceiling.*) Couldn't you manage to pitch your voice in rather a softer key?

HARRY. (*Comes angrily, bills in hand, speaks in a whisper, very rapidly and fiercely.*) Yes! And I say that a woman who goes and runs up bills like these (*Dashing the back of one hand against the bills in the other.*) while her husband is smoking threepenny cigars, will very soon bring herself and him to one of those new palatial workhouses, where, thank heaven, the cuisine and appointments are now organized with a view of providing persons of your taste with every luxury at the ratepayers' expense. Irish lace bolero! (*Turns to another.*) Fur motor coat, fifty-five guineas——

DOLLY. (*Calmly gazing at the ceiling.*) You told me to look as smart as Mrs. Colefield.

HARRY. Not at that price! If I'd known what that motor tour would cost, by Jove! I'd——

DOLLY. You're getting noisy again. You'll wake my father.

HARRY. He ought to be waked! He ought to know what his daughter is saddling me with.

DOLLY. Very well, if you don't care how shabby I look——

HARRY. Shabby! (*Referring to bills.*) Lace demi-toilette! Point de Venise lace Directoire coat! Shabby?

DOLLY. My dear Harry, do you suppose we shall ever agree as to what constitutes shabbiness?

HARRY. No, I'm hanged if we ever shall!

DOLLY. Then suppose we drop the subject! For the future I shall endeavor to please you entirely.

HARRY. Oh, you will?

DOLLY. By dressing so that you'll be ashamed to be seen in the same street with me. I shall make myself a perfect fright—a perfect dowdy—a perfect draggle-tail!

HARRY. Then I shall not be seen in the same street with you.

DOLLY. You won't?

HARRY. No, my dear. Make no mistake about that!

DOLLY. You'll be seen with somebody else perhaps?

HARRY. Very likely.

DOLLY. Have you met Miss Smithson again?

HARRY. Not since the last time.

DOLLY. Have you seen her since we were at Folkestone?

HARRY. What's that to do with your bills?

DOLLY. A great deal. That night at dinner she told you her dress allowance was a hundred and twenty a year, and you said you wished she'd give me a few lessons in economy.

HARRY. I did not.

DOLLY. Pardon me, you did!

HARRY. Pardon me, I did not. I said she might give *some* women *a* lesson in economy.

DOLLY. You did not. I heard every word of your conversation, and you distinctly asked her to give me, your wife, a few lessons in economy.

HARRY. I'll swear I didn't!

DOLLY. Ask my father! He was there.

HARRY. Very well! I'll ask him the first thing in the morning.

DOLLY. No, to-night! You've accused me of deliberately saying what isn't true, and I——

HARRY. I have not!

DOLLY. Yes, you have. And I insist on having it cleared up to-night! I don't suppose he's asleep. Fetch him down!

HARRY. Very well! I will fetch him down!

(*Exit.*)

DOLLY. (*Paces furiously up and down.*) Me! Lessons

in economy! Lessons in economy! Me! Lessons in economy!

(*Re-enter* HARRY.)

HARRY. He'll be down in a minute! Meantime, (*Very angry.*) I want to know what any woman in this world wants with two dozen cache corsets? (*Banging his free hand on the bills.*)

DOLLY. We will clear up Miss Smithson first——

HARRY. No, we will not clear up Miss Smithson——

DOLLY. Because you can't clear up Miss Smithson——

HARRY. I can clear up Miss Smithson——

DOLLY. You cannot clear up Miss Smithson——(MATT *appears at door in dressing-gown, rubbing his eyes and looking very sleepy.*) Dad, you remember Miss Smithson——

MATT. (*Coming in, very sleepy.*) Smithson?

DOLLY. The girl at the hotel at Folkestone, that Harry paid so much attention to.

HARRY. I paid no more attention to Miss Smithson than was absolutely necessary. Did I, Mr. Barron?

DOLLY. Oh! Oh! Dad, you remember——

MATT. Not for the moment——

DOLLY. Not the disgraceful way Harry—there's no other word—carried on!

HARRY. I did not carry on—Mr. Barron, I appeal to you.

DOLLY. Dad!

MATT. My dear, I certainly did not notice——

DOLLY. No, he was far too careful to let anyone notice it, except his own wife!

HARRY. You lay your life, when I do carry on, my wife will be the last person I shall allow to notice it!

DOLLY. I daresay! Dad, did you hear that?

MATT. Yes. (*Rousing himself a little.*) Now, Harry, what about this Miss Smithson?

HARRY. That's what I want to know!

MATT. Who is Miss Smithson?

DOLLY. Surely you remember that lanky girl——

HARRY. Miss Smithson is not lanky——

DOLLY. Not lanky? Not lanky!? You can't have any eyes——

HARRY. That's what I've often thought!

DOLLY. (*Explodes.*) Oh! Oh! Dad!

MATT. Come, Harry, let's clear this up. (*Suddenly.*) Smithson? Oh, yes! The girl who sat on your left at that dinner party——

DOLLY. That's the one!

MATT. I should call her a trifle lanky, Harry.

DOLLY. A trifle? Well, never mind! You remember that dinner party——

MATT. (*Cautiously.*) Ye-es.

DOLLY. You remember how she waited for a lull in the talk, and then she said with that silly, simpering, appealing look——

HARRY. Miss Smithson's look is not silly or simpering.

DOLLY. Well, it's appealing, isn't it?

HARRY. (*With a little chuckle.*) Oh, yes, it's appealing.

DOLLY. (*Enraged.*) Oh! Dad!

MATT. (*Quiets her.*) Shush!—What did she say?

DOLLY. She said with a very marked glance at me, "My dress allowance is a hundred and twenty a year, and I don't understand how any reasonable woman can wish for more!" What do you think of that?

MATT. Well, if she did say that, and if she glanced at you, it——

DOLLY. Yes?

MATT. It wasn't very nice of her.

DOLLY. Nice? It was an insult! A direct, intentional, abominable insult, wasn't it?

MATT. Yes, yes, decidedly, under the circumstances——

DOLLY. And Harry ought to have resented it?

MATT. At his own dinner table he couldn't very well, could he?

DOLLY. Yes! At least, if he couldn't resent it, he ought

to have *shown* that he resented it. Instead of that, he actually asked her to give me a few lessons in economy.

HARRY. I did not!

DOLLY. Pardon me, you did! Me! his wife! Lessons in economy!

HARRY. And a thundering good thing if she had given you a few before you ran up those bills! (*Dashes his hand on to the bills.*)

DOLLY. There! You hear?!

MATT. Come, Harry, you oughtn't to have asked another woman to give your wife lessons in economy.

HARRY. I didn't!

DOLLY. Dad! You were there——

MATT. Yes, but I don't quite remember——

DOLLY. You don't remember? Surely you can remember a simple thing like that when your own daughter tells you it was so.

MATT. Now, Harry, what did you really say to Miss Smithson?

HARRY. I said she might give some women a lesson in economy.

MATT. Not meaning Dolly? (*Gives him a wink to say "No."*)

HARRY. No-o.

DOLLY. Then whom did he mean? Lessons in economy. Whom *could* he mean if he didn't mean me?

HARRY. Just so!

DOLLY. Ah! There! You see, he owns it!

MATT. No, no, I'm sure he doesn't mean it! Did you, Harry? (*Winking at* HARRY.)

DOLLY. Then will he please say what he really does mean.

MATT. Now, Harry, what do you really mean?

HARRY. Well, you remember that night of the dinner party at Folkestone?

MATT. (*Cautiously.*) Ye-es—

HARRY. After they'd all gone you and I went into the smoking room, didn't we?

MATT. (*Cautiously.*) Ye-es.

HARRY. And you said, "Doll's in one of her high gales again!"

DOLLY. High gales? (*Indignant.*) Father! You didn't say that?

MATT. No, no, my dear——

HARRY. Excuse me, those were your exact words: "High gales!"

MATT. I don't remember.

DOLLY. No, you don't remember anything.

HARRY. You said, "What on earth was up between her and Miss Smithson at dinner?"

DOLLY. You see! That proves exactly what I said!

HARRY. No, by Jove, it proves that your father noticed what a confounded, cussed——

DOLLY. Go on! Go on! Say it!

MATT. Shush! Shush! Well, Harry, what did you say?

HARRY. Well, not wishing to give Dolly away——

DOLLY. Ha! ha! Not wishing to give me away!

HARRY. Not then! But, by Jove, if any decent chap were to come along now——

DOLLY. (*Exploding.*) There! There! (*To* MATT.) And you sit there and hear my own husband insult me in my own house!

MATT. No! No!

DOLLY. But there you sit! There you sit!

MATT. (*Jumps up fiercely.*) Now, Harry!

HARRY. (*Fiercely.*) Well, now, Mr. Barron——

DOLLY. Why don't you defend me? Why don't you demand an apology?

MATT. What for?

DOLLY. For everything! For to-night! For that night at Folkestone!

HARRY. That night at Folkestone! Why, your father was quite on my side——

MATT. What?

DOLLY. He wasn't; were you, Dad?

MATT. No—no.

HARRY. What? (*Fiercely.*) Do you remember exactly what passed between us in the smoking-room, Mr. Barron?

MATT. No.

HARRY. Then I'll tell you——

MATT. (*Retreating towards door.*) No—no—I don't want to know——

HARRY. (*Following him up, shouting a little.*) You said, "I know what she's like in her high gales! I remember what the little devil was like at home."

DOLLY. (*Pursuing him up to door.*) Father! You didn't say that?

MATT. No—no, my darling—quite a mistake—quite a mistake—altogether a mistake.

(*Gets thankfully off at back.*)

DOLLY. (*Calls after him.*) Then why don't you stay and tell him so?

HARRY. (*Shouts after* MATT.) It's not a mistake!

DOLLY. (*Calls after* MATT.) It's cowardly of you to leave me here to be insulted!

HARRY. (*Goes up to door, shouts.*) It's not a mistake! You patted me on the back, and said, "Poor chap! Poor chap!" You know you did! (*Closes the door, comes fiercely down to* DOLLY.) It's not a mistake! He could see you had insulted Miss Smithson.

DOLLY. I had not insulted her! I was far too civil to her, considering that the next evening you took her out on the Leas, when you ought to have been at billiards——

HARRY. I took her out on the Leas!

DOLLY. Yes! You weren't in the billiard-room! So where were you? Where were you?

HARRY. I jolly well don't know, and I—I——

DOLLY. Say it! Say it!

HARRY. I damned well don't care!

DOLLY. Ah!

(*She seizes the box, brings it up to him, puts it irritatingly in front of him; he seizes it, they struggle for it, trying to take it out of each other's hands: she screams, he tries to get it; there is a scuffle round the room; he tries to rub her knuckles, she makes a little feint to bite him; in the struggle the box drops on the floor a little below the table, right.*)

DOLLY. Jobling! Jobling! Jobling!

HARRY. Now, madam, for the last time, have I all your bills?

DOLLY. Jobling! Jobling! Jobling!

HARRY. Have I all your bills?

DOLLY. Jobling! Jobling! Jobling!

HARRY. Once more, madam, have I all your bills?

DOLLY. No, you haven't!

HARRY. Then please hand them over to me this instant, so that I may take proceedings.

DOLLY. (*Laughing.*) Proceedings! Ha! Take your proceedings!

HARRY. By Jove! I will take proceedings.

DOLLY. Take them! Take them!

HARRY. (*Walking about furiously with the bills.*) So this is the way the money goes! (*Banging the bills.*) While I have to smoke twopenny cigars! And can't get a decent dinner!

DOLLY. You can't get a decent dinner?

HARRY. No! Look at those messes last night. They weren't fit for a cook-shop.

DOLLY. Oh! Oh! Oh! Get a housekeeper! Get a housekeeper!

HARRY. By Jove! That's what I mean to do!

DOLLY. Have Miss Smithson! Send for her to-morrow morning! I'll hand her over the keys!

HARRY. (*Shouting.*) And please hand me over the rest of your bills! The rest of your bills, madam!

(DOLLY *marches up to the desk.*)

(MATT *appears at door in dressing-gown.*)

MATT. I can't get a wink of sleep——

(DOLLY *takes out about twenty more bills.*)

HARRY. I insist upon seeing the whole lot! So there!

DOLLY. (*Flourishing the bills, strewing them on the floor.*) Well there! And there! And there! And there! Now you've got the whole lot! And I hope you're satisfied! I'm going into Renie's room! (*Exit.*)

HARRY. I insist on your going through these bills——

QUICK CURTAIN.

PICTURE. (MATT *picking up box carefully.*)

*The* CURTAIN *is dropped for a second or two to signify the passing of a year.*

*It rises on the same scene*

## SCENE II

*The Same. A Year Later*

(*Discover* DOLLY *and* MATT.)

(DOLLY *is fideting at desk with bills.* MATT *is reading.*)

MATT. (*Looking up from his book.*) I say, Dolly, what's the matter?

DOLLY. (*Shutting down the desk with a bang.*) Nothing. (*Comes down to him.*) Harry has been bothering me to know if I've got any bills this New Year.

MATT. Well, you haven't?

DOLLY. No, no! Of course not.

MATT. I should hope not—after that tremendous row last year, and after Harry stumping up like a Trojan and paying them all off.

DOLLY. Of course I haven't got any bills. At least——

(MATT *has got up and is looking at her critically.*)

MATT. What? what? what? (*Shakes his head.*) Sad! sad! sad!

DOLLY. Well, of course I've got a few oddments.

MATT. Oddments?

DOLLY. Yes; every woman must have a few oddments of bills, they spring up before you know of it.

MATT. How much?

DOLLY. I don't know. Dad!

MATT. Well?

DOLLY. Now that South Africans have gone up at last, and you won that splendid coup on them last week. . . .

MATT. Well?

DOLLY. You couldn't lend me—a few hundreds—till my allowance comes due? Just a few hundreds?

MATT. (*In a reproachful tone, shaking his head.*) Sad! sad! sad!

DOLLY. (*Listens.*) There's Harry! You will help me, dad—you will?

MATT. I'll see what I can do.

(HARRY *enters cheerfully in evening dress.*)

HARRY. Now, Doll, about these mere oddments of bills.

DOLLY. Not now, dear.

HARRY. Yes, dear, now! (*Very sternly.*) This instant!

DOLLY. Harry, you're going to lose your temper.

HARRY. No. I'm going to keep a firm guard on it, but (*Very sternly.*) let me see those bills.

DOLLY. (*Creeps frightened up to the desk.*) I'm sure you're going to lose your temper.

(*She opens the desk.*)

HARRY. (*Firmly.*) No. I'm quite calm. Whose bill is that? (*She hands him one timorously.*) Fulks and Garner! Artist Furriers!—More artists! (*Looks at total.*) One hundred and twenty-four pounds! Well, I'm——

DOLLY. Ah, Jobling!

HARRY. I should think I am Jobling! And you said you'd never enter their shop again!

DOLLY. I never meant to. But this time it was absolutely necessary.

HARRY. Necessary?

DOLLY. Yes; you see the chief item——

HARRY. (*Reads.*) Chinchilla toque, coat, muff and boa, 80 guineas. 80 guineas!

DOLLY. I got them as a surprise for you when we go South next week.

HARRY. Surprise! Great Heavens! What in the name of all——

MATT. Shush, Harry! Her motive was a good one. She got it to please you.

DOLLY. You haven't seen it yet; it's just outside. I've a great mind to give you a great New Year's treat, and let you see it on!

HARRY. I'm not going to be sweedled——

MATT. Hush, Harry! Let her put it on. Let's have a look at it, and see whether it's worth the money. Put it on, Doll.

(*Exit* DOLLY.)

HARRY. (*Calls after her.*) I tell you I'm not going to be sweedled!

MATT. What is "sweedled?"

HARRY. Sweedling is sweedling! It's part swindling and part wheedling. It's what every d-ee-d good-natured husband like me has to go through, when he's fool enough to put up with it.

MATT. Well, old boy, you'll have to pay, you know. It will come to that in the end.

HARRY. I'm not going to be sweedled!

MATT. And if Dolly has been a little extravagant, I must help her out with it to-morrow morning!

HARRY. No, we'll go into it thoroughly to-night.

MATT. No, Harry. My room is just above here. Besides, the cook is going to give us a special New Year dinner, and I want to enjoy it. This New Year we'll start with a comfortable evening, please!

(DOLLY *enters at back in a very handsome Chinchilla coat.*

HARRY *looks a little sulky. She stands in the middle of the room and displays it.)*

DOLLY. Well? (*He looks at it rather sulkily, walks away: she follows him.*) Well? (*Walking after him.*) Well? Well?

(*He turns, looks at her, she stands and holds out her arms.*)

HARRY. Oh, hang it all! (*Takes her in his arms and kisses her.*) There!

DOLLY. (*Kissing him heartily.*) And there! (*Another kiss.*) And there! (*Another kiss.*) And there! (*Catches sight of the collecting-box, goes to it, furiously, sweeps if off the table on to the floor.*) AND THERE!

CURTAIN.

# THE MAN IN THE BOWLER HAT

A TERRIBLY EXCITING AFFAIR

## A. A. MILNE

A. A. Milne was born at London in 1882. His apprentice years were spent in the world of journalism. He was for eight years, until 1914, assistant editor of "Punch." From 1914-1918 he served in France. His first successful play, "Wurzel Flummery," appeared in 1917. The best known of his plays is "Mr. Pim Passes By," first produced in 1919. It is Mr. Milne's distinction that he has been able to write effectively of the little trifles of life that are in the end not only important but interesting.

The following is a list of Mr. Milne's published plays:

"Wurzel Flummery;" "Mr. Pim Passes By;" "The Boy Comes Home;" "Belinda;" "The Romantic Age;" "The Dover Road;" "The Truth About Blayds;" "The Man in the Bowler Hat;" "The Great Broxopp;" "Success;" "The Artist."

# THE MAN IN THE BOWLER HAT*

CHARACTERS

JOHN
MARY
HERO
HEROINE
CHIEF VILLAIN
BAD MAN

SCENE: *A Sitting-room.*

TIME: *The Present.*

*The scene is* MARY'S *sitting-room—the most ordinary sitting-room in the world.* JOHN *and* MARY, *two of the most ordinary people, he in the early forties, she in the late thirties, are sitting in front of the fire after dinner. He, as usual, is reading the paper; she, as usual, is knitting. They talk in a desultory way.*

MARY. Did I tell you that Mrs. Patchett had just had another baby?

JOHN. (*Not looking up from his paper.*) Yes, dear, you told me.

MARY. Did I? Are you sure?

JOHN. Last week.

MARY. But she only had it yesterday. Mr. Patchett told me this morning when I was ordering the cauliflower.

JOHN. Ah! Then perhaps you told me she was going to have one.


This play is also published separately, paper bound, at 50 cents a copy.

MARY. Yes, I think that must have been it.

JOHN. This is the one that she was going to have?

MARY. It weighed seven pounds exactly.

JOHN. Of course, being a grocer, he would have the scales ready. Boy or girl?

MARY. Boy.

JOHN. The first boy, isn't it?

MARY. The second.

JOHN. (*Sticking to it.*) The first one that weighed seven pounds exactly.

(*They are silent again—he reading, she knitting.*)

MARY. Anything in the paper to-night?

JOHN. (*Turning over the paper.*) A threatened strike of boiler-makers.

MARY. Does that matter very much?

JOHN. It says here that the situation is extremely serious.

MARY. Tell me about it.

JOHN. (*Not very good at it.*) Well, the—er—boiler-makers are threatening to strike. (*Weightily.*) They are threatening not to make any more—er—boilers.

MARY. Kitchen boilers?

JOHN. (*With an explanatory gesture.*) Boilers. They are threatening not to make any more of them. And—well—that's how it is. (*Returning to his paper.*) The situation is extremely serious. Exciting scenes have been witnessed.

MARY. What sort of scenes?

JOHN. Well, naturally, when you have a lot of men threatening not to make any more boilers . . . and—er—a lot of other men threatening that if they *don't* make any—well, exciting scenes are witnessed. *Have* been witnessed by this man, this special correspondent.

MARY. (*After a pause.*) It's a funny thing that nothing exciting ever happens to *us*.

JOHN. It depends what you mean by exciting. I went round in 95 last Saturday—as I think I told you.

MARY. Yes, but I mean something really thrilling—and dangerous. Like in a novel—or on the stage.

JOHN. My dear Mary, nothing like that ever happens in real life. I mean it wouldn't happen to *us*.

MARY. Would you like it if it did?

(*He says nothing for a moment. Then he puts down his paper, and sits there, thinking. At last he turns to her.*)

JOHN. (*Almost shyly.*) I used to imagine things like that happening. Years ago. Rescuing a beautiful maiden and—and all that sort of thing. And being wrecked on a desert island with her. . . . (*He turns away from her, staring into his dreams.*) Or pushing open a little green door in a long high wall, and finding myself in a wonderful garden under the bluest of blue skies, and waiting, waiting . . . for something. . . .

MARY. I used to imagine things too. People fighting duels because of me. . . . Silly, isn't it? Nothing ever really happens like that.

JOHN. (*Still with his thoughts.*) No. . . .

(*At this moment a* STRANGE MAN *comes in. Contrary to all etiquette, he is wearing a Bowler Hat and an overcoat, and has a half-smoked cigar in his mouth. He walks quickly across the room and sits down in a chair with his back to the audience.* JOHN *and* MARY, *deep in their thoughts, do not notice him.*)

MARY. (*Looking into the fire.*) I suppose we're too old for it now.

JOHN. I suppose so.

MARY. If it had only happened once—just for the memories.

JOHN. So that we could say to each other—Good lord! what's that?

(*It was the crack of a revolver. No mistaking it, even by* JOHN, *who has never been much of a hand with revolvers.*)

MARY. (*Frightened.*) John!

(*There is a scuffling noise outside the door. They look*

*eagerly towards it. Then suddenly there is dead silence. The Man in the Bowler Hat flicks some of his cigar ash on to the carpet—*MARY'S *carpet.)*

JOHN. Look!

(*Very slowly the door begins to open. Through the crack comes a long, sinuous hand. The door opens farther, and the hand is followed by a long, sinuous body. Still The Man in the Bowler Hat says nothing. Then the door is closed, and leaning up against it, breathing rather quickly, is the* HERO, *in his hand a revolver.* JOHN *and* MARY *look at each other wonderingly.*)

JOHN. (*With a preliminary cough.*) I—I beg your pardon?

HERO. (*Turning quickly, finger to his lips.*) H'sh!

JOHN. (*Apologetically.*) I beg your pardon!

(*The* HERO *listens anxiously at the door. Then, evidently reassured for the moment, he comes towards them.*)

HERO. (*To* JOHN.) Quick, take this! (*He presses his revolver into* JOHN'S *hand.*)

JOHN. I—er—what do I——

HERO. (*To* MARY.) And you! This! (*He takes another revolver from his hip-pocket and presses it into* MARY'S *hand.*)

MARY. Thank you. Do we——

HERO. (*Sternly.*) H'sh!

MARY. Oh, I beg your pardon.

HERO. Listen!

(*They all listen.* JOHN *and* MARY *have never listened so intently before, but to no purpose. They hear nothing.*)

JOHN. (*In a whisper.*) What is it?

HERO. Nothing.

JOHN. Yes, that's what *I* heard.

HERO. Have you got a—— (*He breaks off and broods.*)

MARY. A what?

HERO. (*Shaking his head.*) No, it's too late now.

JOHN. (*To* MARY.) Haven't we got one?

MARY. I ordered one on Saturday, but it hasn't come.

HERO. You wait here—that will be best. I shall be back in a moment.

JOHN. What do we do?

HERO. Listen. That's all. Listen.

JOHN. (*Eagerly.*) Yes, yes.

HERO. I shall be back directly.

(*Just as he is making for the window, the door opens and the* HEROINE—*obviously*—*comes in. They stand gazing at each other.*)

HEROINE. Oh! (*But with a world of expression in it.*)

HERO. Oh! (*With even more expression.*)

HEROINE. My love!

HERO. My beautiful!

(*They meet and are locked in an embrace.*)

JOHN. (*To* MARY.) I suppose they're engaged to be married.

MARY. Oh, I think they must be.

JOHN. They've evidently *met* before.

HERO. (*Lifting his head for a moment.*) My Dolores! (*He bites her neck again.*)

JOHN. (*To* MARY.) I think this must be both "How do you do" *and* "Good-bye."

MARY. (*Wistfully.*) He is very good-looking.

JOHN. (*Casually.*) Oh, do you think so? Now *she's* pretty, if you like.

MARY. (*Doubtfully.*) Ye-es. Very bad style, of course.

JOHN. (*Indignantly.*) My dear Mary——

HEROINE. (*To* HERO.) Quick, quick, you must go!

HERO. Never—now that I have found you again.

HEROINE. Yes, yes! My father is hot upon your tracks. He will be here at any moment in his two-seater.

HERO. (*Turning pale.*) Your father!

HEROINE. I walked on ahead to warn you. He has come for —IT!

JOHN. (*To* MARY.) What on earth's IT?

HERO. (*Staggering.*) IT.

HEROINE. Yes.

JOHN. (*To* MARY.) Income-tax collector.

HERO. The Rajah's Ruby!

MARY. Oh, how exciting!

HEROINE. Yes, he knows you have it. He is determined to wrest it from you.

HERO. Never!

JOHN. Well done! Bravo! (*Offering his cigarette case.*) Would you care for a——(*But the* HERO *spurns it.*)

HEROINE. There is no mischief he might not do, if once it were in his possession. Three prominent members of Society would be ruined, there would be another war in Mexico and the exchange value of the rouble would be seriously impaired. Promise me you will never give it up.

HERO. I promise.

HEROINE. I must go. I am betraying my father by coming here, but I love you.

JOHN. (*To* MARY.) She does love him. I thought she did.

MARY. How could she help it?

HERO. I adore you!

JOHN. You see, he adores her too. It certainly looked like it.

MARY. I still don't think she's very good style.

HEROINE. Then—good-bye!

(*They embrace again.*)

JOHN. (*After a decent interval.*) Excuse me, sir, but if you have a train to catch—I mean if your future father-in-law's two-seater is any good at all, oughtn't you to be—er——

HERO. (*Releasing* HEROINE.) Good-bye! (*He conducts her to the door, gives her a last long lingering look, and lets her go.*)

MARY. (*To herself.*) Pretty, of course, in a kind of way, but I must say I don't *like* that style.

(*The* HERO *comes out of his reverie and proceeds to business.*)

HERO. (*Briskly to* JOHN.) You have those revolvers?

JOHN. Yes.

HERO. Then wait here, and listen. More than one life depends upon it.

JOHN. How many more?

HERO. If you hear the slightest noise——

JOHN. (*Eagerly.*) Yes?

HERO. H'sh!

(*He goes to the window, waits there listening for a moment, and then slips out. . . .* JOHN *and* MARY *remain, their ears outstretched.*)

JOHN. (*With a start.*) H'sh! What's that?

MARY. What was it, dear?

JOHN. I don't know.

MARY. It's so awkward when you don't quite know what you're listening *for*.

JOHN. H'sh! We were told to listen and we must listen. More than one life depends on it.

MARY. All right, dear.

(*They continue to listen. A little weary of it,* MARY *looks down the barrel of the revolver to see if she can see anything interesting.*)

JOHN. (*Observing her.*) Don't do that! It's very dangerous to point a loaded revolver at yourself. If anything happened, it would be too late to say afterwards that you didn't mean it.

MARY. Very well, John—Oh, look!

(*Again the door opens quickly, and a sinister gentleman in a fur-coat inserts himself into the room. We recognize him at once as the* CHIEF VILLAIN. *Very noiselessly, his back to* JOHN *and* MARY, *he creeps along the wall towards the window.*)

JOHN. (*In a whisper.*) Father-in-law.

MARY. Do we—— (*She indicates the revolver.*)

JOHN. (*Doubtfully.*) I—I suppose—— (*He raises his gun hesitatingly.*)

MARY. Oughtn't you to say something first?

JOHN. Yes—er—— (*He clears his throat warningly.*) Ahem!

(*The* CHIEF VILLAIN *continues to creep towards the window.*)

You sir!

MARY. (*Politely.*) Do you want anything, or—or anything?

(*The* CHIEF VILLAIN *is now at the window.*)

JOHN. Just a moment, sir.

(*The* CHIEF VILLAIN *opens the window and steps out between the curtains.*)

MARY. Oh, he's gone!

JOHN. I call that very bad manners.

MARY. Do you think he'll come back?

JOHN. (*With determination.*) I shall shoot him like a dog if he does. (*Waving aside all protests.*) Like a dog.

MARY. Yes, dear, perhaps that *would* be best.

JOHN. Look out, he's coming back.

(*He raises his revolver as the door opens. Again the* CHIEF VILLAIN *enters cautiously and creeps towards the window.*)

MARY. (*In a whisper.*) Shoot!

JOHN. (*Awkwardly.*) Er—I suppose it *is* the same man?

MARY. Yes, yes!

JOHN. I mean—it wouldn't be quite fair if—— (*He coughs warningly.*) Excuse me, sir!

(*The* CHIEF VILLAIN *is now at the window again.*)

MARY. Quick, before he goes!

JOHN. (*Raising his revolver nervously.*) I ought to tell you, sir—— (*To* MARY.) You know, I still think this is a different one.

(*The* CHIEF VILLAIN *again disappears through the window.*)

MARY. (*In great disappointment.*) Oh, he's gone!

JOHN. (*Firmly.*) It was a different one. The other one hadn't got a moustache.

MARY. He had, John. It was the same man, of course it was.

JOHN. Oh! Well, if I had known that, if I had only been certain of it, I should have shot him like a dog.

A VOICE. (*Which sounds like the* HERO's.) Help, help!

MARY. John, listen!

JOHN. I *am* listening.

A VOICE. He-e-elp!

MARY. Oughtn't we to do something?

JOHN. We *are* doing something. We're listening. That's what he told us to do.

A VOICE. Help!

JOHN. (*Listening.*) That's the other man; the one who came in first.

MARY. The nice-looking one. Oh, John, we *must* do something.

JOHN. If he calls out again, I shall—I shall—do something. I shall take steps. I may even have to shoot somebody. But I will *not* have——

A VOICE. Quick, quick!

MARY. There!

JOHN. Er—was that the same voice?

MARY. (*Moving to the door.*) Yes, of course it was. It sounded as if it were in the hall. Come along.

JOHN. Wait a moment. (*She turns round.*) We must keep cool, Mary. We mustn't be impetuous. Just hold this a moment. (*He hands her his revolver.*)

MARY. (*Surprised.*) Why, what——

JOHN. I shall take my coat off. (*He takes off his coat very slowly.*) I'm going through with this. I'm not easily roused, but when once——

A VOICE. Help! Quick!

JOHN. (*Reassuringly.*) All right, my man, all right. (*Very leisurely he rolls up his sleeves.*) I'm not going to have this sort of thing going on in *my* house. I'm not going to have it. (*Doubtfully.*) I don't think I need take my waistcoat off too. What do *you* think, Mary?

MARY. (*Impatiently.*) No, dear, of course not, you look very nice.

JOHN. (*Very determined.*) Now then, let's have that revolver. (*She gives it to him.*) I shall say "Hands up!"—very sharply, like that—"*Hands up!*"—and then if he doesn't put his hands up I shall—I shall say "Hands up!" again. That will show him that I'm not to be trifled with. Now then, dear, are you ready?

MARY. (*Eagerly.*) Yes!

JOHN. Then——

(*But at that moment the lights go out.*)

MARY. Oh!

JOHN. (*Annoyed.*) Now, why did you do that, Mary?

MARY. I didn't do it, dear.

JOHN. Then who did?

MARY. I don't know. They just went out.

JOHN. Then I shall write to the Company to-morrow and complain. I shall complain to the Company about the lights, and I shall complain to the landlord about the way people go in and out of this house, and shriek and——

MARY. (*In alarm.*) Oh!

JOHN. *Don't* do that! What is it?

MARY. I can feel somebody quite close to me.

JOHN. Well, that's me.

MARY. Not you, somebody else. . . . Oh! He touched me!

JOHN. (*Addressing the darkness.*) Really, sir, I must ask you not to——

MARY. Listen. I can hear breathings all round me!

JOHN. Excuse me, sir, but do you mind *not* breathing all round my wife?

MARY. There! Now I can't hear anything.

JOHN. (*Complacently.*) There you are, my dear. You see what firmness does. I wasn't going to have *that* sort of thing going on in my house.

(*The lights go up and reveal the* HERO *gagged so that only his eyes are visible, and bound to a chair.*)

MARY. (*Clinging to her husband.*) Oh, John!

JOHN. (*With sudden desperate bravery.*) Hands up! (*He levels his revolver.*)

MARY. Don't be silly, how can he?

JOHN. All right, dear, I was only practising. (*He blows a speck of dust off his revolver, and holds it up to the light again.*) Yes, it's quite a handy little fellow. I think I shall be able to do some business with this all right.

MARY. Poor fellow. I wonder who it is.

(*The* HERO *tries to speak with his eyes and movements of the head.*)

JOHN. He wants something. Perhaps it's the evening paper. (*He makes a movement towards it.*)

MARY. Listen!

(*The* HERO *begins to tap with his feet.*)

JOHN. He's signalling something.

MARY. Dots and dashes!

JOHN. That's the Morse Code, that's what that is. Where's my dictionary? (*He fetches it hastily and begins to turn over the pages.*)

MARY. Quick, dear!

JOHN. (*Reading.*) Here we are. "1. Morse—The walrus." (*Looking at the* HERO.) No, that must be wrong. Ah, this is better. "2. Morse code signalling of telegraph-operators—as 'He sends a good morse.'"

MARY. Well? What does it say?

JOHN. Nothing. That's all. Then we come to "Morsel

a small piece of food, a mouthful, a bite. Also a small meal."

MARY. (*Brilliantly.*) A mouthful! That's what he means! He wants the gag taken out of his mouth. (*She goes to him.*)

JOHN. That's very clever of you, Mary. I should never have thought of that.

MARY. (*Untying the gag.*) There! . . . Why, it's the man who came in first, the nice-looking one!

JOHN. Yes, he *said* he was coming back.

(*Before the* HERO *can express his thanks—if that is what he wants to express—the* CHIEF VILLAIN, *accompanied by a* BAD MAN, *comes in.* JOHN *and* MARY *instinctively retreat.*)

CHIEF VILLAIN. (*Sardonically.*) Ha!

JOHN. (*Politely.*) Ha to you, sir.

(*The* CHIEF VILLAIN *fixes* JOHN *with a terrible eye.*)

(*Nervously to* MARY.) Say "Ha!" to the gentleman, dear.

MARY. (*Faintly.*) Ha!

CHIEF VILLAIN. And what the Mephistopheles are *you* doing here?

JOHN. (*To* MARY.) What *are* we doing here?

MARY. (*Bravely.*) This is our house.

JOHN. Yes, this is *our* house.

CHIEF VILLAIN. Then siddown!

(JOHN *sits down meekly.*)

Is this your wife?

JOHN. Yes. (*Making the introduction.*) Eh—my wife—er—Mr.—er—the gentleman——

CHIEF VILLAIN. Then tell her to siddown too.

JOHN. (*To* MARY.) He wants you to siddown.

(*She does so.*)

CHIEF VILLAIN. That's better. (*To* BAD MAN.) Just take their guns off 'em.

BAD MAN. (*Taking the guns.*) Do you want them tied up or gagged or anything?

CHIEF VILLAIN. No, they're not worth it.

JOHN. (*Humbly.*) Thank you.

CHIEF VILLAIN. Now then, to business. (*To* HERO.) Where's the Rajah's ruby?

HERO. (*Firmly.*) I shan't tell you.

CHIEF VILLAIN. You won't?

HERO. I won't.

CHIEF VILLAIN. That's awkward. (*After much thought.*) You absolutely refuse to?

HERO. I absolutely refuse to.

CHIEF VILLAIN. Ha! (*To* BAD MAN.) Torture the prisoner.

BAD MAN. (*Cheerfully.*) Right you are, governor. (*He feels on the lapel of his coat and then says to* MARY.) Could you oblige me with the loan of a pin, Mum?

MARY. I don't think—— (*Finding one.*) Here you are.

BAD MAN. Thanks. (*He advances threateningly upon the prisoner.*)

CHIEF VILLAIN. Wait! (*To* HERO.) Before proceeding to extremities, I will give you one more chance. Where is the Rujah's Raby?

BAD MAN. You mean the Rabah's Rujy, don't you, governor?

CHIEF VILLAIN. That's what I said.

JOHN. (*Wishing to help.*) You *said* the Rubah's Rajy, but I think you meant the rhubarb's——

CHIEF VILLAIN. Silence! (*To* HERO.) I ask you again —where is the Ruj—I mean where is the Rab——Well anyhow, where *is* it?

HERO. I won't tell you.

CHIEF VILLAIN. Proceed, Mr. Smithers.

BAD MAN. Well, you've asked for it, Mate. (*He pushes the pin into the* HERO'*s arm.*)

HERO. Ow!

MARY. Oh, poor fellow!

CHIEF VILLAIN. Silence! Where is——

(*The* HERO *shakes his head.*)

Torture him again, Mr. Smithers.

HERO. No, no! Mercy! I'll tell you.

JOHN. (*Indignantly.*) Oh, I say!

BAD MAN. Shall I just give him another one for luck, governor?

HERO. Certainly not!

JOHN. (*To* MARY.) Personally I think he should have held out much longer.

CHIEF VILLAIN. Very well, then. Where is the Rajah's Ruby?

HERO. In the cloak-room of Waterloo Station. In a hat-box.

CHIEF VILLAIN. (*Doubtfully.*) In the cloak-room at Waterloo Station, you say?

HERO. Yes. In a hat-box. Now release me.

CHIEF VILLAIN. How do I know it's there?

HERO. Well, how do *I* know?

CHIEF VILLAIN. True. (*Holding out his hand.*) Well, give me the ticket for it.

HERO. I haven't got it.

BAD MAN. Now then, none of that.

HERO. I haven't really.

JOHN. I don't think he'd say he *hadn't* got it, if he *had* got it. Do you, Mary?

MARY. Oh, I'm sure he wouldn't.

CHIEF VILLAIN. Silence! (*To* HERO.) Where is the ticket?

HERO. In the cloak-room of Paddington Station. In a hat-box.

CHIEF VILLAIN. The same hat-box?

HERO. Of course not. The other one was at Waterloo Station.

CHIEF VILLAIN. Well then, where's the ticket for the hat-box in the Paddington cloak-room?

HERO. In the cloak-room at Charing Cross. In a hat-box.

CHIEF VILLAIN. (*Annoyed.*) Look here, how many hat-boxes have you got?

HERO. Lots.

CHIEF VILLAIN. Oh! Now let's get this straight. You say that the Rajah's Ruby is in a hat-box in the cloak-room at Paddington——

HERO. Waterloo.

CHIEF VILLAIN. Waterloo; and that the ticket for that hat-box is in a hat-box in the cloak-room at Euston—

HERO. Paddington.

CHIEF VILLAIN. Paddington; and that the ticket for this ticket, which is in a hat-box at Paddington, for the Ruby which is in a hat-box at King's Cross——

BAD MAN. Euston.

JOHN. (*Tentatively.*) St. Pancras?

MARY. Earl's Court?

CHIEF VILLAIN. (*Angrily.*) Oh, shut up! The ticket for this ticket, which is in a hat-box at Paddington, for the Ruby which is in a hat-box at—at——

HERO. Waterloo.

CHIEF VILLAIN. Waterloo, thank you. This ticket is in a hat-box at—er——

JOHN. (*With decision.*) St. Pancras.

MARY. (*Equally certain.*) Earl's Court.

CHIEF VILLAIN. *Shut up!* In a hat-box at——

HERO. Charing Cross.

CHIEF VILLAIN. Exactly. (*Triumphantly.*) Then give me the ticket!

HERO. Which one?

CHIEF VILLAIN. (*Uneasily.*) The one we're talking about.

JOHN. (*Helpful.*) The St. Pancras one.

MARY. The Earl's Court one.

CHIEF VILLAIN. (*In a fury.*) *Will* you shut up? (*To* HERO.) Now listen. (*Very slowly and with an enormous effort of concentration.*) I want the ticket for the hat-box at Charing Cross, which contains the ticket for the hat-box at——

(JOHN'S *lips indicate "St. Pancras" to* MARY, *whose own*

*seem to express a preference for Earl's Court. The* VILLAIN *gives them one look, and goes on firmly.*)
—at Paddington, which contains the ticket for the hat-box at Waterloo, which contains the Rajah's Ruby. (*Proudly.*) There!

HERO. I beg your pardon?

CHIEF VILLAIN. (*Violently.*) I will *not* say it again! Give me the ticket!

HERO. (*Sadly.*) I haven't got it.

CHIEF VILLAIN. (*In an awe-struck whisper.*) You haven't got it?

HERO. No.

CHIEF VILLAIN. (*After several vain attempts to speak.*) Where is it?

HERO. In the cloak-room at Victoria Station.

CHIEF VILLAIN. (*Moistening his lips and speaking faintly.*) Not—not in a hat-box?

HERO. Yes.

CHIEF VILLAIN. (*Without much hope.*) And the ticket for that?

HERO. In the cloak-room at Euston.

CHIEF VILLAIN. (*Quite broken up.*) Also in a hat-box?

HERO. Yes.

CHIEF VILLAIN. How much longer do we go on?

HERO. (*Cheerfully.*) Oh, a long time yet.

CHIEF VILLAIN. (*To* BAD MAN.) How many London stations are there?

JOHN. Well, there's St. Pancras, and——

MARY. Earl's Court——

BAD MAN. About twenty big ones, governor.

CHIEF VILLAIN. Twenty! (*To* HERO.) And what do we do when we've gone through the lot?

HERO. Then we go all round them again.

CHIEF VILLAIN. (*Anxiously.*) And—and so on?

HERO. And so on.

CHIEF VILLAIN. (*His hand to his head.*) This is terrible. I must think. (*To* BAD MAN.) Just torture him again while I think.

BAD MAN. (*Cheerfully.*) Right you are, governor. (*He approaches his victim.*)

HERO. (*Uneasily.*) I say, look here!

JOHN. I don't think it's quite fair, you know——

MARY. (*Suddenly.*) Give me back my pin!

BAD MAN. Must obey orders, gentlemen. (*Coaxingly to* HERO.) Just a little way in! (*Indicating with his fingers.*) That much.

JOHN. (*To* MARY.) I think perhaps "that much" wouldn't matter. What do——

CHIEF VILLAIN. (*Triumphantly.*) I've got it!

(*He rises with an air, the problem solved. They all look at him.*)

JOHN. What?

CHIEF VILLAIN. (*Impressively to* HERO.) There is somewhere—logically, there must be somewhere—a final, an ultimate hat-box.

JOHN. By Jove! That's true!

HERO. Yes.

BAD MAN. (*Scratching his head.*) I don't see it.

CHIEF VILLAIN. Then—where *is* that hat-box?

JOHN. (*Cheerfully.*) St. Pancras.

MARY. Earl's Court.

CHIEF VILLAIN. Shut up! (*To* HERO.) Where is that hat-box?

HERO. In the cloak-room at Charing Cross.

CHIEF VILLAIN. Ah! (*He holds out his hand.*) Then give me the ticket for it.

BAD MAN. (*Threateningly.*) Come on now! The ticket!

HERO. (*Shaking his head sadly.*) I can't.

CHIEF VILLAIN. (*Almost inarticulate with emotion.*) You don't mean to say you've—lost—it?

HERO. (*In a whisper, with bowed head.*) I've lost it.

(*With a terrible shriek the* CHIEF VILLAIN *falls back fainting into the arms of the* BAD MAN. *Instinctively* JOHN *and* MARY *embrace, sobbing to each other "He's lost it!" The* HEROINE *rushes in, crying, "My love, you've lost it!" and puts her arms round the* HERO. *Only the* MAN IN THE BOWLER HAT *remains unmoved. Slowly he removes the cigar from his mouth and speaks.*)

BOWLER HAT. Yes. . . . That's all right. . . . Just a bit ragged still. . . . We'll take it again at eleven to-morrow. . . . Second Act, please.

(*And so the rehearsal goes on.*)

# LONESOME-LIKE

PLAY IN ONE ACT

## HAROLD BRIGHOUSE

Harold Brighouse was born in Lancashire in 1882. He was educated in Manchester, where a number of his characteristic plays were first performed under the direction of Miss Horniman, whose repertory theater (The Gaiety) was the gate through which the so-called "Manchester School" of playwrights made their entrance into the theatrical world. While Mr. Brighouse's score of plays are concerned with a variety of themes, his most significant work is found in the half-dozen whose scenes are laid in his native district. The best of these are the full-length comedy, "Hobson's Choice," and the one-act "Lonesome-Like."

Like all genuine comedies, "Lonesome-Like" is a study in character. Utterly simple in structure, it is a work that appeals in a wistful way to the emotions.

Following is a list of Harold Brighouse's published plays: "The Price of Coal;" "The Doorway;" "Dealing in Futures;" "Graft;" "Lonesome-Like;" "The Oak Settle;" "Spring in Bloomsbury;" "The Scaring-off of Teddy Dawson;" "The Odd Man Out;" "The Game;" "Garside's Career;" "The Northerners;" "Hobson's Choice;" "Converts;" "Followers;" "Zack;" "Maid of France;" "Once a Hero;" "The Happy Hangman;" "Maypole Morning;" "The Paris Doctor;" "The Prince Who Was a Piper;" "The Man About the Place."

References: Preface to "Hobson's Choice" (On the Manchester School); Barrett H. Clark, "A Study of the Modern Drama"; A. E. Morgan, "Tendencies of Modern English Drama."

# LONESOME-LIKE*

## CHARACTERS

SARAH ORMEROD, *An Old Woman*
EMMA BRIERLEY, *A Young Woman*
THE REV. FRANK ALLEYNE, *A Curate*
SAM HORROCKS, *A Young Man*

SCENE: *Room in a Lancashire Cottage.*

TIME: *The present.*

*The scene represents the interior of a cottage in a Lancashire Village. Through the window at the back the grey row of cottages opposite is just visible. The outside door is next to the window. Door left. As regards furniture the room is very bare. The suggestion is not of an empty room, but a stripped room. For example, there are several square patches where the distemper of the walls is of a darker shade than the rest, indicating the places once occupied by pictures. There is an uncovered deal table and two chairs by it near the fire-place right. Attached to the left wall is a dresser and a plate rack above it containing a few pots. The dresser has also one or two utensils upon it. A blackened kettle rests on the top of the cooking range, but the room contains only the barest necessities. The floor is uncarpeted. There are no window curtains, but a yard of cheap muslin is fastened across the window, not coming, however, high enough to prevent a passer-by from looking in should he wish to do so. On the floor, near the fire, is a battered black tin trunk, the lid of which is raised. On a peg behind the door left is a black silk skirt and bodice and an old-fashioned beaded bonnet. The time is afternoon. As the curtain rises the room is empty. Immediately, however, the door left opens and* SARAH ORMEROD, *an old woman, enters carrying clumsily in her arms a couple of pink flannelette night-dresses, folded neatly. Her black stuff dress is well worn, and her wedding-ring is her only ornament. She wears elastic-sided boots, and her rather short skirt shows a pair of grey worsted stockings. A small plaid shawl covers her shoulders.* SARAH *crosses and puts the night-dresses on the table, surveying the trunk ruefully. There is a knock at the outside door and she looks up.*

SARAH. Who's theer?

EMMA. (*Without.*) It's me, Mrs. Ormerod, Emma Brierley.

SARAH. Eh, coom in, Emma, lass. (*Enter* EMMA BRIERLEY. *She is a young weaver, and, having just left her work, she wears a dark skirt, a blouse of some indeterminate blue-grey shade made of cotton, and a large shawl over her head and shoulders in place of a jacket and hat. A colored cotton apron covers her skirt below the waist, and the short skirt displays stout stockings similar to* SARAH'S. *She wears clogs, and the clothes—except the shawl—are covered with ends of cotton and cotton-wool fluff. Even her hair has not escaped. A pair of scissors hangs by a cord from her waist.*)

SARAH. Tha's kindly welcoom. It's good o' thee to think o' coomin' to see an ould woman like me.

EMMA. (*By door.*) Nought o' th' sort, Mrs. Ormerod. Th' mill's just loosed and A thowt A'd step in as A were passin' and see 'ow tha was feeling like.

SARAH. (*Crossing to box.*) Oh, nicely, nicely, thankee. It's only my 'ands as is gone paralytic, tha knaws, an' a weaver's no manner o' good to nobody without th' use o' 'er 'ands. A'm all reeght in masel.' That's worst of it.

EMMA. Well, while A'm 'ere, Mrs. Ormerod, is theer nought as A can do for thee?

SARAH. A dunno as theer is, thankee, Emma.

EMMA. (*Taking her shawl off, looking round and hanging it on a peg in the door.*) Well, A knaws better. What wert doin' when A coom in? Packin' yon box?

SARAH. Aye. Tha sees theer's a two three things as A canna bear thowt o' parting from. A don't reeghtly knaw if they'll let me tak' 'em into workus wi' me, but A canna have 'em sold wi' rest of stuff.

EMMA. (*Crosses below* SARAH *to box, going on her knees.*) Let me help yo.

SARAH. Tha's a good lass, Emma. A'd tak' it kindly of thee.

EMMA. They'd do wi' packin' a bit closer. A dunno as they'd carry safe that road.

SARAH. A know. Its my 'ands tha sees, as mak's it difficult for me. (*Sits on chair* L. C.)

EMMA. Aye. A'll soon settle 'em a bit tighter. (*Lifts all out. Burying her arms in the box and rearranging its contents.*)

SARAH. But what's 'appened to thy looms, lass? They'll not weave by 'emselves while thee's 'ere, tha knows.

EMMA. (*Looking round.*) Eh, looms is all reeght. Factory's stopped. It's Saturday afternoon.

SARAH. So 'tis. A'd clean forgot. A do forget time o' th' week sittin' 'ere day arter day wi' nought to do.

EMMA. So that's all reeght. Tha's no need to worry about me. Tha's got trouble enough of thy own. (*Resuming at the box.*)

SARAH. Aye, th'art reeght theer, lass. Theer's none on us likes to think o' going to workus when we're ould.

EMMA. 'Appen it'll be all reeght after all. Parson's coomin' to see thee.

SARAH. Aye, A knaw 'e is. A dunno, but A'm in 'opes 'e'll do summat for me. Tha can't never tell what them folks can do.

EMMA. (*Kneeling up.*) Tha keep thy pecker oop, Mrs. Ormerod. That's what my moother says to me when A tould 'er A were coomin' in to thee. Keep 'er pecker oop, she says. It's not as if she'd been lazy or a wastrel, she says; Sal Ormerod's bin a 'ard worker in 'er day, she says. It's not as if it were thy fault. Tha can't 'elp tha 'ands going paralytic. (*She continues rummaging in the trunk while speaking.*)

SARAH. Naw. It's not my fault. God knaws A'm game enough for work, ould as A am. A allays knawed as A'd 'ave to work for my living all th' days o' my life. A never was a savin' sort.

EMMA. Theer's nowt against thee for that. Theer's some as can be careful o' theer brass an' some as can't. It's not a virtue, it's a gift. That's what my moother allays says. (*Resumes packing.*)

SARAH. She's reeght an' all. We never 'ad the gift o' savin,' my man and me. An' when Tom Ormerod took an' died, the club money as A drew all went on 'is funeral an' 'is gravestone. A warn't goin' to 'ave it said as 'e warn't buried proper.

EMMA. It were a beautifu funeral, Mrs. Ormerod.

SARAH. Aye.

EMMA. A will say that, beautiful it were. A never seen a better, an' A goes to all as A can. (*Rises.*) A dotes on buryin's. Are these the next? (*Crosses* C. *before table for night-dresses. Takes the night-dresses, and resumes packing.*)

SARAH. Aye. (EMMA *puts them in and rests on her knees listening to* SARAH'S *next speech.*)

SARAH. (*Pause.*) A've been a 'ouseproud woman all my life, Emma, an A've took pride in 'aving my bits 'o sticks as good as another's. Even th' manager's missus oop to factory 'ouse theer, she never 'ad a better show 'o furniture nor me, though A says it as shouldn't. An' it tak's brass to keep a decent 'ouse over your 'ead. An' we allays 'ad our full week's 'ollydayin' at Blackpool reglar at Wakes time. Us didn't 'ave no childer o' our own to spend it on, an' us spent it on ourselves. A allays 'ad a plenty o' good food in th' 'ouse an' never stinted nobody, an' Tom 'e liked 'is beer an' 'is baccy. 'E were a pigeon-fancier too in 'is day, were my Tom, an' pigeon-fancying runs away wi' a mint o' money. No. Soom'ow theer never was no brass to put in th' bank. We was allays spent oop coom wages neeght.

EMMA. A knaw, Mrs. Ormerod. May be A'm young, but A knaw 'ow 'tis. We works cruel 'ard in th' mill, an', when us plays, us plays as 'ard too (*pause*), an' small blame to us either. It's our *own* we're spendin'.

SARAH. Aye. It's a 'ard life, the factory 'and's. A can mind me many an' many's the time when th' warnin' bell went on th' factory lodge at ha'f past five of a winter's mornin' as A've craved for another ha'f hour in my bed, but Tom 'e got me oop an' we was never after six passin' through factory gates all th' years we were wed. There's not many as can say they were never late. "Work or Clem," that were what Tom allays tould me th' ould bell were sayin'. An' 'e were reeght, Emma, "Work or Clem" is God's truth. (EMMA's *head in box.*) An' now th' time's coom when A can't work no more. But Parson's a good man, 'e'll mak' it all reeght. (EMMA's *head appears.*) Eh, it were good o' thee to coom in, lass. A bit o' coompany do mak' a world o' difference. A'm twice as cheerful as A were.

EMMA. A'm glad to 'ear tha say so, Mrs. Ormerod. (*Rises from the box.*) Is theer owt else?

SARAH. A were thinking A'd like to tak' my black silk as A've worn o' Sundays this many a year, but A canna think its reeght thing for workus.

EMMA. Oh, thee tak' it, Mrs. Ormerod.

SARAH. A'd dearly love to. Tha sees A'm noan in debt, nobbut what chairs an table 'ull pay for, and A doan't like thowt o' leaving owt as A'm greatly fond of.

EMMA. Yo doan't, Mrs. Ormerod. Thee tak' it. Wheer

is it? A'll put un in. Theer's lots o' room on top. A'll see un's noan crushed.

SARAH. It's hanging theer behind door. (EMMA *crosses back to door, gets clothes.*) A got un out to show Parson. A thowt A'd ask un if it were proper to tak' it if A've to go. My best bonnet's with it, an' all. (EMMA *goes below table, takes the frock and bonnet, folds it on the table and packs it.*)

EMMA. A'll put un in.

SARAH. A'm being a lot o' trouble to thee, lass.

EMMA. That's nowt, neighbours mun be neighbourly. (*Gets bonnet from table and packs it.*)

SARAH. (*Pause. Looking round.*) Place doan't look much, an' that's a fact. Th' furniture's bin goin' bit by bit, and theer ain't much left to part wi' now.

EMMA. Never mind, it 'ull be all reeght now Parson's takken thee oop.

SARAH. A'm hopin' so. A *am* hopin' so. A never could abide th' thowt o' th' workus—me as 'as bin an 'ard workin' woman. A couldn't fancy sleepin' in a strange bed wi' strange folk round me, an' when th' Matron said "Do that" A'd 'ave to do it, an' when she said "Go theer" A'd 'ave to a' gone wheer she tould me—me as 'as allays 'eld my yead 'igh an' gone the way A pleased masel'. Eh, it's a terrible thowt, the workus.

EMMA. (*Rising.*) Now tha's sure that's all?

SARAH. (*Pause. Considers.*) Eh, if A havna forgot my neeghtcaps. (*Rises, moves* C. *and stops.*) A suppose they'll let me wear un in yonder. A doan't reeghtly think as A'd get my rest proper wi'out my neeghtcaps.

EMMA. Oh, they'll let thee wear un all reeght.

SARAH. (*As she goes.*) A'll go an' get un. (*Exit* R. *Returning presently with the white nightcaps.*) That's all now. (*Giving them to* EMMA, *who meets her* C.)

EMMA. (*Putting them in.*) Yo never 'ad no childer, did yo, Mrs. Ormerod?

SARAH. No, Emma, no—may be that's as broad as 's

long. (*Sits above fire.*) Yo never knaw 'ow they go. Soom on 'em turn again yo when they're growed or they get wed themselves an' forget all as yo've done for 'em, like a many A could name, and they're allays a worrit to yo when they're young.

EMMA. A'm gettin' wed masel' soon, Mrs. Ormerod.

SARAH. Are yo, now, Emma? Well, tha art not one o' them graceless good-for-nowts. Tha'll never forget thy moother, A knaw, nor what she's done for thee. Who's tha keepin' company with?

EMMA. It's Joe Hindle as goes wi' me, Mrs. Ormerod.

SARAH. 'Indle, 'Indle? What, not son to Robert 'Indle, 'im as used to be overlooker in th' factory till 'e went to foreign parts to learn them Roossians 'ow to weave?

EMMA. Aye, that's 'im.

SARAH. Well, A dunno ought about th' lad. 'Is faither were a fine man. A minds 'im well. But A'll tell thee this, Emma, an' A'll tell it thee to they faice, 'e 's doin' well for 'isself is young Joe 'Indle.

EMMA. Thankee, Mrs. Ormerod.

SARAH. Gettin' wed! Think 'o that. Why, it seems as t'were only t'other day as tha was running about in short frocks, an' now tha's growed up and gettin' thasel' wed! Time do run on. Sithee, Emma, tha's a good lass. A've gotten an ould tea-pot in yonder (*indicating her bedroom*) as my moother give me when A was wed. A weren't for packing it in box because o' risk o' breaking it. A were going to carry it in my 'and. A'd a mind to keep it till A died, but A reckon A'll 'ave no use for it in workus.

EMMA. Tha's not gone theer yet.

SARAH. Never mind that. (*Slowly rises.*) A'm going to give it thee, lass, for a weddin'-gift. Tha'll tak' care of it, A knaw, and when thy eye catches it, 'appen tha'll spare me a thowt.

EMMA. Oh no, Mrs. Ormerod, A couldn't think o' takkin' it.

SARAH. Art too proud to tak' a gift from me?

EMMA. No. Tha knaws A'm not.

SARAH. Then hold thy hush. A'll be back in a minute. Happen A'd best tidy masel' up too against Parson cooms.

EMMA. Can A help thee, Mrs. Ormerod?

SARAH. No, lass, no. A can do a bit for masel'. My 'ands isn't that bad, A canna weave wi' 'em, but A can do all as A need to.

EMMA. Well, A'll do box up. (*Crosses to table* R. *and gets cord.*)

SARAH. Aye.

EMMA. All reeght. (*Exit* SARAH. *A man's face appears outside at the window. He surveys the room, and then the face vanishes as he knocks at the door.*) Who's theer?

SAM. (*Without.*) It's me, Sam Horrocks. (EMMA *crosses* L. *and opens door.*) May A coom in?

EMMA. What dost want?

SAM. (*On the doorstep.*) A want a word wi' thee, Emma Brierley. A followed thee oop from factory and A've bin waitin' out theer till A'm tired o' waitin'.

EMMA. Well, tha'd better coom in. A 'aven't time to talk wi' thee at door. (EMMA *lets him in, closes door, and, leaving him standing in the middle of the room, resumes work on her knees at the box.* SAM HORROCKS *is a hulking young man of a rather vacant expression. He is dressed in mechanic's blue dungarees. His face is oily and his clothes stained. He wears boots, not clogs. He mechanically takes a ball of oily black cotton-waste from his right pocket when in conversational difficulties and wipes his hands upon it. He has a red muffler round his neck without collar, and his shock of fair hair is surmounted by a greasy black cap, which covers perhaps one tenth of it.*)

SAM. (*After watching* EMMA's *back for a moment.*) Wheer's Mrs. Ormerod?

EMMA. (*Without looking up.*) What's that to do wi' thee?

SAM. (*Apologetically.*) A were only askin'. Tha needn't be short wi' a chap.

EMMA. She's in scullery washin' 'er if tha wants to knaw.

SAM. Oh!

EMMA. (*Looking at him over her shoulder after a slight pause.*) Doan't tha tak' thy cap off in 'ouse, Sam Horrocks?

SAM. Naw.

EMMA. Well, tha can tak' it off in this 'ouse or get t' other side o' door.

SAM. (*Takes off his cap and stuffs it in his left pocket after trying his right and finding the ball of waste in it.*) Yes, Emma. (EMMA *resumes work with her back towards him and waits for him to speak. But he is not ready yet.*)

EMMA. Well, what dost want?

SAM. Nought. . . . Eh, but tha art a gradely wench.

EMMA. What's that to do wi' thee?

SAM. Nought.

EMMA. Then just tha mind thy own busines, an' doan't pass compliments behind folks' backs.

SAM. A didn't mean no 'arm.

EMMA. Well?

SAM. It's a fine day, isn't it? For th' time o' th' year?

EMMA. Aye.

SAM. A very fine day.

EMMA. Aye.

SAM. (*Desperately.*) It's a damned fine day.

EMMA. Aye.

SAM. (*After a moment.*) Dost know my 'ouse, Emma?

EMMA. Aye.

SAM. Wert ever in it?

EMMA. Not sin' tha moother died.

SAM. Naw. I suppose not. Not sin' ma moother died.

She was a fine woman, ma moother, for all she were bed-ridden.

EMMA. She were better than 'er son, though that's not saying much neither.

SAM. Naw, but tha does mind ma 'ouse, Emma, as it were when she were alive?

EMMA. Aye.

SAM. A've done a bit at it sin' them days. Got a new quilt on bed from Co-op. Red un it is wi' blue stripes down 'er.

EMMA. Aye.

SAM. Well, Emma?

EMMA. (*Over her shoulder.*) Well, what? What's thy 'ouse an' thy quilt to do wi' me?

SAM. Oh nought. . . . Tha doesn't 'elp a feller much, neither.

EMMA. (*Rising and facing him.* SAM *is behind corner table and backs a little before her.*) What's tha gettin' at, Sam Horrocks? Tha's got a tongue in thy faice, hasn't tha?

SAM. A suppose so. A doan't use it much though.

EMMA. No. Tha's not much better than a tongue-tied idiot, Sam Horrocks, allays mooning about in th' engine-house in day-time an' sulkin' at 'ome neeght-time.

SAM. Aye, A'm lonely sin' ma moother died. She did 'ave a way wi' 'er, ma moother. Th' 'ould plaice 'as not bin t' same to me sin' she went. Day-time, tha knaws, A'm all reeght. Tha sees, them engines, them an' me's pals. They talks to me an' A understands their ways. A doan't some'ow seem to understand the ways o' folks like as A does th' ways o' them engines.

EMMA. Tha doesn't try. T'other lads goes rattin' or dog-feeghtin' on a Sunday or to a football match of a Saturday afternoon. Tha stays moonin' about th' 'ouse. Tha's not likely to understand folks. Tha's not sociable.

SAM. Naw. That's reeght enough. A nobbut get laughed at when A tries to be sociable an' stand my corner down at th' pub wi' th' rest o' th' lads. It's no use ma tryin' to soop ale, A can't carry th' drink like t'others. A knaws A've ways o' ma own.

EMMA. Tha has that.

SAM. A'm terrible lonesome, Emma. That theer 'ouse o' mine, it do want a wench about th' plaice. Th' engines is all reeght for days, but th' neeghts is that lonesome-like tha wouldn't believe.

EMMA. Tha's only thasel' to blame. It's nought to do wi' me, choosehow.

SAM. Naw? A'd . . . A'd 'oped as 'ow it might 'ave, Emma.

EMMA. (*Approaching threateningly.*) Sam Horrocks, if tha doan't tell me proper what tha means A'll give tha such a slap in th' mouth.

SAM. (*Backing before her.*) Tha does fluster a feller, Emma. Just like ma moother.

EMMA. A wish A 'ad bin. A'd 'ave knocked some sense into thy silly yead.

SAM. (*Suddenly and clumsily kneels above chair* L. *of table.*) Wilt tha 'ave me, Emma? A mak' good money in th' engine-house.

EMMA. Get oop, tha great fool. If tha didn't keep thasel' so close wi' tha moonin' about in th' engine-'ouse an' never speakin' a word to nobody tha'd knaw A were keepin' coompany wi' Joe Hindle.

SAM. (*Scrambling up.*) Is that a fact, Emma?

EMMA. Of course it's a fact. Bann's 'ull be oop come Sunday fortneeght. We've not 'idden it neither. It's just like the great blind idiot that tha art not to 'a' seen it long enough sin'.

SAM. A wern't aware. By gum, A 'ad so 'oped as tha'd 'ave me, Emma.

EMMA. (*A little more softly.*) A'm sorry if A've 'urt thee, Sam.

SAM. Aye. It were ma fault. Eh, well, A think mebbe A'd best be goin'.

EMMA. (*Lifts box to* L.) Aye. Parson's coomin' to see Mrs. Ormerod in a minute.

SAM. (*With pride.*) A knaw all about that, anyhow.

EMMA. She'm in a bad way. A dunno masel' as Parson can do much for 'er.

SAM. It's 'ard lines on an ould un. Well, yo'll not want me 'ere. A'll be movin' on. (*Getting his cap out.*) No offence, Emma, A 'ope. A'd 'ave asked thee first if A'd knawn as 'e were after thee. A've bin tryin' for long enough.

EMMA. No. Theer's no offence, Sam. Tha's a good lad if tha art a fool, an' mebbe tha's not to blame for that. Good-bye.

SAM. Good-bye, Emma. An' . . . An' A' 'ope 'e'll mak' thee 'appy. A'd dearly like to coom to th' weddin' an' shake 'is 'and. (MRS. ORMEROD *heard off* R.)

EMMA. A'll see tha's asked. Theer's Mrs. Ormerod stirrin'. Tha'd best be gettin'.

SAM. All reeght. Good-bye, Emma.

EMMA. Good-bye, Sam. (*Exit* SAM L. C. MRS. ORMEROD *comes from the inside door. She has a small blue teapot in her hand.*)

SARAH. Was anybody 'ere, Emma? A thowt A yeard someun talkin', only my yearin' isn't what it used to be, an' A warn't sure.

EMMA. It were Sam Horrocks, Mrs. Ormerod.

SARAH. Yon lad of ould Sal Horrocks as died last year? 'Im as isn't reeght in 'is yead?

EMMA. Aye. 'E's bin askin' me to wed 'im.

SARAH. (*Incensed.*) In my 'ouse? Theer's imperence for thee, an' tha promised to another lad, an' all. A'd 'ave set about 'im wi' a stick, Emma.

EMMA. 'E didn't knaw about Joe. It made me feel cruel like to 'ave to tell 'im.

SARAH. 'E'll get ower it. Soom lass'll tak' 'im.

EMMA. A suppose so.

SARAH. (*Coming down, putting the tea-pot in* EMMA'S *hands.*) Well, theer's tea-pot.

EMMA. (*Meets* SARAH R. C., *examining tea-pot.*) It's beautiful. Beautiful, it is, Mrs. Ormerod.

SARAH. Aye, it's a bit o' real china is that. Tha'll tak' care on't, lass, won't thee?

EMMA. A will an' all.

SARAH. Aye. A knaw it's safe wi' thee. Mebbe safer than it would be in workus. A can't think well on yon plaice. A goa cold al ower at thowt of it. (*A knock at the door.*)

EMMA. That'll be Parson.

SARAH. (*Crosses* L. *Smoothing her hair.*) Goa an' look through window first, an' see who 'tis.

EMMA. (*Puts tea-pot on table. Looking through window.*) It's not th' ould Parson. It's one o' them young curate chaps.

SARAH. Well, coom away from window an' sit thee down. It won't do to seem too eager. Let un knock again if it's not th' ould Parson. (EMMA *leaves the window and goes to* R. *of table. The knock is repeated. Raising her voice.*) Coom in so who tha art. Door's on latch. (*Enter the* REV. FRANK ALLEYNE. *He is a young curate, a Londoner and an Oxford man, by association, training, and taste, totally unfitted for a Lancashire curacy, in which he is unfortunately no exception.*)

ALLEYNE. Good afternoon, Mrs. Ormerod.

SARAH. Good day to thee.

ALLEYNE. I'm sorry to say Mr. Blundell has had to go to a missionary meeting, but he asked me to come and see you in his stead.

SARAH. Tha's welcoom, lad. Sit thee down. (EMMA *comes below table* L. *Dusts a chair* L. *of table, which doesn't need it, with her apron.* ALLEYNE *raises a deprecatory hand.* SARAH'S *familiarity, as it seems to him, offends him. He looks sourly at* EMMA *and markedly ignores her.*)

ALLEYNE. Thank you; no, I won't sit, I cannot stay long.

SARAH. Just as tha likes. It's all same to me. (EMMA *stays by* R. *of table.*)

ALLEYNE. How is it with you, Mrs. Ormerod?

SARAH. It might be worse. A've lost th' use o' my 'ands, and they're takkin' me to workus, but A'm not dead yet, and that's summat to be thankful for.

ALLEYNE. Oh yes, yes, Mrs. Ormerod. The—er—message I am to deliver is, I fear, not quite what Mr. Blundell led you to hope for. His efforts on your behalf have—er—unfortunately failed. He finds himself obliged to give up all hope of aiding you to a livelihood. In fact—er—I understand that the arrangements made for your removal to the workhouse this afternoon must be carried out. It seems there is no alternative. I am grieved to be the bearer of bad tidings, but I am sure you will find a comfortable home awaiting you, Mrs.—er—Ormerod.

SARAH. 'Appen A shall an' 'appen A shan't. Theer's no tellin' 'ow you'll favor a thing till you've tried it.

ALLEYNE. You must resign yourself to the will of Providence. The consolations of religion are always with us. Shall I pray with you?

SARAH. A never were much at prayin' when A were well off, an' A doubt the Lord ud tak' it kind o' selfish o' me if A coom cryin' to 'im now A'm 'urt.

ALLEYNE. He will understand. Can I do nothing for you?

SARAH. A dunno as tha can, thankin' thee all same.

ALLEYNE. I am privileged with Mr. Blundell's permission to bring a little gift to you, Mrs. Ormerod. (*Feeling in his coat-tails and bringing out a Testament.*) Allow me to present you with this Testament, and may it help you to bear your Cross with resignation. (*He hands her the Testament.* SARAH *does not raise her hands, and it drops on her lap.* ALLEYNE *takes it again and puts it on the table.*) Ah, yes, of course . . . your poor hands . . . I understand.

SARAH. Thankee kindly. Readin don't coom easy to me, an' my eyes aren't what they were, but A 'll mak' most of it.

ALLEYNE. You will never read that in vain. And now, dear sister, I must go. I will pray for strength for you. All will be well. Good day.

SARAH. Good day to thee. (*Exit* ALLEYNE.)

EMMA. Tha doesn't look so pleased wi' tha gift, Mrs. Ormerod.

SARAH. It's not square thing of th' ould Parson, Emma. 'E should a coom an' tould me 'isself. Looks like 'e were feart to do it. A never could abide them curate lads. We doan't want no grand Lunnon gentlemen down 'ere. 'E doan't understand us no more than we understand 'im. 'E means all reeght, poor lad. Sithee, Emma, A've bin a Church-goin' woman all my days. A was browt oop to Church, an' many's th' bit o' brass they've 'ad out o' me in my time. An' in th' end they send me a fine curate with a tuppenny Testament. That's all th' good yo get out o' they folks.

EMMA. We'm chapel to our 'ouse, an' 'e didn't forget to let me see 'e knaw'd it, but A doan't say as it's ony different wi' chapels, neither. They get what they can outer yo, but yo mustn't look for nothin' back, when th' pinch cooms. (*Clock outside strikes three.*) Sakes alive, theer's clock goin' three. My dinner 'ul be nice an' cold.

SARAH. Eh, what's that, lass? Dost mean to tell me tha's bin clemmin' all this time?

EMMA. A coom 'ere straight from factory.

SARAH. Then tha doesn't move till tha's 'ad summat to eat.

EMMA. My dinner's ready for me at whoam, Mrs. Ormerod.

SARAH. Then just look sharp an' get it, tha silly lass. Tha's no reeght to go wi'out thy baggin'.

EMMA. (*Putting her shawl on.*) All reeght. A'm off. (*Picking up tea-pot.*)

SARAH. Tha's bin a world o' coomfort to me, Emma. It'll be 'arder to bear when tha's gone. Th' thowt's too much for me. Eh, lass, A'm feart o' yon great gaunt building wi' th' drear windows.

EMMA. 'Appen ma moother 'ull coom in. Tha'll do wi' a bit o' coompany. A'll ask her to coom an' fetch thee a coop o' tea by an' bye. (*A knock at the door.*)

SARAH. Who's theer?

SAM. (*Without.*) It's only me, Mrs. Ormerod.

EMMA. A do declare it's that Sam Horrocks again.

SARAH. Sam Horrocks! What can th' lad be after now? (*Calling.*) Hast tha wiped thy boots on scraper?

SAM. Yes, Mrs. Ormerod.

SARAH. Coom in then. (EMMA *in* L. *corner. Enter* SAM.) Tak' thy cap off.

SAM. Yes, Mrs. Ormerod.

SARAH. What dost want?

SAM. A've soom business 'ere. A thowt A'd find thee by thysel'. A'll coom again. (*Bolting nervously for the door.*)

SARAH. Let that door be. Dost say tha's got business 'ere?

SAM. Aye, wi' thee. A'd like a word wi' thee private. (EMMA *moves to open door.*)

SARAH. All reeght. Emma's just goin' to 'er dinner.

EMMA. (*Speaking through door.*) A'll ask my moother to step in later on, Mrs. Ormerod, and thank thee very much for th' tea-pot.

SARAH. A'll be thankful if she'll coom. (*Exit* EMMA *with tea-pot.*) Now, Sam Horrocks, what's the matter wi' thee?

SAM. (*Dropping the cotton waste he is fumbling with and picking it up.*) It's a fine day for th' time o' th' year.

SARAH. Didst want to see me private to tell me that, lad?

SAM. Naw, not exactly.

SARAH. Well, what is it then? Coom, lad, A'm waitin' on thee. Art tongue-tied? Can't tha quit mawlin' yon bit o' waste an' tell me what 'tis tha wants?

SAM. (*Desperately.*) Mebbe it'll not be so fine in th' mornin'.

SARAH. A'll tell thee what A'd do to thee if A 'ad the use o' my 'ands, my lad. A'd coom aside thee and A'd box thy ears. If tha's got business wi' me, tha'd best state it sharp or A'll be showin' thee the shape o' my door.

SAM. Tha do fluster a feller so as A doan't knaw wheer A am. A've not been nagged like that theer sin' my ould moother died.

SARAH. A've 'eerd folk say Sal Horrocks were a slick un wi' 'er tongue.

SAM. (*Admiringly.*) She were that. Rare talker she were. She'd lie theer in 'er bed all day as it might be in yon corner, an' call me all th' names she could put her tongue to, till A couldn't tell ma reeght 'and from ma left. (*Still reminiscent.*) Wonnerful sperrit, she 'ad, considerin' she were bed-ridden so long. She were only a little un an' cripple an' all, but by gum she could sling it at a feller if 'er tea weren't brewed to 'er taste. Talk! She'd talk a donkey's yead off, she would.

SARAH. (*On her mettle.*) An' A'll talk thy silly yead off an' all if tha doan't get sharp to tellin' me what tha wants after in my 'ouse, tha great mazed idiot.

SAM. Eh, but she were a rare un.

SARAH. The lad's daft aboot his moother.

SAM. (*Detachedly, looking at window. Pause.*) Wunnerful breeght the sky is, to-day.

SARAH. Tha great 'ulkin' fool. A'd tak' a broomstick to thee if—if A'd the use o' my 'ands.

SAM. Now, if that isn't just what ma moother used to say.

SARAH. Dang thy moother. An' A doan't mean no disrespect to 'er neither. She's bin in 'er grave this year an' more, poor woman.

SAM. A canna 'elp thinkin' to 'er all same. Eh, but she were wunnerful.

SARAH. An' A'd be wunnerful too. A'd talk to thee. A'd call thee if A were thy moother an' A'd to live aside 'o thee neeght an' day.

SAM. (*Eagerly.*) Eh, by gum, but A wish tha would.

SARAH. Would what?

SAM. Would coom an' live along wi' me.

SARAH. Tha great fool, what dost mean? Art askin' me to wed thee?

SAM. A didn't mean to offend thee, Mrs. Ormerod. A'm sorry A spoke. A allays do wrong thing. But A did so 'ope as tha might coom. Tha sees A got use to moother. A got used to 'earin' 'er cuss me. A got used to doin' for 'er an' A've nought to do in th' evenings now. It's terrible lonesome in th' neeght-time. An' when notion coom to me, A thowt as A'd mention un to thee casual.

SARAH. Dost mean it, Sam Horrocks? Dost tha know what tha's sayin', or is tha foolin' me?

SAM. O' course A mean it. Tha sees A'm not a marryin' sort. Th' lasses won't look at me. A'm silly Sam to them, A knaws it. A've a slate loose, A shan't never get wed. A thowt A'd mebbe a chance wi' yon lass as were 'ere wi' thee, but hoo towld me A were too late. A allays were slow. A left askin' too long an' A've missed 'er. A gets good money, Mrs.Ormerod, but A canna talk to a young wench. They maks me go 'ot and cowld all over. An' when curate towld me tha was to go to workus, A thowt A'd a chance wi' thee. A knaw'd it weren't a big chance, because my plaice ain't much cop after what tha's bin used to 'ere. A've got no fine fixin's nor big chairs an' things like as tha used to 'ave. Eh, but A would 'ave loved to do for thee as A used to do for ma moother, an' when A yeerd thee talkin' now an' callin' me a fool an' th' rest, by gum, A just yearned to 'ave thee for allays. Tha'd fill 'er plaice wunnerful well. A'd just a' loved to adopt thee.

SARAH. To adopt me?

SAM. Ay, for a moother. A'm sorry tha can't see thy way to let me. A didn't mean no offense. (*Turning to the door.*)

SARAH. 'Ere lad, tha tell me this. If A'd said tha might tak' me for thy moother, what wouldst ha' done?

SAM. Why kissed thee, an' takken thee oop in ma arms whoam to thy bed. It's standin' ready in yonder wi' clean sheets an' all, an' a new quilt from Co-op. A 'opes you'll pardon th' liberty o' mentioning it.

SARAH. A new quilt, Sam? What's colour?

SAM. Red, wi' blue stripes down 'er.

SARAH. A'm not a light weight, tha knows.

SAM. A'd carry thee easy—"Strong in th' arm and weak in th' yead." It's an ould sayin', but it's a good un, an' it fits.

SARAH. Wilt tha try, Sam Horrocks? God bless thee, wilt tha try, lad?

SAM. Dost mean it, Mrs. Ormerod? Dost mean tha'll coom? Tha's not coddin' a feller, art tha?

SARAH. No, A'm not coddin'. Kiss me, Sam, my son. (*He kisses her and lifts her in his arms.*)

SAM. By gum, but that were good. A'll come back fur thy box.

SARAH. Carry me careful, tha great luny. A'm not a sack o' flour.

SAM. Eh, but A likes to year thee talk. Yon was real mootherly, it were. (*Exit through door, carrying her.*)

CURTAIN AT CLINK OF LATCH.

# HANGING AND WIVING

A PASSAGE IN THE LIVES OF A GIRL AND A WOMAN

## J. HARTLEY MANNERS

J. Hartley Manners was born at London in 1870. Like many other successful contemporary dramatists, his early training was received on the stage. He first appeared as an actor in Melbourne in 1898. He began writing plays in 1899. For several years he has resided chiefly in America, where his wife, Laurette Taylor, has achieved widespread popularity and success in his plays. The best among these are "Peg o' My Heart," "Happiness," "Out There," "The Harp of Life" and "The National Anthem." Mr Manners is an able craftsman with an expert knowledge of the requirements of the theater. In such plays as "Peg o' My Heart" and "Happiness" he has successfully depicted characters in the poorer walks of life in contradistinction to those more happily endowed and by means of sympathetic and observant treatment produced an appealing type of modern comedy and human drama.

A number of Mr. Manners' plays are in one-act form: among the more striking of them is "Hanging and Wiving," which is here published for the first time.

The following is a list of Mr. J. Hartley Manners' published plays: "Peg o' My Heart," "Happiness," "Out There," "The Harp of Life," "The National Anthem," "The House Next Door," "Wreckage," "The Wooing of Eve," "The Girl in Waiting."

One-act plays: "A Queen's Messenger," "The Woman Intervenes," "Just as Well," "The Day of Dupes," "God's Outcast."

# HANGING AND WIVING*

*"Hanging and Wiving Goes by Destiny."*

CHARACTERS

THE GIRL
A MAID
THE WOMAN
A MAN

SCENE: *Sitting-room of a Furnished Flat in London.*

TIME: *The Present.*

*It is a very ordinary room, such as might be met with in any of a hundred furnished flats in the South-western district of London. Only the intimate touches suggest the occupant: a few of her photographs; some of those of her nearest relatives: one of an officer in uniform; a curious old rug, a cabinet of porcelain—probably a legacy; a rare tapestry also evidently bequeathed. These hint at the individuality of the fair tenant. But what immediately appeals to the eye is eloquent of an impending journey. The floor is littered with trunks standing, sitting and lying. They are labelled, locked and strapped waiting to be removed. When the significance of these silent witnesses of some approaching feat of travel has had time to be appreciated, a bell rings.*

*The* MAID, *a capable, sturdy woman of 45, enters from an inner room and goes out through the door leading into the hall. The low murmur of voices is heard for a few moments. Then the* MAID *re-enters, followed by* THE WOMAN. *The* MAID *closes the door leading to the hall and goes silently back to the inner room.*

*The* WOMAN *would arrest attention in a throng. Framed in the shadow of the door with the tapestry above her, a gleam of sunlight on her face, there is an irresistible halo of fascination around her. The cryptic expression in her eyes makes one yearn for knowledge of her. Sorrowful, mocking, playful, sardonical they change as rapidly as her thoughts. Of commanding height, yet at times she seems as a child. No longer young, yet she embodies most of the allurements of youth. Silver of tongue, perfect in expression, every word she speaks is as clear-cut as a diamond. She makes a dazzling picture as she stands, closely wrapped in furs, surveying the conventional little room. The trunks naturally attract her attention first. There is no avoiding them. She looks down curiously at them, reads the label on one of them and smiles. The photographs finally draw her to them. She looks at the officer but quickly passing him over she is attracted by one of a middle-aged, kindly, happy-looking woman. She takes it quite reverently from its resting-place and polishing the glass with her glove, looks at it and sighs.*

*From the inner room,* THE GIRL *enters. She is as fair as the woman is dark. Both are positive in their opposite coloring. She is below medium height, extremely pretty, and moves easily and gracefully as one accustomed to vigorous exercise. She looks questioningly and in no little wonder at the woman. It is evidently an unwelcome visit.*

THE WOMAN. (*Replacing the photograph on the piano, smiles at the* GIRL, *takes one of her hands in her own two hands and speaking apparently sincerely, yet with the faintest trace of mockery.*) You don't remember me? Why should you? When we last met you were a little pink-and-white baby.

THE GIRL. (*Puzzled, distrustful, timid, taking away her hand.*) Really?

THE WOMAN. I brought you a christening-cup then. Doesn't that seem ridiculous? And now—as you are going to be married tomorrow—(*Searching amongst her furs for something hidden.*)

THE GIRL. (*Amazed and angry.*) What?

THE WOMAN. —as you're going to be married tomorrow I've brought you another little gift. (*Finds a slender case.*) It was an old custom in our family when one of us married to give the bride a gift that would cut. So I've dared to bring you *this.* (*Hands her the case.*)

(*The* GIRL *looks at the* WOMAN *distrustfully, then draws from the sheath a slim, keenedged, curiously wrought knife.*)

Isn't it enchanting? It is so symbolical. (*Touching the blade with her forefinger.*) They cut quarrels, tempers, jealousies *and* sometimes the marriage-tie itself.

THE GIRL. Who are you?

THE WOMAN. (*Nodding towards the photograph on the piano.*) Your mother was one of my bridesmaids. Doesn't it seem absurd? And *that* was a wedding-present from an uncle. (*Indicating the knife.*) He was a bachelor. Poor dear. But he was right. It *cut*—cut beautifully. You will make me so happy by accepting it.

THE GIRL. I don't want it. (*Holding it out.*)

(*The* WOMAN *protests with a gesture.*)

Here! (*Forces it into* THE WOMAN'S *hands.*)

THE WOMAN. How disappointing of you!

THE GIRL. (*Glaring at* THE WOMAN.) How do you know I am going to be married?

THE WOMAN. Aren't you?

THE GIRL. How did you know?

THE WOMAN. I came all the way from France to give you this. (*Holding up knife.*) And you refuse it.

Cruel of you. Your husband-that-may-be would adore it.

THE GIRL. What is your name?

THE WOMAN. I had no time to write. I only heard two days ago. And I rushed over. Rushed, my dear. So you marry tomorrow. Wonderful! *And* in Holland. How priceless. The dear quaint people. Such a novel idea. Adorable. How did you ever think of it? Perhaps *he* thought of it? It would be *so* like him. Fancy being married in Dutch! The service won't seem so awful, will it?

THE GIRL. (*Angrily and insistently.*) How did you hear I am going to be married?

THE WOMAN. Nothing is secret today, my dear. We're all living in glass houses. Especially if we're in love. That is the one condition between two people that quickens everyone's curiosity. Rich and poor, happy and miserable. The unending mystery. "How will it turn out?" We all love to guess. Don't we? "Hanging and wiving goes by destiny!" Doesn't it?

THE GIRL. (*Furiously.*) Who are you?

THE WOMAN. I believe you're angry with me. *Are* you?

THE GIRL. Yes, I am.

THE WOMAN. That makes me so unhappy. Don't you like me?

THE GIRL. No.

THE WOMAN. How frank. Now I like you. I wasn't prepared to. In fact, when I heard of you I *dis*liked you. And you were such a nice baby. But I was wrong. (*Looking at and approaching her.*) Yes, I like you. And I am going to protect you from doing a very stupid thing.

THE GIRL. *Protect* me?

THE WOMAN. I *can.* And now that I like you I *will.*

THE GIRL. From what?

THE WOMAN. From going tomorrow to Holland.

THE GIRL. (*Indignantly.*) Oh!

THE WOMAN. My dear, he's not going to marry you. He couldn't. If he *did* he'd be taken away from you and put into a horrid prison. Wouldn't that be wretched? Of course, *some* wives wouldn't mind. But you would. Wouldn't you?

THE GIRL. (*Very white, very nervous, gasping to control her breathing.*) What do you mean?

THE WOMAN. A stupid restriction, my dear. But there it is. Until a man gets rid of one wife, he can't take another. It's so annoying.

THE GIRL. His wife is dead.

THE WOMAN. Did he tell you that?

THE GIRL. Yes.

THE WOMAN. How misleading of him. My dear, all lovers are liars.

THE GIRL. (*Dazed.*) She's not dead?

THE WOMAN. (*Shakes her head.*) Isn't it a pity?

THE GIRL. How do I know you're speaking the truth?

THE WOMAN. Ah! If you hadn't refused my little gift you *would* have known. (*Taking out the knife and pointing to some lettering on the blade.*) There's the date of his marriage, his name and his wife's. See? (THE GIRL *looks at it excitedly.*) *That's my* name, my dear. (THE GIRL *looks at her in horror.*)

THE GIRL. (*Dully.*) You!

THE WOMAN. (*Putting knife back in sheath.*) Yes. I suppose you think it's a shame I've lived so long! You look as if you did.

THE GIRL. (*Vehemently.*) I don't believe it.

THE WOMAN. (*Sitting down coolly, loosening her furs and relaxing.*) Very well. I'll wait here until he calls.

THE GIRL. (*Frightened.*) No, no.

THE WOMAN. Then you *do* believe it?

THE GIRL. (*Distractedly.*) You've not been a wife to him.

THE WOMAN. Did he tell you that, too?

THE GIRL. You treated him cruelly, shamefully.

THE WOMAN. Ah! And then he killed me so as to marry you.

THE GIRL. He thought you were dead.

THE WOMAN. Did he really? It's extraordinary the number of men who have thought their wives dead and taken nice, new, fresh ones. Only to find the disagreeable people were alive. And then the tiresome police have interfered. Such a shame. So you see, my dear, you mustn't go to Holland tomorrow.

THE GIRL. (*Walking up and down distractedly.*) If you hated him so much why didn't you divorce him or let him divorce you?

THE WOMAN. I don't want to marry again. (*With a gesture of disgust.*) Not after *him*. Why should I divorce him?

THE GIRL. Then let him divorce you.

THE WOMAN. How heartless of you! Divorce *me!* My dear! Then he might *really* marry you. I don't dislike you enough to allow that. So I came to stop you.

THE GIRL. (*Vehemently.*) You can't stop me. I love him. And I'm going with him. I want no marriage-service. I want to be with him always. We would be *really* married.

THE WOMAN. You're very young, my dear, aren't you?

THE GIRL. (*Hotly.*) I'm old enough to decide for myself.

THE WOMAN. Oh, I can see that.

THE GIRL. What was *your* marriage? A mockery. You tied to a man you hated: he bound to a woman he—he —(*Stops.*)

THE WOMAN. Oh, don't stop.

THE GIRL. I don't want any such tie. We'll both be free. If he tires of me he can go. And we both can begin again and no harm done.

THE WOMAN. It all sounds so delightfully *new*. How *did* you think of it?

THE GIRL. Oh, you may sneer. Human beings can make their own standards of morality. The Sacrament has brought you both misery. I'll have none of it. And I'll be just as moral as the best of you. *Better*—since there will be no pretence in our relationship. No lying. I have a right to give my body where I please.

THE WOMAN. *Have* you?

THE GIRL. We all have. Men *and* women.

THE WOMAN. Only there's this difference, my dear. A man can give *his* as often as *he* pleases, and still retain his position. He can fill the highest posts and so long as he is fairly discreet he is secure. In some circles he is even given an added glamor. The dear, gay fellow. But the woman, thanks to our advanced civilization, is branded for just one tiny, little slip. Just one. She is branded by one of the oldest words in the language. She is a harlot, my dear. And she shares the distinction with the poor, drab street-walker. (THE GIRL *shivers*: THE WOMAN *watches her closely*.) Cruel, isn't it? But there it is, my dear. You mustn't do that. Really, you mustn't. What would your life be, living either openly or in hiding with him? Frightened to have children. If you *did*, marking them at birth with an unfair handicap. Think of it. And don't imagine you'd be the first. It's been tried. It's being tried now. And what are the women like who do this splendid, daring, flying-in-the-face-of-convention thing? Have you ever seen them? *I* have. Haggard, furtive, hunted. As they walk they dread the expectant hand on their shoulders. As they look at you the secret of it is in their eyes. And it's not a happy secret, believe me, my dear. It's nasty any way you look at it. Isn't it, my dear?

THE GIRL. I love him. (*Covers her eyes with her hands*.) He loves me.

THE WOMAN. Isn't that too wonderful! Some men age so slowly. They attract as much in middle-life as they did when they were young men. No wonder the birth-rate is stationary. I was just about your age—perhaps a little younger—*very* little, my dear, when I said "I love you." And to the same man. Odd, isn't it? And still he's going about saying it today just as if the years meant nothing. Marvellous. He said: "I love you" to me for just six months. Then he said it to someone else and I've only glimpsed him since. And you're the last—so far as we know.

THE GIRL. (*Hurt and outraged, gives a cry and walks away.*)

THE WOMAN. (*Goes to her, changes her whole tone to one of pity.*) Don't mind me, dear. I've been hurt *so* much in my life and rather than show it, I mock at everything. I want to be kind to you. I want you to like me. Your mother and I were such good friends. Where is she?

THE GIRL. (*Faintly, emotionally.*) She's dead. My father, too.

THE WOMAN. Do you live here alone?

THE GIRL. (*Nods.*) For the last few months. Oh! I don't know what to do. (*Suddenly.*) Who told you?

THE WOMAN. Someone who is very fond of you wrote to me.

THE GIRL. Who?

THE WOMAN. Your maid. She was with me for ten years. Lucky you found her, wasn't it?

(*Bell rings in the distance.*)

THE GIRL. Why didn't she tell me?

THE WOMAN. Even maids have their code. And she's devoted to you. She felt she really should write me. Such a loyal soul. So at a great deal of personal inconvenience I decided the nicest thing for all of us would be to have a delightful little chat. It's so refreshing for two women to have a heart-to-heart talk about a man. Isn't it?

(*Enter* THE MAID *from inner room.*)

THE GIRL. I'm not in to anyone.

THE MAID. No, madam. (*Goes to door.*)

THE GIRL. Wait. You leave here tonight.

THE MAID. Yes, madam. (*Opens door.*)

THE WOMAN. Bridges! Would you like to come back to me?

THE MAID. Yes, madam.

THE WOMAN. Delightful. (*To* THE GIRL.) My maid reads all my letters. *So* tantalizing. Steams them over a kettle and seals them up again. I *do* like letters *first* hand. (*To* THE MAID.) I hope you haven't acquired that habit?

THE MAID. No, madam.

THE WOMAN. I'm at the Berkeley.

(*Bell rings again.*)

THE MAID. Yes, madam. (*Goes out.*)

THE WOMAN. Such good manners. It *will* be nice, having my correspondence private again. It's a shame you're losing her. You can have mine if you like but I can't give her a character.

THE GIRL. (*Opens the door.*) I want you to go. Go now. I can't bear your being in this room.

THE WOMAN. Oh, but I can't go. Really, I can't (*Sits.*)

(THE MAID *re-enters, stands inside the door. Enter* THE MAN. THE MAID *goes into the inner room.* THE GIRL *moves quickly and looks at him in astonishment. He is a tall, handsome man of some* 46 *years of age. His manner is quiet and courtly. He goes straight to the* GIRL *entirely innocent of* THE WOMAN'S *presence.*)

THE MAN. What is the matter, dear? Why did you telephone?

THE GIRL. (*Startled.*) I didn't telephone.

THE MAN. Your maid said you wanted to see me in half an hour and that it was most urgent.

THE WOMAN. (*Rises: coming down.*) I asked her to. (THE MAN *turns and sees his wife. He stares at her as at a ghost.*) Hello, Kit. Well, really I *might* have been dead and come to life judging by the way you stare at me. (*Looks from one to the other.*) Why did you tell this child I was dead?

THE MAN. I hoped you were.

THE WOMAN. Did you really? Well now that you know I'm not what are you thinking of doing?

THE MAN. I haven't had time to think.

THE WOMAN. One thing—you will not take her to Holland tomorrow?

THE MAN. No.

THE WOMAN. She is perfectly willing though to live with you as your wife, if you are agreeable. Are you?

THE MAN. (*Looks at* THE GIRL *who, in turn, looks piteously at* THE WOMAN.) That is very brave of you, dear.

THE WOMAN. You said that to me when I was her age —or younger. That I was brave for *marrying* you. (*To* THE GIRL.) The braver we are the more we attract him. He certainly *does* test our courage. He's testing yours now. So am I. (*To* THE MAN.) The dear child doesn't believe I am your wife. Do convince her I am. You *did* marry me, didn't you?

THE MAN. Unfortunately.

THE WOMAN. And left me six months afterwards?

THE MAN. I did.

THE WOMAN. For another woman.

THE MAN. That's what you thought.

THE WOMAN. Well? *Didn't* you?

THE MAN. No. After six months with you my one wish was to be free of *all* women.

THE WOMAN. What subtle flattery.

THE MAN. It's the plain God's truth.

THE WOMAN. From the time you left me you have never been near me. Have you?

THE MAN. Did you want me to be?

THE WOMAN. No. But it would have been nice to have

given me the option. Since you left me I have heard of you occasionally, always discreditably. Usually in connection with another woman. Do you deny that?

THE MAN. I don't deny your *hearing* about them.

THE WOMAN. There *have* been other women?

THE MAN. Besides you? Good God, yes. But I've never given them the chance to treat me as you did.

THE WOMAN. (*To* THE GIRL.) You see? There *have* been other women, my dear, but he never gave them the chance of marrying him that he hoped to give to you. (*To* THE MAN.) How dull of you to try to deceive this beautiful child! You always *were* dull. You have achieved one part of your destiny. You have *wived.* You certainly deserve *hanging.*

THE MAN. Had I stayed with you I most probably would have been hanged—

THE WOMAN. Then I should have insisted on keeping you.

THE MAN. —for justifiable homicide.

THE WOMAN. At least it would have shown some spirit.

THE MAN. (*To* THE GIRL.) Do you wonder I left her?

THE GIRL. No. I *hate* her.

THE WOMAN. Oh! My dear! And I like you *so* much.

THE GIRL. (*To* THE MAN.) You were quite right. How *could* you have married her?

THE WOMAN. He *didn't. I* married *him.* As a matter of fact he tried to *avoid* me. That piqued me. So I gave him my pure, young, girlish heart. He looked *so* well in uniform. (*To* THE MAN.) You should never wear anything else. I loathe you in *those.* (*Shudders.*) You never could choose a tailor. Dreadful. (*As she looks at his clothes.*) Aren't they, my dear? He really seemed to have a good figure as an officer in the Hussars, and I adored good figures when I was a girl. And he said "I love you" so convincingly. (*Sweetly.*) I am sure he does still. But he had no conversation, my dear. He talked constantly and said nothing. Deathly! (*Taps her lips, stifling a yawn.*) When I think of those nerve-destroying months of married deadlock. And I always detested *yawning*. It's so unbecoming. Isn't it?

THE MAN. (*To* THE GIRL.) It's as though there were some evil spirit in her. There was nothing she did not jibe at. Nothing! At first it was amusing. Unusual. Fascinating. A woman with a dead soul. A beautiful face: a distorted mind. But to *live* with! To hear her constantly! Mocking at breakfast. Jibes at lunch. Sneers at dinner. An evil thought on every clean subject. Gross jibes about the most sacred things. It was revolting! It couldn't last! One of us had to go. And I liked life too well to end it for her. So I cleared out. She spoke of my discreditable life. Why? I took care to have stories carried to her. Because I wanted to be free of her. I wanted her to take the chance to be free of me. But she wouldn't. I sent my lawyer to her repeatedly. She refused. *She* didn't want to marry. So she'd prevent *me*. Then for years I heard nothing of her. I *did* try to find her. She had gone. No trace. Then I made up my mind. Why should my life be made unbearable? Why shouldn't I be free to marry when at last I found someone I loved and who loved me? She had her chance. She wouldn't take it. She deserted *me*. It was impossible to find her. She knew where to find me. I'm in the Army List. I told you as much as I dared. Not all the truth. Most of it. I kept the vital fact back. I was afraid. I would have told you tomorrow. I'd have left the decision to you. Believe me I would. Well, I'm glad now I waited. Because you have met her. You've heard her. In *that* lies my justification. There have been no other women. Just you, dear. I love you. Different from anything I've ever known. True. Honest. Burning. But now it's hopeless. I know that. Hopeless. I'm to be punished all my life for having met that—that——

THE GIRL. (*Vehemently.*) No! You're not. I believe you and *I* love *you*. True. Honest. Burning. With everything of me. Take me. I couldn't be happy away from you. You can't be away from me. Don't let that evil woman torture us. I don't want any ceremony. I'm willing to be your lover if I can't be your wife. Take me.

THE MAN. Oh, my dear, I love you too much to let you do that. (*Wearily.*) I've seen it. It burns out. The uncertainty. Insults. Sneered at. Belittled. She'd see to it. And it would fall heaviest on you. At the last you might hate me. (*Shivers.*) I've seen it. Silent, implacable hatred. Mute reproaches. It would be too ugly. No. (*To* THE WOMAN.) You've beaten me. (*Mutters distractedly under his breath: staring dully.*) God! I don't know what to do now. I'm all astray. Licked. Done.

THE GIRL. (*Distractedly.*) If you let that woman separate us you'll never see me again. Never. You mustn't. I can't bear it! I can't! I can't! (*Shudders.*) It isn't fair to me. Or to yourself. (*Breaks down, cries bitterly.*) I wish I were dead! I wish I were dead.

THE MAN. (*Goes to her.*) Don't do that, dear. Don't. (*Puts his hand on her shoulder: tears stream down his cheeks: he bends down and whispers to her.*)

THE GIRL. (*Faintly.*) Send—her—away. I can't bear her looking at me. I can't breathe with her in the room. *Do* send her away.

(THE WOMAN *has turned her back to the two people.* THE MAN *turns to speak to her. At the same moment* THE WOMAN *turns too: motions him not to speak. She goes to* THE GIRL. THE MAN *tries to stop her She goes to the other side of* THE GIRL *and puts her hand gently on her shoulder.*)

THE WOMAN. I know you'll think me ridiculous—and

please don't look at me. Because you've made *me* cry. (*Gets out her handkerchief and blows her nose: then searches in her vanity case and cannot find what she is looking for.*) And I've no powder. (*Looks at herself in little mirror in vanity case.*) And my nose reddens *so* easily *now*. You poor little thing. Life is a tragedy because you can't marry him. It was my tragedy that I *did*. And *his*. Isn't it *too* ridiculous. (*Closes vanity case: arranges furs around her neck.*) I'm going to do something perfectly absurd. You'll both hate me for it some day. It will make you very miserable. And you'll deserve to be. I'm going to let you marry. (THE MAN *and* THE GIRL *look at her unbelievingly.*) Yes, I am. It's weak of me. I know. But you took an unfair advantage of me. I detest tears. Especially a child's. You poor, silly little thing. Crying over Kit. Too fantastic. (*Sniffles and uses her handkerchief.*) Don't waste any more. Keep 'em until you're married to him. (*Turns to* THE MAN.) Go through the usual, degrading rigmarole. Room at an hotel. Pretty lady. Chambermaid to see you go into the room. Detective to find you in it. I'll sue for my rights. You refuse to live with me. Horrid thing! Then the divorce-court. Decree. Six months of impatience. A quiet, *very* quiet wedding. There you are. Stick to Holland. (*To* THE GIRL.) It *must* have been your idea, my dear. Kit could never think farther than the four-mile radius. And—that's that. (THE GIRL *looks at her joyfully: goes to her timidly.*) Don't kiss me, my dear. We're both too damp. (*Puts both her hands on* THE GIRL'S *shoulders.*) I suppose I *am* a terrible person. I lost my faith when I was *very* young and I've scoffed ever since. You'll never lose yours.

THE GIRL. Never.

THE WOMAN. I can see that. Oh! May I? (*Takes up* THE GIRL'S *vanity-case and takes out powder puff.*)

Sure you don't mind? (*Powders her nose.*) Sweet of you. We have at least *one* thing in common. I don't see why you shouldn't be very happy—for a while. (*Looking in the little mirror.*) When he talks, my dear, do what I did: *don't listen.* It's so much simpler than trying to follow him. Conversationally he's all blind-alleys. He'd land you in a cul-de-sac. Thank you so much. (*Hands back vanity case to* THE GIRL.)

(THE MAID *comes in dressed for the street.*)

MAID. (*Quietly to* THE GIRL.) May I go now, madam?

THE GIRL. Yes. I'll send your wages to you tomorrow.

MAID. Thank you, Madam. I'm sorry I displeased you. But I couldn't help——

THE GIRL. That will do.

MAID. Yes, Madam. (*Goes to door.*)

THE WOMAN. Bridges. You may as well come with me. Wait for me.

MAID. Yes, Madam. (*Goes out.*)

THE WOMAN. I've lost a husband and regained a maid. A fair exchange. Good for ill. Good-bye, child. (*Pats* THE GIRL'S *cheek: turns to* THE MAN.) Maynard & Maynard, Conduit Street will give you every assistance in the immoral divorce. Be nice to her. Well, as nice as you can. She's much too good for you. Much. Still, men *are* scarce. Don't bore her, Kit. Odd! She loves you. I *hated* you. (*Opens door: as she passes out.*) Oh, Bridges, you must put me to bed. I'm twitchy. Isn't it horrid? I *do* hope your hands are still *cool.* And *dry.* If there's one thing I abhor it's moist, warm fingers touching me. (*Her voice dies away.*)

(THE GIRL *stands looking in front of her: thinking.*)

(THE MAN *closes the door shutting out the sound of* THE WOMAN'S *voice. He comes down.*)

THE MAN. She makes me feel unclean! Ashamed! (*Shivers.*)

THE GIRL. I wonder if she's quite as cruel as she would like you to believe she is?

THE MAN. What do you think?

THE GIRL. I don't think she is, somehow. I believe she loved you.

THE MAN. My darling!

THE GIRL. And then something happened. You disappointed her.

(*The Curtain begins to fall.*)

If she didn't love you why did she never marry again?

(*The Curtain reaches the Stage.*)

THE END OF THE PASSAGE.

# 'OP-O'-ME-THUMB

PLAY IN ONE ACT

## FREDERICK FENN and RICHARD PRYCE

Frederick Fenn was born at Bishop Stortford in 1868, and is best known in the English theater as a writer of amusing and sentimental plays. He has likewise adapted a number of dramas. Many of his works are written in collaboration with the novelist and playwright, Richard Pryce. His first successful play, "Judged by Appearances," was performed by the popular English actor, James Welch. "'Op-o'-Me-Thumb," written with Richard Pryce, is by all odds the best known work of these dramatists. It was acted by Maude Adams.

Richard Pryce was born at Boulogne, France. Although he is better known as a novelist, he has written a few original plays and adapted a number of others.

Following is a list of published plays by Frederick Fenn:

"'Op-o'-Me-Thumb," "The Convict on the Hearth," "The Nelson Touch."

By Richard Pryce:

"A Privy Council," "The Dumb Cake," "Little Mrs. Cummin," "The Visit."

# 'OP-O'-ME-THUMB*

## CHARACTERS

MADAME JEANNE MARIE NAPOLEON DE GALLIFET DIDIER.
CLEM (MRS.) GALLOWAY.
ROSE JORDAN.
CELESTE.
AMANDA AFFLICK.
HORACE GREENSMITH.

SCENE: *Working-room in a Laundry.*

TIME: *The Present.*

SCENE. *Working room at* MADAME DIDIER'S *Laundry in Soho. In front of the large shop window that gives on to the street there hangs a lace curtain. Upon the glass of the upper half of a door "Madame Didier, Blanchisserie Française" may be read backwards.*

*It is Saturday evening before an August bank-holiday.* MADAME *with goffering irons is finishing a cap at stage back* L. ROSE JORDAN *stands on a chair putting paper packets of collars and cuffs into pigeon holes.* CLEM (MRS.) GALLOWAY *is mending socks, etc., at small table* R. CELESTE *is sitting on centre table marking off collars, etc., in account book, or slipping pink tissue paper into a stack of shirts, and singing as she swings her feet.*

CELESTE. Eve in her garden she was a lady,
*She* never grew old n' fady.
*She* might 'a' bin there to-day-dy,
But *she* was inquisitive.

---



This play is also published separately at 30 cents a copy.

*I'd* never 'a bin s' crazy,
*You* wait till I'm 'alf a daisy,
*See* me with a chance to be lazy.
I'd keep you all alive!

MADAME. You have make out zose bills, Celeste?

CELESTE. (*Nodding.*)
Oh wait till I'm 'alf a daisy,
Snakes! I'd send 'em all back to blazy.
*You* give me the chance to be lazy,
I'd——

CLEM. Couldn't be much lazier than what you are now, I should think—daisy or no daisy.

CELESTE. Couldn't I? I'd have a bit of a try!
(*Resumes.*)
Oh when I'm a real lady,
*In* a barouche I shall parady—(*She breaks off suddenly.*) Where's Amanda?

CLEM. (*Sarcastically.*) Want a little 'elp with y' singin'?

CELESTE. Where *is* Amanda?

ROSE. Gone to Strahan's.

CELESTE. What for?

ROSE. They never sent them things they wrote about.

CELESTE. (*Stopping in her work.*) Do they expect us to do 'em this time o' day?

MADAME. (*Coming down.*) No. No. Like always you excite yourself for nothing. Go on. Go on. What is Monday? 'Oliday, is it not? Very well. They close. I close. I 'ave the things 'ere for Tuesday, hein? You mind your business. Always wanting to know.

CELESTE. (*Appeased.*) Well, you never do know with shops. It wouldn't be the first time. It was Strahan wanted the collars dressed in two hours last week, wasn't it, for some customer or other. I wouldn't 'a' done 'em, I know. Oh ho. (*She hums to herself for a moment or two.*) Well, well. When I'm married and 'ave a 'usband to keep me—

MADAME. Keep you! Bah, you know nothing, you. A man wants a wife who will work. Mon Dieu, if one is to be lazy it will not be the wife. Look at me.

CLEM. (*Who has gone up to table at back to fetch more things and who now comes down.*) You're right, Madame. 'Usbands is all very well in their way, as I should be the first to deny, me of course bein' different and independent so to speak, but when it comes to which is to do the work—

CELESTE. Listen to Clem.

CLEM. Not so much of y'r Clem. Mrs. Galloway, if you please. You seem to forget who I am. I've got me ring, I 'ave, *and* me lines if I do come 'ere to oblige—Mr. Galloway 'avin' poor 'ealth—besides private means, bein' a pensioneer.

CELESTE. Pensioneer! Four pence a day, isn't it, dear? —and gone before twelve, they tell me, at the Pig and Whistle. A fine pensioneer! You wait until I bring mine along.

CLEM. Yes, I daresay there'll be some waitin' to do. What's your 'usband goin' to be if I may make so bold to inquire?

CELESTE. 'Aven't quite made up me mind. But I'm just about tired of this. I'm not sure as I shan't go and be a actress for a change, and stand in the lime-light and 'ave bokays thrown at me—'ere chuck us some of those things, Rose—(*Begins to work frantically.*)—and—and 'ave lords waitin' at the stage door to take the 'orses out of me carriage—

CLEM. (*Laughs.*) You'll be wantin' to be a child of myst'ry next, like Amanda.

CELESTE. (*Pausing, seriously.*) Do you think she is?

CLEM. Is what?

CELESTE. A child of myst'ry—what she says I mean. You know—all that about 'er father and about them jewels as somebody gives 'er. Do you know she washed that there shirt again last week. She says it'll be fetched one of these days and then there'll be a surprise for us.

ROSE. Surprise! Garn! A little image like 'er? Ain't room for much up 'er sleeve. Little 'aporth o' mist'ry!

CELESTE. (*Thoughtfully.*) Well I don't know. Things *do* 'appen, y' know. I wonder 'oo 'er father reely is. (*Mystified.*) She's so close about 'im, ain't she? And then there *is* that shirt—there's no goin' against that.

CLEM. (*Shortly.*) Lots of customers forgets things.

CELESTE. Yes, but the care she takes of it. It's bin 'ere best part of a year, and I don't know 'ow many times she 'asn't dressed it. There may be something in it, y' know.

ROSE. (*Pulling a long paper parcel out of one of the large pigeon holes—reading.*) "Mr. 'Orris Greensmith, to be called for." (*Opening the paper a little and looking inside.*) Blest if I don't believe she's done it up again. It 'ad pink paper in last week and now it's blue. 'Ve we got any blue paper, madam? No. I thought not.

CLEM. (*Interested.*) She must 'a' bought it.

CELESTE. There.

ROSE. Well! *It'll* never be fetched. If 'e's 'er mash why doesn't 'e come 'ere and fetch it?

CELESTE. She says it's a sort of a token, see? while 'e's away. Something to 'old by, she says. And then, 'e does send 'er things.

CLEM. (*Weightily.*) 'As any body seen 'em?

CELESTE. N-no, but there was a brooch, I b'lieve, and a necktie.

CLEM. (*Coming to the table* C. *to fetch scissors* L. *and pausing in her work to gossip.*) Well, why doesn't she wear 'em? That's it, y' see. Why doesn't she wear 'em?

CELESTE. (*As if struck by this for the first time.*) Yes. Why doesn't she?

CLEM. (*Sits at table* R. *and talks confidentially.*) That's where the test comes in. Why doesn't she wear 'em—'stead of that bit of crape, say? Not that I've anything to say against that. She 'as plenty of deaths in 'er family—that I will say for 'er.

ROSE. (*Contemptuously.*) Lots of people 'as relations die. Any one can.

CLEM. (*Generously.*) No, give everybody their due, I say, and she does 'ave her afflictions. I've been bereaved meself and I know what it is.

ROSE. Crape's cheap enough. And she don't ask us to none of 'er funerals.

CLEM. (*Forgetting* AMANDA *and showing an inclination to lose herself in pleasant retrospect.*) Fun'rals— the fun'rals I've been to in my time! There was me sister's 'usband (*She goes back to her place* R. *as she speaks.*) —all my family's married well, that I am thankful to say—and when she lost 'im she done the thing 'andsome I tell y'. (*To* CELESTE.) Gimme them vests—no—there by the socks. Under y' nose, stupid! There was as many as three mournin' coaches an' a 'earse with plumes—and the 'atbands!—well—and afterwards we—

CELESTE. That'll do, Clem. We know all about that—and y' cousins too as died at 'Ighb'ry. It's Amanda I'm talking about, not you. I wonder whether she could show us one of them presents. Good mind to ask 'er. Why don't she come in?

ROSE. Gone a errand, I tell y'.

CELESTE. Well, she might be back be now, I should think. Talk about 'ares and tortoise shells! I'd 'a' done it on me 'ead. She's a fair crawler, Amanda is.

ROSE. (*Laconically.*) Legs is short.

CELESTE. So's time, and I don't want to be 'ere all night.

MADAME. (*Coming down.*) She is little, but she is good. She work. She does not talk, talk, talk. She is not singing when she should be working. Where should

I be, me, with another like you? And this Saturday and I forced to go out at five! Five, mon Dieu, and it wants but ten minutes. (*She goes up* L. R.)

CELESTE. (*Absently.*) I wonder whether she's got any body to take 'er out a Monday. Think she 'as?

ROSE. It'd be a funny sort o' feller as 'd want to. (*She looks over her shoulder towards the glass door.*) 'Ere she is. 'Ere's Mandy.

(*The door* R. *is pushed open and* AMANDA AFFLICK *comes in backwards pulling after her a washing basket nearly as large as herself. She is an odd, forlorn looking little figure with big eyes and a pathetic expression. She has yet an air of being quite capable of taking care of herself.*)

ROSE. Well, Crapie.

MADAME. Ah, you have come back. You have brought the money? (AMANDA *hands her a paper and some loose change.*) That is right. Now I may go and you will help these good for nothings to finish. (*She takes the cap on its stand and puts it on end of table back, then goes into inner room* L. *whence she returns a moment or two later with her cloak.*)

CELESTE. (*To* AMANDA.) Didn't 'appen to meet ch' father, did y'?

CLEM. We thought perhaps as you was gone s' long that you'd ran away with that mash o' yours—'im as goes without 'is shirt. 'Orris Whatsaname.

AMANDA. Oh. Did y'? (*She sidles past* CLEM *who is leaning over a basket and giving her an intentional "shove," sends her sprawling across it.*) Now then, Mrs., can't y' make room for a lady?

CLEM. (*Getting up, and angry.*) They don't teach y' manners in the work'us, do they Clumsy?

AMANDA. You'll find out when you get there, dear.

ROSE. (*Linking arms with* CELESTE L., *coming towards* AMANDA *in front of table* C.) We've got a new bow to-day. (*She points to a band of black crape around* AMANDA'S *arm.*)

CELESTE. So she 'as! Where did y' git that, S'rimp? (AMANDA *arranges the bow on her arm, pulling out the ends.*)

AMANDA. I've been doin' a little shoppin' this afternoon, and I bought this Rembrandt in case you was took off sudden, S'leste. S'leste! (*She gives a little chuckle.*) It is a name, ain't it? Where did y' git it? Off the front of a shop, eh?

Pretty Celeste
'Ad a very weak chest.
If 'er chest 'd been stronger
Me tale 'd been longer.

(*She hoists herself on the table.*)

(CLEM *and* ROSE *laugh shrilly.* CELESTE *flushes.*)

CELESTE. Weak chest y'self. What's wrong with my chest?

AMANDA. (*Sitting on table.*) Bit narrer, dear, isn't it? But p'raps it's the cut o' y' bodice. Some of those bodices-'ands can spoil things a treat, can't they?

CELESTE. What do y' know about it? You shut y' face. You! you ain't got no figger, you never dresses, you ain't got enough 'air to go in a locket, and every feller I know says as you're a bloomin' little monkey without a stick. So, now, there!

MADAME. (*Bustling into outdoor things and interposing to prevent the quarrel developing.*) Now, now, now! One would think that in life there was nothing to do. You quarrel, you talk, you sing. Do I sing? Mon Dieu, no. Celeste she sing till she make my 'ead ache, and then it is you. (*To* AMANDA, *who gets off table.*) And you all talk, talk, talk like I don't know what. For shame. Now I go, and you, Celeste, will go to Madame Jones with 'er things—they are listed, eh?—and Mrs. Galloway will take M. Gigot 'is waistcoat, and Rose, you will not forget Miss Smeet's dress. She must 'ave it to-night. Now quick all of you. Amanda will wait for me. I shall not be long. Now attention! No more singing, do you 'ear? You can sing if you want, in the street, and then you will be run in for drink to punish you. (*She goes out* L.) (ROSE *jumps off her chair.*)

ROSE. Is she gone? Lord, I wish it was Monday! I shan't git up all to-morrow so's to rest meself. Do 'ope it'll be fine.

CLEM. I expect it will. Makes such a difference, bank 'oliday, don't it? P'tickler when it's 'Am'stead.

ROSE. Course it's 'Am'stead. What d' *you* think.

CLEM. (*Crossing to* ROSE *and* CELESTE R.) We should 'a' gone there too, only for Mr. Galloway 'avin' a aunt at Greenwich—though of course bein' married I'm different, so to speak. We shall go be tram, I expect, and then there 's th' 'ill in the Park, an' the 'eath close by an' all. But I don't know as I shouldn't like to be goin' with y'.

ROSE. (*Half ignoring her.*) Wish you was, dear. (*Turning to* CELESTE.) S'leste, you an' Albert will be ready, won't you? You must be 'ere first thing, cause of me and my friend pickin' y' up.

(CLEM *goes up* L., *presently returns to her work* R.)

CELESTE. We'll be ready. Rather. What ho! (*Seeing* AMANDA, *who has been looking from one to another and who stands a little bit wistfully outside the group.*) Well, Mandy, got someone to take y' out Monday, eh?

AMANDA. (*Starts and pulls herself together.*) I—I don't know as I can go out at all a Monday. Y' see prop'ly speakin' I'm in mournin'.

CELESTE. You're always in mournin' 'oliday time—you was at Easter, too. I believe meself——

AMANDA. (*Quickly.*) Well, so I was. I lost me aunt on the mother's side just before Good Friday. This (*she touches crape bow*) is for me cousin's niece as passed away quietly last week in—in Kensington. We—we 'ad been estranged for some time, but now she is gone I bear 'er no malice, and she shall never 'ave it to say as I didn't pay 'er proper respect. And besides I don't know as I care to go out in my circumstances.

CELESTE. Your circumstances! What are they?

AMANDA. Oh, well—till—till 'e comes for me, y' know.

ROSE. Till 'e comes for 'is shirt, eh?—the tall 'andsome stranger as none of us 'as never seen—n' never won't. (*She jumps on a chair again and takes out parcel.*) Garn. You've made it all up about 'im, I believe. "Mr. 'Orris Greensmith, to be called for!" "Miss Amanda Afflick, to be called for!" That's more like it. 'Ere, Clem! Ketch. (*She pitches parcel to* MRS. GALLOWAY.)

AMANDA. (*Starting forward.*) Give it 'ere.

CLEM. (*Holding it high.*) Y' been washin' it again, Crapie, 'aven't y'?

AMANDA. Give it 'ere. 'Tain't yours.

CLEM. Ketch, S'leste. (*She throws it to* CELESTE.)

CELESTE. Better not wash it any more. It's gettin' so thin it 'll blow away one of these days.

AMANDA. (*Fiercely.*) Give it me.

CELESTE. Not so fast.

AMANDA. Give it to me!

CELESTE. Tell us the truth then. You been coddin' us about it all this time, 'avent you? 'Orris or whatever 'e's called 'as left it 'ere didn't take no notice of y' at all, now did 'e?

AMANDA. (*At back of centre table as* CELESTE *dances round with shirt.*) Didn't 'e? P'raps 'e's never wrote to me neither, letters and letters on scented paper with crests and coats o' arms—and sealing wax too. You're jealous all the lot o' y'! Give it 'ere. You'll mess it. Oh (*half crying*) you'll mess it and 'e might come for it to-day. Give it 'ere.

CLEM. Let 'er 'ave it, S'leste.

CELESTE. (*Holds it high.*) If I do will y' show me that brooch?

AMANDA. What brooch?

CELESTE. You know. The one you told us about. The minnycher set in diamonds.

AMANDA. (*Affecting unconcern.*) Oh, 'aven't I shown it to y'?

CELESTE. No, n' none of 'is presents. If I give it y', will y'?

AMANDA. (*Hesitates.*) I—I don't know where I put it.

CELESTE. Well then the bracelet with the turquoise.

AMANDA. I—I lent that to me cousin for 'er niece's funeral. She 'asn't sent it back yet.

CELESTE. Well then one of the other things then—some present as 'e's give y', will y'?

AMANDA. Give me my shirt.

CELESTE. Will y' then?

AMANDA. All right.

CELESTE. There y' are, Kipper! Ketch! (AMANDA *catches the shirt and with her back to the others gently fondles it for a moment as a mother might fondle a child. Then pulling a chair forward and climbing it she puts the parcel safely away on a shelf.*)

CELESTE. Seein's believin' y' know, and when we've seen —no 'anky-panky mindje!—some jewel or something.

AMANDA. All right.

CLEM. (*Indulgently.*) Let 'er alone, S'leste. That'll do.

AMANDA. (*Standing on chair to put away the shirt, turns fiercely.*) 'Ere what's it got to do with you? You keep your oar out of my wheel. I can take care of meself, Mrs. Clementina William Galloway. You think just because I'm not twelve feet 'igh and six foot round like some people as I can't 'old me own with a pack of chatterin' girls like S'leste 'ere and Rose Allelujah Jordan. One more river to cross! What ho! I spurn the lot of you. You're no more to me than a herd of buzzin' flies. (*Quieting down.*) I go 'ome from 'ere and I set on the sofa and read 'is letters, and all what 'appens in this 'ouse o' bondage is no more to me than a dream of the night!

CLEM. Does 'e know what your temper is?

ROSE. Little spitfire!

AMANDA. There dear, I don't mean it. Only y' see when y'r 'ead's full of more important things and there's wonderful changes loomin' before y' it's apt to make y' a bit 'asty. There, Clem (*goes to her*) I didn't mean to be cross. One of these days you shall know all.

CELESTE. (*Impressed in spite of herself.*) When did y' 'ear from 'im last?

AMANDA. Wednesday week—no, Tuesday it would be.

ROSE. Did 'e send y' anything then?

AMANDA. 'E's goin' to.

CELESTE. Something nice! (AMANDA *nods.*)

CELESTE. Is it a ring?

AMANDA. No.

CLEM. 'E's too sharp for that, eh Mandy?

AMANDA. Better than that. (*Gets on the table again.*) It's—it's a hairloom—one of those things you wear at the op'ra.

CELESTE. I know—a tarara.

AMANDA. Yes. (*The girls stop working and loll on the table listening open-mouthed.*) It sticks in y'r 'ead with spikes and it's got diamonds and em'rals and stars all round—it sticks up like a crown and it glitters—fit to blind y'.

CELESTE. 'E must 'ave a lot o' money.

ROSE. Seems to chuck it about, don't 'e?

CELESTE. But you ain't *seen* 'im again?

AMANDA. No. But 'e's comin'.

CELESTE. 'Ere?

AMANDA. Yes. There's a understandin', y' see. There's clouds on the horizon—that's why there's all this mystery. But when 'e fetches 'is shirt—it's a sort of a sign, see—I shall know that bright days are in store.

CLEM. (*Joining the table group after affecting indiffer-*

*ence.*) But what I want to know is—me of course 'avin' a 'ome of me own and bein' in a responsible p'sition so to speak—what I want to know—is 'e going to marry y'?

AMANDA. When 'e's asked me father.

ROSE. Asked y' father?

AMANDA. Everybody respectable does that. A young fella comes along and 'e says, isn't she beautiful, 'e says, I'd die for 'er, I wish she'd walk on me, through me 'eart first. But 'e don't say nothing to 'er, not till 'e's been to 'er father—if 'e's any class, y' know.

ROSE. But you're not beautiful. I'm a lot better lookin' than what you are and I shouldn't like any chap to go to my father.

AMANDA. (*Sweetly.*) Of course if y' father 'appens to be doin' a bit in 'Olloway it makes a difference.

ROSE. 'Olloway! Jail bird y'self! I don't believe a word of it. I don't believe—

CELESTE. Easy, Rose. (*Pulling her away.*) Let's 'ear. (*To* AMANDA.) 'As 'e seen y' father?

AMANDA. Not yet—because—because of law suits, and then there's a missin' will, y' see.

CELESTE. Missin' will?

AMANDA. (*Setting herself again on table* C.) Well, there should be be rights, but I think we've got over that. Y' see it's like this: My father wanted me to grow up without any rank or pearls or carriages so as I shall be loved just for myself alone—

CLEM. She's coddin'. She's only a workus girl and never 'ad no father.

AMANDA. I'm not. It's true. I've thought about it and dreamt about it till I know it's true. Besides you'll see. I'm goin' to 'im in oh such a little while.

CELESTE. And what about 'Orris?

AMANDA. I shall ask 'im if 'e loves me passionately, and if 'e says yes, I shall lay one white jew'ld 'and in 'is, and look into 'is pleadin' eyes and say, 'Orris, because you loved me truly when I was pore and in disguise, you shall 'ave your reward.

CELESTE. (*To the others.*) It sounds all right, don't it?

CLEM. (*Rises.*) 'Ere, come along, girls. What's the good o' 'angin' about listenin' to all this rubbish when we got these things to take 'fore we can go. 'Ere, bustle up, S'leste. The old woman 'll be back again mongdewing like Lord-save-us-all if she finds they ain't gone. (CELESTE *and* ROSE *go into inner room to put on their hats and coats.*) You show us that present, Corpsies, or find some one to take y' out a Monday, and then p'raps we'll see about believin' y'. Come, Rose. (*She goes into inner room* L.)

AMANDA. (*Absently and waving her hand.*) I have always loved you, 'Orris. Now your patience is rewarded. Rise and take me to my carriage.

ROSE. (*Putting on her hat and helping* CELESTE *with her coat as she and* CLEM. *reappear with their things.*) Carriage! You find somebody with a moke and a barrer to take y' to 'Amstead.

AMANDA. (*Loftily.*) I'm not goin' on Monday. Bank 'olidy! It's just for ordinary people as 'ave no prospex and nothing better to think of.

ROSE. Oh, indeed. (*She picks up basket back centre.*) Well I 'ope, Miss Amander Afflick, as you'll enjoy yours all alone by y'r own self with nobody asked y' to go with em!

CLEM. Don't git run away with by a earl or anything like that while we're out.

CELESTE. So long, Corpsie. Y' got to show us one of them presents, y' know. 'Ere, wait for me, Rose.

(*They troop out* L. *with their packages.*)

AMANDA. (*When the door has closed behind them sits still for a moment or two. When she lifts her face it is seen to be working. To herself.*) Monday! I should like to be goin' to 'Amstead—or anywheres. They might 'a' asked me to go with 'em. Somebody might. Nobody never won't. Never, never, never. 'Oo wants me? 'Oo could? I couldn't. Oh, well.

(*She sniffs drily and getting up and moving to rack climbs the chair again and takes down the rescued shirt. Very carefully and lovingly she refolds it in its covering, holds it to her for a moment and puts it back on the shelf. She is turning once more to the room when the door is flung open and* HORACE GREENSMITH *enters* R. *He is a young workman of sufficiently ordinary appearance, the type of navvy who may always be seen in London breaking up main thoroughfares with sledgehammer and wedge.*)

HORACE. 'Ere, two-foot-nothing. Where's Mother Didier?

AMANDA. (*Getting off chair quickly.*) Oh, Mr. Greensmith! I thought you was dead. Oh! (*Sits.*) Oh!

HORACE. Mr. Greensmith! You know my name. And who might you be to think I was dead?

AMANDA. Oh—you must excuse me—but I did indeed. (*She puts her hand over her heart.*)

HORACE. Did y'. Well, I'm jolly well not.

AMANDA. (*Faintly.*) Oh, it's like one from the grave. I shall be all right in a minute.

HORACE. Well be quick about it. Now are y' better! Very well then, touchin' a shirt I left 'ere. Has the old woman sold it or lost it? Is she goin' to fork it out or does she want me to summons her for it? Go an' arsk 'er. Look slippy.

AMANDA. It's all right, Mr. Greensmith. It's been took pertikler care of. (*Fetches it, and undoing the paper in which it is wrapped, displays the shirt to him proudly.*)

HORACE. Jeroosalem! Did y' wash it yesterday?

AMANDA. Yes, Mr. Greensmith.

HORACE. Not so much o' y' Mr. Greensmith. 'Oo told

y' to wash it yesterday! Did the old woman twig I was comin'?

AMANDA. No, Mr.—Orris. I've washed it every week, *ever* since you left it so as to 'ave it ready for you.

HORACE. S'help me Jimmy, you must be 'ard up for something to do? Y' don't think I'm going to pay for all that, do y'?

AMANDA. Oh, no, Mr. Greensmith. If you was to stuff the money down me throat wild horses wouldn't make me swallow it.

HORACE. H'm! Well; I ain't going to. What's the damage, anyhow?

AMANDA. We don't want you to pay anything, reelly.

HORACE. Oh, we don't, don't we! That suits me A1. You may stick over the door then, Washers by appointment to Orris Greensmith, Esquire. Do you do all y'r work like that? Is this a charitable institution or what is it?

AMANDA. Oh, no, Mr. Orris, we aren't charitable, oh, not at all. You see we—that is *I* thought we should never see you no more. You'd been away so long—there seemed nothing else to think—

HORACE. Well, I'm jiggered. Deaders on the free list eh? 'Oly Moses!

AMANDA. You don't think it was a liberty, do you?

HORACE. (*Looks at her a moment and then bursts out laughing.*) Strike me silly if I ever came across anything quite as dotty before. I was dead, was I, and this was a blasted souvenir. 'Oo the blazes wanted a blasted souvenir of me? Not you!

AMANDA. I know it was a liberty, Mr. Greensmith.

HORACE. 'Ere, 'andle me carefully. I shall faint.

AMANDA. I'm very sorry if you're angry.

HORACE. Was you 'ere when I come before?

AMANDA. (*Eagerly.*) Oh, yes, Mr. Orris. It was at a quarter to five one Wednesday—don't you recklekt? It was in October, the 15th and there was a crool fog all the morning. You was coughin' and sayin' things about the weather.

HORACE. Was I?

AMANDA. Don't you remember?

HORACE. I remember the fog—but then I remember a lot o' fogs.

AMANDA. I've thought of it every day since.

HORACE. 'Ere, what are you anyway?

AMANDA. I'm a orphin. I don't say so but I am—only to you I mean. I—what'll you think of me, Mr. Greensmith?—I—I was born in the Union.

HORACE. I got no call to think one way or the other.

AMANDA. I wouldn't 'a' told no one else. But I couldn't tell you—well, what I tell the others.

HORACE. The others? Are there any more 'ere like you?

AMANDA. Oh, no, I don't think there's any others anywhere like me.

HORACE. No, I dessay not.

AMANDA. Of course, I'm not very tall. We don't grow much in the work'ouse—but some o' them large girls is very fickle, don't you think so, Mr. Greensmith?

HORACE. No girls is any good.

AMANDA. Oh, Mr. Orris, you ain't married, are y'?

HORACE. Not much.

AMANDA. (*Relieved.*) Oh—I thought jes fer a moment —you mustn't mind me. Oh, I am glad.

HORACE. Married. Yah. Knows too much about it.

AMANDA. I'm glad ye're not married, any way. Y' see, Mr. Greensmith, if you won't think it a liberty what I am telling you, I always thought of you as a sort of fairy prince, y' see; and they aren't never married, are they?

HORACE. (*Stretches out one leg and looks at it dubiously.*) 'Ere, my 'ead 'll go if I stop much longer. A fairy—you've been ill, 'aven't you?

AMANDA. Oh *no*, Mr. 'Orris, I'm never ill. I'm very

strong, and work! Well, you should see me on a busy day! It's only—

HORACE. Only what?

AMANDA. Well, when you ain't got much of y'r own you do dream about beautiful things, don't you? That's how I came to think of you.

HORACE. Thank you—very kind of you, don't mention it. (*Pause.*) Well chuck us the shirt.

AMANDA. (*Brings it to him slowly.*) I suppose you'll send us some other things.

HORACE. Don't know; can't say.

(AMANDA *furtively wipes one eye.*)

HORACE. Hello. What's the matter with y'?

AMANDA. Oh, nothing.

HORACE. What's that crape for?

AMANDA. I *say* it's for relations.

HORACE. Oh, well, pull up your socks and grin, y' can't 'ave y' relations always, y' know.

AMANDA. I never 'ad no relations.

HORACE. Well what d' y' wear the bow for then? Y' don't know what y're talking about. Y' wears it for your relations and you never 'ad none. Rottin' sort of goin' into mourning that. Where's y' father? (AMANDA *shakes her head.*) Oh, well—where's y' mother, anyway?

AMANDA. She's dead—she died when I was quite little—oh well, littler than I am now. But it ain't for 'er.

HORACE. 'Oo is it for?

AMANDA. You won't tell the other girls, will y'?

HORACE. No. What should I want t' go jawin' about you for?

AMANDA. You see, I tell *them* that I got a father who's rich—ever so rich—and who's coming to take me away, see, like in a story. I'm in disguise now, but one day 'e'll come and say "Apparel 'er in ermine," and then I shall go away and be a lady. I used to think he would really come, but now I guess 'e's dead, though I tell them 'e's comin'. I don't wear it for 'im though. I keep on changin' 'oo it's for. Y' see I felt I must wear it. (*Looks up shyly.*) But I can take it off now, Mr. 'Orris. (*A pause.*)

HORACE. Well of all. Give us the shirt.

AMANDA. Are y' goin' at once?

HORACE. Well, since you are so pressin' I got about 'alf a minute t' waste. *Now* then.

AMANDA. Nothin', I jes wanted to see you. Y' can smoke if y' like.

HORACE. Make meself at 'ome, eh, and what for! (*Sits on table.*)

AMANDA. (*Coming near to him* L. *standing beside him.*) Y' said y' wasn't married. Are y' in love, Mr. Greensmith?

HORACE. Oh, chuck it. What's that to do with you?

AMANDA. I want to know pertickler.

HORACE. Well, I ain't jes' now.

AMANDA. I expect lots o' girls is in love with you.

HORACE. Oh, yes. I can't 'ardly get down the street for 'em.

AMANDA. You wouldn't say I was pretty, would y' Mr. Greensmith?

HORACE. I 'aven't thought about it.

AMANDA. You wouldn't think about it, would y'?

HORACE. (*Indulgently.*) W-ell—

AMANDA. Eh? but looks ain't everything, are they? Some o' them pretty girls they ain't content when one feller likes 'em, they wants a lot o' chaps to say as they're beautiful.

HORACE. Don't I know it? 'Orris Greensmith ain't goin' to be one of them.

AMANDA. You ain't very 'asty, are you?

HORACE. Middlin'. What's up?

AMANDA. I don't hardly like to tell y'.

HORACE. 'Ere, what y' been doin' of? (*Stops in act of lighting pipe and stares at her with match in his hand.*)

AMANDA. (*Wriggling in front of him.*) I want to tell y', Mr. Greensmith, but I'm afraid you won't like it.

HORACE. Not knowing, can't say. Stand still, can't y'?

AMANDA. Y' might turn round, will y', and look out the winder? I don't like bein' looked at—then I'll tell y'.

HORACE. (*Stares at her hard a minute.*) Well, there ain't much to look at, is there? Now then. (*Turns round and lights up pipe.*)

AMANDA. Y' see—y' see—it's like this, Mr. 'Orris. You comin' in and seein' me last year and never comin' 'ere again all the girls what's 'ere says as 'ow you were in love with me.

HORACE. (*Turning round promptly.*) What! Me! Wodder they take me for? In love—! Lord save us.

AMANDA. Y' know girls will talk, Mr. 'Orris.

HORACE. Yuss, they talks right enough if you give them 'alf a chance. Well, is that what y' wanted to tell me, 'cause if so y' could 'a' kep' it to y'self.

AMANDA. That ain't all.

HORACE. 'Ope y' jolly well told 'em I wasn.

AMANDA. No. I didn't tell 'em that.

HORACE. D'y' mean to tell me a pack o' girls thinks as I—? (*Roars with laughter.* AMANDA *stands shamefaced and nervous.*)

AMANDA. I 'oped y' wouldn't laugh, Mr. 'Orris.

HORACE. Wouldn't laugh. Ho no! but it is a bit thick, isn't it! So I'm in love with you, am I? Would y' like t' get on the table and then y'r lovin' 'usband could give y' a kiss. (AMANDA *begins to get on table.*)

HORACE. (*Amazed.*) Did y' think I was really goin' to kiss y'?

AMANDA. I should like y' to kiss me, Mr. 'Orris.

HORACE. (*Sinks into chair.*) Phew. Ere, I'm gettin' 'ot. Give us a chance. You go too quick fer me.

AMANDA. (*Squatting on the table and smoothing her

*dress and pulling it over her boots.*) I didn't know as gentlemen didn't like bein' kissed.

HORACE. 'Ere, let's look at y'. (*Pause.*)

AMANDA. (*Looking at him diffidently.*) You are 'andsome, aren't you, Mr. 'Orris, but I s'pose you know that.

HORACE. I've 'eard something about it.

AMANDA. That ain't all what I told 'y jes now.

HORACE. What!

AMANDA. All the other girls they've got fellers to give 'em things.

HORACE. You don't say so. Well, you ain't goin' to catch me—

AMANDA. Oh, no, but I didn't like their sayin' as nobody ever giv' me anything, so I bin tellin' them as you gave me lots an' 'eaps o' things—diamonds and joolery and watches—'andsome, y' know. I didn't know as you'd come back. I'd waited so long—and at last I went into mournin'—but I kep' on sayin' about the presents and letters, and now I 'aven't even anything to be in mournin' for, and they'll say as they always knew as I was kiddin', and (*Sniffs.*) they didn't—they reelly thought it was true what I told them. I know it was a liberty, Mr. 'Orris, but I 'oped you wouldn't mind.

HORACE. (*Whistles. Slowly.*) They thinks as I've been stuffing you up with presents?

AMANDA. Yes, Mr. 'Orris.

HORACE. Well you've just about made a nice mess of things, ain't y'?

AMANDA. Couldn't you—

HORACE. Couldn't I do it really? Not much.

AMANDA. I didn't mean that, but as you ain't dead couldn't you go on saying nothin' and let me go on pretendin'?—

HORACE. No.

AMANDA. It wouldn't cost y' nothin'. Why won't y'?

HORACE. Yes. Why won't I?

AMANDA. (*Walking away very much downcast.*) I thought you might like to oblige a lady.

HORACE. What next?

(AMANDA *goes up to window and dries her eyes with her apron.*)

HORACE. What 'r y' snuffling about, y' little beggar?

AMANDA. Nothin', Mr. 'Orris.

HORACE. They must be a precious lot o' mugs them girls if they swaller a tale like that. I never heard o' such a thing. (*He leans against table with his back to audience.*)

AMANDA. They didn't believe it for a long while, but now they believes it, an' about me father, too.

HORACE. Father! Didn't y' say he was a gonner?—

AMANDA. (*Faintly and tearfully.*) I don't know, though I guess. But (*Rather proudly.*) they think I've got a father as rich as ever 'e could be, and 'andsome, more 'andsome even than you.

HORACE. Pretty sort o' father to leave you in this 'ole then.

AMANDA. They think 'e's comin' to fetch me.

HORACE. Best 'urry up I should say.

AMANDA. (*Gives a little gesture.*) Oh, don't you see! I got nothing, Mr. 'Orris—nothing. (*She subsides and burying her face in the hollow of her arm cries silently.*) (*Pause.*)

HORACE. 'Ere, funny, you needn't drown the place out. Tell 'em what you blasted well like. I don't care. (*Kicks a clothes basket.*) I don't care.

AMANDA. Oh, Mr. 'Orris.

HORACE. Yes, oh, Mr. 'Orris, but you don't catch me coming 'ere no more.

AMANDA. You won't come 'ere again!

HORACE. No fear. Is it likely? What d'ye take me for?

AMANDA. Then I don't know as I'll tell 'em anything then.

HORACE. Suit yourself.

AMANDA. I'd rather—oh, I don't care what they think.

HORACE. Look 'ere, nipper. (*He comes to her.*) I'm goin' to talk like a father to you. You're puttin' y'r money on the wrong 'orse—not as I'm a wrong'un mindye, but if you was to talk to some chaps like this—

AMANDA. (*Quickly.*) Oh, but I wouldn't.

HORACE. That's all right then. Now you give me my shirt and I'll be off. (*Generously.*) You tell those girls just what you damn well please.

AMANDA. (*Looking at the parcel lingeringly.*) You're goin' to take it.

HORACE. Time I did, isn't it?

AMANDA. I shan't 'ave nothin' to remember y' by.

HORACE. Would y' like a lock o' me 'air? 'Ere—'ere's a present for y'. (*He takes a pin out of his tie.*) Gold pin, 42 carat, diamond mounted, pearl centre, em'rald border encrusted with rubies. (*Polishes it on his sleeve.*) New cut 2-9. There, my dear.

AMANDA. (*Delighted.*) Oh, Mr. 'Orris!

HORACE. Now we're quits.

AMANDA. (*Excitedly.*) I did want something to show to S'leste, and it is lovely, lovely, but—but—

HORACE. What now?

AMANDA. It means as you're goin' for ever. Couldn't—couldn't you keep it and not—

HORACE. Not what?

AMANDA. Not go. It—it's like you dyin' all over again.

HORACE. Well of all the treats—

AMANDA. (*With a new thought.*) Where are y' goin' now?

HORACE. 'Ome, I s'pose.

AMANDA. We—we do send things—

HORACE. What are y' drivin' at?

AMANDA. Say I was to bring y' this. Or if you'd wait a little bit I might carry it out for you. It's nice strollin' in the summer evenin's, Mr. 'Orris, and it'd be no trouble.

HORACE. (*Stooping, with his hands on his knees, and thus bringing his face on to a level with hers.*) Come with me, d'y' mean?

AMANDA. Yes.

HORACE. Yes. We could go for strolls every evenin', eh?

AMANDA. (*With a long breath.*) Oh—ye-es.

HORACE. (*Mimicking her.*) Ye-es! What d' y' think my friends 'd say? Why, as we was walkin' out.

AMANDA. *I* wouldn't mind, Mr. 'Orris.

HORACE. But what price me?

AMANDA. I shouldn't expect y' to marry me.

HORACE. Much obliged. Thank y'.

AMANDA. I didn't even dream as y'd marry me really.

HORACE. Well then, if you was to come messin' about with me what'd your girls 'ere say? You don't want to lose y' character, I s'pose.

AMANDA. *I* wouldn't mind, Mr. 'Orris.

HORACE. So 'elp me Bob. You don't seem to mind anything. (*He walks half-way to the door and pauses.*) 'Ere. Are all o' you girls goin' out a Monday?

AMANDA. The others are, Rose and S'leste and Clem—that's Mrs. Galloway.

HORACE. But what about you?

AMANDA. I—I'm supposed to be in mournin'.

HORACE. 'As nobody asked y'? (AMANDA *hangs her head.*) 'As nobody asked y'?

AMANDA. I—(*She bites her lip.*)—I can't pretend any more. (*Breaking down.*) No. Nobody's never asked me. (*She sobs.*) I s'pose now nobody never will. I see 'em all start times and times with their fellas. Oh, it don't matter. Only I didn't mean as *you* should know. (*Sits.*)

HORACE. Where are they goin'?

AMANDA. (*Sobbing gently.*) 'Amstead. Oh, it don't matter, Mr. 'Orris.

HORACE. Yes it do. (*He moves about restlessly for a minute, then stares at her intently.*) Look 'ere. Shall I take y'?

AMANDA. D' y' mean it?

HORACE. Did I say it? Very well then.

AMANDA. Oh, Mr. 'Orris.

HORACE. I'll get a trap and we'll go to 'Amstead.

AMANDA. (*In ecstasy.*) Oh, Mr. 'Orris.

HORACE. All right. That's settled. I'll call for you 'ere at nine sharp Monday morin'.

AMANDA. Y' won't change y' mind?

HORACE. No. If I say I'll do a thing I'll do it.

AMANDA. And I may tell S'leste and the others?

HORACE. Tell the 'ole world if y' like. Tell all Soho.

AMANDA. (*Dancing and clapping her hands and singing.*) Oh, it'll be joyful, joyful, joyful! I'll wear me blue dress that buttons up the back, and I've got a 'at as I 'hardly worn yet. Won't the other girls stare! Not one of 'em's got a fella like you. Rose's Jim—why 'e's not much bigger than me. And S'leste's Albit—'e's only a dustman. And as for Mr. Galloway—if 'e's sober be nine o'clock in the mornin' Clem'll 'ave something to be thankful for. Oh, Mr. 'Orris. Sat'dy, Sundy, Mondy. A 'ole day to look forward in. There won't be a 'appier lady anywhere Monday than what I shall be. You'll be 'ere be nine. (*Coming back to him.*) That's when the others go.

HORACE. D' they start from 'ere?

AMANDA. Yes.

HORACE. (*Shifting his feet.*) Nine o'clock, that's all right, but I think it'd be better to meet by the Dispens'ry, see—in Paul street.

AMANDA. (*Her face falling a little.*) Paul street—right down there?

HORACE. What's the matter with Paul street? Everyone knows the Dispens'ry. It's a good place to meet, ain't it.

AMANDA. I should 'a' liked you to come 'ere.

HORACE. What's the difference?

AMANDA. (*Reluctantly.*) I should 'a' liked 'em all to see me goin' off with y'. They won't more than 'alf believe else.

HORACE. Paul street's much more convenient.

AMANDA. There won't be the crowd there is 'ere.

HORACE. No. That's it. We don't want no crowds, do we? It'll be much better to go quietly from Paul street, won't it? You *be* there at nine and I'll come along and pick y' up. Then we shan't 'ave no waitin' about.

(AMANDA *looks at him slowly.*)

HORACE. You could be at the corner, couldn't you, where that little court is, and come out when I whistled?

AMANDA. (*Still looking at him.*) Yes. I needn't show meself till you come.

HORACE. That's right. (*A little pause.*) And er—I was thinkin' there's such 'undreds of people goes to 'Amstead. We don't want to go there, do we? What'd y' say to the forest?

AMANDA. Eppin'?

HORACE. Yes. I know a nice quiet little bit of it where we could go.

AMANDA. (*Meekly.*) I don't mind, Mr. 'Orris. (*She walks away from him.*)

HORACE. All right then. Monday, nine o'clock. Paul street. Blest if I wasn't goin' without me shirt after all. Ta-ta. (*Is about to go.*)

AMANDA. (*Calling him back just as he is at the door.*) Mr. 'Orris.

HORACE. Yes.

AMANDA. I—I can't go after all.

HORACE. (*Coming back.*) Can't go!

AMANDA. No.

HORACE. What d' y' mean, can't go?

AMANDA. What I say—(*Recovering herself with an effort.*)—I been pretendin'. Just to see what you'd do.

HORACE. Pretendin'!

AMANDA. Yes. (*Nervous and excited, but gaining con-*

*fidence as she proceeds.*) You see I shouldn't be allowed to go out with strangers. My people wouldn't let me. I've been brought up different. I'm afraid you'll be very angry, but none of that about me bein' a orphin or born in the Union is true. I'm the child of poor but respectable parents, and I've bin very strictly brought up, and so, though I'm very much obliged to you, Mr. Greensmith, I mustn't accept your kind invitation.

HORACE. Strike me pink!

AMANDA. You don't mind me 'avin' a bit of a lark with y', do y'? It was so dull 'ere while the others was out. I couldn't 'elp it. Ha, ha, ha. If you was to seen y'r own face! You got a soft 'eart, that I will say. Ha, ha, ha.

HORACE. Made a fool of me, 'ave y'. All right my girl. Wait till I bring y' more washin' to do.

AMANDA. There, don't be angry.

HORACE. Angry. 'Oo's angry? It's enough to make anyone angry. Why—

AMANDA. Garn. You know very well as it's a relief.

HORACE. Relief?

AMANDA. (*Half hysterical.*) Not to 'ave to take me out—a little 'op-o'-me-thumb like me. Ain't it now? And 'ave everybody laughin' at y', and askin' y' what it was, and where y'd picked it up, and why they 'adn't drowned it when it was born. Ho, ho. It'd be a poor world, eh, if we didn't git a bit o' fun out of it some'ow, and some of us was meant to supply all the fun for the others, it's my opinion. Lord, when you thought I was cryin' I thought I should 'a died. Laugh! Whenever I think of it I shall most split meself. Y' don't mind, old man, do y'?

HORACE. I've a good mind to wring y' neck for y'.

AMANDA. No, don't do that. May I keep the pin?

HORACE. Keep what y' like.

AMANDA. I will then. Now say y' ain't angry before y' go.

HORACE. I'll be blowed if I do.

AMANDA. Jes' to show there's no ill feelin'.

HORACE. Git out.

AMANDA. Say it. (*She stands looking up at him tremulously.*)

HORACE. 'Ere. (*Stares at her hard, then takes her hands and pulls her round to the light.*) Why! What'r-ye playin' at? Tell the truth and shame the devil. Twig? I was a fool to say as I'd take y'. We wasn't made for each other—what d'ye call yerself 'op-o'-me-thumb? but you're a game little 'un, and 'Orris Greensmith's goin' to sling 'is bloomin' 'ook. See! Now gi' us that kiss I asked y' for. (*Kisses her quickly and in shame-faced manner, but very kindly, then whips up hat and shirt and goes out quietly. She stands for a moment or two swaying. When she looks up he is gone.*)

AMANDA. 'E kissed me! (*Wonderingly.*) 'E kissed me. O-oh. (*She looks round and begins mechanically to put the room tidy. Presently she bethinks her of the pin. She takes it out of the bosom of her dress where she has stuck it.*) 'E was ashamed of me, too. I s'pose I ought to spurn it. I ought really to 'a thrown it at 'is false feet and said: "Take back the jew'ls with which you 'ave loaded me, they are poisonin' me," but (*Shaking her head and rubbing the stones on her sleeve to make them shine.*) I can't. Oh, Mr. 'Orris, you've broken me 'eart and stuck a pin in it. But you did kiss me. You can't take back y' kiss. I shan't wait to hear their talk. Me pretendin's over and done with. (*She pulls off her crape bow and holds it to her lips.*) There's nobody—nobody now for me to pretend. Oh, Mr. 'Orris—Mr. 'Orris. (*She crouches in a shabby little heap in the middle of the empty room as the curtain falls.*)

CURTAIN.

# PHIPPS

COMEDY IN ONE ACT

## STANLEY HOUGHTON

Stanley Houghton, the most brilliant and promising member of the so-called "Manchester School" of English dramatists, was born at Ashton-upon-Mersey in 1881. Until he reached the age of thirty he worked in his father's law office in Manchester, but in 1912, after the success of "Hindle Wakes," he was able to devote all his time to the writing of plays. He was destined, however, to spend less than two years as an independent artist; toward the end of 1913, after a trip through Europe, he returned to Manchester to die.

Houghton was one of the most significant of the younger English playwrights. His half-dozen important plays are studies in middle-class English life and character. He was especially fond of the one-act form, developing it with skill and insight. "Phipps" is a well-rounded, amusing and biting satire of contemporary life.

Following is a list of Stanley Houghton's published plays: "Hindle Wakes;" "The Younger Generation;" "Independent Means;" "Phipps;" "The Fifth Commandment;" " Fancy Free;" "The Dear Departed;" "Marriages in the Making;" "Partners;" "The Perfect Cure;" "The Old Testament and the New;" "The Master of the House."

References: T. H. Dickinson, "The Contemporary Drama of England"; Barrett H. Clark, "A Study of the Modern Drama."

# PHIPPS*

## CHARACTERS

PHIPPS, *a Butler*
LADY FANNY
SIR GERALD

SCENE: *Sir Gerald's Library*

TIME: *The Present*

SCENE. *The library of* SIR GERALD'S *London house is a handsome, comfortable place, with very few books in it. There are plenty of easy chairs, rugs, rich hangings and good water-colours.*

SIR GERALD *and* LADY FANNY *are discovered in the midst of an absorbing, if not a heated, colloquy. Both are about thirty, and extremely good-looking; they wear evening clothes, which cause them to look even less than thirty and more good-looking than ever.* SIR GERALD *is slight in build, and his enemies might call him a bit of a dude. He is a pleasant enough fellow, nevertheless.* LADY FANNY *is gorgeous and shimmering, acute and witty, full of hasty enthusiasms and queer impulses. You like her, but she is a disconcerting woman, all the same. You never know what she is going to say next.* SIR GERALD *is standing in the middle of the room, and* LADY FANNY *is leaning forward in an arm-chair. Suddenly she rises and sweeps towards* SIR GERALD *with a superb gesture.*)

LADY FANNY. Verv well then, hit me! Hit me! Hit me, do you hear?


This play is also published in "Five One-Act Plays" by the same author. Price, 75 cents a copy.

(SIR GERALD *steps forward as if about to strike her, and raises his arm; but instead of hitting her he merely scratches his head in a perplexed way.*)

LADY F. Well, why don't you hit me? I'm waiting to be hit. (*She turns her cheeks meekly towards him, as if it were a kiss she is expecting and not a blow.*)

SIR GERALD. Er—yes. But I don't think that's quite the—er—quite the idea.

LADY F. You are reluctant to strike a woman, even if she is your wife?

SIR G. On the contrary. If I must strike a woman, I prefer that she be my wife. I have no objection to striking you, my dear; only it is no good doing it in private. In that case, you would be unable to prove my cruelty.

LADY F. The judge ought to take my word for that. Indeed, if the case comes before Sir Frederick Mitchie, I am sure he will, because I know him so well.

SIR G. Sir Frederick is a model of courtesy, and I am certain that he will spare you all the trouble he possibly can; but I am afraid that he will confirm my view that the law insists upon my being cruel to you in public.

LADY F. It will not be necessary, I trust, for you to strike me at the Opera or the Ritz.

SIR G. That would be overdoing it. It would betray the amateur. Reticence is the mark of the true artist. But if you wish to get a divorce there must be a witness of some sort when I strike you.

LADY F. Ring for the servants.

SIR G. (*Shocked.*) The servants! My dear! Perhaps I am prudish and even old-fashioned, but the servants—

LADY F. Then *one* of the servants.

SIR G. Which one?

LADY F. What do you think about Cook?

SIR G. I *never* think about Cook.

LADY F. I mean as a witness.

Sir G. Oh! I am afraid that Cook might be inclined to talk.

Lady F. Perhaps you are right. She is naturally a gossip. I suggested her because she has already been married three times, and would probably make an interested and even a sympathetic spectator.

Sir G. Why not your maid?

Lady F. Robinson? No. Robinson knows quite enough about me already.

Sir G. There's that parlour-maid—the one with frizzy hair.

Lady F. She is *much* too young. I should prefer Phipps.

Sir G. Phipps! My dear Fanny, do you think Phipps would like it?

Lady F. You might hint to him that we would consider it in his wages.

Sir G. But Phipps is a most respectable man.

Lady F. That is why I should prefer him. He is discreet. I could place myself in his hands without reserve.

Sir G. He is certainly a perfect butler.

Lady F. Will you ring for him, dear?

Sir G. Willingly.

(SIR GERALD *rings the bell.*)

Lady F. You absolutely decline to give me those pearls?

Sir G. Absolutely.

Lady F. Very well. As soon as Phipps arrives, you will be good enough to strike me.

Sir G. Certainly. That is the idea, I believe.

Lady F. Yes. I think about here—(*She chooses a position in the middle of the room, and places* SIR GERALD *conveniently opposite to her.*) That will do nicely. By the way, Gerald, you won't hurt me, will you?

Sir G. I am a gentleman, Fanny. I hope that I shall always behave as one, no matter what provocation you offer me.

Lady F. Thank you, Gerald.

Sir G. At the same time, Fanny, I must remind you

that although I shall not use actual violence, it will be necessary for you to convey the impression that I am hurting you.

LADY F. Oh, I see. Of course. (*She nods.*) Very well. I promise you I'll do that. Hush, here he is.

(*They take up their attitudes again.*)

(PHIPPS, *a large, pleasant, discreet man of forty-five, enters and stands by the door.*)

LADY F. (*As before.*) Very well then, hit me! Hit me! Hit me, do you hear? (SIR GERALD *steps forward and strikes* LADY FANNY. *Crying out.*) Oh! oh! You've hit me! You coward!

(LADY FANNY *collapses into the easy chair, sobbing. Her prostration is so complete that she might have been run over by a steam-roller, instead of having been rather delicately slapped upon the shoulder. As she cowers in the chair,* SIR GERALD *steps forward with a threatening air, evidently intending to strike her again.* PHIPPS, *however, rapidly advances, hits* SIR GERALD *a sound blow under the jaw, catches him by the coat collar and flings him aside, tripping him up as he does so in such wise that* SIR GERALD *tumbles on to the floor in a heap.* PHIPPS *stands calmly over the prostrate baronet, in the attitude of a butler awaiting orders.*)

PHIPPS. You rang, my lady. (LADY FANNY *stares open-mouthed at* PHIPPS.) Was this what you rang for, my lady? (*He indicates the figure of* SIR GERALD.)

LADY F. (*Admiringly.*) Phipps! How strong you are! I never knew before that you were so strong.

(SIR GERALD *attempts to get up.*)

PHIPPS. I beg your pardon, sir, but if you don't lie quiet I shall be obliged to knock you down again; with all respect to you, sir.

SIR G. Do you know that you've nearly broken my jaw?

PHIPPS. I am aware, sir, that I have taken rather a liberty with you, but, as man to man, you will understand that I had no alternative.

SIR G. Confound you! Will you let me get up? (SIR GERALD *sits on his haunches and scowls up at* PHIPPS.)

PHIPPS. I think it would be better, sir, if you would retain your present position for the moment.

SIR G. (*To* LADY FANNY.) This is all your fault, Fanny. It was your idea to ring for Phipps. (*To* PHIPPS.) Go away, and send Cook here.

PHIPPS. I am sorry, sir, but unless I can have some assurance that you will behave yourself, I cannot trust you with any woman, not even with Cook.

LADY F. But what do you propose to do now, Phipps? We cannot prolong this situation indefinitely.

PHIPPS. I propose to remain here until I have Sir Gerald's word of honour that he will strike neither you, my lady, nor Cook, for whom he asks in his wrath; in the hope, no doubt, that I shall permit him to treat her differently from you because of her inferior station. It is true that Cook's father is a green-grocer in the Edgware Road, and that yours, my lady, is a Duke. But though I am a sound Conservative in politics, I confess that I am unable to consider distinctions of rank where a woman is in distress or danger. In such a case as this I am not a butler, but a man, and as a man I feel that I stand in *loco parentis* both to you, my lady, and to Cook. I represent Mr. Perkins, the green-grocer, as well as his Grace.

LADY F. Phipps! How blind I have been! You have been a perfect butler for three years without my ever suspecting that you were a man.

PHIPPS. Yes, my lady, that is the secret of my success as a butler. (SIR GERALD *makes an attempt to get up.*) Do you mind remaining in a semi-recumbent posture, sir? (*To* LADY FANNY.) I am extremely sorry that I have forgotten myself on this occasion, my lady, but I can assure you that I shall try and not let it occur again.

SIR G. For Heaven's sake, Fanny, make the fellow let me get up.

LADY F. Oh, yes, Phipps, you must allow Sir Gerald to get up now. I undertake that he will behave himself.

PHIPPS. Very good, my lady. (PHIPPS *assists* SIR GERALD *to rise.*) I can take your word for it, I am sure.

(PHIPPS *takes a small clothes-brush out of a desk drawer, and brushes* SIR GERALD'S *coat.*)

LADY F. We are very much obliged to you, Phipps—perhaps I should say *I* am very much obliged to you—for the devotion you have shown to-day. It is painful for me to have to tell you that it is mistaken. You have been deceived by appearances.

PHIPPS. (*Brushing.*) Appearances, my lady?

LADY F. Perhaps I should say by my talent for acting. You never saw me play in the theatricals at Tatsworth in the old days, did you?

PHIPPS. I never had that pleasure, my lady.

(PHIPPS *replaces the brush, and stands attentively by* LADY FANNY.)

LADY F. On more than one occasion I was mistaken for a professional.

PHIPPS. A professional actress, my lady?

LADY F. Certainly.

PHIPPS. I am not surprised, my lady; it is surprising how little experience some of our best-known actresses possess.

SIR G. Damn it all, we seem to be drifting into a discussion about the stage now.

LADY F. One moment, Gerald. Phipps, I find, is an intelligent critic of modern acting. (*To* PHIPPS.) You never realized that when Sir Gerald struck me my emotional outburst was assumed?

PHIPPS. Not for one moment, my lady.

LADY F. He is an *extremely* intelligent critic of acting!

Sir Gerald did not hurt me, Phipps. At least, not very much.

PHIPPS. I cannot imagine Sir Gerald hurting anybody very much. (*To* SIR GERALD.) I beg your pardon, sir; I'm sure you did your best.

SIR G. Don't apologize to me, pray. I can't help feeling that you would be able to discuss my character more freely if you would allow me to retire.

PHIPPS. Not at all, sir. Your presence does not embarrass us in the least.

LADY F. I asked Sir Gerald to strike me.

PHIPPS. Ah, my lady, it is good of you to try and shield Sir Gerald. You'll be telling me next that you rang for me in order to come and see him strike you.

LADY F. As a matter of fact, that is precisely what did occur. We were in a slight domestic difficulty, and we required your assistance.

SIR G. Look here! Is there any need to tell all this to Phipps?

PHIPPS. If I am to be of any use, sir, it will be necessary for you to tell me everything. Otherwise I can hardly give you the full benefit of my advice.

LADY F. I have just had a violent quarrel with Sir Gerald.

PHIPPS. I have observed with regret that you have had a great many quarrels with Sir Gerald of late.

LADY F. This is by far the worst that we have ever had. Sir Gerald complains that I am extravagant.

SIR G. I appeal to you, Phipps, as a married man—you *are* married, aren't you?

PHIPPS. Not at present, sir. I *was* married. My wife divorced me.

LADY F. Oh, dear! How was that?

SIR G. My dear—ought we to ask?

PHIPPS. There were very excellent reasons for the step.

LADY F. How glad I am that we decided to have you

in, Phipps. Your experience will be most useful. I am going to divorce Sir Gerald.

PHIPPS. Oh, my lady! Reflect. I hold no brief for Sir Gerald, but after all he is your husband.

LADY F. Yes. That is why I am going to divorce him.

PHIPPS. I hope you will think twice before doing so, my lady.

LADY F. We have not shocked you, I trust, Phipps?

PHIPPS. No, my lady. I have lived with you too long to be easily shocked. But since you have been good enough to take me into your confidence, I beg leave to urge you most strongly to make it up with Sir Gerald.

SIR G. Look here, Phipps. We didn't invite you here to give us a lecture.

PHIPPS. Then, sir, may I ask why you *did* ring for me?

LADY F. We rang for you to be a witness. From your past experience you must be aware that it is necessary for a woman to prove both adultery and cruelty before she can obtain a divorce.

PHIPPS. Or desertion and cruelty.

LADY F. There is no difference. The one implies the other. *Now* do you understand our difficulty?

PHIPPS. Forgive me, my lady, if I say that the difficulty does not seem to me an insuperable one.

LADY F. Oh, the desertion or what-do-you-call-it would be easy enough, of course, especially to Sir Gerald. It is the cruelty that presents the difficulty. You see, whatever Sir Gerald has done, he has never made a practice of hitting me.

SIR G. I hope I know where to draw the line.

LADY F. We were expecting that you would understand everything, and would help to make things all so easy for us. Phipps, am I to be disappointed in you, after all?

PHIPPS. No, my lady. That shall never be. (*To* SIR

GERALD.) You and her ladyship have definitely decided to separate?

SIR G. Yes.

PHIPPS. Nothing I can say will prevent you?

SIR G. Nothing.

LADY F. Nothing.

PHIPPS. There is—excuse me—no other lady?

SIR G. Certainly not. I can't afford to keep her ladyship, let alone anybody else.

LADY F. You shall not have to reproach me with that much longer.

PHIPPS. Then may I point out that you have selected a most unpleasant mode of accomplishing your object. To divorce Sir Gerald, it will be necessary for you to transact a lot of cumbersome legal business, to appear in court and have your photograph in the papers, and generally to go through a great deal of disagreeable publicity.

LADY F. All that is quite true, but I don't see how it can be avoided.

PHIPPS. Quite easily, my lady.

LADY F. How?

PHIPPS. By letting Sir Gerald divorce you.

LADY F. Divorce me!—But I have given him no reason to do so.

PHIPPS. Ah, my lady, don't let a little thing like that stand in the way.

SIR G. Eh?

PHIPPS. It is all so simple. You have only to order Robinson to pack for you; to select a congenial companion; and to leave the country. Sir Gerald does the rest. It is as easy as taking a Kodak photograph.

LADY F. Really, Phipps, there is something in what you say. Gerald, what do you think?

SIR G. Well—it's an idea.

(*They consider the matter for a moment.*)

LADY F. There is only one thing troubling me. The choice of the—what did you call him, Phipps?

PHIPPS. The congenial companion, my lady.

LADY F. Yes. The congenial companion. What a charming way of putting it.

PHIPPS. If you would permit me to suggest a name, my lady—the Earl of Skye——

LADY F. Tony? I'm very fond of Tony. (*She considers.*) H'm! Ho, Phipps, Lord Skye is going to Norway salmon fishing on Saturday. We could hardly expect him to put off his trip just to oblige us in this trifling matter. Gerald! Can't you think of some one?

SIR G. What about Harry Roughwood?

LADY F. No go! He's down with measles.

SIR G. Ow! Bad luck. (*He scratches his head.*) I dunno *who* we could get.

LADY F. It's too bad of you, Gerald. You *are* stupid.

(*They all reflect with the utmost earnestness.*)

PHIPPS. I wonder, my lady, if in this emergency you would allow me to make another suggestion?

LADY F. Of course, Phipps. Have you thought of some other man?

PHIPPS. I have, my lady.

LADY F. But is he available? He may have some other engagement.

PHIPPS. Whether he is available depends upon you and Sir Gerald, my lady.

LADY F. Why! Who is he?

PHIPPS. I was referring to myself, my lady.

LADY F. You!

SIR G. You!

(*There is a pause.*)

LADY F. Oh, but, Phipps, we could hardly expect you to undertake a responsibility of this sort, especially at your present wages.

PHIPPS. It is true, my lady, that you have only engaged me as your butler, but seeing that you are placed in a difficulty, I should be perfectly happy to make myself useful in any capacity.

SIR G. It's jolly good of you, Phipps, it is indeed; but we couldn't think of giving you so much trouble.

PHIPPS. No trouble at all, Sir Gerald. On the contrary, it would be a pleasure.

SIR G. Oh! would it?

LADY F. This is quite an idea. I'm sure, Gerald, that you would prefer a nice respectable man like Phipps to go with me. We must think it over thoroughly. Sit down, Phipps.

PHIPPS. If it's all the same to you, my lady, I should feel more comfortable standing.

LADY F. I insist. Sit here by me.

(LADY FANNY *crosses to a settee, and makes room for* PHIPPS *on it by her side.* PHIPPS *unwillingly takes the seat indicated.*)

LADY F. You said it would be a pleasure. What did you mean by that?

PHIPPS. My lady, now that I know that you and Sir Gerald are estranged, I can speak freely. For the past three years I have cherished an ardent affection for your ladyship.

SIR G. (*Startled.*) Eh! What's that?

LADY F. Phipps! Do you really mean it?

PHIPPS. I know it is a great liberty, my lady, to entertain such sentiments towards you, but even a butler is capable of a human attachment; and under the circumstances I hope that you will be inclined to overlook it this time.

LADY F. And you have managed to conceal your feelings all these years?

PHIPPS. It has been a struggle, my lady. I have been torn between conflicting emotions. My duty seemed to be to give you a month's notice; but then came the reflection that if I did so I should never see you again.

Lady F. My poor Phipps! My heart bleeds for you. What devotion!

Phipps. You do not mind, my lady?

Lady F. I have never been loved like this before. It is a new sensation. Tell me more about yourself. Why did your wife divorce you?

Phipps. Well, my lady——

Sir G. (*Who has been roaming about behind the settee in some agitation of mind.*) I say, I'm afraid I'm in the way here.

Phipps. Not at all, sir.

Sir G. I'll go into another room if I am disturbing you.

Phipps. Believe me, sir, I had clean forgotten you were there.

Lady F. Be quiet, Gerald. I don't mind you stopping here if you won't talk. Go on, Phipps. What is it that you propose?

Phipps. That instead of divorcing Sir Gerald, you adopt the far easier course of going away with me and allowing Sir Gerald to divorce you. That would be much pleasanter for all parties. I should never have dared to suggest such a thing, if it were not that your ladyship and Sir Gerald have given each other notice as it were; leaving you, so to speak, temporarily without a place. I can give you no diamonds, no pearls, my lady. All I can offer is the sincere and pent-up devotion of a man of forty-five, in good health and preservation. Could you bring yourself to accept it, my lady?

Lady F. (*Closing her eyes in rapture.*) Oh, this is wonderful! Gerald, you never speak to me like this.

Phipps. You could hardly expect him to do so, my lady, seeing that you are his wife.

Lady F. *Dare* I go with you? What would it be like to love a man for himself alone. (*Looking at him earnestly.*) Phipps—you fascinate me—strangely.

Sir G. May I ask what you propose to live on? Will Phipps support you on the emoluments he gains as butler, or do you yourself intend to take up a position as lady's maid?

PHIPPS. There you touch the main difficulty. I fear that her ladyship will find herself in rather poor circumstances for a time, unless you, sir should think of making her a settlement.

SIR G. I'm damned if I'll make her a settlement.

LADY F. Gerald, there is no need to get angry, even if you *are* ashamed of being mean.

SIR G. I'm not mean.

LADY F. Oh, yes, you are. First you refuse to buy me the pearls, and now you refuse to make us a settlement. I call it *worse* than mean. You are a perfect dog in the manger.

SIR G. I didn't refuse to buy you the pearls. I said I couldn't afford to buy them unless I sold Cleveleys.

LADY F. That comes to much the same thing as refusing, doesn't it?

PHIPPS. My lady. I am waiting for your answer.

SIR G. (*Eagerly.*) Hold on a bit. One moment, please, Phipps.

PHIPPS. (*Bowing.*) I beg pardon, sir. (*He steps back a pace.*)

SIR G. Look here, Fanny. If I sell Cleveleys and buy you the pearls, will you promise not to ask me for anything else for a whole year?

LADY F. A year is too long. I might consider six months.

SIR G. Six months. (*He looks at* PHIPPS *and reflects.*)

(PHIPPS, *under the impression that he may now speak, takes a step forward.* SIR GERALD *intercepts him quickly.*)

All right. Six months.

LADY F. And you'll buy me the pearls? That's a promise.

SIR G. Yes.

LADY F. Then there will be no need for us to get divorced at all, will there?

PHIPPS. (*Anxiously.*) My lady——

LADY F. Oh, yes, Phipps. I am sorry to disappoint you, Phipps.

PHIPPS. You have decided to remain with Sir Gerald, my lady?

LADY F. For the present. It will be so much less trouble, after all. But we need not regret the circumstances which caused us to invite your co-operation. It has enabled us to become more closely acquainted than I had thought possible. I am intensely obliged to you for all your kindness. You see how valuable your advice has proved. I hope we shall have the benefit of it on many future occasions.

PHIPPS. No, my lady.

SIR G. No?

PHIPPS. Never again, my lady.

LADY F. Oh, but why not, Phipps?

PHIPPS. I regret, my lady, that I cannot remain any longer in your service.

LADY F. But why? To leave us just when we were beginning to know each other more intimately!

PHIPPS. That is just it, my lady. I have been so perfect a butler to you for three years, that you never suspected that I was a man. Now you know that I am a man, I shall never be a perfect butler to you again. I give you a month's notice, my lady. (PHIPPS *bows and goes out of the room.*)

SIR G. (*Wiping his brow in relief.*) What a man!

LADY F. Oh, Gerald! If only you would try to be more like him.

(*The Curtain falls quickly, leaving* SIR GERALD *staring at* LADY FANNY *in surprise.*)

CURTAIN.

# SPREADING THE NEWS

COMEDY IN ONE ACT

## LADY GREGORY

Lady Augusta Gregory was born at Roxborough, Ireland, in 1859. She became a dramatist in order to furnish the Abbey Theater in Dublin with plays of a light character. There were few such works available, and though Lady Gregory's first dramatic idea came to her as a serious play, she determined to try the theme in the vein of comedy.

Lady Gregory has written a number of plays, mostly one-act comedies, which are without doubt among the very finest specimens of pure comedy that have been written in modern times. She perhaps more closely approaches the spirit of Molière than any other dramatist now writing in the English language.

Lady Gregory was one of the founders of the Abbey Theater, through which the modern Irish dramatic movement was enabled to come into being.

Following is a list of Lady Gregory's published plays: "Spreading the News;" "Kincora;" "The White Cockade;" "Hyacinth Halvey;" "The Gaol Gate;" "The Canavans" "The Jackdaw;" "The Rising of the Moon;" "Dervorgilla;" "The Workhouse Ward;" "The Image;" "The Travelling Man;" "The Full Moon;" "Coats;" "The Deliverer;" "Mac Darragh's Wife;" "The Bogie Men;" "Damer's Gold;" "The Golden Apple;" "The Dragon;" "Aristotle's Bellows;" "The Jester;" "The Wrens;" "Shanwalla;" "Hanrahan's Oath."

References: Ernest Boyd, "The Contemporary Drama of Ireland"; Lady Gregory, "Our Irish Theater"; Barrett H. Clark, "A Study of the Modern Drama."

# SPREADING THE NEWS*

## CHARACTERS

BARTLEY FALLON
MRS. FALLON
JACK SMITH
SHAWN EARLY
TIM CASEY
JAMES RYAN
MRS. TARPEY
MRS. TULLY
A POLICEMAN (JO MULDOON)
A REMOVABLE MAGISTRATE

PLACE: *The Outskirts of a Fair.*

TIME: *The Present.*

SCENE. *The outskirts of a Fair. An Apple Stall. Mrs. Tarpey sitting at it. Magistrate and Policeman enter.*

MAGISTRATE. So that is the Fair Green. Cattle and sheep and mud. No system. What a repulsive sight!

POLICEMAN. That is so, indeed.

MAGISTRATE. I suppose there is a good deal of disorder in this place?

POLICEMAN. There is.

MAGISTRATE. Common assault?

POLICEMAN. It's common enough.

MAGISTRATE. Agrarian crime, no doubt?

POLICEMAN. That is so.

MAGISTRATE. Boycotting? Maiming of cattle? Firing into houses?

---



This play is also obtainable in separate form, paper bound, at 50 cents a copy.

POLICEMAN. There was one time, and there might be again.

MAGISTRATE. That is bad. Does it go any farther than that?

POLICEMAN. Far enough, indeed.

MAGISTRATE. Homicide, then! This district has been shamefully neglected! I will change all that. When I was in the Andaman Islands, my system never failed. Yes, yes, I will change all that. What has that woman on her stall?

POLICEMAN. Apples mostly—and sweets.

MAGISTRATE. Just see if there are any unlicensed goods underneath—spirits or the like. We had evasions of the salt tax in the Andaman Islands.

POLICEMAN. (*Sniffing cautiously and upsetting a heap of apples.*) I see no spirits here—or salt.

MAGISTRATE. (*To* MRS. TARPEY.) Do you know this town well, my good woman?

MRS. TARPEY. (*Holding out some apples.*) A penny the half dozen, your honour.

POLICEMAN. (*Shouting.*) The gentleman is asking do you know the town! He's the new magistrate!

MRS. TARPEY. (*Rising and ducking.*) Do I know the town? I do, to be sure.

MAGISTRATE. (*Shouting.*) What is its chief business?

MRS. TARPEY. Business, is it? What business would the people here have but to be minding one another's business?

MAGISTRATE. I mean what trade have they?

MRS. TARPEY. Not a trade. No trade at all but to be talking.

MAGISTRATE. I shall learn nothing here.

(JAMES RYAN *comes in, pipe in mouth. Seeing* MAGISTRATE *he retreats quickly, taking pipe from mouth.*)

MAGISTRATE. The smoke from that man's pipe had a greenish look; he may be growing unlicensed tobacco at home. I wish I had brought my telescope to this district. Come to the post-office, I will telegraph for it. I found it very useful in the Andaman Islands.

(MAGISTRATE *and* POLICEMAN *go out left.*)

MRS. TARPEY. Bad luck to Jo Muldoon, knocking my apples this way and that way. (*Begins arranging them.*) Showing off he was to the new magistrate.

(*Enter* BARTLEY FALLON AND MRS. FALLON.)

BARTLEY. Indeed it's a poor country and a scarce country to be living in. But I'm thinking if I went to America it's long ago the day I'd be dead!

MRS. FALLON. So you might, indeed. (*She puts her basket on a barrel and begins putting parcels in it, taking them from under her cloak.*)

BARTLEY. And it's a great expense for a poor man to be buried in America.

MRS. FALLON. Never fear, Bartley Fallon, but I'll give you a good burying the day you'll die.

BARTLEY. Maybe it's yourself will be buried in the graveyard of Cloonmara before me, Mary Fallon, and I myself that will be dying unbeknownst some night, and no one a-near me. And the cat itself may be gone straying through the country, and the mice squealing over the quilt.

MRS. FALLON. Leave off talking of dying. It might be twenty years you'll be living yet.

BARTLEY. (*With a deep sigh.*) I'm thinking if I'll be living at the end of twenty years, it's a very old man I'll be then!

MRS. TARPEY. (*Turns and sees them.*) Good morrow, Bartley Fallon; good morrow, Mrs. Fallon. Well, Bartley, you'll find no cause for complaining to-day; they are all saying it was a good fair.

BARTLEY. (*Raising his voice.*) It was not a good fair, Mrs. Tarpey. It was a scattered sort of a fair. If we didn't expect more we got less. That's the way with me always; whatever I have to sell goes down and whatever I have to buy goes up. If there's ever any misfortune coming to this world, it's on myself it pitches, like a flock of crows on seed potatoes.

MRS. FALLON. Leave off talking of misfortunes and listen to Jack Smith that is coming the way, and he singing.

(*Voice of* JACK SMITH *heard singing.*)

I thought, my first love,
  There'd be but one house between you and me,
And I thought I would find
  Yourself coaxing my child on your knee.
Over the tide
  I would leap with the leap of a swan,
Till I came to the side
  Of the wife of the Red-haired man!

(JACK SMITH *comes in. He is a red-haired man, and is carrying a hayfork.*)

MRS. TARPEY. That should be a good song if I had my hearing.

MRS. FALLON. (*Shouting.*) It's "The Red-haired man's wife."

MRS. TARPEY. I know it well. That's the song that has a skin on it!

(*She turns her back to them and goes on arranging her apples.*)

MRS. FALLON. Where's herself, Jack Smith?

JACK SMITH. She was delayed with her washing; bleaching the clothes on the hedge she is, and she daren't leave them, with all the tinkers that do be passing to the fair. It isn't to the fair I came myself, but up to the Five Acre Meadow I'm going, where I have a contract for the hay. We'll get a share of it into tramps to-day. (*He lays down hayfork and lights his pipe.*)

BARTLEY. You will not get it into tramps to-day. The rain will be down on it by evening, and on myself too. It's seldom I ever started on a journey but the rain would come down on me before I'd find any place of shelter.

JACK SMITH. If it didn't itself, Bartley, it is my belief you would carry a leaky pail on your head in place of a hat, the way you'd not be without some cause of complaining.

(*A voice heard, "Go on, now, go on out o' that. Go on I say."*)

JACK SMITH. Look at that young mare of Pat Ryan's that is backing into Shaughnessy's bullocks with the dint of the crowd! Don't be daunted, Pat, I'll give you a hand with her.

(*He goes out, leaving his hayfork.*)

MRS. FALLON. It's time for ourselves to be going home. I have all I bought put in the basket. Look at there, Jack Smith's hayfork he left after him! He'll be wanting it. (*Calls.*) Jack Smith! Jack Smith!—He's gone through the crowd—hurry after him, Bartley, he'll be wanting it.

BARTLEY. I'll do that. This is no safe place to be leaving it. (*He takes up fork awkwardly and upsets the basket.*) Look at that now! If there is any basket in the fair upset, it must be our own basket! (*He goes out to right.*)

MRS. FALLON. Get out of that! It is your own fault it is. Talk of misfortunes and misfortunes will come. Glory be! Look at my new egg-cups rolling in every part—and my two pound of sugar with the paper broke——

MRS. TARPEY. (*Turning from stall.*) God help us, Mrs. Fallon, what happened your basket?

MRS. FALLON. It's himself that knocked it down, bad manners to him. (*Putting things up.*) My grand sugar that's destroyed, and he'll not drink his tea without it. I had best go back to the shop for more, much good may it do him!

(*Enter* TIM CASEY.)

TIM CASEY. Where is Bartley Fallon, Mrs. Fallon? I want a word with him before he'll leave the fair. I was afraid he might have gone home by this, for he's a temperate man.

MRS. FALLON. I wish he did go home! It'd be best for me if he went home straight from the fair green, or if he never came with me at all! Where is he, is it? He's gone up the road (*Jerks elbow.*) following Jack Smith with a hayfork.

(*She goes out to left.*)

TIM CASEY. Following Jack Smith with a hayfork! Did ever anyone hear the like of that. (*Shouts.*) Did you hear that news, Mrs. Tarpey?

MRS. TARPEY. I heard no news at all.

TIM CASEY. Some dispute I suppose it was that rose between Jack Smith and Bartley Fallon, and it seems Jack made off, and Bartley is following him with a hayfork!

MRS. TARPEY. Is he now? Well, that was quick work! It's not ten minutes since the two of them were here, Bartley going home and Jack going to the Five Acre Meadow; and I had my apples to settle up, that Jo Muldoon of the police had scattered, and when I looked round again Jack Smith was gone, and Bartley Fallon was gone, and Mrs. Fallon's basket upset, and all in it strewed upon the ground—the tea here—the two pound of sugar there—the egg-cups there—Look, now, what a great hardship the deafness puts upon me, that I didn't hear the commencement of the fight! Wait till I tell James Ryan that I see below; he is a neighbour of Bartley's, it would be a pity if he wouldn't hear the news!

(*She goes out. Enter* SHAWN EARLY *and* MRS. TULLY.)

TIM CASEY. Listen, Shawn Early! Listen Mrs. Tully, to the news! Jack Smith and Bartley Fallon had a falling out, and Jack knocked Mrs. Fallon's basket into the road, and Bartley made an attack on him with a hayfork, and away with Jack, and Bartley after him. Look at the sugar here yet on the road!

SHAWN EARLY. Do you tell me so? Well, that's a queer thing, and Bartley Fallon so quiet a man.

MRS. TULLY. I wouldn't wonder at all. I would never think well of a man that would have that sort of a mouldering look. It's likely he has overtaken Jack by this.

(*Enter* JAMES RYAN *and* MRS. TARPEY.)

JAMES RYAN. That is great news Mrs. Tarpey was telling me! I suppose that's what brought the police and the magistrate up this way. I was wondering to see them in it a while ago.

SHAWN EARLY. The police after them? Bartley Fallon must have injured Jack so. They wouldn't meddle in a fight that was only for show!

MRS. TULLY. Why wouldn't he injure him? There was many a man killed with no more of a weapon than a hayfork.

JAMES RYAN. Wait till I run north as far as Kelly's bar to spread the news! (*He goes out.*)

TIM CASEY. I'll go tell Jack Smith's first cousin that is standing there south of the church after selling his lambs. (*Goes out.*)

MRS. TULLY. I'll go telling a few of the neighbors I see beyond to the west. (*Goes out.*)

SHAWN EARLY. I'll give word of it beyond at the east of the green. (*Is going out when* MRS. TARPEY *seizes hold of him.*)

MRS. TARPEY. Stop a minute, Shawn Early, and tell me did you see red Jack Smith's wife, Kitty Keary, in any place?

SHAWN EARLY. I did. At her own house she was, drying clothes on the hedge as I passed.

MRS. TARPEY. What did you say she was doing?

SHAWN EARLY. (*Breaking away.*) Laying out a sheet on the hedge. (*He goes.*)

MRS. TARPEY. Laying out a sheet for the dead! The Lord have mercy on us! Jack Smith dead, and his wife laying out a sheet for his burying! (*Calls out.*) Why didn't you tell me that before, Shawn Early? Isn't the deafness the great hardship? Half the world might be dead without me knowing of it or getting word of it at all! (*She sits down and rocks herself.*) O my poor Jack Smith! To be going to his work so nice and so hearty, and to be left stretched on the ground in the full light of the day! (*Enter* TIM CASEY.)

TIM CASEY. What is it, Mrs. Tarpey? What happened since?

MRS. TARPEY. O my poor Jack Smith!

TIM CASEY. Did Bartley overtake him?

MRS. TARPEY. O the poor man!

TIM CASEY. Is it killed he is?

MRS. TARPEY. Stretched in the Five Acre Meadow!

TIM CASEY. The Lord have mercy on us! Is that a fact?

MRS. TARPEY. Without the rites of the Church or a ha'porth!

TIM CASEY. Who was telling you?

MRS. TARPEY. And the wife laying out a sheet for his corpse. (*Sits up and wipes her eyes.*) I suppose they'll wake him the same as another. (*Enter* MRS. TULLY, SHAWN EARLY, *and* JAMES RYAN.)

MRS. TULLY. There is great talk about this work in every quarter of the fair.

MRS. TARPEY. Ochone! cold and dead. And myself maybe the last he was speaking to!

JAMES RYAN. The Lord save us! Is it dead he is?

TIM CASEY. Dead surely, and the wife getting provision for the wake.

SHAWN EARLY. Well, now, hadn't Bartley Fallon great venom in him?

MRS. TULLY. You may be sure he had some cause. Why would he have made an end of him if he had not? (*To* MRS. TARPEY, *raising her voice.*) What was it rose the dispute at all, Mrs. Tarpey?

MRS. TARPEY. Not a one of me knows. The last I saw

of them, Jack Smith was standing there, and Bartley Fallon was standing there, quiet and easy, and he listening to "The Red-haired Man's Wife."

MRS. TULLY. Do you hear that, Tim Casey? Do you hear that, Shawn Early and James Ryan? Bartley Fallon was here this morning listening to red Jack Smith's wife, Kitty Keary that was! Listening to her and whispering with her! It was she started the fight so!

SHAWN EARLY. She must have followed him from her own house. It is likely some person roused him.

TIM CASEY. I never knew before, Bartley Fallon was great with Jack Smith's wife.

MRS. TULLY. How would you know it? Sure it's not in the streets they would be calling it. If Mrs. Fallon didn't know of it, and if I that have the next house to them didn't know of it, and if Jack Smith himself didn't know of it, it is not likely you would know of it, Tim Casey.

SHAWN EARLY. Let Bartley Fallon take charge of her from this out so, and let him provide for her. It is little pity she will get from any person in this parish.

TIM CASEY. How can he take charge of her? Sure he has a wife of his own. Sure you don't think he'd turn souper and marry her in a Protestant church?

JAMES RYAN. It would be easy for him to marry her if he brought her to America.

SHAWN EARLY. With or without Kitty Keary, believe me it is for America he's making at this minute. I saw the new magistrate and Jo Muldoon of the police going into the post-office as I came up—there was hurry on them—you may be sure it was to telegraph they went, the way he'll be stopped in the docks at Queenstown!

MRS. TULLY. It's likely Kitty Keary is gone with him, and not minding a sheet or a wake at all. The poor man, to be deserted by his own wife, and the breath hardly gone out yet from his body that is lying bloody in the field! (*Enter* MRS. FALLON.)

MRS. FALLON. What is it the whole of the town is talking about? And what is it you yourself are talking about? Is it about my man Bartley Fallon you are talking? Is it lies about him you are telling, saying that he went killing Jack Smith? My grief that ever he came into this place at all!

JAMES RYAN. Be easy now, Mrs. Fallon. Sure there is no one at all in the whole fair but is sorry for you!

MRS. FALLON. Sorry for me, is it? Why would any one be sorry for me? Let you be sorry for yourselves, and that there may be shame on you for ever and at the day of judgment, for the words you are saying and the lies you are telling to take away the character of my poor man, and to take the good name off of him, and to drive him to destruction! That is what you are doing!

SHAWN EARLY. Take comfort now, Mrs. Fallon. The police are not so smart as they think. Sure he might give them the slip yet, the same as Lynchehaun.

MRS. TULLY. If they do get him, and if they do put a rope around his neck, there is no one can say he does not deserve it!

MRS. FALLON. Is that what you are saying, Bridget Tully, and is that what you think? I tell you it's too much talk you have, making yourself out to be such a great one, and to be running down every respectable person! A rope, is it? It isn't much of a rope was needed to tie up your own furniture the day you came into Martin Tully's house, and you never bringing as much as a blanket, or a penny, or a suit of clothes with you, and I myself bringing seventy pounds and two feather beds. And now you are stiffer than a woman would have a hundred pounds! It is too much talk the whole of you have. A rope is it? I tell you the whole of this town is full of liars and schemers that would hang you up for half a glass of whiskey. (*Turn-*

*ing to go.*) People they are you wouldn't believe as much as daylight from without you'd get up to have a look at it yourself. Killing Jack Smith indeed! Where are you at all, Bartley, till I bring you out of this? My nice quiet little man. My decent comrade! He that is as kind and as harmless as an innocent beast of the field! He'll be doing no harm at all if he'll shed the blood of some of you after this day's work! That much would be no harm at all. (*Calls out.*) Bartley! Bartley Fallon! Where are you? (*Going out.*) Did any one see Bartley Fallon? (*All turn to look after her.*)

JAMES RYAN. It is hard for her to believe any such a thing, God help her! (*Enter* BARTLEY FALLON *from right, carrying hayfork.*)

BARTLEY. It is what I often said to myself, if there is ever any misfortune coming to this world it is on myself it is sure to come! (*All turn round and face him.*)

BARTLEY. To be going about with this fork and to find no one to take it, and no place to leave it down, and I wanting to be gone out of this—Is that you Shawn Early? (*Holds out fork.*) It's well I met you. You have no call to be leaving the fair for a while the way I have, and how can I go till I'm rid of this fork? Will you take it and keep it until such time as Jack Smith—

SHAWN EARLY. (*Backing.*) I will not take it, Bartley Fallon, I'm very thankful to you!

BARTLEY. (*Turning to apple stall.*) Look at it now, Mrs. Tarpey, it was here I got it; let me thrust it in under the stall. It will lie there safe enough, and no one will take notice of it until such time as Jack Smith——

MRS. TARPEY. Take your fork out of that! Is it to put trouble on me and to destroy me you want? putting it there for the police to be rooting it out maybe. (*Thrusts him back.*)

BARTLEY. That is a very unneighborly thing for you to

do, Mrs. Tarpey. Hadn't I enough care on me with that fork before this, running up and down with it like the swinging of a clock, and afeard to lay it down in any place! I wish I never touched it or meddled with it at all!

James Ryan. It is a pity, indeed, you ever did.

Bartley. Will you yourself take it, James Ryan? You were always a neighborly man.

James Ryan. (*Backing.*) There is many a thing I would do for you, Bartley Fallon, but I won't do that!

Shawn Early. I tell you there is no man will give you any help or any encouragement for this day's work. If it was something agrarian now——

Bartley. If no one at all will take it, maybe it's best to give it up to the police.

Tim Casey. There'd be a welcome for it with them surely! (*Laughter.*)

Mrs Tully. And it is to the police Kitty Keary herself will be brought.

Mrs. Tarpey. (*Rocking to and fro.*) I wonder now who will take the expense of the wake for poor Jack Smith?

Bartley. The wake for Jack Smith!

Tim Casey. Why wouldn't he get a wake as well as another? Would you begrudge him that much?

Bartley. Red Jack Smith dead! Who was telling you?

Shawn Early. The whole town knows of it by this.

Bartley. Do they say what way did he die?

James Ryan. You don't know that yourself, I suppose, Bartley Fallon? You don't know he was followed and that he was laid dead with the stab of a hayfork?

Bartley. The stab of a hayfork!

Shawn Early. You don't know, I suppose, that the body was found in the Five Acre Meadow?

Bartley. The Five Acre Meadow!

Tim Casey. It is likely you don't know that the police are after the man that did it?

Bartley. The man that did it!

MRS. TULLY. You don't know, maybe, that he was made away with for the sake of Kitty Keary, his wife?

BARTLEY. Kity Keary, his wife! (*Sits down bewildered.*)

MRS. TULLY. And what have you to say now, Bartley Fallon?

BARTLEY. (*Crossing himself.*) I to bring that fork here, and to find that news before me! It is much if I can ever stir from this place at all, or reach as far as the road!

TIM CASEY. Look, boys, at the new magistrate, and Jo Muldoon along with him! It's best for us to quit this.

SHAWN EARLY. That is so. It is best not to be mixed in this business at all.

JAMES RYAN. Bad as he is, I wouldn't like to be an informer against any man. (*All hurry away except* MRS. TARPEY, *who remains behind her stall. Enter magistrate and policeman.*)

MAGISTRATE. I knew the district was in a bad state, but I did not expect to be confronted with a murder at the first fair I came to.

POLICEMAN. I am sure you did not, indeed.

MAGISTRATE. It was well I had not gone home. I caught a few words here and there that roused my suspicions.

POLICEMAN. So they would, too.

MAGISTRATE. You heard the same story from everyone you asked?

POLICEMAN. The same story—or if it was not altogether the same, anyway it was no less than the first story.

MAGISTRATE. What is that man doing? He is sitting alone with a hayfork. He has a guilty look. The murder was done with a hayfork!

POLICEMAN. (*In a whisper.*) That's the very man they say did the act; Bartley Fallon himself!

MAGISTRATE. He must have found escape difficult—he is trying to brazen it out. A convict in the Andaman Islands tried the same game, but he could not escape my system! Stand aside—Don't go far—have the handcuffs ready. (*He walks up to* BARTLEY, *folds his arms, and stands before him.*) Here, my man, do you know anything of John Smith?

BARTLEY. Of John Smith! Who is he, now?

POLICEMAN. Jack Smith, sir—Red Jack Smith.

MAGISTRATE. (*Coming a step nearer and tapping him on the shoulder.*) Where is Jack Smith?

BARTLEY. (*With a deep sigh, and shaking his head slowly.*) Where is he, indeed?

MAGISTRATE. What have you to tell?

BARTLEY. It is where he was this morning, standing in this spot, singing his share of songs—no, but lighting his pipe—scraping a match on the sole of his shoe——

MAGISTRATE. I ask you, for the third time, where is he?

BARTLEY. I wouldn't like to say that. It is a great mystery, and it is hard to say of any man, did he earn hatred or love.

MAGISTRATE. Tell me all you know.

BARTLEY. All that I know— Well, there are three estates; there is Limbo, and there is Purgatory, and there is——

MAGISTRATE. Nonesense! This is trifling! Get to the point.

BARTLEY. Maybe you don't hold with the clergy so? That is the teaching of the clergy. Maybe you hold with the old people. It is what they do be saying, that the shadow goes wandering, and the soul is tired, and the body is taking a rest— The shadow! (*Starts up.*) I was nearly sure I saw Jack Smith not ten minutes ago at the corner of the forge, and I lost him again— Was it his ghost I saw, do you think?

MAGISTRATE. (*To* POLICEMAN.) Conscience-struck! He will confess all now!

BARTLEY. His ghost to come before me! It is likely it was on account of the fork! I to have it and he to have no way to defend himself the time he met with his death!

MAGISTRATE. (*To* POLICEMAN.) I must note down his words. (*Takes out notebook.*) (*To* BARTLEY.) I warn you that your words are being noted.

BARTLEY. If I had ha' run faster in the beginning, this terror would not be on me at the latter end! Maybe he will cast it up against me at the day of judgment— I wouldn't wonder at all at that.

MAGISTRATE. (*Writing.*) At the day of judgment——

BARTLEY. It was soon for his ghost to appear to me— is it coming after me always by day it will be, and stripping the clothes off in the night time?— I wouldn't wonder at all at that, being as I am an unfortunate man!

MAGISTRATE. (*Sternly.*) Tell me this truly. What was the motive of this crime?

BARTLEY. The motive, is it?

MAGISTRATE. Yes: the motive; the cause.

BARTLEY. I'd sooner not say that.

MAGISTRATE. You had better tell me truly. Was it money?

BARTLEY. Not at all! What did poor Jack Smith ever have in his pockets unless it might be his hands that would be in them?

MAGISTRATE. Any dispute about land?

BARTLEY. (*Indignantly.*) Not at all! He never was a grabber or grabbed from any one!

MAGISTRATE. You will find it better for you if you tell me at once.

BARTLEY. I tell you I wouldn't for the whole world wish to say what it was—it is a thing I would not like to be talking about.

MAGISTRATE. There is no use in hiding it. It will be discovered in the end.

BARTLEY. Well, I suppose it will, seeing that mostly everybody knows it before. Whisper here now. I will tell no lie; where would be the use? (*Puts his hand to his mouth, and* MAGISTRATE *stoops.*) Don't be putting the blame on the parish, for such a thing was never done in the parish before—it was done for the sake of Kitty Keary, Jack Smith's wife.

MAGISTRATE. (*To* POLICEMAN.) Put on the handcuffs. We have been saved some trouble. I knew he would confess if taken in the right way. (POLICEMAN *puts on handcuffs.*)

BARTLEY. Handcuffs now! Glory be! I always said, if there was ever any misfortune coming to this place it was on myself it would fall. I to be in handcuffs! There's no wonder at all in that. (*Enter* MRS. FALLON, *followed by the rest. She is looking back at them as she speaks.*)

MRS. FALLON. Telling lies the whole of the people of this town are; telling lies, telling lies as fast as a dog will trot! Speaking against my poor respectable man! Saying he made an end of Jack Smith! My decent comrade! There is no better man and no kinder man in the whole of the five parishes! It's little annoyance he ever gave to any one! (*Turns and sees him.*) What in the earthly world do I see before me? Bartley Fallon in charge of the police? Handcuffs on him! O Bartley, what did you do at all at all?

BARTLEY. O Mary, there has a great misfortune come upon me! It is what I always said, that if there is ever any misfortune——

MRS. FALLON. What did he do at all, or is it bewitched I am?

MAGISTRATE. This man has been arrested on a charge of murder.

MRS. FALLON. Whose charge is that? Don't believe them! They are all liars in this place! Give me back my man!

MAGISTRATE. It is natural you should take his part, but you have no cause of complaint against your neighbors. He has been arrested for the murder of John Smith, on his own confession.

MRS. FALLON. The saints of heaven protect us! And what did he want killing Jack Smith?

MAGISTRATE. It is best you should know all. He did it on account of a love affair with the murdered man's wife.

MRS. FALLON. (*Sitting down.*) With Jack Smith's wife! With Kitty Keary! Ochone, the traitor!

THE CROWD. A great shame, indeed. He is a traitor, indeed.

MRS. TULLY. To America he was bringing her, Mrs. Fallon.

BARTLEY. What are you saying, Mary? I tell you——

MRS. FALLON. Don't say a word! I won't listen to any word you'll say! (*Stops her ears.*) O, isn't he the treacherous villain? Ohone go deo!

BARTLEY. Be quiet till I speak! Listen to what I say!

MRS. FALLON. Sitting beside me on the ass car coming to the town, so quiet and so respectable, and treachery like that in his heart!

BARTLEY. Is it your wits you have lost or is it I myself that have lost my wits?

MRS. FALLON. And it's hard I earned you, slaving, slaving—and you grumbling, and sighing, and coughing, and discontented, and the priest wore out anointing you, with all the times you threatened to die!

BARTLEY. Let you be quiet till I tell you!

MRS. FALLON. You to bring such a disgrace into the parish. A thing that was never heard of before!

BARTLEY. Will you shut your mouth and hear me speaking?

MRS. FALLON. And if it was for any sort of a fine handsome woman, but for a little fistful of a woman like Kitty Keary, that's not four feet high hardly, and not three teeth in her head unless she got new ones! May God reward you, Bartley Fallon, for the black treachery in your heart and the wickedness in your mind, and the red blood of poor Jack Smith that is wet upon your hand!

(*Voice of* JACK SMITH *heard singing.*)

The sea shall be dry,
The earth under mourning and ban!
Then loud shall he cry
For the wife of the red-haired man!

BARTLEY. It's Jack Smith's voice—I never knew a ghost to sing before—. It is after myself and the fork he is coming! (*Goes back. Enter* JACK SMITH.) Let one of you give him the fork and I will be clear of him now and for eternity!

MRS. TARPEY. The Lord have mercy on us! Red Jack Smith! The man that was going to be waked!

JAMES RYAN. Is it back from the grave you are come?

SHAWN EARLY. Is it alive you are, or is it dead you are?

TIM CASEY. Is it yourself at all that's in it?

MRS. TULLY. Is it letting on you were to be dead?

MRS. FALLON. Dead or alive, let you stop Kitty Keary, your wife, from bringing my man away with her to America!

JACK SMITH. It is what I think, the wits are gone astray on the whole of you. What would my wife want bringing Bartley Fallon to America?

MRS. FALLON. To leave yourself, and to get quit of you she wants, Jack Smith, and to bring him away from myself. That's what the two of them had settled together.

JACK SMITH. I'll break the head of any man that says that! Who is it says it? (*To* TIM CASEY.) Was it you said it? (*To* SHAWN EARLY.) Was it you?

ALL TOGETHER. (*Backing and shaking their heads.*) It wasn't I said it!

JACK SMITH. Tell me the name of any man that said it!

ALL TOGETHER. (*Pointing to* BARTLEY.) It was *him* that said it!

JACK SMITH. Let me at him till I break his head! (BARTLEY *backs in terror. Neighbors hold* JACK SMITH *back.*)

JACK SMITH. (*Trying to free himself.*) Let me at him! Isn't he the pleasant sort of a scarecrow for any woman to be crossing the ocean with! It's back from the docks of New York he'd be turned (*trying to rush at him again*), with a lie in his mouth and treachery in his heart, and another man's wife by his side, and he passing her off as his own! Let me at him can't you. (*Makes another rush, but is held back.*)

MAGISTRATE. (*Pointing to* JACK SMITH.) Policeman, put the handcuffs on this man. I see it all now. A case of false impersonation, a conspiracy to defeat the ends of justice. There was a case in the Andaman Islands, a murderer of the Mopsa tribe, a religious enthusiast——

POLICEMAN. So he might be, too.

MAGISTRATE. We must take both these men to the scene of the murder. We must confront them with the body of the real Jack Smith.

JACK SMITH. I'll break the head of any man that will find my dead body!

MAGISTRATE. I'll call more help from the barracks. (*Blows Policeman's whistle.*)

BARTLEY. It is what I am thinking, if myself and Jack Smith are put together in the one cell for the night, the handcuffs will be taken off him, and his hands will be free, and murder will be done that time surely!

MAGISTRATE. Come on! (*They turn to the right.*)

CURTAIN.

# A MINUET

### A LITTLE PLAY IN VERSE

## LOUIS N. PARKER

Louis N. Parker was born at Calvados, France, in 1852. He was educated at various musical schools and was for nearly twenty years Director of Music at Sherborne School, Dorset, during which time he composed many cantatas and other musical works. At the age of forty he resigned from this position in order to devote himself entirely to the writing of plays. Although he has written and produced several pageants, he is also the author of a large number of plays, chiefly of a historical and romantic character. Among these the most successful are "Rosemary," "Pomander Walk," "Disraeli," and "The Cardinal."

Among his few one-act plays, "A Minuet" is the most interesting. Mr. Parker's gift of incisive dialogue and his ability to delineate character under the stress of extraordinary circumstances is nowhere better seen than in this little play.

Following is a list of Mr. Parker's published plays:

"Disraeli;" "Joseph and His Brethren;" "The Cardinal;" "Summer Is A-Comin' In;" "The Aristocrat;" "Drake;" "Rosemary;" "Pomander Walk;" "Mavourneen;" "The Man in the Street;" "A Minuet;" "Beauty and the Barge."

# A MINUET*

DEDICATED TO ELSIE LESLIE

## CHARACTERS

THE MARQUIS
THE MARCHIONESS
THE GAOLER

SCENE: *Living-room in the Gaoler's quarters of the Conciergerie, Paris.*

TIME: *During the Terror—French Revolution*

SCENE: *The living-room in the* GAOLER'S *quarters in the prison of the Conciergerie. There is only one door, and that is at the back. In an angle is a window, heavily barred inside and out. Through this the upper stories of houses can be seen. These are lighted up now and then with a wavering glare as of passing torches. The room is but sparsely furnished. There is a rickety table toward the spectator's left, with a straw-bottomed chair beside it. There are two or three other similar chairs. In one corner is a small iron stove, with a chimney which meanders deviously, and finally goes out through one of the top panes of the window. In another corner is a minute metal washing-apparatus. It is night. The room is lighted by a hanging-lamp with a green shade, suspended from the ceiling. On the walls are caricatures of the king, Revolutionary placards, and a pleasing picture of the guillotine.*

THE MARQUIS, *elegantly, but soberly, dressed, is seated at the table, reading in a small, calf-bound book.*

THE MARQUIS. (*Reading.*)

---



This play is also obtainable in separate form, paper bound, at 50 cents a copy.

"Is there an after-life, a deathless soul,
A heaven, to which to aspire as to a goal?
Who shall decide what nobody may know?
Science is dumb; Faith has no proofs to show.
Men will dispute, as autumn leaves will rustle:
The soul is an idea; the heart, a muscle."

(*He leaves off reading.*)

Well said, Voltaire! This philosophic doubt
Has ruled my life, and now shall lead me out;
'Tis this has helped me to a mind serene
While I await the gentle guillotine.

(*He closes the book and lays it aside.*)

What's to be hoped for, what is to be dreaded,
Whether I die in bed or be beheaded?
I've lived; I've loved; enjoyed; and here's the end.
I'll meet my death as I should meet a friend;
Or, better, as a nobleman of France
Salutes his mistress in a courtly dance.

(*He rises and walks to and fro, with his hands behind him.*)

I am alone; no soul will sorrow for me;
My enemies dread me; and my friends—abhor me.
For all I know, my wife—the ugly word!—
Is in Coblentz, attended by absurd,
Perfumed and mincing abbés. She and I,
I'm proud to say, lived as I mean to die,
With never a trace of middle-class emotions;
I went my way; she followed her own notions;
And when she hears I'm dead, so fine her breed,
She'll arch her eyebrows, and exclaim, "Indeed?"

(*The door is flung open, and* THE GAOLER *appears.*)

*The Gaoler:*

(*Brutally.*)
Citizen!

*The Marquis:*

Joseph?
(*He sits.*)

Is the tumbril here?

*The Gaoler:*

Not yet, aristocrat; but have no fear.
The widow never missed—

*The Marquis:*

The—widow?

*The Gaoler:*

Aye,
The guillotine.

*The Marquis:*

(*With a shrug.*)
The people's wit!

*The Gaoler:*

I say,
She never missed an assignation yet.
One down, t'other come on! She'll not forget.

*The Marquis:*

Yet she's a woman! Wonderful!

*The Gaoler:*

You seem
As though you thought your doom was but a dream.
(*Roughly.*)
Aristocrat, you are to die!

*The Marquis:*

(*Calmly.*)
How true.
And so are you, my friend, and so are you,
Sooner or later. In your case, I think
It will be sooner, owing to the drink.

*The Gaoler:*

(*Coming at him threateningly.*)
You dare—!

*The Marquis:*

(*Warding him off with a delicate hand.*)
Oh, please, let's have no vulgar quarrel!
And I apologize for seeming moral.
You've been so courteous as to—*lend*—your room

In which to await my, as you call it, "doom."
(*Handing him a coin.*)
Take my last louis, friend, and go away.

*The Gaoler:*

I spit on it!

*The Marquis:*

And pocket it. Good day.

*The Gaoler:*

(*Pointing to the door.*)
I came to tell you that a woman's there,
Asking to see you.

*The Marquis:*

What?

*The Gaoler:*

She's young and fair,
And, judging by the richness of her dress,
Some heretofore aristo, nothing less.

*The Marquis:*

(*With grave reproof.*)
All women are aristocrats by birth;
No old or ugly woman treads the earth.

*The Gaoler:*

Ho! you should see my wife!

*The Marquis:*

I should be proud.

*The Gaoler:*

Shall I admit her?

*The Marquis:*

Yes.

*The Gaoler:*

It's not allowed.
Nevertheless—

*The Marquis:*

(*Handing him a jeweled snuff-box.*)
My snuff-box. From
(*He springs to his feet and kisses it.*)
The king!

*The Gaoler:*

I spit on it.

*The Marquis:*

(*Deprecatingly.*)

You spit on everything.

That's low.

*The Gaoler:*

The widow will spit out your head.

(*He stumps out, leaving the door open.*)

*The Marquis:*

(*With disgust.*)

And that's my equal! Pah!

(*He picks up a hand-glass and arranges his jabot, etc.*)

Why do I dread

This meeting? Who can be the fair
Who ventures hither to this loathsome lair?
The Duchess of Saint-Maur? A heart of ice.
The Countess of Durance? A cockatrice.
The Marchioness of Beaurepaire? Alas!
Her love and faith were brittle as this glass.
The Lady of Bougency?

(*He laughs.*)

But she had

Three other lovers, while she drove me mad.
Not one would risk her head to say good-bye
To a discarded lover soon to die.
Can it be Jenny of the Palais Royal?
I never met a woman half so loyal.
She brought her innocence into my life;
She almost loved me—for a while.

(*In the glass he is still holding he sees the Marchioness, who now appears in the doorway.*)

My wife!

(*The Marchioness comes in, and the door swings to with a clang. She makes a magnificent and elaborate curtsey.*)

*The Marchioness:*

Marquis!

*The Marquis:*

(*With an equally elaborate bow.*)
Ah! Marchioness!

*The Marchioness:*

(*Brightly.*)
Milord O'Connor
Kindly escorted me.

*The Marquis:*

Oh! too much honor!

*The Marchioness:*

(*Looking round the room; with a dainty sigh.*)
Ah, what a world, where gentlemen are treated
Like vulgar criminals!

*The Marquis:*

Won't you be seated?

*The Marchioness:*

(*Ceremoniously taking her seat.*)
I greatly fear I must cut short my visit;
Time is so precious nowadays.

*The Marquis:*

(*With a whimsical smile.*)
Ah! Is it?
How did you hear that I must soon—go hence?

*The Marchioness:*

A charming abbé told me in Coblentz.

*The Marquis:*

(*Leading her on.*)
What did you say?

*The Marchioness:*

I scarce gave any heed.
I arched my eyebrows, and exclaimed, "Indeed?"

*The Marquis:*

Ah!—I'm distressed you chose to undertake
A long and tiresome journey for my sake.

*The Marchioness:*

(*Volubly.*)
Oh, I had charming company. Time passed away
Quite quickly, thanks to ombre and piquet.
(*With a pretty pout.*)
I lost a deal of money.

*The Marquis:*

My regrets.
I've squandered my last coin.

*The Marchioness:*

And then at Metz
A charming man, an Irishman—such grace!
Such wit! Such—

*The Marquis:*

Never mind.

*The Marchioness:*

Begged for a place
Beside me in my coach.

*The Marquis:*

His name?

*The Marchioness:*

Milord
O'Connor.

*The Marquis:*

To be sure. He—touched a chord?

*The Marchioness:*

(*Enthusiastically.*)
Oh, yes!

*The Marquis:*

(*Insidiously.*)
And you were—kind?

*The Marchioness:*

(*Roguishly.*)
To him or you?

*The Marquis:*

(*With a polite protest.*)
Oh, dying men don't count.

*The Marchioness:*

(*Thinking it over.*)

That's very true.

*The Marquis:*

No doubt he's waiting for you now?

*The Marchioness:*

(*Carelessly.*)

No doubt.

*The Marquis:*

You must not strain his patience; 'twill wear out.
(*With great courtesy, but a dangerous gleam in his eyes.*)
And when you join him, tell him I regret
I'm not at liberty. We might have—met.

*The Marchioness:*

You would have liked each other very much.
Such conversation! Such high spirits! Such—

*The Marquis:*

(*Rises.*)
This prison is no place for you. Farewell!

*The Marchioness:*

The room *is* ugly. I prefer my cell.

*The Marquis:*

(*Arrested as he is moving toward the door.*)
Your—cell?

*The Marchioness:*

(*Matter of fact.*)
Of course. I am a prisoner, too.
That's what I came for.

*The Marquis:*

What?

*The Marchioness:*

(*Very simply.*)

To die with you.

*The Marquis:*

To die with me!

*The Marchioness:*

(*Rises.*)

A Beauclerc could not fail.

*The Marquis:*

But—

*The Marchioness:*

Yes?

*The Marquis:*

The guillotine!

*The Marchioness:*

(*Brushing it aside as of no consequence whatever.*)

A mere detail.

*The Marquis:*

(*Recovering.*)

Pardon me, Marchioness, but I confess
You almost made me show surprise.

*The Marchioness:*

What less
Did you expect of me?

*The Marquis:*

We've lived apart
So long, I had forgotten—

*The Marchioness:*

I'd a heart?
You had forgotten many things beside:—
The happy bridegroom and the happy bride.
And so had I. At court the life we lead
Makes love a frivolous pastime.

*The Marquis:*

(*Gravely.*)

And we need
The shock of death to show us we are human.

*The Marchioness:*

Marquis and Marchioness? No! Man and woman.
(*Pause.*)
Once you were tender.

*The Marquis:*

Once you were sincere.

*The Marchioness:*

So long ago!

*The Marquis:*

So short a time!

*The Marchioness:*

Oh, dear!

Our minds are like a potpourri at dusk,
Breathing dead rosemary, lavender, and musk;
Things half forgotten, silly things—sublime!
A faded ribbon, withered rose, a rhyme;
A melody of old Provence, whose lilt
Haunts us as in a dream, like amber, spilt
God knows how long ago!

*The Marquis:*

Do you remember
How first I wooed you by the glowing ember
Of winter fires?

*The Marchioness:*

Ah, you were passionate then!

*The Marquis:*

I was the proudest, happiest of men.

*The Marchioness:*

I, the most innocent of maids.

*The Marquis:*

Alas!
How the years change us as they come and pass!

*The Marchioness:*

(*Very tenderly.*)
*Do you remember, by the Rhone,
The gray old castle on the hill,
The brambled pathway to the mill?
You plucked a rose. We were alone;

*The following thirty-four lines form a "Ballade" with a double refrain and the "Envoi." They must be spoken lyrically and consecutively, with a slight stress on the refrains, so that the hearer may appreciate the shape of the poem. —L. N. P.

For cousins need no chaperon.
How hot the days were, which the shrill
Cicada's chirping seemed to fill:
A treble to the mill-wheel's drone!
*Ah, me! what happy days were those!*
*The Marquis:*
*Gone, with the perfume of the rose.*

I called you Doris, for I own
'Meg' on my fancy cast a chill.
*The Marchioness:*
I called you Amadis! You will
Admit no knightlier name is known.
We were like fledglings newly flown.
*The Marquis:*
Like little children: Jack and Jill.
*The Marchioness:*
With many a scratch and many a spill
We scrambled over stick and stone.
*The Marquis:*
*Ah, me! what happy days were those!*
*The Marchioness:*
*Gone, with the perfume of the rose.*
*The Marquis:*
Over lush meadows, thickly strown
With daisy and with daffodil,
We ran at dawn to catch the trill
Of larks on wild wing sunward blown!
*The Marchioness:*
In orange-groves we heard the moan
Of love-lorn nightingales; until
You pressed my hand. A tender thrill
Was in your touch and in your tone.
*Ah, me! what happy days were those!*

*The Marquis:*
*Gone, with the perfume of the rose.*

*The Marchioness:*

Marquis, might we not yet atone
  For all our errors, if we chose?

*The Marquis:*

But—Doris, *all the perfume's gone.*

*The Marchioness:*

(*Producing a withered rose from her bosom.*)
*But—Amadis, I've kept the rose!*

*The Marquis:*

You've kept the rose! But will it bloom again?

*The Marchioness:*

Perhaps in heaven.

*The Marquis:*

(*With a shrug.*)
Is there a heaven?

*The Gaoler:*

(*Appearing at the door.*)
You twain
Aristocrats, the tumbril waits!
(*He disappears.*)

*The Marchioness:*

(*Swaying a moment.*)
Ah, me!

*The Marquis:*

(*Eagerly.*)
Is there a heaven, Doris?

*The Marchioness:*

(*Recovering, smiles bravely, and holds out her hand.*)
Come and see.
(*As the Marquis takes her hand and they go out.*)

CURTAIN.

# THE GHOST OF JERRY BUNDLER

PLAY IN ONE ACT

## W. W. JACOBS and CHARLES ROCK

W. W. Jacobs was born at London in 1863. He began life as an employee in the Civil Service, but he later turned his hand to the writing of a series of novels and stories depicting the characteristic incidents, chiefly humorous, in the life of seafaring-folk. His best books have become semi-classics of their kind. Mr. Jacobs' humor and originality are fortunately as effective in his plays as they are in his books and stories. "Beauty and the Barge," and "The Monkey's Paw," written with Louis N. Parker, are among his most successful plays, though "The Boatswain's Mate," "Admiral Peters" and "The Ghost of Jerry Bundler," are more in the manner of the novels and stories.

Following is a list of W. W. Jacobs' published plays:

"The Gray Parrot;" "The Boatswain's Mate;" "The Changeling;" "Beauty and the Barge;" "The Monkey's Paw;" "Admiral Peters;" "A Love Passage;" "The Ghost of Jerry Bundler."

# THE GHOST OF JERRY BUNDLER*

CHARACTERS

PENFOLD
MALCOLM
HIRST
SOMERS
DOCTOR LEEK
BELDON
GEORGE (*a waiter*)

SCENE: *Commercial Room in an Old-fashioned Hotel.*

TIME: *The Present.*

*The Commercial Room in an old-fashioned hotel in a small country town. An air of old-fashioned comfort is in evidence everywhere. Old sporting prints on the walls. On the table up* C. *are half a dozen candlesticks, old-fashioned shape with snuffer attached. Two pairs of carpet slippers are set up within fender. Red curtains to window recess. Shutters or blinds to windows. Armchair and about six other chairs in the room. One old-fashioned settle. One small table. Clock. Decanter of water, half a dozen toddy tumblers. Matches, etc. The only light is a ruddy glow from the fire. Kettle on hob. Moonlight from* R. *of window when shutter is opened. Practical chandelier from ceiling or lights at side of mantelpiece.* DOCTOR'S *coat and muffler on chair up* L., *his cap on mantelpiece.*

---



This play is also published separately, paper bound, at 30 cents a copy.

*All lights out, dark stage. Opening music. Curtain rise —ticking of clock heard. Wind, then church clock chimes, the lights come very slowly up, when the red glow is seen in the fireplace the low murmurs of the characters heard, and gradually get louder as lights come up to when* SOMERS' *voice tops all.*

*The stage occupied by all characters except* GEORGE *the waiter. Discovered,* PENFOLD, *sitting in arm chair* L. *of fire, above it.* DOCTOR LEEK *standing above fire and leaning on mantelshelf.* HIRST *sitting on settle below fire and nearest to audience.* SOMERS *seated on settle with him but above him.* MALCOLM *and* BELDON *on chairs* R. C., *facing fire.* ALL *are smoking, and drink from their respective glasses from time to time.* SOMERS *has just finished a story as Curtain rises.*

OMNES. Oh, I say, that sounds impossible, etc.

SOMERS. Haunted or not haunted, the fact remains that no one stays in the house long. It's been let to several tenants since the time of the murder, but they never completed their tenancy. The last tenant held out for a month, but at last he gave up like the rest, and cleared out, although he had done the place up thoroughly, and must have been pounds out of pocket by the transaction.

MALCOLM. Well, it's a capital ghost story, I admit, that is, as a story, but I for one can't swallow it.

HIRST. I don't know, it is not nearly so improbable as some I have heard. Of course it's an old idea that spirits like to get into the company of human beings. A man told me once, that he travelled down by the Great Western, with a ghost as fellow passenger, and hadn't the slightest suspicion of it, until the inspector came for tickets. My friend said, the way that ghost tried to keep up appearances, by feeling in all its pockets, and even looking on the floor for its ticket, was quite touching. Ultimately it gave it up, and with a loud groan vanished through the ventilator.

(SOMERS, MALCOLM *and* LEEK *laugh heartily.*)

BELDON. Oh, I say come now, that'll do.

PENFOLD. (*Seriously.*) Personally I don't think it's a subject for jesting. I have never seen an apparition myself, but I have known people who have, and I consider that they form a very interesting link between us and the after life. There's a ghost story connected with this house, you know.

OMNES. Eh! Oh? Really!

MALCOLM. (*Rising and going to mantelpiece, takes up his glass of toddy.*) Well, I have used this house for some years now. I travel for Blennet and Burgess—wool—and come here regularly three times a year, and I've never heard of it. (*Sits down again on his chair, holding glass in his hand.*)

LEEK. And I've been here pretty often too, though I have only been in practice here for a couple of years, and I have never heard it mentioned, and I must say I don't believe in anything of the sort. In my opinion ghosts are the invention of weak-minded idiots.

PENFOLD. Weak-minded idiots or not, there is a ghost story connected with this house, but it dates a long time back.

(GEORGE, *the waiter, enters* D. L. *with tray and serviette.*) Oh, here's George, he'll bear me out. You've heard of Jerry Bundler, George?

GEORGE. (C.) Well, I've just 'eard odds and ends, sir, but I never put much count to 'em. There was one chap 'ere, who was under me when fust I come, he said he seed it, and the Guv'nor sacked him there and then. (*Goes to table by window, puts tray down, takes up glass and wipes it slowly.*) (MEN *laugh.*)

PENFOLD. Well, my father was a native of this town, and he knew the story well. He was a truthful man and a steady churchgoer. But I have heard him declare that once in his life he saw the ghost of Jerry Bundler in this house; let me see, George, you don't remember my old dad, do you? (GEORGE *puts down glasses over table.*)

GEORGE. No, sir. I come here forty years ago next Easter, but I fancy he was before my time.

PENFOLD. Yes, though not by long. He died when I was twenty, and I shall be sixty-two next month, but that's neither here nor there. (GEORGE *goes up to table* C. *tidying up and listening.*)

LEEK. Who was this Jerry Bundler?

PENFOLD. A London thief, pickpocket, highwayman—anything he could turn his dishonest hand to, and he was run to earth in this house some eighty years ago. (GEORGE *puts glass down and stands listening.*) He took his last supper in this room. (PENFOLD *leans forward.* BELDON *looks round to* L. *nervously.*) That night soon after he had gone to bed, a couple of Bow Street runners, the predecessors of our present detectiv force turned up here. They had followed him from London, but had lost scent a bit, so didn't arrive till late. A word to the landlord, whose description of the stranger who had retired to rest, pointed to the fact that he was the man they were after, of course enlisted his aid and that of the male servants and stable hands. The officers crept quietly up to Jerry's bedroom and tried the door, it wouldn't budge. It was of heavy oak and bolted from within. (OMNES *lean forward, showing interest.*) Leaving his comrade and a couple of grooms to guard the bedroom door, the other officer went into the yard, and, procuring a short ladder, by this means reached the window of the room in which Jerry was sleeping. The Inn servants and stable hands saw him get on to the sill and try to open the window. Suddenly there was a crash of glass, and with a cry, he fell in a heap on to the stones at their feet. Then in the moonlight, they saw the face of the highwayman peering over the sill. (OMNES *move uneasily.*) They sent for the blacksmith, and with his sledge-hammer he battered in the strong oak panels, and the first thing that met their eyes was the body of Jerry Bundler dangling from the top of the four-post bed by his own handkerchief. (OMNES *sit back, draw their breath, and are generally uneasy. Slight pause.*)

SOMERS. I say, which bedroom was it? (*Earnestly.*)

PENFOLD. That I can't tell you, but the story goes that Jerry still haunts this house, and my father used to declare positively that the last time he slept here, the ghost of Jerry Bundler lowered itself from the top of his four-post bed and tried to strangle him.

BELDON. (*Jumps up, gets behind his chair, twists chair round; nervously.*) O, I say that'll do. I wish you'd thought to ask your father which bedroom it was.

PENFOLD. What for?

BELDON. Well, I should take jolly good care not to sleep in it, that's all. (*Goes to back.*)

(PENFOLD *rising, goes to fire, and knocks out his pipe,* LEAK *gets by arm-chair.*)

PENFOLD. There's nothing to fear. I don't believe for a moment that ghosts could really hurt one. (GEORGE *lights candle at table.*) In fact, my father used to say that it was only the unpleasantness of the thing that upset him, and that, for all practical purposes, Jerry's fingers might have been made of cotton wool for all the harm they could do.

(GEORGE *hands candle, gets to door and holds it open.*)

BELDON. That's all very fine, a ghost story is a ghost story, but when a gentleman tells a tale of a ghost that haunts the house in which one is going to sleep, I call it most ungentlemanly.

(*Beldon places his chair to* L. *of table* R. PENFOLD *goes up to* C. LEEK *sits in arm chair.* BELDON *goes to fire-place.*)

PENFOLD. Pooh! Nonsense. (*At table up* C.)

(*During his speech* GEORGE *lights one of the candles.*)

Ghosts can't hurt you. For my part, I should rather like to see one.

OMNES. Oh, come now——etc.

PENFOLD. Well, I'll bid you good-night, gentlemen.

(*He goes towards door* L. GEORGE *opens it for him; he passes out as they all stay.*)

OMNES. Good-night.

(HIRST *rises, crosses to* L. C.)

BELDON. (*Up* R., *calling after him.*) And I hope Jerry'll pay you a visit.

MALCOLM. (*Rises, goes to fire.*) Well, I'm going to have another whisky if you gentlemen will join me. I think it'll do us all good after that tale. George, take the orders.

(GEORGE *comes down with salver to table* R., *gathers up glasses.*)

SOMERS. Not quite so much hot water in mine.

MALCOLM. I'll have the same again, George.

BELDON. A leetle bit of lemon in mine, George.

LEEK. Whisky and soda for me, please.

HIRST. Whisky!

(GEORGE *goes to table* R., *collects glasses, crosses to door* L. *speaks.*)

GEORGE. (*To* MALCOLM.) Shall I light the gas, Mr. Malcolm? (*At door.*)

MALCOLM. No, the fire's very comfortable, unless any of you gentlemen prefer the gas.

OMNES. No, not at all—etc.

MALCOLM. Never mind, George. (*This to* GEORGE *as no one wants the gas.*) The firelight is pleasanter.

(*Exit* GEORGE *for orders* L.)

(BELDON *gets* C.)

MALCOLM. (*At fire.*) Does any gentleman know another——?

SOMERS. (*Seated* R.) Well, I remember hearing——

BELDON. (*Up* C.) Oh, I say—that'll do.

(OMNES *laugh.*)

LEEK. Yes, I think you all look as if you'd heard enough ghost stories to do you the rest of your lives. And you're not all as anxious to see the real article as the old gentleman who's just gone.

HIRST. (*Looking to* L.) Old humbug! I should like to put him to the test. (C.) (*Bus.*) I say, suppose I dress up as Jerry Bundler and go and give him a chance of displaying his courage? I bet I'd make the old party sit up.

MALCOLM. Capital!

BELDON. A good idea.

LEEK. I shouldn't, if I were you.

HIRST. Just for the joke, gentlemen.

SOMERS. No, no—drop it, Hirst.

HIRST. Only for the joke. Look here, I've got some things that'll do very well. We're going to have some amateur theatricals at my house. We're doing a couple of scenes from "The Rivals," Somers, (*pointing to* SOMERS.) and I have been up to town to get the costumes, wigs, etc., to-day. I've got them up-stairs—knee-breeches, stockings, buckled shoes, and all that sort of thing. It's a rare chance. If you wait a bit, I'll give you a full dress rehearsal, entitled "Jerry Bundler, or the Nocturnal Stranger." (*At door* L.)

LEEK. (*Sneeringly.*) You won't frighten us, will you?

HIRST. I don't know so much about that—it's a question of acting, that's all.

MALCOLM. I'll bet you a level sov, you don't frighten me.

HIRST. (*Quietly.*) A level sov. (*Pauses.*) Done. I'll take the bet to frighten you first, and the old boy afterwards. These gentlemen shall be the judges. (*Points to* LEEK *and* BELDON.)

BELDON. (*Up* C.) You won't frighten us because we're prepared for you, but you'd better leave the old man alone. It's dangerous play. (*Appeals to* LEEK.)

HIRST. Well, I'll try you first. (*Moves to door and pauses.*) No gas, mind.

OMNES. No! no!

HIRST. (*Laughs.*) I'll give you a run for your money.

(GEORGE *enters, holds door open.*)

(*Exit* HIRST.)

(GEORGE *passes drinks round. Five drinks.* SOMERS *takes the one ordered for* HIRST *and puts it on the table* R. BELDON *sits* R. C. GEORGE *crosses to table, puts two drinks down, goes to fire and gives drinks, then up to table, puts tray down, takes up glass and begins to wipe it, gets down* L. *for lines.*)

LEEK. (*To* MALCOLM.) I think you'll win your bet, sir, but I vote we give him a chance. Suppose we have cigars round, and if he's not back by the time we've finished then I must be off, as I have a quarter of an hour's walk before me. (*Looks at watch.*) He's a friend of yours, isn't he?

SOMERS. Yes, I have known him a good many years now, and I must say he's a rum chap; just crazy about acting and practical joking, though I've often told him he carries the latter too far at times. In this case it doesn't matter, but I won't let him try it on the *old gentleman*. You see we know what he's going to do, and are prepared, but he doesn't, and it might lead to illness or worse; the old chap's sixty-two and such a shock might have serious consequences. But Hirst won't mind giving up that part of it, so long as he gets an opportunity of acting to us.

LEEK. (*Knocks pipe on grate.*) Well, I hope he'll hurry up. It's getting pretty late. (*To* SOMERS.)

MALCOLM. Well, gentlemen, your health!

SOMERS. Good luck.

LEEK. Hurrah!

BELDON. Chin-chin!

LEEK. By the way, how is it you happen to be here to-night?

SOMERS. Oh, we missed the connection at Tolleston Junction and as the accommodation at the Railway Arms there was rather meagre, the Station Master advised us to drive on here, put up for the night, and catch the Great Northern express from Exton in the morning. (*Rises, crosses to* L.) Oh, George, that reminds me—you might see that "Boots" calls us at 7 sharp.

(BELDON *rises, goes up to them to fire.*)

GEORGE. Certainly, sir. What are your numbers?

SOMERS. 13 and 14.

GEORGE. I'll put it on the slate, special, sir. (*Goes to door* L.)

LEEK. I beg pardon, gentlemen, I forgot the cigars; George, bring some cigars back with you.

BELDON. A very mild one for me.

GEORGE. Very well, sir. (*Takes up tray from side-board.*)

(*Exit* L.)

(SOMERS *sits* R. C.)

MALCOLM. I think you were very wise coming on here. (*Sits on settee* R.) I stayed at the Railway Arms, Tolleston, once—never again though. Is your friend clever at acting?

SOMERS. I don't think he's clever enough to frighten you. I'm to spend Christmas at his place, and he's asked me to assist at the theatricals he spoke of. Nothing would satisfy him till I consented, and I must honestly say I am very sorry I ever did, for I expect I shall be pretty bad. I know I have scarcely slept a wink these last few nights, trying to get the words into my head.

(GEORGE *enters backwards, pale and trembling.*)

MALCOLM. Why! Look—what the devil's the matter with George? (*Crosses to* GEORGE.)

GEORGE. I've seen it, gentlemen. (*Down stage* L. C.)

OMNES. Seen who?

(BELDON *down* R. *edge of table* R. LEEK *up* R. C. SOMERS *up* R.)

GEORGE. The ghost. Jer—Bun—

MALCOLM. Why, you're frightened, George.

GEORGE. Yes, sir. It was the suddenness of it, and besides I didn't look for seeing it in the bar. There was only a glimmer of light there, and is was sitting on the floor. I nearly touched it.

MALCOLM. (*Goes to door, looks off, then returns—to others.*) It must be Hirst up to his tricks. George was out of the room when he suggested it. (*To* GEORGE.) Pull yourself together, man.

GEORGE. Yes, sir—but it took me unawares. I'd never have gone to the bar by myself if I'd known it was there, and I don't believe you would, either, sir.

MALCOLM. Nonsense, I'll go and fetch him in. (*Crosses to* L.)

GEORGE. (*Clutching him by the sleeve.*) You don't know what it's like, sir. It ain't fit to look at by yourself, it ain't indeed. It's got the awfullest deathlike face, and short cropped red hair—it's—

(*Smothered cry is heard.*)

What's that? (*Backs to* C. *and leans on chair.*)

(ALL *start, and a quick pattering of footsteps is heard rapidly approaching the room. The door flies open and* HIRST *flings himself gasping and shivering into* MALCOLM'S *arms. The door remains open. He has only his trousers and shirt on, his face very white with fear and his own hair all standing on end.* LEEK *lights the gas, then goes to* R. *of* HIRST.)

OMNES. What's the matter?

MALCOLM. Why, it's Hirst. (*Shakes him roughly by the shoulder.*) What's up?

HIRST. I've seen—oh, Lord! I'll never play the fool again. (*Goes* C.)

OTHERS. Seen what?

HIRST. Him—it—the ghost—anything.

MALCOLM. (*Uneasily.*) Rot!

HIRST. I was coming down the stairs to get something I'd forgotten, when I felt a tap—(*He breaks off suddenly gazing through open door.*) I thought I saw it again—Look—at the foot of the stairs, can't you see anything? (*Shaking* LEEK.)

LEEK. (*Crosses to door peering down passage.*) No, there's nothing there. (*Stays up* L.)

(HIRST *gives a sigh of relief.*)

MALCOLM. (L. C.) Go on—you felt a tap——

HIRST. (C.) I turned and saw it—a little wicked head with short red hair—and a white dead face—horrible.

(*Clock chimes three-quarters.*)

(*They assist him into chair* L. *of table* R.)

GEORGE. (*Up* C.) That's what I saw in the bar—'orrid—it was devilish. (*Coming* C.)

(MALCOLM *crosses to* L. HIRST *shudders.*)

MALCOLM. Well, it's a most unaccountable thing. It's the last time I come to this house. (*Goes to* R. *of* LEEK.)

GEORGE. I leave to-morrow. I wouldn't go down to that bar alone—no, not for fifty pounds. (*Goes up* R. *to arm-chair.*)

SOMERS. (*Crosses to door* R. *then returns to* R. C.) It's talking about the thing that's caused it, I expect. We've had it in our minds, and we've been practically forming a spiritualistic circle without knowing it. (*Goes to back of table* R.)

BELDON. (*Crosses to* R. C.) Hang the old gentleman. Upon my soul I'm half afraid to go to bed.

MALCOLM. Doctor, it's odd they should both think they saw something.

(*They both drop down* L. C.)

GEORGE. (*Up* C.) I saw it as plainly as I see you, sir. P'raps if you keep your eyes turned up the passage you'll see it for yourself. (*Points.*)

(*They all look.* BELDON *goes to* SOMERS.)

BELDON. There—what was that?

MALCOLM. Who'll go with me to the bar?

LEEK. I will. (*Goes to door.*)

BELDON. (*Gulps.*) So—will I. (*Crosses to door* L. *They go to the door. To* MALCOLM.) After you. (*They slowly pass into the passage.* GEORGE *watching them. All exit except* HIRST *and* SOMERS.)

SOMERS. How do you feel now, old man?

HIRST. (*Changing his frightened manner to one of assurance.*) Splendid!

SOMERS. But—(*A step back.*)

HIRST. I tell you I feel splendid.

SOMERS. But the ghost—(*Steps back to* C.)

HIRST. Well, upon my word, Somers—you're not as sharp as I thought you.

SOMERS. What do you mean?

HIRST. Why, that I was the ghost George saw. (*Crosses to* L. C.) By Jove, he *was* in a funk! I followed him to the door and overheard his description of what he'd seen, then I burst in myself and pretended I'd seen it too. I'm going to win that bet—(VOICES *heard. Crosses to* R.) Look out, they're coming back. (*Sits.*)

SOMERS. Yes, but——

HIRST. Don't give me away—hush!

(*Re-enter* MALCOLM, LEEK, BELDON *and* GEORGE L.)

(BELDON *and* GEORGE *go up to back* C.)

HIRST. Did you see it? (*In his frightened manner.*)

MALCOLM. (C.) I don't know—I thought I saw something, but it might have been fancy. I'm in the mood to see anything just now. (*To* HIRST.) How are you feeling now, sir?

HIRST. Oh, I feel a bit better now. I daresay you think I'm easily scared—but you didn't see it.

MALCOLM. Well, I'm not quite sure. (*Goes to fire.*)

LEEK. You've had a bit of a shock. Best thing you can do is to go to bed.

HIRST. (*Finishing his drink.*) Very well. Will you, (*Rises.*) share my room with me, Somers?

(GEORGE *lights two candles.*)

SOMERS. (*Crosses to* L. C.) I will with pleasure. (*Gets up to table* C. *and gets a candle.*) Provided you don't mind sleeping with the gas full on all night. (*Goes to door* L.)

LEEK. (*To* HIRST.) You'll be all right in the morning.

HIRST. Good night, all. (*As he crosses to door.*)

OMNES. Good night.

(ALL *talking at fire, not looking to* L. *as* HIRST *and* SOMERS *exeunt,* HIRST *chuckles and gives* SOMERS *a sly dig.*)

SOMERS. Good night.

MALCOLM. (*At fireplace.*) Well, I suppose the bet's off, though as far as I can see I won it. I never saw a man so scared in all my life. Sort of poetic justice about it. (LEEK *with revolver in his hand, is just putting it into his pocket. Seeing him.*) Why, what's that you've got there?

LEEK. A revolver. (*At fire.*) You see I do a lot of night driving, visiting patients in outlying districts—they're a tough lot round here, and one never knows what might happen, so I have been accustomed to carry it. I just pulled it out so as to have it handy. I meant to have a pot at that ghost if I had seen him. There's no law against it, is there? I never heard of a close time for ghosts.

BELDON. Oh, I say, never mind ghosts. Will *you* share my room? (*To* MALCOLM.)

(GEORGE *comes down a little, holding candle.*)

MALCOLM. With pleasure. I'm not exactly frightened, but I'd sooner have company, and I daresay George here would be glad to be allowed to make up a bed on the floor.

BELDON. Certainly.

MALCOLM. Well, that's settled. A majority of three

to one ought to stop any ghost. Will that arrangement suit you, George?

GEORGE. Thank you, sir. And if you gentlemen would kindly come down to the bar with me while I put out the gas. I could never be sufficiently grateful, and when (*At door.*) We come back we can let the Doctor out at the front door. Will that do, sir?

LEEK. All right; I'll be getting my coat on. (GEORGE *gets to door. They exit at door* L. LEEK *picks up his coat off chair up* L., *puts it on and then turns up trousers. Footsteps heard in flies, then goes to the window* R., *pulls curtain aside and opens the shutters of the window nearest the fire. A flood of moonlight streams in from* R. *Clock strikes twelve.*) By Jove, what a lovely night. That poor devil did get a fright, and no mistake. (*Crossing down to fireplace for his cap which is on the mantlepiece.* MALCOLM, BELDON *and* GEORGE *return—the door closes after them.*) Well, no sign of it, eh?

MALCOLM. No, we've seen nothing this time. Here, give me the candle, George, while you turn out the gas.

LEEK. All right, George, I'll put this one out. (*Turns out gas below fire.*)

(MALCOLM *and* BELDON *are up at sideboard,* GEORGE *having put the other gas out, goes up to them and is just lighting the candles for them. The* DOCTOR *is filling his pipe at mantel-shelf, and stooping to get a light with a paper spill.* LEEK *whistles and lights spill. The handle of the door is heard moving.* OMES *stand motionless—* MALCOLM *and* BELDON *very frightened. They all watch. The room is lit only by the fire-light which is very much fainter than it was at the beginning of the play, by the candle which* GEORGE *holds, and by the flood of moonlight from the window.*)

(*The door slowly opens, a hand is seen, then a figure appears in dark breeches, white stockings, buckled shoes, white shirt, very neat in every detail, with a long white or spotted handkerchief tied round the neck, the long end hanging down in front. The face cadaverous, with sunken eyes and a leering smile, and close cropped red hair. The figure blinks at the candle, then slowly raises its hands and unties the handkerchief, its head falls on to one shoulder, it holds handkerchief out at arm's length and advances towards* MALCOLM.)

(*Just as the figure reaches the place where the moonbeams touch the floor,* LEEK *fires—he has very quietly and unobtrusively drawn his revolver.* GEORGE *drops the candle and the figure, writhing, drops to the floor. It coughs once a choking cough.* MALCOLM *goes slowly forward, touches it with his foot, and kneels by figure, lifts figure up, gazes at it, and pulls the red wig off, discovering* HIRST. MALCOLM *gasps out* "DOCTOR." LEEK *places the revolver on chair, kneels behind* HIRST. MALCOLM *is* L. C., *kneeling. At this moment* SOMERS *enters very brightly with lighted candle.*)

SOMERS. Well, did Hirst win his bet? (*Seeing* HIRST *on floor, he realizes the matter.*) My God, you didn't—I told him not to. I told him not to!! I told him—(*Falls fainting into arms of* GEORGE.)

CURTAIN.

# WEALTH AND WISDOM

COMEDY IN ONE ACT

## OLIPHANT DOWN

Oliphant Down was born in 1885 at Bridgewater, Somersetshire, and was educated at Warminster School in Wiltshire. He first came to London in 1902 and went to work in an office for a few years, after which he became a journalist and professional writer. He enlisted in the British Army in 1914 and in May, 1917, was killed in France. Down is the author of half a dozen one-act plays of a fantastic and poetic character, among which "The Maker of Dreams" is undoubtedly the most popular. "Wealth and Wisdom," however, is an outstanding example of the author's talent as a commentator on human character and a writer of entertaining and poetic plays. It has never been published before.

Following is a list of Oliphant Down's published plays:

"The Maker of Dreams;" "The Quod Wrangle;" "Tommy-by-the-Way;" "Bal Masque;" "Wealth and Wisdom;" and "The Idealist."

# WEALTH AND WISDOM*

## CHARACTERS

PEGGY KEEMAN, *Owner of a Small Dairy Farm.*
JIM WYMAN, *A Young Englishman.*

SCENES: *Room fitted up like a small dairy, in a small Irish village.*

TIME: *The Present.*

*Room in a small house, fitted somewhat after the manner of a dairy. There is a door in the side wall on the spectator's right. A latticed window at the back allows a view of a sweep of broad hills, though their distance suggests a valley between. There is a stout deal table center on which stands a lead-glaced pair of scales. A churn is in the corner of the room on the left. Caddles and grease-proof paper are on the table. There is a grandfather clock to the right of the window. Outside brilliant sunshine.* PEGGY KEEMAN *discovered, unscrewing lid of churn. She dips her arms in and scoops round with her hand. From the churn she produces a large lump of butter which she places on dish and takes to table. She is dressed in light colored clothes, the sleeves of her blouse being rolled well above the elbow. A sleeveless holland overall gives her a cool and pleasing appearance. She begins to coddle the butter. Knocking at door.*

PEGGY. You're welcome.

(*Door opens and* JIM WYMAN *enters. His appearance, smart cut suit, brown shoes, handkerchief-tie, and green felt hat—suggests the masher without making him altogether a brainless idiot.*)

JIM. Mornin', Peggy.

PEGGY. Oh, and it's you, is it. Well, you can't come in, so just go out with the door shut and nothing said.

JIM. (*Imitating.*) You won't turn me from the door and me walking bareheaded in the sunshine.

PEGGY. It's the blessed sunshine of the butter you'll be walking your fingers into.

JIM. (*Advancing to table.*) I've come to help you, Peggy.

PEGGY. That never was in all the days I've known you. (JIM *is playing with a weight.*) Now leave those weights, I'm telling you, and get you along. When I close my doors and the air full of sunshine, it's to keep tramps out.

JIM. Oh, I say, tramps! But I suppose I am a bit of a beggar, Peggy. . . .

PEGGY. That's the third "Peggy."

JIM. When a fellow's proposed about four hundred times, he's not going to stop over a name.

PEGGY. And is it so many as four hundred you've asked me?

JIM. Twice a day for seven weeks.

PEGGY. (*Calculating on slate.*) Two times forty nine. It's ninety eight.

JIM. It was three times last Tuesday, so that's ninety-nine. And how can I help it when you go patting the butter with hands as white as the milk the cow hid the cream in.

PEGGY. Is that the hundredth, or is it just talk?

JIM. Peggy, I'm desperate now. You know what day it is.

PEGGY. Know what day it is and Michael O'Cullen waiting on the road under the hill every Thursday for five years, and me taking the butter to him! It's yourself's been sleeping in the wet grass and the lone people's drawn your brains out.

Jim. But it's *the* Thursday! The last day! You forget what happens to-day!

Peggy. And it's me is it that's been lying in the wet grass with nothing between me and the stars but a windy night. I'm knowing what Thursday it is, and you shall hear it. It's to-day you're to get your wife before ever it's twelve on the clock, or you'll not get forty thousand pounds from your uncle. And a daft old fool it must be he is, to have given you six months to do it in, and I'm thinking you're a near relation of his to have let the time go by and all.

Jim. It's you who've wasted the time. I've been asking you for weeks.

Peggy. And now you've got five minutes left to find her in. But it'll not be me that'll marry you. What should my like be doing with forty thousand pounds! Get about you and ask someone else.

Jim. It would jolly well serve you right if I took you at your word.

Peggy. I'm asking you to do that same.

Jim. If there was another woman here I would!

Peggy. (*Glancing towards the door which has been open since* jim *came in.*) There's Maggie Hanaghan coming along the road. I've seen her this three minutes. She's a decent body and twenty-two in a month that will be.

Jim. Peggy, I'll give you a last chance! Come now.

Peggy. Maggie is nigh the gate. Ask her.

Jim. You mean it?

Peggy. I'm saying it.

Jim. (*Warningly.*) I'm in earnest!

(peggy, *by way of answer, goes to the door.*)

Peggy. (*Calling.*) Maggie, me darlin', there's a man I have with a bit to tell you. Unlift the gate.

(*There is a pause, during which* JIM *stands nervously. Noise at gate.*)

JIM. It's all right, Miss Hanaghan. I had a letter for post, but I've left it behind. (*He shuts door quickly and stands with his back to it.*)

PEGGY. (*Looking at him with ironical admiration.*) It's a fine liar ye are, Jim Wyman, and I'm thinking it's a saintlier woman than myself you're needing, or you're lost entirely.

JIM. I'd be a poor man if I couldn't tell a lie to save the woman who's to be my wife.

PEGGY. Oh, you're not quit of that yet.

JIM. And I never shall be.

PEGGY. What should I be doing with forty thousand pounds, I'm saying? I'd be a lost woman without the butter and the eggs and the crowing of the cocks to tell me there was someone coming over the hills with a lamp, and me knowing it was the dawn.

JIM. But what a nest egg we should have against bad times. It would take your old hens a bit of trouble to lay forty thousand pounds.

PEGGY. I'm not wanting nest eggs; not of that sort. And leave go of that butter! If you must have a toy-thing put your fingers round one of these. (*Referring to basket of eggs.*)

JIM. Say, Peggy, have you never wanted to get married. I don't say to me, to anyone?

PEGGY. It's as curious as a fidgetty crow you are, and him letting fall a marrow bone into a hollow tree, and not knowing what was become of it at all.

JIM. That's no answer.

PEGGY. Oh, there was a time I'm recalling, the moonshine got into my head, and I looked at the little stars and let on they was speakin' to me, and they just twinkling where they was put in the beginnings. But the Holy Fathers was good to me the day and I broke my shins on a milk-stool and was a sane woman from that on.

JIM. Ah, but when there's a cross wind and a low, beating rain against the window panes and they rattling, isn't it you would be glad to have a man put up the latch of the door fast, and him and you on the inside and no heed to the weather? (*The clock whirs, preparatory to striking.*)

PEGGY. Providence and mercy, tis the time come and the hour ready for the striking, and you a poor man with the sound of it.

JIM. (*Almost angrily.*) Well, let it strike! I don't care.

PEGGY. (*Humourously.*) 'Twould want St. Patrick himself to stop it, I'm thinking, and the sun up over going its way on. (*The clock strikes twelve.*) (*At the conclusion,* JIM *takes off his collar and tie. He then goes out and closes door. After brief pause, knocking heard.*)

PEGGY. (*As before.*) You're welcome. (JIM *re-enters and stands just inside the door, with his hands one on top of the other, in a humble attitude.*) What's the trouble of it now?

JIM. (*In a plaintive voice.*) It's a poor man, God help him, would speak with the lady of the house.

PEGGY. And is it a fool the poor man thinks she is. Let him begone, and him drawing in the air from the sweet peas and they bursting their little souls with flowering.

JIM. (*Dropping Irish.*) Oh hang it all!

PEGGY. I'm not wanting to twit you now and your misfortune, but aren't you a poor soft loon to carry on the way you do and all, and you just let a woman's smile melt up a great fortune.

JIM. What other way would you have me carry on? I'm a penniless man now; a real beggar. I must either work or starve and starving is not much in my line. I'm going to work. I want you to give me some work.

PEGGY. Is it me?

JIM. Surely there's some little job you could let me do.

PEGGY. And is it much money you'd be wanting?

JIM. I'll take the same as any other man would take.

PEGGY. (*Aghast.*) The same is it you'd take . . .!

JIM. Yes, I'm not proud. I've had an education, I admit, but I'm content to take no more than an ordinary man.

PEGGY. Oh, the shamelessness of the poor daft! Take no more, is it, and you not knowing a m'norca from a speckly wy'ndot. And an educated man, is it! May be you'd be after teaching the ignorant old hens to write scripture sayings on the eggs. (JIM *is somewhat crest-fallen at her ridicule.*) But there, I'll not hold you to scorn and you with good intentions. I'll take you on for a week and pay you what may be you're worth and the week ended.

JIM. Good! You take me on; that's something.

PEGGY. But it's not me will promise that there will be much owing to you when the time's come.

JIM. (*Taking off coat and rolling up shirt sleeves.*) I'm content. Ho, ho! Now for my first job. Start me off, Peggy.

PEGGY. Aye, but hold your whist! Is it Peggy I am to every man of a bad lot comes tramping the country? It's Mistress Keeman I'm after telling you. Now get about you with a broom and make clean the stone steps. (JIM *takes broom by clock and commences to brush violently up and down the room.*) Oh, saints in Paradise. Wasn't it the stone steps, I said? Is it the butter you're wanting to make as black as the dun cow itself?

JIM. Sorry. Excess of zeal, that's all. I'll do the steps.

PEGGY. Give the broom into my hand. May be you'd forget to close the door to.

JIM. What else shall I do then?

PEGGY. Lord help us, what is there you can do?

JIM. I can wrap the butter up.

PEGGY. Give me a look at your hands. (JIM *holds them out.*)

JIM. Clean as a high rock in a windy place.

PEGGY. They're passing clean for a man.

JIM. And for a woman either. They're as clean as yours for all your two hands are the prettiest in Ireland.

PEGGY. (*Pleased.*) Is it Joseph you are, to pay compliments and tempt your mistress?

JIM. Sure, it was meself thought the mistress tempted Joseph.

PEGGY. Well, maybe it was. Father Bevan always held the like of that was not fit chapters for a good Catholic. So it's yourself would know it better than me.

JIM. Well, what do I do now?

PEGGY. When I put the butter up into pats, I put them down so. (*Illustrating by moving a pat between the coddles and placing it on the grease proof paper.*) Then fold it up so. (*Illustrates.*)

JIM. That's easy. (*There's a silence, whilst* PEGGY *weighs out another pound, pats it up and lays it on the paper. She watches* JIM. *His wrapping up is not very successful.*)

JIM. That doesn't look right somehow. How was it you did it?

PEGGY. It's an ignorant one you are for an educated man. That's a paper spoiled. (*Throws it away.*) You'll waste more in a day than you'll earn in a month. Now watch you closer and maybe you'll learn things and you not entirely wanting. (*Folds up pat.*)

JIM. I'll get it better next time. (*Another pat weighed out, etc. This time he wraps it better.*) How long d'you think 'twould take me to learn farming?

PEGGY. Oh, most like you'd spend your life at it and not know much about it.

JIM. I'll know something about it in six months or my name's not Jim Wyman! I've absolutely made up my mind. I'll go across the ferry to Colly Grigan's farm and he shall teach me the tricks of the trade.

PEGGY. Colly Grigan's farm, is it! A nice omahdun he to teach a man farming. There's more stones on his rye patch than in all the houses in the valley, and they a half score. Colly Grigan indeed!

JIM. Well, who else is to teach me?

PEGGY. What's wrong with my ways of farming? Isn't it meself can teach as much as any man, and you choosing to stop here?

JIM. Ah, but what would the neighbors say? They're the devil and all his angels to take away a girl's character.

PEGGY. I'm thinking you're a strange one. Here some minutes you've been and not a word said of will you marry.

JIM. Oh, that's off for a bit. When the money was there 'twas a different matter. I haven't got more 'n about thirty bob in the world, so I don't ask any girl to marry me yet awhile.

PEGGY. For an educated man it's little you understand the ways of women, Jim Wyman. Is it a girl you think wouldn't marry for a straight body and a kind word? Why there's some I could name with enough for two and the right man coming down the road.

JIM. It's little *you* understand of the ways of men, Peggy. You don't suppose a decent fellow would be content to live on his wife's money. At any rate, I'm not one of them. Perhaps in a year I shall have a bit of property and then I'll talk again. But till then I keep my mouth shut and my heart locked up—I'm waiting for another pat of butter.

PEGGY. Is it a year you'd be after waiting. Arrah, that's a mighty long time and none to say what might happen in the passing of it. Why, a widow woman might get on the blind side of you. A widow woman's a queer thing to a lone man, and him not knowing in the ways of such. I'm thinking you'd be better not be risking it for a year.

JIM. Widows or not, I've made up my mind to earn my living without any woman's help.

PEGGY. Let you not be a fool, Jim Wyman, but come you along and be my man.

JIM. What, you'd take me penniless?

PEGGY. It's a distracted man you are this day or you'd not act this queer.

JIM. (*Advancing to her.*) Peggy, you mean it? (*He is about to catch hold of her, but stops.*) No, I'm hanged if I do! You've made a fool of me once and I'm jolly well going to wait until I can come and show you a farm as big as yours. Then we'll talk.

PEGGY. It's a nice talker you are. Wait till a month goes over then see if your heart's not sad with emptiness and you wanting to come up to the pathway and kiss me.

JIM. I'll not kiss you till I've got my farm.

PEGGY. Maybe, but we'll see anyhow.

JIM. Look here, Peggy, I don't understand you a bit. What made you let me lose that money of my uncle's if you intended marrying me all the time?

PEGGY. How would a poor lone man follow the workings of a woman's heart? How was I to know was you wanting me for my own self or was it just to put a hand on your Uncle's great wealth and me a comely body would do as well as any?

JIM. (*Amused.*) So you doubted me!

PEGGY. And it wasn't that I doubted like any common woman and she jealous, but I wanted to see just for the joy of seeing. Maybe it was like wet paint and you knowing it, yet you must put out your finger and make sure.

JIM. Well, I'm glad the money's lost. Now for work and the joys of life. I'm quit of the waster. I'll have my own house with nine bean-rows and a hive for the honey bee. Yes, by jove, and a water-butt with clematis climbing round it and hens clucking on the door step!

PEGGY. And me to tell you which is the good layers and which . . .

JIM. Oh no, that's in the future when I've made my mark. Till then you take your chance with the widow woman for all I say. (*The latch of the gate is heard.*) Is that one coming now?

PEGGY. (*Looking out of the door.*) It's the postboy; maybe it's a letter. (*She runs out and returns almost at once.*) It's a telegram for you. (JIM *takes and opens it.*)

JIM. Hullo! "Congratulations on engagement. Only just in time, you young dog. Benjamin." What the devil's he getting at?

PEGGY. Maybe he's heard you's engaged.

JIM. But he can't have!

PEGGY. Maybe a body telegraphed him.

JIM. Nonesense! Who could have!

PEGGY. Sure, I did.

JIM. You!

PEGGY. Me very own self. I sent it to him this morning before you came in, telling you was engaged to Peggy Keeman and she a decent body.

JIM. Good Lord!

PEGGY. You see, after a hundred odd times of asking and me willing it seemed like one of the family I was and all that money going for the want of a little message.

JIM. (*After a pause.*) You've spoiled my idyll. I won't touch a confounded penny.

PEGGY. (*Soothingly.*) It'll be a nice thing to fall back upon, and school fees and all so heavy. Maybe some seasons will be good and some bad, but it's not in me to let the children run wild and no education along of a poor harvest.

JIM. I'm hanged if I give up the waterbutt with the

clematis! I'm jolly well going to earn my living by the sweat of my brow.

PEGGY. Well, you can work still. Isn't it now that you can buy a farm of your own and work till the sweat of your brow makes furrows down your face in the dust of day. Sure, you can buy my farm and I'll teach you all about it, and no widow woman waiting to waylay you and your heart beating low for a kind word.

JIM. I'll buy it! I'll give you five hundred for it, lock stock and barrel.

PEGGY. It's not worth more than two hundred.

JIM. Five's my offer!

PEGGY. The farm's yours then.

JIM. Pon my soul, you've made a man of me. You've taught me wisdom and the joys of life.

PEGGY. Then will you kiss me now?

JIM. Faith I will!

CURTAIN.

## LIST OF ONE-ACT PLAYS FOR READING AND PERFORMANCE

### AMERICAN ONE-ACT PLAYS

Lewis M. Beach.

**Four One-Act Plays** (N. Y., 1921), includes **The Clod, A Guest for Dinner, Love Among the Lions, and Brothers.**

Alice Brown.

**One-Act Plays** (N. Y., 1919), includes **The Hero, Doctor Auntie, The Crimson Lake, Milly Dear, The Web, The Loving Cup, Joint Owners in Spain, The Sugar House,** and **The March Wind.**

Colin Campbell Clements.

Plays for a Folding Theater (Cincinnati, 1923), includes **Pierrot in Paris, Columbine, The Return of Harlequin, Three Lepers of Suk-el-Garab, The Desert, The Siege,** and **Moon Tide.**

**Job** (N. Y., 1923.)

**You** (N. Y., 1924.)

**Pirates** (N. Y., 1922.)

Zona Gale.

**The Neighbors** (N. Y., 1923.)

Susan Glaspell.

**Plays** (Boston, 1920), contains the following one-act plays: **Trifles, The People, Suppressed Desires, Close the Book, The Outside, Woman's Honor,** and **Tickless Time.**

George Kelly.

**Finders Keepers** (Cincinnati, 1922.)

Lawrence Langner.

**Five One-Act Comedies** (Cincinnati, 1922), includes **Matinata, Another Way Out, The Family Exit, Pie,** and **Licensed.**

George Middleton.

Following plays in separate reprints: **Embers, Madonna, Tradition, A Good Woman, The Groove, The Cheat of Pity, Mothers, The Man Masterful, Their Wife, On Bail, Waiting, Back of the Ballot.**

Percy MacKaye.

**Yankee Fantasies** (N. Y., 1912), includes: **Sam Average, Chuck, Gettysburg, The Cat-Boat,** and **The Antick.**

**George Washington at the Delaware** (N. Y., 1920.)

Philip Moeller.

**Five Somewhat Historical Plays** (N. Y., 1918), includes: **Helena's Husband, The Little Supper, Sisters of Susannah, The Roadhouse in Arden,** and **Pokey.**

**Two Blind Beggars and One Less Blind** (N. Y., 1918.)

Christopher Morley.

**One-Act Plays** (N. Y., 1924), includes **Thursday Evening, Rehearsal, Bedroom Suite, On the Shelf, Walt,** and **East of Eden.**

Kenyon Nicholson.

**A Hint to Brides** (New York, 1923.)

**Garden Varieties** (New York, 1924) includes **White Elephants, The Bug Man, Confession, The Anonymous Letter, The Casino Gardens, The Marriage of Little Eva,** and **So This Is Paris Green.**

Mark O'Dea.

**Red Bud Women** (Cincinnati, 1922), includes **The Song of Solomon, Shivaree, Miss Myrtle Says "Yes,"** and **Not in the Lessons.**

Eugene O'Neill.

**The Moon of the Caribbees,** etc., (N. Y., 1924), includes besides the title play, **Bound East for Cardiff, In the Zone, The Long Voyage Home, Where the Cross Is Made,** and **'Ile.**

Booth Tarkington.

**The Trysting Place** (Cincinnati, 1923.)

**The Ghost Story** (Cincinnati, 1922.)

Juliet Wilbor Tompkins.

**Tired** (N. Y., 1924.)

Stuart Walker.

**Portmanteau Plays** (Cincinnati, 1917), includes **The Trimplet, Nevertheless, The Medecine Show, The Six Who Pass While the Lentils Boil.**

**More Portmanteau Plays** (Cincinnati, 1919), includes **The Very Naked Boy.**

## ENGLISH AND IRISH ONE-ACT PLAYS

Elizabeth Baker.

**Miss Tassey** (London, 1913.)

H. Granville Barker.

**Three Short Plays** (Boston, 1917), includes **Rococo, Vote by Ballot,** and **Farewell to the Theater.**

Sir James Barrie.

**Half Hours** (N. Y., 1914), includes **The Twelve Pound Look, Rosalind, Pantaloon, The Will.**

**Echoes of the War** (N. Y., 1918), includes **The Old Lady Shows Her Medals, The New Word, Barbara's Wedding,** and **A Well-Remembered Voice.**

Arnold Bennett.

**Polite Farces** (N. Y., no date), includes **The Stepmother, A Good Woman,** and **A Question of Sex.**

George Calderon.

**Eight One-Act Plays** (London, 1922), includes **Peace, The Little Stone House, Derelicts, Geminae, Parkin Brothers, The Two Talismans, The Prince Who Was a Piper,** and **The Man About the Place.**

Gilbert Cannan.

**Four Plays** (London, 1913), includes **James and John, Miles Dixon, Mary's Wedding,** and **A Short Way With Authors.** (All these also separately, in paper.)

Harold Chapin.

**Three One-Act Plays** (London, 1921), includes **It's the Poor that 'Elps the Poor, The Autocrat of the Coffee Stall,** and **Innocent and Annabel.**

**The Dumb and the Blind** (London, 1914.)
**Augustus in Search of a Father** (London, 1911.)
**Muddle Annie** (London, 1921.)
**The Philosopher of Butterbiggens** (N. Y., 1921.)
**The Threshold** (N. Y., 1921.)

Ernest Dowson.

**The Pierrot of the Minute** (N. Y., no date.)

John Drinkwater.

**Pawns** (Boston, 1920), includes **The Storm, The God of Quiet, X=O: A Night of the Trojan War,** and **Cophetua.**

Lord Dunsany.

**Five Plays** (N. Y., 1914), includes **The Golden Doom, The Glittering Gate,** and **The Lost Silk Hat.**

**Plays of Gods and Men** (Boston, 1917), includes **The Queen's Enemies** and **A Night at an Inn.**

**Plays of Far and Near** (N. Y., 1923), includes **The Compromise of the King of the Golden Isles, The Flight of the Queen, Cheezo, A Good Bargain, If Shakespeare Lived Today,** and **Fame and the Poet.**

(All these plays, except those in **Five Plays,** are published separately in paper.)

John Galsworthy.

**Six Short Plays** (N. Y., 1921), includes **The First and the Last, The Little Man, Hall Marked, Defeat, The Sun,** and **Punch and Go.**

St. John Hankin.

**The Constant Lover** (N. Y., 1912.)

Laurence Housman.

**False Promises** (N. Y., 1923), includes **The Christmas Tree, The Torch of Time, Moonshine, A Fool and His Money,** and **The House-Fairy.**

**The Wheel** (N. Y., 1920), includes **Apollo in Hades, The Death of Alcestis,** and **The Doom of Admetus.**

**Followers of St. Francis** (Boston, 1924), includes **Cure of Souls, Lovers Meeting, The Fool's Errand, and The Last Disciple.**

**As Good as Gold** (N. Y., 1916.)
**Bird in Hand** (N. Y., 1916.)
**The Return of Alcestis** (N. Y., 1916.)
**The Lord of the Harvest** (N. Y., 1916.)
**Nazareth** (N. Y., 1916.)
**A Likely Story** (N. Y., 1916.)
**The Snow Man** (N. Y., 1916.)

Hermon Ould.

**Joan the Maid** (N. Y., 1924.)
**Columbus** (N. Y., 1924.)

Gertrude Robins.

**Makeshifts and Realities** (London, no date), includes the plays mentioned.

**Loving as We Do** (London, no date), includes **Loving as We Do, The Return, After the Case, and 'Ilda's Honorable.**

Bernard Shaw.

**The Man of Destiny.**
**How He Lied to Her Husband.**
**Press Cuttings.**
**The Shewing up of Blanco Posnet.**
(The above separately, N. Y., no date.)
**Misalliance**, etc., (N. Y., 1914), includes **The Dark Lady of the Sonnets.**
**Heartbreak, House**, etc., (N. Y., 1919), includes **Augustus Does His Bit, O'Flaherty V. C., and Annajanska.**

Alfred Sutro.

**Five Little Plays** (N. Y., 1912), includes **The Man in the Stalls, A Marriage Has Been Arranged, The Man on the Kerb, The Open Door, and The Bracelet.** (Also separately, in paper.)

The following, separately, in paper (N. Y., 1902):

**A Game of Chess, The Salt of Life, Mr. Steinmann's Corner, Ella's Apology, The Gutter of Time, The Correct Thing, A Maker of Men, Carrots, The Marriage Will Not Take Place.**

Githa Sowerby.

**Before Breakfast** (London, 1913.)

John M. Synge.

**Riders to the Sea** (Boston, 1916.)
**The Shadow of the Glen** (Boston, 1916.)

William Butler Yeats.

**The Land of Heart's Desire** (N. Y., no date.)
**The Pot of Broth.**
**Cathleen ni Houlihan.**
**The Hour Glass.**
(Above three plays in one volume, N. Y., 1904.)

## COLLECTIONS AND ANTHOLOGIES

The following collections and anthologies of One-Act plays include valuable reference lists as well as numerous texts of American, Irish, and English modern one-act plays:

**Representative One-Act Plays by British and Irish Authors,** edited by Barrett H. Clark, (Boston, 1921.)

**Representative One-Act Plays by American Authors,** edited by Margaret G. Mayorga. (Boston, 1919.)

**One-Act Plays by Modern Authors,** edited by Helen Louise Cohen. (N. Y., 1921.)

**The Atlantic Book of Modern Plays,** edited by Sterling Andrus Leonard. (Boston, 1921.)

**The Atlantic Book of Junior Plays,** edited by Charles Swain Thomas. (Boston, 1924.)

**Twelve Plays,** edited by Edwin Van B. Knickerbocker. (N. Y., 1924.)

**A Treasury of Plays for Women,** edited by Frank Shay. (Boston, 1922.)

**A Treasury of Plays for Men,** edited by Frank Shay. (Boston, 1923.)

**Twenty-Five Short Plays** (International), edited by Frank Shay. (N. Y., 1925.)

**Twenty Contemporary One-Act Plays** (American), edited by Frank Shay. (Cincinnati, 1922.)

**Fifty Contemporary One-Act Plays,** edited by Frank Shay and Pierre Loving. (Cincinnati, 1920.)

**Contemporary One-Act Plays,** edited by B. Roland Lewis. (N. Y., 1923.)

**Short Plays by Representative Authors,** edited by Alice M. Smith. (N. Y., 1922.)

## LIST OF REFERENCES ON MODERN PLAYS AND PRODUCTION

Several of the books on the modern theater and drama treat of the one-act play as an independent art form, but there are two devoted entirely to the subject: B. Roland Lewis' **The Technique of the One-Act Play** (Boston, 1918) and Percival Wilde's **The Craftsmanship of the One-Act Play** (Boston, 1923. Among the general works treating the subject are Clayton Hamilton's **Seen on the Stage** (N. Y., 1920); Barrett H. Clark's **A Study of the Modern Drama** (N. Y., 1925), and Ludwig Lewisohn's **The Drama and the Stage** (N. Y., 1922.)

For references on the American drama in general see:

**The American Dramatist**, by Montrose J. Moses (Boston, 1917.)
**The New American Drama**, by Richard Burton (N. Y., 1911.)
**Dramatists of the New American Theater**, by Thomas H. Dickinson (N. Y., 1925.)
**Our American Theater**, by Oliver M. Sayler (N. Y., 1923.)
**A Study of the Modern Drama**, by Barrett H. Clark (N. Y., 1925.)
**The Modern Drama**, by Ludwig Lewisohn (N. Y., 1915.)

For references on the English drama in general, see:

**The Contemporary Drama of England**, by Thomas H. Dickinson (Boston, 1917.)
**The English Stage**, by Augustin Filon (N. Y., 1898.)
**The English Stage of Today**, by Mario Borsa (N. Y., 1908.)
**The Renascence of the English Drama**, by Henry Arthur Jones (N. Y., 1895.)
**The New Drama and the Old**, by William Archer (Boston, 1923.)
**Dramatic Portraits**, by P. P. Howe (N. Y., 1913.)
**Tendencies of Modern English Drama**, by A. E. Morgan (N. Y., 1924.)
**The Twentieth Century Theater**, by Frank Vernon (Boston, 1924.)
**A Study of the Modern Drama**, by Barrett H. Clark (N. Y., 1925.)

For references on the Irish drama, see:

**Irish Plays and Playwrights**, by Cornelius Weygandt (Boston, 1913.)
**The Contemporary Drama of Ireland**, by Ernest Boyd (Boston, 1917.)
**The Celtic Dawn**, by L. R. Morris (N. Y., 1917.)
**Our Irish Theater**, by Lady Gregory (N. Y., 1913.)
**Essays**, by W. B. Yeats (N. Y., 1924.)
**Literature in Ireland**, by Thomas MacDonough (N. Y., 1916.)
**The Modern Drama**, by Ludwig Lewisohn (N. Y., 1922.)
**A Study of the Modern Drama**, by Barrett H. Clark (N. Y., 1925.)
**Aspects of Modern Drama**, by F. W. Chandler (N. Y., 1914.)

For guidance in the producing of plays see:

**How to Produce Amateur Plays**, by Barrett H. Clark.
**How to Produce Children's Plays**, by Constance D'Arcy MacKay.
**The New Movement in the Theater**, by Sheldon Cheney.